Better Birding

Better Birding

Tips, Tools, and Concepts for the Field

George L. Armistead
and
Brian L. Sullivan

PRINCETON UNIVERSITY PRESS
PRINCETON AND OXFORD

Copyright © 2016 by Princeton University Press
Published by Princeton University Press, 41 William Street, Princeton, New Jersey 08540
In the United Kingdom: Princeton University Press, 6 Oxford Street, Woodstock, Oxfordshire OX20 1TW

nathist.princeton.edu

ISBN (pbk.) 978-0-691-12966-2

Library of Congress Cataloging-in-Publication Data

Armistead, George L.
     Better birding : tips, tools, and concepts for the field / George L. Armistead & Brian L. Sullivan.
        pages cm
     Includes bibliographical references and index.
     ISBN 978-0-691-12966-2 (pbk. : alk. paper) 1. Birds—United States—Identification. 2. Birds—Canada—
Identification. I. Sullivan, Brian L. II. Title.

   QL682.A76 2015
      598—dc23
   2015012196

British Library Cataloging-in-Publication Data is available

This book has been composed in Minion Pro and Myriad Pro
Printed on acid-free paper. ∞

Printed in China

10 9 8 7 6 5 4 3 2 1

For Dad,
Thanks, Pops
—GLA

To Sophie and Ella,
For helping me see the big picture
—BLS

Contents

Acknowledgments

We received tremendous assistance and support over the course of this project. First and foremost we wish to thank our publisher, Princeton University Press, and in particular Robert Kirk, for bearing with the growing pains of two evolving authors.

A turning point in this project came after Edward S. "Ned" Brinkley reviewed the manuscript and refocused our efforts. Without Ned's input we may not have succeeded in bringing the writing and organizing of this book to an agreeable finish. Ned has served in the multiple roles of friend, colleague, mentor, and editor as nimbly as anyone possibly could. Likewise, Steve Howell provided invaluable advice on the direction of the early manuscript, steering us toward what you see here today.

We are indebted to many friends and colleagues who provided input and editing on various parts of the book. We wish to thank in particular Alvaro Jaramillo, Dan Lane, and Louis Bevier for reviewing significant portions of the manuscript. Also, Henry T. Armistead, Chris Benesh, Dr. Robert Curry, Jesse Fagan, Marshall J. Iliff, Tom Johnson, Paul E. Lehman, Steve Mlodinow, Michael O'Brien, Brian Patteson, Michael Retter, Dr. Nate Rice, Fletcher Smith, and Richard Webster reviewed parts of the manuscript, providing important input and information.

For access to museum collections we thank Carla Cicero at the Museum of Vertebrate Zoology at Berkeley, Maureen Flannery at the California Academy of Sciences, and Paul Sweet at the American Museum of Natural History.

Thanks also to our photographers, who contributed hundreds of images to the book. They are: Mike Andersen (MA), George Armistead (GLA), Danny Bales (DB), Glenn Bartley (GB), Daniel Behm (DBe), Louis Bevier (LB), Gerard W. Beyersbergen (GBe), Shawn Billerman (SB), Tom Blackman (TB), Dan Casey (DC), Oleg Chernyshov (OC), Ashley Cohen (AC), Robin Corcoran (RC), Jan Crites (JC), Mike Danzenbaker (MD), Ian Davies (ID), David Dillon (DD), Laura Erickson (LE), Sam Fason (SF), Sam Galick (SG), Alan Garner (AGa), Reinhard Geisler (RG), Brian Gibbons (BG), Doug Gochfeld (DG), António A. Gonçalves (AAG), Jamie Goodspeed (JG), Michael Gray (MG), António Guerra (AG), Nic Hallam (NH), Larry Hancock (LH), Ned Harris (NHa), Randy Harrod (RH), Hugh Harrop (HH), David Hollie (DH), Steve N. G. Howell (SNGH), Bill Hubick (BH), Alex Hughes (AHu), K. K. Hui (KKH), Adam Hutchins (AH), Dave Irving (DI), Melissa James (MJ), Alvaro Jaramillo (AJa), Ashley Jensen (AJe), Andy Johnson (AJ), Tom Johnson (TJ), Kevin Karlson (KK), Marcin Kojtka (MK), Stephen Kolbe (SK), Paul Kusmin (PK), Iain H. Leach (IHL), Tony Leukering (TL), Jerry Liguori (JL), Kevin Lin (KL), Aaron Maizlish (AM), Larry Manfredi (LM), Curtis Marantz (CM), Jimmy McMorran (JM), Edwin Mercado (EM), Ryan Merrill (RM), Martin Meyers (MM), Steve Mlodinow (SM), Brennan Mulrooney (BM), Michael O'Brien (MOB), Ryan O'Donnell (RO), Greg Page (GP), Ilya Povalyaev (IP), Jeff Ritz (JR), Raybel Robles (RR), Kerry Ross (KR), Cameron Rutt (CR), Michaela Sagatova (MSa), Ryan Sanderson (RSa), Larry Sansone (LS), Ed Schneider (ES), Peter Schoenberger (PS), Scott Schuette (SS), Ryan Shaw (RS), Tania Simpson (TS), Ken Slade (KS), Chris Sloan (CS), Brian Small (BS), Daniel Smith (DS), Graham Smith (GS), Jan Willem Steffelaar (JWS), Matt Studebaker (MSt), Brian Sullivan (BLS), Mark Szantyr (MS), Monte Taylor (MT), Tinyfishy (T), Jeremiah Trimble (JT), John Turner (JTu), David Vander Pluym (DV), Gerrit Vyn (GV), Christopher L. Wood (CLW), Teri Zambon (TZ).

Any mistakes that remain in this volume are solely the responsibility of the authors.

GLA: Thanks are due to Matthew F. Sharp, who once whimsically suggested, "I know a book you should do." My colleagues at the Academy of Natural Sciences of Philadelphia (ANSP), particularly from 1995 to 2002, including Matthew F. Sharp, Doug Wechsler (VIREO: Visual Resources for Ornithology), Dr. Nate Rice, Robert S. Ridgely, Bill Mathews, and Dr. Frank Gill, all helped provide a foundation for my study of birds, particularly in framing my understanding of biodiversity and taxonomy. Delaware Valley Ornithological Club meetings held at ANSP (now the Academy of Natural Sciences of Drexel University) cemented what I learned in the Ornithology Department.

It was my work as a guide at Field Guides, Inc. (2002–2012) that crystallized for me the way to approach writing this book. Particular thanks are owed to Jan Pierson and Peggy Watson, who taught me much about how to best help other birders. And while guiding tours for Field Guides I spent a lot of time picking the brains of hundreds of tour participants, and especially those of my coguides: Chris Benesh, John Coons, Megan Crewe, Jesse Fagan, Phil Gregory, Alvaro Jaramillo, Dan Lane, John Rowlett, Rose Ann Rowlett, Dave Stejskal, Terry

Stevenson, Jay Vandergaast, Richard Webster, and Bret Whitney. The office staff there, including Maggie Burnett, Sharon Mackie, Teresa Paschall, and Karen Turner, also influenced my approach. My experiences at Field Guides had a direct impact on my approach to this project.

Brian Patteson (Seabirding Pelagic Trips) and Ned Brinkley have taught me a tremendous amount about my favorite habitat, the ocean. The honor of serving as a guide on so many of Brian's pelagic trips gave me the opportunity to familiarize myself with many species I would not have encountered elsewhere and allowed me to develop my skills as a guide.

My work on this book has benefited greatly from conversations and communications with Alvaro Jaramillo, Louis R. Bevier, Ned Brinkley, Marshall J. Iliff, Brian Patteson, Jeff Gordon, Paul Lehman, Chris Benesh, Steve N. G. Howell, Kate Sutherland, Ted Floyd, Matthew F. Sharp, Todd M. Day, Todd Fellenbaum, Tony Leukering, Nikolas Haas, Dan Lane, and Henry T. Armistead.

Thanks are due my colleagues at the American Birding Association, particularly Jeff Gordon, Bill Stewart, Liz Gordon, Ted Floyd, Greg Neise, Michael Retter, John Puschock, and Nate Swick, for our thoughtful discussions about birds and how to better serve birders.

Special thanks are owed to my family, all of whom have supported me, and without whom it is doubtful I'd have had the perseverance to complete my part in this project. Heartfelt thanks go to my mother, Mary E. Armistead, and my sisters and their husbands, Anne and Derek Ayres and Mary and Michael Solomonov. Most of all I wish to thank my father, Henry T. Armistead. Pops, I can't thank you enough. I had no idea that the family trip you organized for us to Churchill, Manitoba, in 1984 would so alter the course of my life. Birds have proven fascinating to me.

Of course more than anyone, I owe coauthor Brian Sullivan a massive debt of gratitude and appreciation. Coauthorship tested our friendship, more than either of us could have expected. We navigated sensitive territory extremely well. I'm proud of that, and of having had the honor to work with Brian on this project. It's been a long and fantastic journey.

BLS: I've been lucky to have the support of family and a host of birding mentors over the years. To my family I am greatly in debt. My mom, Joyce Sullivan; dad,

Ken L. Sullivan; and brother, Ken C. Sullivan, endured many windswept days on Hawk Mountain with me, shivering as a procession of Red-tailed Hawks drifted past. I was captivated; they were freezing. But they had the foresight to see a growing passion. Without the patience and support of my parents I would never have discovered my true course in life. And without the love and warmth of my wife and daughter, I wouldn't realize why any of this matters. Thanks, Sophie and Ella, for helping me see the big picture.

So many birders have impacted the way I think about birds and perceive nature that to single any one person out would be a discredit to the rest. Though they are too many to name, I've learned from everyone I've worked with over many years in the field, and most recently at the Cornell Lab of Ornithology. My colleagues there, especially Chris Wood, Marshall Iliff, Jessie Barry, Andrew Farnsworth, Steve Kelling, John Fitzpatrick, Tim Lenz, Will Morris, and Jeff Gerbracht, have shown me what it means to have a true passion for birds, and I try to do my best to reach the high bar they and everyone at the Lab constantly nudges upward.

I've learned a great deal from working with a small team of coauthors on another project: *The Princeton Guide to North American Birds*. This team of writers, including Steve N. G. Howell, Michael O'Brien, Chris Wood, Ian Lewington, and Robert Kirk, has taught me to strive for excellence in observation, research, and writing.

Over the years, Jerry Liguori has been an excellent friend, mentor, and collaborator, teaching me how to look at hawks from a different angle, and constantly pushing the limits in the domain of raptor identification.

George and I met one blustery winter day twenty years ago at Barnegat Inlet in New Jersey. We became good friends and over the coming years spent much time birding together. We frequently talked about the idea of helping people become better birders, and George took that on as a full-time job in his tour-leading profession. I went in another direction, toward fieldwork and then toward eBird. But we circled back to the idea and conceived of this book. It wasn't easy. The idea took time to really form itself, and over the years we've pushed this project in many directions. We are proud of the outcome, and I'm proud to have a friendship with George that can persevere through good times and bad.

Introduction

You walk into a coffee shop. It's about half filled, mostly with college-age people. The barista is talking loudly on the phone as he prepares an espresso for a mother of two. Behind them in line is an older man carrying his Jack Russell terrier. The terrier is looking at you imploringly. Seated unobtrusively in the rear of the café, removed from all social interaction and as far away from the rasping of the espresso machine as possible, is someone facing away from you. As soon as you walk in the door, with only a cursory glance, you know this is your best friend, Holly.

You can't even see the face, yet you know it's her. How can you be sure this person is Holly? How did you even spot her there in the first place? It's a pretty impressive feat you've just performed, actually, considering all the distractions. There's the murmur and bustling of the patrons, the loud barista fluttering about, the cute Jack Russell, a bevy of attractive college students, and a raucous espresso machine, all demanding your attention. Yet you noticed and identified Holly right away.

Maybe you spotted Holly because that is where Holly always sits. But that alone would not confirm her identity. The fact that a person is sitting there does not mean that person is Holly, after all. Maybe it's Wednesday afternoon and you know that Holly always spends Wednesday afternoons at this coffee shop. But there are probably other people who do, too. You know it's Holly based on this information about her habits, combined with a few telltale field marks. These might include the color of her hair, the favorite sweater she is wearing, the red headphones, or her signature black handbag. But there are yet more subtle characters you process. You know Holly so well that without even realizing it, you recognize the angle at which she holds her head as she reads, the way her foot dangles loosely when her leg rests on her knee, and the general shape she takes while seated. All of these things taken together equal Holly—and you are an expert on her.

This process is what expert birders go through each time they identify a bird. It happens hundreds or even thousands of times a day during a birding outing, though most of it is subconscious. When they see a soaring Red-tailed Hawk and identify it with the naked eye, they can do so partly because they know there is often a Red-tailed Hawk in that spot, partly because it's moving like one, and partly because it just *looks* like one. Combine these factors in a split second (habits,

movement, appearance), and you have reached an identification. When "good birders" do this, people marvel at their skill. But in reality we all do this, all the time. It's the same way you recognized Holly. And the way you recognize your cousin as she walks toward you on a beach, even three-quarters of a mile away. And it's the same way that after just the first few notes of your favorite song, you recognize it instantly. Because you *know* it—you know it *really* well. Here we hope to teach you to learn to recognize birds in this way, and take your birding to the next level.

Purpose of This Book

Our primary goal for this book is to help you develop a solid foundation for building your field skills. We will hit on the typical field marks but will also steer you toward behavioral cues and hints on habitat, which, combined with the natural history and taxonomic notes, will provide a broader way in which to view birds. In the process of examining the twenty-four groups treated herein, you will lay strong structural support for your birding; you will take a more ground-up and wide-angle approach to it. By providing information about a bird's habits, we hope to offer you a better chance of encountering sought-after species, but more importantly a better chance of *knowing* a species, as we've described above. Woven into each chapter are lessons that will help organize your thinking about a group of species, which in turn we hope will lead you to become more adept at finding, identifying, and knowing what you see in the field.

How to Use This Book

Despite how it may appear, the selection of groups treated in these chapters was not arbitrary, though it certainly was subjective. We chose groups from the continental United States and Canada (the American Birding Association Area, hereafter "the ABA Area") that fit one of three criteria: (1) we thought the group represented a good opportunity to build core birding skills, (2) we thought the group could use a refreshed treatment, or (3) we thought the group was interesting and we wanted to present it using this format.

Each chapter begins with brief bits of information on the approximate age at which the species treated make their first breeding attempts, what their breeding strategies are, and how long they may live. This is meant to give you a sense of the scope of a bird's life; the lifespan is usually the number of years a long-lived bird in this group might live, but many individuals live much shorter lives. This information is followed by an essay that provides background context for the group treated, including a brief discussion of its natural history, taxonomy, and identification problems. The **Focus on** section contains a short list of things to focus your attention on when learning the species in a group, or when seeing them in the field. **Hints and Considerations** provides brief contextual information on potentially confusing species, general range and distribution, useful notes on seasonality, and ID tricks specific to that group. The **Identification** section begins with an overview of the plumages associated with the group and its members. This often involves a rudimentary discussion of molt strategy, age, and plumage progression. Following this overview are the species accounts, which typically begin with a broad outline of the species and then become progressively more specific about how to distinguish a particular species. After the accounts, in some cases, are short summaries of rare vagrant species within the group that have appeared in the ABA Area. Also evident in most chapters are shaded text boxes containing either a "Taxonomic Note" or "Natural History Note." Both of these are meant to add more information about a bird's or a group's identity, useful in the context of identification. Chapters end with a list of the references cited in the text.

Wide-Angle Birding:
Be the Bird, See the Bird

There's a Japanese proverb that says, "Don't study something. Get used to it."[1] And so it is with any subject in which you hope to achieve expertise. To study is to begin down the path toward expertise, and having some structure and focus for your study is important. Armchair study is helpful preparation, but you must combine it with field experience in order to achieve expertise. The proverb indicates that the best way to really become expert about something is simply to be around it, and be mindful of it. Certainly this is true of birds. And it is wise to vary your approach between focusing on feather by feather details and seeing a more holistic picture.

Too often, beginning and intermediate birders focus so closely and intensely on a bird or group of birds that they actually narrow their view too much. More advanced birders make use of what they call GISS, which is an acronym for general impression, size, and shape. Both a strength and weakness of the modern field guide are the arrows highlighting salient field marks. These are, of course, helpful handles for birders, but these signature field characters can also act as a crutch, limiting any expanded understanding of the bird. You learn more when you can also zoom out and see the big picture—see the bird in context. Sometimes you have to lower your binoculars and step away from the scope, look at your surroundings and the habitat the bird is in, consider the conditions, and use your ears. Relying too much on the view through your optics can actually hinder your attempts at identification. It is possible to miss the forest for the trees in bird identification. A wide-angle approach is just as important. Identification is very much about identity, but too often our study of a species ends with the acquisition of a single signature field mark. A bird's appearance is but one part of its identity. Expertise is gained only by looking at the bird as a whole. And the whole includes not just a bird's plumage, shape, behavior, and flight style but also its habitat, seasonal habits, range, and natural history. Truly expert birders know not only what the bird is, but *why* the bird is.

Anna Botsford Comstock elucidated this well when she said, "The identification of birds is simply the alphabet to the real study." We forget at times that birds are not just a conglomeration of field marks: they are creatures with lives, still evolving, that possess a constellation of instinctual needs and learned behaviors. Understanding these needs and the associated behaviors brings a birder up to a higher level: the *next* level.

Of course there is no quick way to become an expert, even with some natural acumen. Becoming great at bird identification takes dedication and work. The idea that certain people are naturally gifted is exaggerated. We birders are like so many other subcultures in that we have our heroes. We enjoy marveling at the skill of certain superb field birders, but the truth is these superbirders didn't get that good overnight. They became good because they love studying birds and dedicate their time to it, and they continue to learn with open eyes and minds every time they go into the field. In his book *Outliers*, Malcolm Gladwell points out that real expertise accrues only after approximately ten thousand hours of study.[2] For a beginning or intermediate birder, this sounds daunting. Ten thousand hours is a lot of time to devote to anything. But at the same time, that's all it takes: an investment of time, and a focused approach. And in a way, that's liberating. Becoming an expert birder is about dedication, and indeed, if you have read this far, you likely possess the necessary elements to become one.

What Is a "Good Birder"?

How can someone be good at birding? And what exactly is a "good birder"? What do people mean when they say so-and-so is a good birder? What skills are brought to bear by a good birder, as opposed to an average birder? First let's consider exactly what a birder is.

Generally a birder is someone who enjoys birds. Designating oneself a birder connotes a certain level of commitment to the pastime. Some people enjoy arguing about the differences between "birder" and "bird-watcher." It may be that there is no real value in making a distinction between the two. If we all like birds, and both are noble pursuits, then what's the difference, right? But it is an interesting exercise to explore the terms and think about how they might differ in their meaning. One distinction might be that a birder sounds more active and less passive than a bird-watcher. Bird-watching sounds like something anyone might do, even while feeding pigeons in a park or feeding ducks at a suburban pond. Falling into this same category would be the thousands of people who enjoy birds at their feeders, content not knowing the species involved, and happy watching whatever is there. Bird-watching sounds relaxing and casual.

"Birding" is different. It involves active expectation about what you might encounter. It involves preparation. Birders are not always content to see whatever happens to cross their path; just as often they leave their front door with a specific agenda. A birder sets goals. For a bird-watcher it is the act of observation itself that is rewarding, but for the birder, field time is best rewarded by the thrill of the hunt and the element of discovery. Birders go looking for warblers, or they go hawk watching; they embark on a pelagic trip, or they go on a rarity chase. They have a sense of what they want to see, and they also have a sense of what the odds are of seeing it.

Perhaps the following definitions are suitable for the two terms:

bird-watcher: someone who enjoys watching birds.

birder: a wild bird enthusiast; someone who actively pursues an interest in wild birds by studying bird identification and habits, investing time searching for specific species, and keeping a record of sightings over time.

There is an element of fanaticism to birding that doesn't exist within the realm of bird-watching. As noted, both are noble pursuits; there is no intent here to imply a superiority of one over the other, and surely there are shades of gray between the two. But let's try to clarify the terms and achieve a more precise definition of the word "birder."

If we accept the statements above, essentially all birders are also bird-watchers, yet not all bird-watchers are birders. To become a good birder, you must also be a good bird-watcher. Birders enjoy the aesthetics involved in bird-watching, too, but take it a step further. They prepare for the field, studying for their next venture outside, daydreaming about certain species and hoping for discoveries. Very often keeping a list of species sighted during your life, during a given year, or within your yard provides parameters for discoveries. A list of sightings serves as a sort of diary for a birder. Listing is a valuable and deeply engrained aspect of birding.

So, returning to the question of what makes someone a "good birder" and using the definition above, *a good birder is (a) well versed in the habits, range, seasonal occurrence, and identification of birds; (b) good at finding birds; and (c) skilled at recording information about them.*

Becoming a "Good Birder":
Understanding the Basics

Distribution

The word "distribution" is used to describe the typical range of a bird: in other words, where and when a species is expected to occur. The "range maps" in any field guide give a good general idea about this. Generally, most birds are resident or migratory. The degree to which birds migrate varies widely, even within a species. Some species are more nomadic or irruptive, moving in patterns that are less predictable than typical annual migrations.

Climate and geography act in concert to produce what we call "bioregions." Understanding the general distribution of these regions is helpful for birders, as many species (and subspecies) separate along these lines. As we examine the North American continent, discrete bioregions are visible: mountains, forest types, grasslands, deserts, wetlands, and other areas as well. Many bird ranges adhere closely to these biogeographic boundaries.

Using chickadees in the East as an example, Boreal Chickadees are birds of northern coniferous forests, while Carolina Chickadees are birds of the eastern deciduous/pine-oak forests of the Southeast. Black-capped Chickadees are birds mostly of the northern hardwoods, but they overlap in places with both of the other species. Mostly, these birds replace each other within a given bioregion, with just one species likely across vast expanses of the continent. Similar patterns hold true for other species groups like Mallard and Monochromatic "Mallards," in which the more closely related Mottled, Mexican, and American Black ducks overlap little, essentially replacing one another, while the more generalist (and less closely related) Mallard overlaps to some extent with all. In some cases, the ranges of related species fit together like puzzle pieces, but in others they overlap, and then segregate by ecological niche or habitat preferences.

Elevation often influences the extent of a species' range. Many birds are dependent on plants and insects, and factors affecting plant growth and composition as well as food availability and abundance also affect bird distribution. Temperature is one such factor; as you climb in elevation and it becomes cooler, the vegetation changes, and with it, bird species composition. The breeding ranges of some Arctic or boreal species extend south into higher elevations of the Rockies or Appalachians, where alpine tundra provides habitat similar to that found in the Arctic. Look at any range map of the American Pipit as an example.

Compared with the Appalachians, the geologically young Rocky Mountains are taller and more dramatic in their topography, offering a wider range of habitats. From scrubby foothills to aspen and ponderosa pine forests to timberline and alpine tundra, species composition changes according to the habitat within each elevational band. In the eastern United States, some species favor the Appalachian ridges, others the foothills and piedmont below, and others the coastal plain; some do not occur away from the immediate coast (sea level). Related species often separate along elevational bands, so that one species is present at lower elevation but is replaced by another at higher elevation. Mountains, just like deserts, treeless plains, and large water bodies, act as barriers for separating and isolating species.

Distribution plays a key role in identification. Many species, such as the chickadees, have ranges that overlap only slightly with each other, with broad expanses of the continent having only a single chickadee species. Knowing which chickadee, or chickadees, occur in your region can greatly speed identification, especially if only one species is likely. Boreal Chickadee, AK, May (BLS).

Species that occupy broad geographic ranges, such as the Red-tailed Hawk, often showcase Gloger's Rule to good effect with the variation in their subspecies. Krider's Red-tailed Hawk (left) occupies a breeding range on the northern Great Plains, where many species have paler subspecies. Krider's differs from other Red-tailed Hawks in its whiter head, reduced dark markings below, and white-based tail. Harlan's Red-tailed Hawk (right) breeds in the humid boreal forest of Alaska and western Canada and averages much darker and blacker overall than most Red-tailed Hawks. Adult Harlan's can even have a mainly blackish tail, unlike most other adult Red-tailed Hawks (BLS).

Three rules (applied in animal studies) are helpful to keep in mind when you consider a bird's appearance and range:

Gloger's Rule: Species inhabiting humid areas tend to be darker overall than those inhabiting arid areas.

Darker feathers contain more melanin and so appear blacker, but melanin also helps fortify feathers, making them stronger and more resistant to degrading bacteria. Many largely white birds, like gulls, snow geese, and others, have evolved dark wing tips. The tips of a bird's wings take a lot of wear and tear, and increased concentrations of melanin there prevent more rapid wear.

Bergmann's Rule: Populations of a species in colder areas (e.g., higher latitudes) tend to be larger than those in warmer areas.

This is particularly noticeable in widespread species and is thought to relate to thermoregulation. An animal that is larger has less surface area per unit mass and so is able to remain warmer, which is important in colder climes. The inverse is true as well, so that in warm areas where remaining cool in hot conditions can be critical, a smaller animal is able to cool itself more efficiently than a larger one. Compare the massive ravens in the Arctic to those in the Lower 48.

Allen's Rule: Animals in colder climates have smaller appendages than those in warmer climates.

Heat is easily lost through appendages; they have lots of surface area and usually lack fur, feathers, and so forth. Smaller appendages are easier to protect from the cold. Look at a Hoary Redpoll, Ross's Gull, or Rough-legged Hawk. All possess relatively tiny bills and feet.

Seasoning Your Expectations

Habitat very often dictates behavior. A Northern Harrier glides and swoops low over fields and marshes, periodically flapping and hovering. It behaves this way because it hunts rodents and this kind of low, cruising flight allows it to more easily detect prey. A Harrier's long wings allow it to navigate in open, windy areas, and its long legs allow it to pluck rodents cleanly from grassy cover. Harriers have evolved just so, to nimbly take advantage of these open habitats, including during migration. An appreciation of these qualities allows good birders to recognize a Harrier by its structure or movements from considerable distances. Species evolve to take best advantage of their environment. Birds such as wrens and rails that occur in dense habitats are often darker in plumage (helpful for hiding in shadows), have shorter tails, and produce loud, penetrating vocalizations. Species of open grassland or desert are often paler (helpful for hiding in bright light) and are nimble on the ground and in the air.

The way habitat shapes a bird's behavior is often (though not always) obvious. The use of a particular habitat by a species often leads to specific behavioral habits that help birders separate similar species. While Brandt's and Pelagic cormorants overlap in breeding areas, they select different kinds of nest sites, with Brandt's nesting in flatter areas and Pelagic nesting on cliff edges. At breeding colonies when the birds are too distant to be identified by physical characters, behavioral differences like this can be used to separate them. Other species differ in courtship display or in nest construction, and these differences can be instructive.

Understanding habitat, range, and seasonality, collectively termed distribution, can greatly improve the identification process simply by limiting the choices. If, for example, you're birding in New York and are faced with a drab December warbler flitting about the bushes, an understanding of distribution takes you quickly from considering a few dozen possible warbler species to focusing on a limited few; most wood warblers have left New York State by December. By considering the likely species first (is it an Orange-crowned Warbler or a Yellow-rumped Warbler?),

experts can often arrive at split-second identifications that are correct. This process is sometimes called birding by probability, and an ugly truth in birding is that not every bird identified is examined critically— nor is this possible. It's important to understand that while it's not always the ideal approach, birding by probability is commonplace and helpful. Though probability is derided at times, every good birder uses it as a guide. It allows you to temporarily remove unlikely or rare species from contention and to first consider more likely species.

Behavioral cues are significant in separating species. Some are obvious, but others are less so. An actively foraging Reddish Egret, with all of its antics, can scarcely go unnoticed, but you may walk right past the furtive Sprague's Pipit, as it scurries away mouse-like amid the grassy cover. Some species are conspicuous, social, or animated, but others are retiring, solitary, or sluggish. Watch the way a bird moves. Note what it eats and how it obtains food. When it is flying, observe its course, how it holds its wings, and how it flaps and glides. If you are observing a flock of birds, note how the flock behaves and moves as an entity, and whether individuals feed, roost, and bathe in the same area, or whether they use discrete sites for each activity. If a bird walks, does it just walk, or does it hop, run, or scurry

In late afternoon light, a raptor teeters from side to side low over open country, changing direction quickly in the fading light. Most experienced birders would glance at this bird in the field and immediately identify it as a Northern Harrier based on a combination of habitat, behavior, and a general impression of shape and size, or "GISS," even without noting any diagnostic field marks (BLS).

in bursts? Does it bob its tail, perform short flights, or move in yet some other manner? If it's a diving species, does the whole body come out of the water prior to diving? How much of its body does it expose when swimming? Such factors are helpful in distinguishing similar species, and if you keep considering these features of the birds you observe, you may soon find yourself teaching the experts a thing or two.

Birds, like humans, are creatures of habit. On a morning walk you might see the same individual bird, day after day, singing from the exact same perch again and again. That bird is on territory, defending its patch of land from competing males and trying to attract a mate. Many species are sedentary, remaining in the same place year-round, but just as sedentary birds have routines, most migrants adhere to predictable patterns, using well-known routes with consistent annual timing. Some species may occur in an area only during a narrow two-week window each year. Knowing these windows increases your chances of finding these birds and identifying them correctly. The best birders combine probability with traditional field marks to arrive at fast, accurate identifications. Using probability is a good first step, but it is not a field mark in itself. You should use it as a tool in the identification process, while always remembering to look at birds closely when possible.

Rarities—When You Hear Hoofbeats, Think Horses, but Consider Zebras

One of the most exciting aspects of birding is finding a rarity. As birders we canvass our favorite birding sites, often combing through common birds to find something unusual. Finding a rarity can be rewarding on many levels. It's great to receive positive feedback from the birding community after finding (and documenting) a rarity, but there is also great self-satisfaction in knowing that you were prepared for the unexpected, and you were skilled enough to recognize something unusual when it presented itself. One thing you'll see over and over is that good birders find the most rarities. They put in the time in the field. By spending lots of time in the field, they increase their chances of happening across rarities. Good birders know how to be in the right place at the right time. More than anything, good birders are prepared for the unexpected. Instead of glossing over a large flock of pipits on the California coast in October, a good

birder knows that the conditions and season are right to check for the rare Red-throated Pipit. Chance favors the prepared mind. In this book you'll find lots of common birds and quite a few rarities. As you work through these groups, concentrate on learning how to identify the horses, but make sure to learn when and where to expect zebras, too!

eBird—Tools for Birders

eBird (www.ebird.org) is a free, online global database of bird records gathered by hundreds of thousands of birders and used by millions of birders, researchers, and conservationists worldwide. eBird allows you to report what you see, put your observations into the context of others, and discover patterns of bird distribution by looking at what's being reported around you. eBird's bar charts help you know what to expect in a given region or location, thereby improving your ability to use probability as an identification tool (see above). If you are a beginning or intermediate birder, keeping track of what you see in the field might seem daunting. But eBird makes it easy, and you learn a lot in the process. You can use eBird's online tools to enter your observations, but these days more birders are using mobile phones to enter their observations as they are making them from the field. Keeping track of what you see in this way improves your birding skills on many levels. It certainly makes it easier to keep more comprehensive species lists for each birding site you visit, and it makes it easy to keep track of birds because you can add them as you go. A quick look on the "My eBird" page will allow you to see all your observations neatly arranged into helpful lists, including your life list, state, county, and site-level lists, and more. Most importantly, using eBird puts your observations into the hands of scientists and conservationists who are helping research and protect birds and their habitats. Make your birding count—enter your observations into eBird.

Using and Learning Bird Sounds

Birders, like so many people, are visually oriented. Almost always the thing that triggers one's interest in birds is a bird's beauty or its dynamic behavior. "Spark birds" are the birds that kick-start someone's interest in birds. All birders can trace their fascination with birds back to a transformative moment or several moments when a bird interrupted their day, demanding attention.

Are these "bird watchers" or "birders" scanning the cliffs on Alaska's Pribilof Islands? (GLA)

From an American Goldfinch feeding on a purple thistle flower, to a captivating flock of Cattle Egrets, to a Pileated Woodpecker hammering on a tree trunk, a spark bird may take many forms. Most often it is what we see of these birds that grabs our attention, but sometimes it is their voice that stops us in our tracks. If you hear a Willow Ptarmigan, a Common Loon, a Hermit Thrush, a Bewick's Wren, or a Barn Owl before knowing what it is, your curiosity will likely be piqued.

Birdsong is one of the most fascinating areas to explore in ornithology and remains a rich topic for research, one in which amateur birders and recordists can still make a real impact. Yes, there is a lot to learn. From a birding standpoint, if you can tune in to bird sounds you will have a whole new set of tools at your disposal. Learning to "bird by ear" is an essential field skill, and it is one of the easiest ways for beginning and intermediate birders to make significant strides in improving their personal field skills. Often a whole new side of a bird's identity is revealed in the process of learning its sounds.

The manner in which a bird delivers its song, as well as where and how often it sings, can tell us a lot about its habits. Understanding these habits puts us in a better position to know how to find and see the bird. Start listening *actively*, rather than passively. Consider the purpose of a particular sound and ask yourself, is this a contact call between individuals, or is it a scold note being directed at an intruder (maybe you)? Is it an alarm note? Or is it a song, designed to attract a mate and drive away rivals? Think about what the bird is trying to communicate with its sounds. *Be the bird, see the bird.*

Birders who learn bird sounds usually begin with a bird's song. Songs differ from "calls" in that songs are longer, often more complex vocalizations. In most birds (though not all) songs are given by males, usually on the breeding territory, and serve the dual purpose of attracting females and driving away rival males. In some species both males and females sing. When females sing, it is less often about attracting males (though it probably does help strengthen pair bonds) and usually more about territorial defense against neighboring pairs. Often, the species in which females sing are less migratory or resident, so territories require year-round defense from rivals. Some birds possess more than one song type, and some species' song varies considerably from one individual to the next. Other birds, like doves, have limited repertoires, and stereotyped songs that vary little.

Generally, all birds are divided into two groups: the nonpasserines and the passerines. The passerines are often called songbirds (or perching birds). Nonpasserines produce vocalizations as well, but songbirds have a more complex singing apparatus, and the musculature of the syrinx (the organ used to produce vocalizations, akin to the larynx in humans) is more complex. Passerines are further subdivided into oscines and suboscines. In the ABA Area, only the tyrant-flycatchers (e.g., kingbirds, flycatchers, phoebes, etc.) are classified as suboscines, which are believed to be more primitive than the more specialized oscines. Oscine songbirds learn their songs, while many of their calls are believed to be innate inherited expressions. Suboscine birds do not learn their songs but are born innately knowing how to sing them. Since oscines learn their songs from their parents, sometimes they make mistakes. Occasionally, particularly in warblers but sometimes in other birds as well, a bird will learn the song of a neighboring species instead of its parents' song. It is not unheard of for a Common Yellowthroat to belt out the song of a Pine Warbler, for example. The learning of songs by oscine songbirds means that there is variation as well, and local "dialects" have been documented in various species.

As noted, however, songs are just one type of vocalization. More often, in migration and in winter, birds give calls or call notes. These are shorter expressions and so can be harder to learn, but once learned they are a wonderful tool for finding species. Many skulking birds or species that occur only in low densities are detected much more frequently by their calls. Birders able to learn these sounds increase dramatically the diversity of species on their daily lists. Start by learning one bird really well, and then it becomes easier to move on and learn others. Don't try to do too much too soon, or you'll run out of steam. In the course of your study, make an effort to take one bird at a time. For a more thorough treatment on how to learn and appreciate bird sounds, examine Don Kroodsma's *The Singing Life of Birds.*[3]

One area of bird sounds receiving renewed study today is "mechanical sounds." These are sounds made by birds that snap their bills or clap their wings together, or move through the air in such a way that they produce sounds with their wings or tail feathers. The known number of birds that use mechanical sounds to communicate is growing by the day. Examples include drumming woodpeckers; ducks and owls that

Few birders could mistake the "bouncing ball" song of the Black-chinned Sparrow as it echoes across the canyonlands of the Southwest. But many birds have a suite of other distinctive vocalizations that aid identification, including chip notes and flight calls. Becoming proficient at birding by ear, even with the common species in your area, will vastly improve your ability to detect birds, and to pick up on a rarity when one is present (BLS).

clap their wings together; owls that snap their bills; hummingbirds that perform aerial displays in which they produce hums, snaps, and whirrs; winnowing snipes; and many others. The Arctic Warbler produces an impressive "wing rattle" when on territory to intimidate rival intruders.

Recordings and Playback

There is no substitute for learning bird sounds in the field, but a great way to fortify what you've learned, and also to prepare for the field, is to listen to recordings of bird sounds. Between the Cornell Lab of Ornithology's Macaulay Library (www.macaulaylibrary.org/) and Xeno-Canto (www.xeno-canto.org/), a plethora of sounds are available for you to study. At various points in the text we offer Macaulay Library catalog numbers (e.g., ML Cat# 1234) of recordings we recommend studying as typical examples of a species' sound. While there is no better way to learn bird songs than the old fashioned way (active listening in the field), we make an effort in our species accounts to treat bird sounds. Yet attempts to phonetically spell out a complex bird song or describe it in words can frustrate reader and writer alike. We all form our own associations with a bird's sounds, so having authors impose their own can stunt the learning

process. We've made more than a token effort, but we urge developing birders to study sounds in the field, to listen to recordings, and to visit websites such as www. earbirding.com. There is much to be learned via these avenues that cannot be effectively taught in the pages of a book. Probably the best way of all to learn bird sounds is to make your own bird sound recordings, thus marrying your field experience to the study of recording. We need more recordists!

"Playback" is a hot-button issue. Playback is the practice of broadcasting a recording of a bird's sound to attract an individual bird. Typically this is done to bring a bird out of hiding and into view, which can be thrilling for birders. It is not uncommon to hear a bird singing repeatedly but never see it show itself. Sometimes playing back a recording of the bird's song will bring it quickly into view. Some birds respond to playback vigorously by moving toward the origin of the sound, while others may be frightened away, and still others are indifferent.

Playback has its costs and benefits. Many people see playback as disturbing to birds and thus deem it unethical. Often such people condemn any birder who employs the practice. Others use playback frequently. Many birders are perfectly happy without it and have no opinion one way or the other. Hysterical reactions are not productive in any debate, but these crop up in the debate over the ethics of playback, particularly from those against it, who see it as a disturbance created by listers who put their own needs ahead of the bird's security. Those in favor of playback make the case that humans themselves typically represent a disturbance just by their presence alone. If we accept that there will always be humans interfacing with nature, and if using playback minimizes a bird's exposure to certain humans, then this is actually a benefit of playback. Both arguments have some validity. More often, birding instances in which playback might be desirable fall into a gray area between these extremes. There are no rigorous studies on the impact of playback on birds, and initiating such research would be difficult, as birds vary so much in their response, and the impacts of birders and other humans also vary wildly from place to place. Controlling for these variables and making meaningful conclusions would be a real challenge. An all-out ban on playback is not only impractical but also probably unethical, so in the end education and common sense are the only ways to govern such situations.

One thing is certain: if you have never tried playback before, you should not try it without some guidance. Talk to someone experienced with it before trying it yourself. Going out into the field and using playback with no experience would be almost like getting behind the wheel of a car for the first time and pulling out onto the highway. In reality, few birders are truly qualified to teach other birders the proper techniques by which to use playback, and even many experienced birders don't really understand how to use playback properly. Professional birding guides by and large have the most experience, and because they have a vested interest both in seeing birds and in being sure the birds are there to be seen again in the near future, they have a healthy and nuanced approach to playback. If you are interested in using playback, seek out a professional guide and ask for advice on how to wade into the practice.

In the end, a bird will have one of several reactions to playback: it will be attracted, indifferent, or frightened. Generally birds that are strongly territorial respond most vigorously. Before employing playback, a birder must consider (a) the bird, (b) the surroundings, (c) if a sound is going to be introduced, what that sound should be, and (d) to what extent it should be deployed.

(a) The bird:
Is this an endangered species? Are you putting the bird at risk? If the answer to either of these questions is yes, than obviously initiating playback is a very bad idea. Using playback with an endangered species is illegal. Even if the bird is not endangered, is it really important for you to see it? If so, why? Is there a reason to see it beyond personal satisfaction? Would seeing it confirm something extraordinary?

(b) The surroundings:
Do laws or rules of the area forbid playback? (In federally protected areas, broadcasting sound is generally forbidden.) Will you disrupt other birders? Are you on a busy highway where the bird might be hit by a car? Is there a hawk or other predator nearby that might take this opportunity to capture the bird you are trying to attract? Given the habitat, cover, and conditions, is there even a realistic chance of seeing this bird?

(c) Using the correct sound:
You need to consider what sound you should broadcast. Should it be a type of song or a type of call? Different situations call for different sounds.

Many birders don't realize that some species will respond to sounds from other species. Some birds will respond aggressively to the sounds of other, similar species, as they don't want competition. So simply seeing a bird respond to your playback doesn't mean you are seeing the bird you are seeking. For example, certain species of rails and tyrant-flycatchers will respond aggressively to the sounds of other rails or tyrant-flycatchers because the sounds are roughly similar, or perhaps because they simply do not want to face competition for food or other resources. In these instances playback may not offer much benefit.

(d) Using sound appropriately: When is enough enough?
"Trolling" is a method of playback in which a birder broadcasts a certain species' sound repeatedly, trying to determine the presence of a bird. (As in fishing, you are dragging a line to see if you "catch" something.) You have to be careful about trolling. A common mistake for new users of playback is to sit in one spot, put the speaker volume on high, and play the same recording over and over again for minutes on end. This will not endear you to anyone who happens to be nearby (human or bird), and it does constitute bird (birder?) harassment. There is no need to blast a bird's ears out, and you are probably less likely to see the bird if you do broadcast at high volume. You'll likely scare it away or into silence. If you are going to

troll, do so carefully and strategically and follow the guidelines below.

Keep your ears open! Another mistake new users of playback make is that they play a bird's song and await a particular response, failing to realize that the agitated calls they are hearing all around them are actually from the bird they are searching for. Birds exposed to playback sometimes respond with songs but just as often respond with aggressive call notes or scold notes, or even "whisper songs." Whisper songs given on breeding territories, though they sound like subdued expressions of the typical song, are actually expressions of extreme aggression. If you hear a whisper song in response to playback, a bird is saying, "Back off!" Listen to it.

If a bird responds to playback by moving closer and continuing to vocalize, then it's doing its best to be seen. In this case the bird has done its part, so don't keep broadcasting your recording but instead take the opportunity to spot it by homing in on the area it's calling from. Even experienced birders will sometimes sit in one spot playing sound and waiting for a bird to appear precisely where they want it to rather than trying to actively spot it in the area it's already frequenting.

If a bird doesn't respond to playback within a couple of minutes, the odds are that it's not going to respond, or that if it does you have harassed it to the point that it felt it had no choice. When you use playback, do so at a reasonable volume while actively listening for responses, and if that doesn't work after a minute or two, move on.

As with anything else, if you use playback you are going to make mistakes here and there. Minimize them. Remember, too, that many birders are not at all forgiving of those who use playback (even of those who use it responsibly), so be measured in your actions and stay mindful of your surroundings. The following are good general guidelines for using playback:

- Use it strategically, carefully, and sparingly.
- Always obey the laws or regulations for the area you are birding in.
- Don't use it on individual birds that are vulnerable.
- Don't use it if you are in areas where birder traffic is moderate or heavy.
- Save it for use in group birding situations, rather than when you are alone or with just a couple of friends.

For more on this issue, read David Sibley's considered post "The Proper Use of Playback in Birding" on his blog (www.sibleyguides.com/).[4]

Molt: It's Not So Bad, Really . . .

Birders often shy away from learning about molt. Molt is the process by which birds replace their feathers, and all birds undergo some kind of molt each year. Molting birds are confusing to birders, not only because feathers are missing or growing but because the actual shape of a bird's wing appears different when

Freshly molted Pink-footed Shearwater, CA, Sep (BLS); molting Pink-footed Shearwater, CA, May (BLS). Note the uniform upperwings of the freshly molted bird compared with the highly patterned wings of the actively molting bird. Also note the two-toned secondaries on the molting bird: the gray bases to these feathers were covered by the greater coverts, which have now been shed, and the exposed feather tips are browner. This is a good example of how fresh feathers change color when exposed to the elements over the course of a year.

molting. The typical flight style may become labored if a bird is missing lots of feathers. Molt can also produce confusing contrasts between fresh, colorful feathers and worn, bleached feathers that have been exposed to the sun and the elements for nearly a year. These differences sometimes produce striking patterns that are not depicted in typical field guides. Understanding at least the basic patterns and rules of molt is really useful. Knowing these provides an understanding of a bird's life history, and if you are armed with that, identification becomes easier. Molting requires three things: time, safety, and ample resources. So birds fit this process into their lives when they can and typically avoid overlapping extensive molt with migration and breeding. Learning when birds undergo these processes is not only fascinating but also helps you distinguish similar species that differ in molt timing.

Birds have evolved different molt strategies to best fit their natural history requirements. Many birds undergo a complete or partial molt after breeding and before fall migration (if they migrate). This molt is called the "prebasic" molt. It generally results in a uniformly fresh plumage in most birds for fall and winter. Some species then undergo a "prealternate" molt to attain more colorful plumage before breeding. Juveniles of most species undergo a "preformative" molt, which takes place in late summer through early winter and results in a change from an identifiable juvenile plumage to an adultlike plumage that is typically indistinguishable from that of adults in the field. In this book you'll see the terms "prebasic" and "preformative" molts quite a bit, and it's helpful to understand that these refer mainly to adults and juveniles, respectively. For an excellent discussion on molt, consult Steve N. G. Howell's landmark text *Molt in North American Birds*.[5]

Molting Brant, CA, Aug (BLS). Note the very pale underparts that are bleached and worn, and the old brown feathers on the head and neck being replaced by new black ones. Consider the effects of bleaching and wear on the typical, expected plumages one sees in field guides, and be prepared to see birds that look like this. Understanding molt and how birds change their appearance throughout the year is key to accurate identification.

Taxonomy

Taxonomy is the science of organizing and naming life forms; in this case, birds. It is an ugly word for many birders. The "authorities" are forever changing common names, scientific names, and family groupings, and then splitting species, only to lump them again; and it all seems to happen too fast, or not fast enough. What ever happened to the Oldsquaw, Cabot's Tern, Water Pipit, Golden Swamp Warbler, Holboell's Grebe, Pigeon Hawk, Black-breasted Woodpecker, the ungainly Saltmarsh Sharp-tailed Sparrow, the confounding Sutton's Warbler, or the mysterious Cox's Sandpiper? Being a taxonomist is a pretty thankless job, and there isn't much money in it, either. Armchair experts criticize taxonomists for not moving quickly enough, while traditionalists bemoan changes to bird names they've held dear for decades. Making these decisions is usually a lose/lose situation. Everyone is a critic.

Most Americans and Canadians follow the official checklist of the American Ornithologists' Union. A more global treatment can be found in the Clements Checklist of Birds of the World (overseen by the Cornell Lab of Ornithology) or the IOC World Bird List (produced by the International Ornithological Committee, now the International Ornithologists' Union). These authorities publish annual updates with new arrangements of species, names, or family assemblages. This is probably never going to change. Birders often lament the endless changes, but in fact these only reflect newly published, peer-reviewed research. We'll be peeling back the layers of avian evolution and relationships for centuries. Rather than lament this, we should celebrate the inspiring work that is leading us to a better understanding of birds.

The species is the "currency" of taxonomy (akin to the dollar in the US economy). Species have binomial scientific names, first a genus (capitalized) and then a species, which are both in italics (except when surrounded by italic text). Humans, for example, are *Homo sapiens*. The binomial system was first devised by the Swedish botanist Carl Linnaeus in the eighteenth century, and it is universally accepted among biologists as the means by which to name and catalog all life forms. Scientific binomials are rooted in classical languages, especially Latin and ancient Greek, but many bird names have words borrowed from other languages or the names of people or places. Often they are tongue twisters, even for those who name them.

The pronunciation of these names varies, even among experts, so don't fear attempting to pronounce them yourself. Go for it.

The species concept itself remains debated. Many biologists contend that a species is a thing as real as a car or a table, and that while not all living things are neatly defined or categorized, most are, and unambiguously so. In fact, the species is actually the least subjective category that scientists use, but it is important to remember that it is a human construct. It exists only conceptually at a fixed point in time. It is just a tool, and like any tool it has its limitations, but currently it's our best device for categorizing life forms. It is one part of an information retrieval system. Using it we attempt to freeze a life form in time and examine its similarities to and differences from other forms. One shortcoming of this system is that life forms are not static but evolve, some changing faster than others. Consequently, some do not fit neatly into our system of categorization, and some defy it altogether. A cursory study of large gulls and various wrens, corvids, mallards, and others shows how limiting or inadequate the species concept can be at times. In these cases we can only do our best with our chosen methodology. In his excellent textbook *Ornithology*, Dr. Frank Gill notes that "the arrangements of species . . . are not fixed, because a classification is more than an authoritative basis for orderly communication about birds. It is also a set of working hypotheses about the relationships, similarities, and differences among birds."[6]

What a species is, and how that definition is applied, are subjective. Some populations are clear, discrete "species," but others are in the midst of differentiating. Several species concepts attempt to address this complexity, sometimes resulting in competing interpretations.

Species Concepts

In 1859, Charles Darwin and Alfred Russel Wallace coauthored a short paper that described, for the first time, the concept of natural selection as the driving force behind the evolution of organisms. Most taxonomists agree that a species is a population of organisms that share a single evolutionary history and can freely interbreed and produce viable offspring. Determining whether two populations are separate species depends on what "species concept" is used. Presently, the two species concepts most often employed in bird taxonomy are the following:

Biological Species Concept (BSC): a species is a group of interbreeding natural populations that is reproductively isolated from other such groups.[7]

Phylogenetic Species Concept (PSC): a species is the smallest diagnosable cluster of individual organisms that share a common ancestor and possess a diagnosable character.[8]

Ernst Mayr's landmark BSC is still the most widely accepted concept. First posited in 1942, the BSC says that sibling populations of an ancestral form evolve and differentiate, and over time mechanisms arise that prevent interbreeding. At that point they are considered species. In this concept, the idea of "subspecies" is an important one, rooted in the idea that what distinguishes species is their ability to interbreed. It postulates that as populations diverge (as one splits into two), the intermediate stages involve sibling populations that are different but not yet reproductively isolated (i.e., given an opportunity, they may interbreed). At these stages distinctions that are often visible or audible exist between the populations and they may be defined as different "taxa," but they are not so different as to be considered separate species. Taxa (taxon, when singular) are nameable taxonomic groups such as families, genera, species, or, as above, subspecies. Today, while still considered important, reproductive isolation is seen as but one distinguishing feature. Taxa may interbreed for various reasons with various outcomes. Some birds (not even necessarily the closest of relatives) may share an ancestral ability to interbreed but are evolving independently of one another along diverging paths. Others may interbreed occasionally or even regularly, but despite this gene flow they maintain their integrity as separate, distinct entities. (A modification of the BSC, called the Comprehensive Biological Species Concept, addresses this.)[9] Streaking on the flanks of a Hermit Warbler may be evidence of recent hybridization in its family history with the closely related Townsend's Warbler, or it may indicate a character still somewhat shared by the two species.

For the PSC, note that no mention is made of the ability to interbreed with sibling populations. And the subspecies concept is discarded. The PSC emphasizes that species are distinct evolutionary units (on different trajectories), and populations are deemed distinct or not. Identifying a species requires that 95 percent of the individuals in a population be diagnosable and of a common evolutionary origin (identifiable by one or a suite of characters, and without a gene pool tainted by individuals not belonging to that population—-i.e., regular hybridization). There are no subspecies in the PSC, just species, so if populations do not widely interbreed, and 95 percent of the individuals of each population are identifiable (either physically or genetically), they are raised to the level of species. (Gambel's and Eastern White-crowned Sparrows would be one example.) If populations are not easily definable (physically or genetically) and there is evidence of rampant interbreeding, they are not considered separate species. This is the case with birds like Downy Woodpecker and Song Sparrow that show geographic variation along a cline.

What Darwin wrote in 1859 of the species concept remains true today: "No one definition has as yet satisfied all naturalists; yet every naturalist knows vaguely what he means when he speaks of a species." Given the varying opinions on what constitutes a species, it is unlikely that taxonomists will unite around one definition in the near future, and given how speciation occurs (in fits and starts), perhaps they shouldn't. But as our understanding of genetics and birds improves, it is probably something to strive for, if only because the exercise is instructive.

Trends in Taxonomy

Over the decades, certain taxonomic trends are obvious in ornithology, and in certain periods taxonomists preferred "splitting" species, but at other times they more often merged or "lumped" them. Between about 1950 and 1970, when Mayr's BSC became popular, lumping was in vogue. Today, we are in the midst of a splitting era. The study of genetics has blossomed and, combined with a better understanding of evolution, has produced an evolved view of species. Many "cryptic species" are now being recognized, and it is hard to imagine the onset of another lumping era soon. Prior to about 1970, those deemed experts on a particular group of birds made these decisions. (Not infrequently the experts were working with specimens brought from distant lands, and while considered experts they often lacked field experience with the species.) Rarely were they called on to provide evidence for their taxonomic decisions, and it was not unusual for subsequent experts to reverse their decisions or rearrange taxa in another way. In hindsight many decisions appear arbitrary, and often they were simply judgment calls. Biologists today have more tools at their disposal. Since 1970, taxonomic authorities have relied largely on evidence published in peer-reviewed journals before enacting changes. This is slower and at times less efficient, but it helps ensure that decisions are more likely to stand the test of time.

The breakthroughs in genetic research in recent decades have been dramatic and revealing, offering yet another means by which to attack such questions as: Who is related to whom? And how closely related are they? For taxonomists, the primary purpose of genetics is to offer a data set with which to study evolutionary relationships. One issue that often clouds taxonomic study is convergent evolution, which occurs when two organisms evolve similar traits despite having evolved from separate lineages. For instance, both bats and birds are capable of flight, but this is the result of convergence because they do not share a close relationship. An example within birds is the long-perceived relationship between hawks and falcons. Formerly all hawks and falcons were placed together in the order Falconiformes, but recent genetic work has shown that falcons are more closely related to parrots than they are to hawks. The relatively similar habits and appearance of falcons and hawks led biologists to believe they were related when in fact this isn't the case at all. Were it not for the genetic work possible today, who knows when the actual relationships would have been realized? A genetic data set may allow a taxonomist to delineate relationships using important biological information. For instance, the habit of caching food in winter is specific to certain members (chickadees, tits) of the Paridae family, and it is considered an important evolutionary trait and a breakthrough adaptation that allowed certain species to flourish.

Yet, understanding a bird's DNA is not always so wholly informative in distinguishing species as you might think. Genetic studies do not always solve taxonomic problems once and for all. Sometimes taxa may differ dramatically in appearance yet share nearly identical DNA, while other times their genetics may differ substantially yet the taxa appear essentially identical. DNA is complex in both its structure (the genes it contains) and its history (and that of the organism that carries it). It offers clues, but scientists still must make subjective decisions when interpreting results. Some of the biologists who conduct such research are familiar with the birds under study, but some are not, and this can affect how the data are interpreted. Having some knowledge about the natural history of the birds in question (e.g., behavior, voice, molt strategy, habitat preference, etc.) almost always helps to better interpret genetic evidence.

Taxonomy as a Tool for Birders

Taxonomy is a tool for all of us. It allows us to place similar, related birds into groups. Emberizid sparrows, tyrant-flycatchers, and gulls each represent groups of related species; they are taxa, and each of these includes smaller groups (also taxa) that can pose identification problems for birders. But if you can identify a bird as a tyrant-flycatcher, you narrow your choice of species. If you know this tyrant-flycatcher is not a kingbird (genus Tyrannus), that further narrows your choices. What if it is one of those dreaded small olive-gray jobs with wing bars and an eye ring? How do you communicate this to another birder without having to say, "It's one of those small olive-gray jobs with wing bars and an eye ring?" It's a lot easier and more informative to say, "There's an *Empidonax.*" *Empidonax* is the genus that contains Least, Acadian, Yellow-bellied, Alder, Willow, Dusky, Hammond's, Gray, Pacific Slope, Cordilleran, and Buff-breasted flycatchers and also other species found outside the ABA Area. They are notoriously difficult to identify, so if you cannot identify a particular individual, you can at least indicate its genus so that other birders know what you are talking about. Genus names are useful handles, facilitating communication among birders, especially for complexes of similar species like the *Plegadis* ibis, *Accipiter* hawks, *Archilochus* and *Selasphorus* hummingbirds, *Empidonax* and *Myiarchus* flycatchers, *Catharus* thrushes, and *Ammodramus* sparrows. Familiarizing yourself with families and genera improves your ability to narrow choices when identifying a mystery bird and aids in communication.

Birders can also improve their skills in some instances by trying to determine subspecies. Many subspecies are well marked and easily identified, and though they may not count on your list as something new, learning how to identify them increases your understanding of the variation in appearance, seasonal status, and migration routes of the species. Subspecies identification may lead to the discovery of hidden vagrants, too. Some birders dismiss or ignore birds not deemed to be species, but appreciating subspecies and geographical and individual variation is useful, if not for potentially important conservation reasons, then because a curious mind is an active one. David Sibley emphasized this when he wrote that "any distinguishable population is noteworthy, whether classified as a species or not."[10]

As in any pursuit, in the taxonomy of birds it is always important to think for yourself. Question the authorities. Most of us do not have access to genetic laboratories, but take a split or a lump, or examine a few subspecies and test them yourself. How do they differ? Do they differ morphologically? Vocally? Behaviorally? Consider molt, the progression of age-related plumages, and breeding or migration strategies. All of these are instructive and can tell you a lot about a bird and its relatives.

Climate, geography, elevation, and habitat are examples of "isolating mechanisms." Gene flow is *the* critical factor in speciation, and so discussions of a bird's distribution often focus on its breeding range because genes are exchanged during breeding, and the extent of gene flow among similar species determines whether they will remain distinct or become a single taxon.

Isolating mechanisms also exist away from breeding grounds. Waterfowl such as mallards and swans form pairs on the wintering grounds, and the timing and location of pair formation can be another important isolating mechanism: if courtship and pairing happen on the wintering ground, then overlap in species' winter ranges becomes a critical factor for speciation. This leads us to another, perhaps obvious consideration of bird distribution: while birds are indeed distributed across space, they are also distributed across time.

And finally, when it comes to the names used by taxonomists, don't allow the English names to lead you astray. The Common Nighthawk is not a hawk. The Olive Warbler is not a warbler (and not olive!). In fact, the wood warblers of North America aren't even related to the Old World families that were the original "warblers" (a group now being split into multiple families). The Upland Sandpiper, once called the Upland Plover, is more closely related to curlews but is in a monotypic genus. And what the heck is a Yellow-breasted Chat, or a Dickcissel? English names are handles that facilitate easy communication about birds, but they can be misleading about how birds are actually related to one another.

Birding Mentors

Most of all, birding should be fun. For an increasing number of people, it may actually represent a profession (and thus work), but for most enthusiasts it is a pastime. Regardless of your personal birding goals, it's important to expose yourself not just to new places and new birds, but also to new birders. All expert birders have had a mentor, and usually they've had several. Finding new people to expand your thinking about birds and nature can ignite new ideas and illuminate whole new arenas of thought or a provide a fresh approach. Mentors don't need to be older than you, either. Often people your own age or younger can teach you a lot. Keep a lookout for new mentors and consider being one yourself.

Why Birding Is Cool

Though birding has perhaps never been more socially acceptable than it is today, nonbirders are still often puzzled by the idea. They have trouble understanding what it is about birding that is satisfying. They imagine birders in khakis and pith helmets making crazy bird sounds, feverishly pursuing birds with nary another care. This is the unfortunate caricature so often portrayed by the media. They want to show ravenous fanaticism and are less interested in the depth and breadth of mind and personality present in so many birders.

Nonbirding friends who are curious about your hobby may ask, "What is it specifically that you like about birding?" And birders have trouble answering this question, because in our mind the real answer is, what's not to like? You get to be outside in the elements. You are attuned to the weather and your surroundings, and this affords you the perspective to consider your own place on the planet—a refreshing, humbling experience. You are reminded how small your worries often are, and how valuable your time here really is. You can go birding virtually anywhere, escape from worry, and simply be present in the moment. And in that moment, you are often presented with something beautiful, mysterious, and exhilarating, and you can make thrilling discoveries. At times there is also frustration and defeat, but typically there is something satisfying in almost any piece of time spent afield. Other times it's simply reassuring, like checking in with old friends. Typically birding is at least a pleasant activity, and at times it is utterly thrilling. As with any subculture we have our fringe fanatics, but on the balance birders tend to be kind, curious, intelligent, and philosophical people. Maybe that's why we don't make the news too often.

Various poets have written on the restorative power of nature (Dickinson, Coleridge, Wordsworth, Neruda, and Frost, to name a few), and birds are one of nature's most conspicuous elements. They provide a window into the natural world, and nature and its workings, unlike so many human preoccupations, are undeniably meaningful. Floods, droughts, fires, storms, landslides, volcanic eruptions, earthquakes, and yes, even climate change are undeniably powerful events in the earth's history. An examination of birds provides a filter by which to view such events in time and space. As Pablo Neruda reminds us in his poem "Art of Birds," there is much wisdom to be gained through a life spent in pursuit of birds. Yes, aside from some pesky insects, some occasionally adverse weather, and the odd annoying person, ultimately there is very little to dislike about birding.

References

[1] Brooks, D. 2011. The Social Animal: The Hidden Sources of Love, Character and Achievement. New York: Random House.

[2] Gladwell, M. 2008. Outliers: The Story of Success. New York: Little, Brown.

[3] Kroodsma, D. 2007. The Singing Life of Birds. New York: Houghton Mifflin.

[4] Sibley, D. A. 2013. The proper use of playback in birding. http://www.sibleyguides.com/2011/04/the-proper-use-of-playback-in-birding/

[5] Howell, S.N.G. 2010. Molt in North American Birds. New York: Houghton Mifflin.

[6] Gill, F. B. 2006. Ornithology. 3rd ed. New York: W. H. Freeman.

[7] Mayr, E. 1942. Systematics and the Origin of Species, from the Viewpoint of a Zoologist. Cambridge, MA: Harvard University Press.

[8] Cracraft, J. 1983. Species concepts and speciation analysis. Current Ornithology 1:159–87.

[9] Johnson, N. K., J. V. Remsen Jr., and C. Cicero. 1999. Resolution of the debate over species concepts in ornithology: A new comprehensive biologic species concept. In Proceedings of the 22nd International Ornithological Congress, Durban, edited by N. J. Adams and R. H. Slotow, 1470–82. Johannesburg: BirdLife South Africa. http://www.int-ornith-union.org/files/proceedings/durban/Symposium/S26/S26.1.htm

[10] Sibley, D. A. 2000. The Sibley Guide to Birds: National Audubon Society. New York: Alfred A. Knopf.

Waterbirds

Loons

Swans

Mallard and Monochromatic "Mallards"

White Herons

Waterbirds in this case are a general grouping of birds that are not particularly coastal but are generally large and rather obvious and so good subjects for study. They provide a good starting point for a more considered examination, as one or more species are seen nearly throughout the ABA Area. While plumage characters are of course helpful, plumages are generally simple, but structure, range and habitat, and behavior are important keys to examine.

Loons

Red-throated Loon (*Gavia stellata*)

Pacific Loon (*Gavia pacifica*)

Arctic Loon (*Gavia arctica*)

Common Loon (*Gavia immer*)

Yellow-billed Loon (*Gavia adamsii*)

First Breeding:	~2–4 years old
Breeding Strategy:	Seasonally monogamous; solitary, territorial
Lifespan:	Over 20 years

Graceful aquatic birds, loons are pursuit divers that propel themselves through the water with powerful webbed feet. Awkward and vulnerable on land, they are at home in the water, nimbly seizing fish using their powerful, dagger-shaped bills. They typically make land only to breed, nesting primarily across the high Arctic and boreal forest, building their nests at the edges of lakes or on small islands within lakes. They winter mainly in coastal marine waters, migrating along both coasts during spring and fall. During migration along both coasts (mainly March–April, November–December), loons become more social, sometimes aggregating in large, loose flocks (they do not fly in V

formations). If you watch at coastal migration points you may find opportunities to study large numbers of loons in a relatively short time. There, most loons are seen in flight or at a distance, and this is a great way to learn the GISS of each species. Coastal locations hold the largest numbers in migration and winter, but loons can be found on any large body of open water, fresh or salt.

All five of the world's loons occur in North America, and also in parts of temperate and Arctic Eurasia (where they are known as "divers"). Common and Yellow-billed loons are closely related,[1] and they have a similar large build. Arctic and Pacific loons would appear closely related[2] based on their general similarities, but Pacific may actually be more closely related to Common and Yellow-billed.[3] Red-throated Loon appears to be more distantly related to the others,[2] yet all five species share the genus *Gavia*.

Loons are confused mostly with each other, but occasionally they are mistaken for grebes, mergansers, and especially cormorants. While beautiful and distinctive in breeding plumage, winter loons are more challenging identification subjects, clad in subdued grays, black, and white. At close range most loons are relatively straightforward, and a good study of head pattern, bill shape, and general plumage characters will help confirm identification. But loons always prefer open water, so distance and visibility often complicate identification. In addition, immature loons show variable and confusing plumages. Some one- to two-year-old loons oversummer on the wintering grounds, and these immatures can be especially difficult to identify because of age-related plumage variation and muted plumage patterns from sun bleaching or wear.

Common Loon breeds farther south than the others on wooded lakes across the northern United States and Canada, so it is particularly familiar to North American birders. It is a Hollywood favorite, and its call is frequently inserted into movie soundtracks to denote wilderness of any kind—often including, most inappropriately, the jungle! Common Loon's elegant features and distinctive voice lend it a mysterious and popular place in human society. Its likeness appears on the Canadian one-dollar coin, affectionately known as the "loonie." Indeed, the mournful wails of Common Loon are among the most moving sounds in the animal kingdom.

Breeding-plumage Pacific Loon, Churchill, MB, May (GB).

Focus on: *Structure, Head/neck pattern, Bill shape, Flank pattern*

upper back

scapulars

flank pattern

rump

bill shape

neck pattern

foot projection

upperwing coverts

Juvenile Pacific Loon, CA, Jan (BLS).

head shape

neck pattern

scapulars

wing coverts

bill shape

flanks

Adult winter Red-throated Loon, CA, Feb (BLS).

Note the structural differences between these two loons. The Common Loon (left) is larger and more heavily built, with a blocky head and large, stout bill held parallel with the water. The Red-throated Loon is smaller and slimmer overall, with a finer, uptilted bill and a flatter head (both photos BLS).

First-summer Common Loon, CA, Jul (BLS). Understanding the seasonal and age-related variation in loons is important. Many first- and second-year loons oversummer on the wintering grounds, and their variable and often bleached plumages cause ID headaches. On this bird note the pale bill and bleached head and neck, which make using plumage characters difficult. When confronted with a worn or bleached loon, use structural cues for ID.

Hints and Considerations

- Common Loon is the default species inland or along the Gulf Coast. Red-throated Loon is rare inland, but common along both the Pacific and Atlantic coasts. Pacific Loon is rare inland and on the Atlantic Coast. Arctic and Yellow-billed loons are rarities anywhere outside Alaska, and scarce even there.
- Structure is key in loon identification, for all ages and plumages. Focus on the bill, head, and neck. Note the plumage pattern (light vs. dark areas) of the head, neck, back, and flanks.
- It is helpful to think about a mystery loon as belonging to one of two groups: "large loons" or "small loons." Generally, loons are big birds, but Common and Yellow-billed loons are especially large, with blocky heads, heavy bills, and robust bodies. In flight they flap more slowly than smaller loons (consider wind), have thicker necks and big feet, and at times hold their bills agape. The "small loons," Pacific and Red-

Juvenile Common Loon, NJ, Dec (BLS) (left). Note evenly pale-fringed upperparts, with tapered or rounded scapulars. Bill is usually dull silver with a darker culmen but lacks dark blotches of older ages. First-summer Common Loon, CA, Jul (BLS) (right). Generally like a washed-out first-winter, with little sign of breeding plumage. Occasional birds have a few pale-spotted scapulars. Note pale bill without dark blotches.

Second-winter Common Loon, CA, Jan (SNGH) (left). Much like adult winter, but bill generally lacks dark blotches. Determining the age of second-winter loons requires assessing the pattern of the lesser upperwing coverts. Note the small patch of dark feathers with small white spots (see adult). Second-summer Common Loon, CA, Jul (SNGH) (right). Highly variable, some like second-winters, some like breeding adults. Typical individuals, such as this one, look like molting spring adults.

Adult winter Common Loon, CA, Mar (BLS) (left). Note upperwing covert pattern: adults have black coverts with bold white spots year-round, but this can be difficult to see with folded wings. Breeding adult, CA, Mar (BLS) (right). Striking pattern is typical of all breeding adult loons. Small white flecks on face will soon be replaced by dark feathers.

throated, are slimmer overall and smaller billed, with sleek heads and necks. Arctic Loon falls somewhere between the two groups, with males quite large and heavy, and females approaching Pacific Loon in structure. Identify any putative Arctic Loon only with great care.

- All loons may "uptilt" their head or bill, but Red-throated, Yellow-billed, and Arctic loons do so most frequently. Common and Pacific usually hold the bill more horizontally.
- Immature loons wander more often than adults and are confusing, especially in summer, when feather wear, bleaching, and patches of adult breeding plumage confound identification.

Identification

Males and females are similar, but males average slightly larger. A loon's plumage varies depending on both season and age. In all species except Yellow-billed, breeding birds show black bills, while nonbreeding and immature birds have grayish bills with a darker culmen. Below, breeding plumage is described briefly first, followed by nonbreeding and immature plumages, as appropriate.

Adults are categorized as being in either breeding or nonbreeding plumage. Immatures attain adult appearance in the third fall, acquiring full breeding plumage in the third spring. Distinguishable plumages include: juvenile, first spring/summer, second winter, and second spring/summer. Second-summer loons appear highly variable, with some looking similar to winter adults, and others appearing similar to breeding adults but often retaining signs of immaturity (e.g., white blotches on face/neck). Second-winter loons are often indistinguishable from adults in the field.

While determining the age of loons is helpful in identification, all individuals are best identified based on structural characters, regardless of age. The species are ordered from smallest to largest.

RED-THROATED LOON: Our most distinctive loon, Red-throated is also the smallest and slimmest, with a small head and bill, and an almost serpentine appearance in the water. Only slightly smaller than Pacific, the most likely confusion species in the West, Red-throated can also be confused with the larger and bulkier Common Loon. On the water, its pin-head with strongly sloped forehead and flat crown, its skinny neck, and its usually uptilted bill are good indicators. In flight, the wings are slender and swept back, and the head is held low, often lower than the body, but at times bobs almost rhythmically with the wings. The wingbeats are noticeably faster than in the larger loons. Red-throated's overall paler appearance is also noticeable in flight. This is the only loon that can take flight from land, though this is seldom observed.

Adult Red-throated Loon, Arctic coastal plain, AK, Jun (GV). Note the uniform dark back, unlike that of other breeding loons, obvious even at a distance.

Adult winter Red-throated Loon, CA, Jan (BLS). Note fine, uptilted bill, flat crown, and strong, smooth demarcation between white and dark gray on sides of neck. The white-faced and white-necked appearance is typical of adults; this combined with size and structure should allow most birds to be identified, even at a distance.

Juvenile Red-throated Loon, CA, Nov (BLS) (left). Note dusky grayish neck, lacking strong contrast of adult. Back evenly fringed pale, and feathers more tapered than in adult. First-spring Red-throated Loon, CA, Apr (BLS) (right). Variable, some becoming white-necked like adult, some remaining darker necked. Typical birds are washed dusky but show contrast.

Adult winter Red-throated Loon, CA, Feb (BLS) (left). Note strongly white-necked appearance in flight; darker crown and upper neck are often difficult to see altogether. Juvenile Red-throated Loon, CA, Oct (BLS) (right). Darker necked than adult, inviting confusion with Pacific (which see). Distinguishable from Pacific by uniformly dark lower neck (always pale on Pacific).

Breeding: More uniform and dark backed than other breeding loons, these have a dark chestnut-brown throat contrasting with a gray head, and white upper chest and underparts. Their breeding habitat differs from that of other loons in that Red-throateds prefer small, fishless ponds and lakes, from which they commute to larger lakes or coastal areas to forage. Breeding birds frequently give a croaking call when flying. *Adult nonbreeding:* These are paler overall than other loons, especially on the face, neck, and sometimes also on the flanks (but the latter is posture dependent). They are white faced, usually with white surrounding the eye, or at least rimming the front of it. Red-throateds have a narrow, dark crown. There is some white flecking on the back, but the "spots" are fine and very small (tough to discern at a distance); other adult winter loons have largely dark, unmarked backs. Compared to Pacific Loon, it shows less contrast between the extensively pale foreneck and the darker hindneck, and the hindneck and upperparts are less blackish and more grayish. *Immatures:* In Red-throated, a juvenile-like plumage is held through the end of a bird's first summer. These appear similar to nonbreeding adults but are more gray faced, and drabber gray overall, showing little contrast between the whitish foreneck and the pale gray hindneck. Some first-winter and especially first-summer birds can be very pale on the neck, at times appearing nearly entirely white headed at a distance; some can retain an overall gray-headed and gray-necked appearance (similar to fall juveniles) through the first summer. For nonbreeding and immature birds, the frequently upturned bill may accentuate the pale throat/foreneck and the stretched-out, rangy appearance. In flight, they appear mostly pale necked, while Pacific Loons appear mostly dark necked, with a more isolated whitish throat patch.

PACIFIC LOON: This medium-small loon has a compact build that usually shows a smoothly rounded crown. It is both more marine and more social than the others, at times migrating in flocks, sometimes 1,000+ strong. Extremely similar to the rare Arctic Loon, it overlaps in North America far more often with Common and Red-throated loons, so it is more often confused with those two species. Compared to Common Loon, Pacific is slimmer and more compact, with a rounded crown and finer bill. Pacific

Taxonomic Note:

Until 1985 Arctic and Pacific loons were considered the same species.[4] Vagrant records from the East Coast of North America prior to this split all appear to pertain to Pacific Loons. Today, Arctic Loon is the only loon species that is polytypic, comprising two subspecies:[5] (1) *G. a. viridigularis*, breeding in eastern Siberia and extreme western Alaska, and (2) nominate *G. a. arctica*, breeding in Arctic Europe and western Siberia.[6] To date, *G. a. arctica* remains undocumented in North America but seems a good candidate for vagrancy to the East Coast. It averages smaller, and breeding adults have a purplish throat patch (compared to a greenish one in *G. a. viridigularis*), but these throat patches are dependent on lighting and are seldom useful in the field.

Migrating Pacific Loons, CA, Nov (BLS). Flocks often number in the hundreds, unlike those of other loons on the West Coast.

Adult winter Pacific Loon, CA, Feb (BLS). Note fine bill, usually held more horizontally than in Red-throated, as well as more rounded crown, puffy nape, and darker hindneck. Black "chin strap" is a good field mark if present, but not all show it. Note even blackish back and wing coverts, typical of adult and second-winter birds. Second-winters may average paler naped.

Juvenile Pacific Loon, CA, Nov (BLS) (left). Note evenly pale-fringed upperparts and strong, smooth, white/dark gray sides of neck. Smoothly rounded crown and level bill typical. Adult winter Pacific Loon, CA, Nov (BLS) (right). Dark necked at a distance but always has white foreneck (can be hard to see). Adult usually shows stronger neck pattern.

Juvenile Pacific Loon, CA, Nov (BLS) (left). In flying birds note compact proportions (for a loon), dark gray hindneck, and white-throated look. Juvenile shows evenly pale-fringed upperparts. Second-winter Pacific Loon, CA, Sep (BLS) (right). Many immatures oversummer on wintering grounds. Note pale-washed nape, but dark sides of neck and pale foreneck still evident.

Adult breeding Arctic Loon, Meynypil'gyno, Russia, Jun (GV). Most birders will see their lifer in breeding plumage near Nome, Alaska. Note the blocky head shape with peaked forecrown, uptilted bill, and darker gray, more concolorous head than in Pacific. Also note differences in the neck pattern where it meets the breast.

Adult winter Arctic Loon, CA, Jan (BLS) (left). Note bulkier carriage than in Pacific, with uptilted bill, knobbed forecrown, and white flank patch. Structurally between Pacific and Common. First-winter Arctic Loon, CA, Jan (BLS) (right). Note evenly pale-fringed back and scapulars, indicating juvenile plumage. Also note large, obvious white flank patch when bird is riding high on water.

First-summer Arctic Loon, CA, Jun (SNGH) (left). Best identified by combination of structure and obvious white flank patch. Note peaked forecrown and long, uptilted bill. Adult Arctic Loon, AK, May (MM) (right). Distinguishable from Pacific in flight with caution. Note broad white flank patch, darker-headed appearance, and knobbed forecrown.

has an elegant carriage and shows a straight, even, dagger-shaped bill; when swimming it holds its bill horizontal (rarely uptilted). In flight Pacific is more often confused with Red-throated, but Pacific appears darker and thicker necked, with a slightly bulbous head and broader wings. On flying birds, the head is held even with the body, or just below it. *Breeding:* The contrasting silvery-whitish nape/hindneck combined with the round crown is distinctive from quite a distance. The face is dark, the bill is black, and the black upperparts are noticeably spotted white, especially on the scapulars and upper back. The dark throat usually appears black but occasionally shows a greenish or purplish sheen. At reasonably close range, white vertical neck stripes are apparent. Note that these are cut off from those on the shoulder, chest, and sides by the black from the throat, which touches that of the upper back (compare with Arctic Loon). Breeding occurs mostly in small or medium-sized tundra ponds (again compare with Arctic). *Nonbreeding/Immatures:* Nonbreeding adults and immatures resemble one another somewhat. Juveniles, especially when fresh in fall, show nice pale whitish fringes on the back and scapulars, whereas adults are more evenly dark above. Nonbreeding Pacifics are generally darker overall than other loons (ignoring Arctic Loon for the moment; see below); all are dark headed and dark necked, with a dusky face and a dark cap that surrounds the eye (or nearly so). The dark hindneck contrasts sharply with the white foreneck and throat, the latter being noticeable in flight. Compared to Common Loon, Pacific shows a neater, more crisply contrasting neck pattern, darker upperparts, and a duskier face. The oft-touted "chin-strap" is a good field mark when present, but some adults lack it, as do many first-year birds. Generally, winter Pacifics prefer more open ocean and relatively turbulent waters, though migrants may make use of calmer waters.

ARCTIC LOON: Very rare in North America, and very similar to Pacific Loon, it is heavier overall and has distinctive white flank patches in all plumages, though this character requires careful interpretation. Posture affects the prominence of the flank patch, so this character should be used in concert with other features. The white flanks are most obvious when a bird is at rest on the water, or swimming slowly. Then, depending on how much of the bird's flanks are visible above the water, you may see either a broad, arching swath of white along the sides, or only a small, restricted white patch just at the rear flanks. Flank pattern and head shape are less easily assessed on active or foraging loons. Any loon of any species that is bathing, preening, or rolling on its side may suddenly reveal white underparts that can be misinterpreted as white flank patches. Structurally, Arctic is intermediate between Pacific and Common loons but is closer to Pacific. Compared to Pacific, it is chunkier, with a thicker neck and a blockier and more angular head, usually with a prominent forehead bump. The bill is thick and even, larger and stouter than Pacific's, and is often held slightly uptilted (rarely so in Pacific). Separating the two species in flight is possible only with experience and great care, using overall structure and flank/rump pattern. *Breeding:* Compared to Pacific, Arctic shows a darker, more concolorous lead-gray head and nape, and a broad white flank patch. The vertical neck stripes are broader and bolder than on Pacific and also connect with those on the shoulders and chest-sides. In Alaska, Arctic Loons prefer sheltered bays rather than isolated tundra ponds and are rarely, if ever, found in the latter. *Nonbreeding/Immatures:* Again, similar to Pacific, these are clean cut, dark dorsally, and pale ventrally. The black and white on the neck sides contrast sharply, and the dark back contrasts with the white flank patch. The "chin-strap" present on some Pacific Loons is always lacking on Arctic, which also seems to prefer less open ocean waters and is more often found on sheltered bays; it may also make use of large lakes more than Pacific.

COMMON LOON: Our most widespread and familiar loon, it is also probably the most frequently misidentified, mainly by overeager birders who do not understand its seasonal and age-related variation. As with all loons, structure varies in appearance depending on behavior, angle, distance, and lighting, so prolonged study helps ensure accurate identification. Common Loon is bulky and heavy billed, and the head usually shows a prominent bump at the forecrown, lending it a blocky-headed look. It is most similar to Yellow-billed Loon in nonbreeding plumage, especially when reflected sunlight or glare off the silvery bill makes the bill appear paler. Common Loon overlaps frequently with Pacific and Red-throated loons but is the only expected species on inland lakes. Heavily built, in flight it shows large feet projecting behind the tail; it often flies higher than other loons and is regularly seen flying

Adult winter Common Loon, CA, Nov (BLS). Note bulky structure with blocky head, and dagger-shaped bill held level. Unlike other loons, Commons usually show a wedge intruding into the otherwise smooth demarcation of light and dark on the sides of the neck. This whitish wedge can appear as a pale collar on some birds but may be less prevalent on others.

First-winter Common Loon, CA, Nov (BLS) (left). Beware of changing head shape and structure on actively feeding birds. Loons generally appear more streamlined when feeding. First-spring Common Loon, AK, May (BLS) (right). Note pale-collared look at a distance, and white face. Juveniles molt their flight feathers synchronously during the first summer; older birds do so in spring.

1.23. Adult Common Loon, CA, Dec (BLS) (left). Heavily built compared to other loons; note thick neck with pale wedge, pale face, and large feet projecting past tail. Juvenile Common Loon, CA, Oct (BLS) (right). Similar only to Yellow-billed in structure, but bill is typically pale silvery, not yellow. Strong collared effect typical of most Common Loons.

Adult Common Loons on breeding lake, MN, Jun (GB). Breeding across the boreal forest on calm, wooded lakes, Common Loons are more easily encountered during summer than their tundra-breeding relatives.

over land. *Breeding:* Familiar, distinctive, and beautiful, adults at this season show a black head and bill, and black upperparts that are heavily spotted white on the back. The underparts are white and the neck has white striping on the sides. This pattern is similar only to that of Yellow-billed, but the latter breeds only in the high Arctic, whereas Common breeds in more populated latitudes, on placid lakes across the northern United States and Canada. *Nonbreeding/Immatures:* Blackish, or gray brown above, these have a unique neck pattern with a triangular white "wedge" pointing backward, above a darker half collar that rests just above the neck base. Basically, this is a shadow of the breeding plumage pattern. A broken whitish eye ring makes the face appear whiter than on a Pacific or Arctic loon. The bill is usually gray or pale grayish blue, with a darker culmen and darker cutting edges. Juveniles and first-winters have broad whitish edges to the upperparts, and first-summers are generally like first-winters. Second-winters are adultlike but second-summers are highly variable, with some like second-winters, and others similar to breeding adults but usually with blotchy white patches on the neck and face.

YELLOW-BILLED LOON: This is the largest loon, with a thick neck and a heavy, pale yellowish bill in all ages. It is rarely seen, particularly away from the Pacific Northwest, where it is scarce or rare along the coast (from Alaska to Washington) in winter. But Yellow-billed Loons, especially first-winter birds, are increasingly being found as vagrants at inland lakes across the West. The big head usually shows an obvious peaked forecrown, and even at a good distance, a distinctive pale bill, which averages palest at the tip. The culmen is straight, but the mandible is slightly recurved, producing an uptilted look. The bill is straw yellow during breeding, but yellowish white otherwise, sometimes appearing gray based (especially on first-winters). In flight Yellow-billed is most similar to Common Loon, being heavily built and generally flying higher than other species. It's best distinguished from flying Commons by the head and bill patterns. *Breeding:* Similar to Common, but they have broader white neck stripes (widest in the middle) and larger white back spots. *Nonbreeding/Immatures:* Paler overall than Common, Yellow-billed has a notably paler head and neck, often showing a distinct, darkish auricular spot. The darker areas of the head and upperparts are usually grayish or more sandy brown than on Common Loon. Especially problematic are first-summer Common Loons with pale bills. While Common Loons can have very pale silvery bills, note the differences in bill shape and general carriage. Common Loon usually shows an evenly pale bill, whereas Yellow-billed is typically paler on the tip.

Breeding Yellow-billed Loon, AK, Jun (CR). Yellow-billeds nest on small tundra ponds on the Arctic coastal plain, well north of the habitat of Common Loon. Note the straw-yellow, uptilted bill, blocky head shape, and white neck bands that are widest in the middle.

Molting adult Yellow-billed Loon, BC, Oct (IP) (left). Adults arrive mostly in breeding plumage in early fall and become progressively whiter faced during late fall/winter. Adult Yellow-billed Loon transitioning to basic plumage, CA, Oct (BLS) (right).

First-winter Yellow-billed Loon, CA, Feb (BLS) (left). Fresh-plumaged fall juveniles have scaly pale-fringed upperparts that wear away by late winter. Note pale face, dark auricular spot, and dull bluish bill base. Adult Yellow-billed Loon, AK, Jun (CR) (right). Built like a Common Loon, big and bulky, with thick neck and big feet. Note striking pale bill, even at a distance.

Second-summer Yellow-billed (left) and Common loons, CA, Jul (SNGH). When these are seen together, the differences in posture are striking. Note the uptilted bill of the Yellow-billed, and its slightly larger overall size.

First-winter Arctic Loon (back) and adult Pacific Loon, CA, Jan (BLS). Structurally, note the Arctic's slightly uptilted bill, blockier head, and slightly larger size. When these are seen together, the white flank patch of Arctic is obvious.

Adult Common Loon, side-rolling, CA, Dec (BLS) (left). When preening, loons often roll on their sides and can remain that way for some time. Beware of white-flanked appearance (cf. Arctic). Adult winter Pacific (top) and Red-throated loons (BLS) (right). Note similar size and build, but when these are seen together Red-throated often has whiter-necked appearance in flight (juveniles can be dusky).

References

[1]Evers, D. C., J. D. Paruk, J. W. McIntyre and J. F. Barr. 2010. Common Loon (*Gavia immer*). The Birds of North America Online. A. Poole, ed. Ithaca, NY: Cornell Lab of Ornithology. http://bna.birds.cornell.edu/bna/species/313

[2]Boertmann, D. 1990. Phylogeny of the divers, family Gaviidae (Aves). Steenstrupia 16:21–36.

[3]Lindsey, A. R. 2002. Molecular and vocal evolution in loons. PhD diss., University of Michigan, Ann Arbor.

[4]American Ornithologists' Union. 1985. Thirty-fifth supplement to the American Ornithologists' Union Check-list of North American Birds. Auk 102:680–86.

[5]Storer, R. W. 1979. Order Gaviiformes. In Check-list of Birds of the World. Vol. 1, 2nd ed., edited by E. Mayr and G. W. Cottrell, 135–39. Cambridge, MA: Museum of Comparative Zoology.

[6]Russell, R. W. 2002. Pacific Loon (*Gavia pacifica*). The Birds of North America Online. A. Poole, ed. Ithaca, NY: Cornell Lab of Ornithology. http://bna.birds.cornell.edu/bna/species/657a

Swans

Mute Swan (*Cygnus olor*)

Tundra Swan (*Cygnus columbianus*)

Trumpeter Swan (*Cygnus buccinator*)

Also: Whooper Swan (*Cygnus cygnus*)
Bewick's Swan (*Cygnus columbianus bewickii*)

First Breeding:	~3 years old
Breeding Strategy:	Monogamous; territorial
Lifespan:	Over 20 years

Instantly recognizable, swans are romantic symbols of elegance and grace. They are the largest of the waterfowl, and their long, supple necks and immaculate white plumage make them dramatic sights to behold. Inhabiting wetlands, lakes, and bays, they feed on aquatic plant matter (grains, tubers, roots) but also venture into farm fields to uproot stalks and graze grass. On the water they upend, submerging their front ends and using their long necks to reach for submerged vegetation. Swans are heavy birds, and in fact the Trumpeter Swan is the heaviest North American bird. When a swan passes overhead, the whistle of each wingbeat can often be heard, and their calls are a pleasing array of hollow hoots or trumpeting honks.

All six of the world's swans are in the genus *Cygnus*, and they are members of the oldest remaining avian lineage, the waterfowl family Anatidae. This diverse and cosmopolitan family comprises some 150 species. Hybridization is common among waterfowl in general and has been documented among swans. Unlike the more sexually dimorphic ducks, but similar to geese, swans pair for life,[1] though "divorce" occurs on occasion, especially after a failed breeding attempt. Successful pairs remain with their young through migration and winter.

In North America three swan species are common, while a fourth occurs as a rare vagrant. Additionally, Eurasian swan species and the Black Swan of Australia are popular among aviculturists, and all are found intermittently as escapees. On the breeding grounds identification is normally straightforward, as there is little overlap in geographic range and habitat. During winter and migration, however, swan species may occur together at the same location, causing identification headaches for birders. The Mute Swan is a nonnative Eurasian species that has been widely introduced in North America and now enjoys stable "wild" populations in several regions. The Mute Swan is distinctive and seldom confused with other swans. Trumpeter and Tundra swans are native, occurring over a broad range; they are common at certain wetland pockets, but sparse or scarce over much of the continent.

Identifying a bird as a swan is usually easy enough. Deciding which *species* you're looking at is the hard part! Distinguishing between Tundra and Trumpeter swans can be very difficult, and separating them from vagrant or escaped Eurasian swans is a challenge, too. Occasionally individual injured or ill swans cannot migrate and so oversummer in areas that normally do not host summering swans. These birds, as well as lone migrants, distant swans, and first-year swans, provide the most regular identification challenges for birders. All species overlap in habitat, but most have tendencies in their habits that are helpful to consider. The bill is always the key feature to study, but also pay attention to size, shape, season and range, and sounds.

Hints and considerations

- The distinctive Mute Swan is nonmigratory, confined mostly to the Midwest, Great Lakes, and the Mid-Atlantic Coast. It wanders occasionally, and escapees can be found nearly anywhere.
- The native swans, Tundra and Trumpeter, are similar, and separating them from Eurasian swan species (escapees or vagrants) is also a challenge. Tundra and Trumpeter can be distinguished from each other by voice.
- Tundra Swan largely vacates the Lower 48 and southern Canada from June until October, only occasionally oversummering.
- Bill structure is a key character in swan identification. Profile views are most useful for studying face pattern. Note the location of the eye, the narrowness of the lores, and the pattern of feathered versus bare parts on the face. On immatures, note the pattern of the pale skin on the bill.
- Trumpeter attains its white adult plumage later than Tundra does. Generally, first-spring swans with extensive dark gray plumage seen in the months between February and June are Trumpeters. Tundra is paler gray even in its first fall.

Tundra Swans with White-fronted Geese, UK, Feb (BLS). Swans as a group are easily identified by their large size, white plumage, and long, graceful necks, but determining the species of swan can be a lot harder!

Focus on: *Bill structure and pattern, Size, Voice, Age/plumage, Date*

Head and bill details for Trumpeter (top left and right), Tundra (middle left and right), Bewick's (lower left), and Whooper (lower right) swans. Adult Trumpeter (top left, GV; top right, BH) typically shows a long, sloping head profile with a long, straight, heavy bill, broad facial skin in front of the eye, a prominent pink cutting edge to the bill, and no yellow spot. Note the angular lines of Trumpeter's bill, especially the base, which runs straight from the gape to the eye. Heads and necks of Trumpeters are often stained brownish orange. Adult Tundra (middle left, SM; middle right, LS) shows a shorter bill with a curved culmen, and usually a more curved line of facial skin between the gape and the eye. Tundra usually shows some yellow in front of the eye, but this varies from extensive to absent; a small spot is typical. Eurasian Tundra Swans, usually called Bewick's Swans (bottom left, MS), show more extensive yellow in the bill, but not as much as in the larger and straighter-billed Whooper Swan (bottom right, HH), which typically has yellow extending in front of the nostril. Both species are vagrants to North America and should be looked for among large groups of Tundra and Trumpeter swans.

Identification

Adults appear the same across the seasons. The sexes are similar, but males average slightly larger. Adult plumage is attained near the end of the first year in mid to late summer for Mute and Tundra swans, but some Trumpeters may take two to three years to achieve the pure white adult plumage. Juveniles are distinguished from adults by their grayer plumage and by the color of their bare parts. (Nostril position may be a useful character but needs further study.) Juveniles undergo a preformative molt that begins in their first fall, and depending on the species (and the individual), this continues into winter or even into spring.[5] Fresh juveniles are especially gray. The three species differ in their first-cycle molt schedule, though, becoming white at different times of the year. By the end of the preformative molt, Mute Swans and some Tundra Swans will appear largely similar to adults (the adult pattern of the bare parts may develop later); but some Tundra and Trumpeter swans retain some grayish feathers into their second winter.[3, 6] Adult swans of all species may show rusty-brown staining about the head and neck, from tannins in water or iron in submerged substrates where they feed.[3, 6, 7] As far as voice, note that immature swans, which vocalize less (especially Trumpeters), sound higher pitched than adults.

MUTE SWAN: A nonnative species, Mute Swan inhabits ponds in suburban parks or along the coast, loafs around golf courses, and is also seen on larger water bodies, including slow-moving rivers, lakes, estuaries, lagoons, and bays. They generally prefer shallow waters with a good crop of submerged aquatic vegetation. Feral birds and escapees may occur almost anywhere, but populations have toeholds on Vancouver Island and are flourishing in parts of the Midwest, the Great Lakes, the Ohio River Valley, and the Mid-Atlantic Coast (from Chesapeake Bay to New Hampshire).

Large, with a thick neck and long tail, adults have a distinctive bill, which is always reddish orange with a black knob at the base. At rest, Mute Swans frequently show a rather curved neck. When agitated, they take on a unique and intimidating aggressive posture, erecting their neck feathers and flexing their wings, appearing even larger and really puffed up. If you see this posture, keep your distance!

Adults: Note the distinctive bill pattern and structure mentioned above. Adults are white, with longer tails

Natural History Note:

Mute Swan is a Eurasian species, introduced to North America, and is rather aggressive. Though lovely in appearance, they outcompete native waterbirds for food and nesting habitat. They also inadvertently destroy nests of native birds, including declining species such as Least Terns and American Black Ducks.[2] Controlling or eliminating such populations is a "sticky wicket" politically, but it has been accomplished in some areas rather quietly. Note that Mute Swans are not only a threat to other native wildlife in North America, but (like other swans)[3] they also occasionally attack humans that approach nests or young too closely.[4]

Despite their name, Mute Swans do vocalize, yet they are quiet enough that the folktale of the "swan song" developed. According to legend, Mute Swans remain silent until at death's doorstep, at which point they sing forth with tremendous voice, giving their "swan song." In reality, they do not ever "sing," but they do emit several sounds.

than other swans. Size is often difficult to assess, but Mute is large and roughly similar in size to Trumpeter. Be aware that distant immature swans of the other species, showing a noticeable pale area in the bill, might be confused with this species. In such cases, focus on the bill pattern and head structure, consider the habitat, and note the tail. *First-years:* Juveniles occur in a white morph and a gray morph. The white morph is common in North America, and such birds are white upon fledging.[7] Gray morphs become whiter with age and are usually entirely white or mostly white by November or December, and totally white in January or February. The bill is largely grayish to pinkish, becoming increasingly colorful with age. The lores are black, as is the area from the gape to the tip of the bill. *Voice:* They are mostly silent, but they give a snorting, wheezy sneeze, and adults hiss when defending the nest.

TUNDRA SWAN: Formerly known as Whistling Swan, this migratory species breeds on Arctic tundra lakes and wetlands but uses a wide variety of wetlands and farm fields during migration and winter across much of the continent. Approximate migration peaks for the northern Lower 48 are in November and March. Tundra is the smallest North American swan and is easily separated from Mute Swan by its bill color and

Mute Swan does not typically pose an identification problem and is easily separated from the other swans by its orange bill with a large black knob (adult), or a pinkish-orange bill with a small black knob (immature). Also note the thick, curved neck and long tail typical of this species (top, BH; middle and bottom, GLA).

pattern. Separation from the larger, but quite similar, Trumpeter Swan is more challenging. Size is often difficult to assess unless the two species are side by side, but Tundra does possess a shorter and slimmer neck. Most adult Tundra Swans show a variable pale yellow loral spot, but this is not a character you can entirely rely on (see below). Focus on the structure and patterns of the head and bill. Tundra grazes dry fields (e.g., corn, soy, etc.) or fields with emergent grass. It sometimes occurs in the same habitat with Trumpeter Swan in migration and during winter, but Trumpeter is often found in muddier corn fields, digging up stalks.

Tundra shows a concave head profile, sloping down from the forehead to the bill tip. Study the intersection of the face with the feathers of the head. Because of the narrower lores, Tundra has a more isolated eye. The forehead is rounded where it meets the bill. The bill is smaller overall as well, compared to that of the bigger-headed Trumpeter. Usually the feather border between the eyes and the gape is more curved than it is on Trumpeter Swan. Tundra has a more rounded crown. At rest on water, Tundra seems a little more goose-like; it sits higher and shows a more strongly arched back than Trumpeter, but posture varies.

Adults: A pale yellowish loral patch below the eye is present on most adults. Birders too often use this as a clinching mark to identify a swan as a Tundra, but this is a variable character. On some individuals it is greatly reduced and not visible from a distance, while others (rarely) lack it entirely. Even when present it is not diagnostic, as the occasional Trumpeter shows some yellow in the lores, too. But the yellow on Tundra is usually at its clearest and richest right next to the eye, appearing almost like a tear pooling up . Perhaps as many as 10 percent or more of individuals lack a yellow loral patch, while for another 4 percent it may be so extensive it covers 10 percent of the bill.[9] The remainder have a loral patch somewhere between these extremes, with "typical" individuals showing a small teardrop below the eye. *First-years:* Fresh juveniles are pale dusky gray. By December some are still gray, but most have molted some of their large scapular feathers, so that large blotches of pure white are evident on the back. By mid-January nearly all individuals show the new pure-white scapular blotches on the back, unlike Trumpeter. Trumpeter Swan is not only a darker gray but remains more extensively gray longer into the spring, often appearing largely gray (especially on the back) into summer. By April, first-year Tundra Swans

appear largely white bodied, but some have dusky feathers on the head, neck, and upper back. Bill color varies, becoming increasingly black as winter wears on; some juveniles are mostly black billed by November, while others retain a pinkish bill into March. In Tundras that are extensively pink billed, most show a pinkish base to the bill (base is blacker in Trumpeter). Some start to show a yellow loral spot (pale yellow white) as early as February. *Voice:* Calling at night in migration, and when flying during the day, these birds are often heard before they are seen. Remember that the old name is "Whistling" Swan. They give pleasant, whistled, hollow "woo!" hoots that may somewhat recall the sound of Snow Goose in quality.[10]

TRUMPETER SWAN: This is the largest waterfowl species on earth, with a long, heavy bill and a long neck and large head. Trumpeter is resident in much of the southern portion of its range, but when it nests farther north, as in Alaska, it is migratory. Once a concern among conservationists, it is now regarded as a species of "least concern" by Birdlife International, and for over twenty-five years Trumpeter Swans have been released in an effort to establish new breeding populations, especially around the Great Lakes. The success of such efforts is producing lots of records of wandering birds (in some areas they now outnumber Tundras). Most such birds are the progeny of released birds, but they are not banded, neck collared, or wing tagged as the released birds were. These offspring are becoming so widespread that any lone black-billed swan must be considered a potential Trumpeter. Breeding mainly on wooded lakes and bogs, in migration and during winter it overlaps in places with Tundra, but Trumpeter prefers more freshwater situations (e.g., peat bogs, forested lakes, slow-moving rivers). In Washington and southern British Columbia, it forages together with Tundra in farm fields, Trumpeter often preferring moist, muddy fields and digging into the soil more than Tundra (which usually grazes).

Compared to Tundra, Trumpeter rests lower in the water and holds its neck mostly straight, offering a curve only at the base of the longer neck. In part because of its heavier body, it also moves more deliberately than Tundra and appears shorter legged, with larger feet. These differences are typically hard to judge, and really the two species are best separated using head features (or voice). The profile from forehead to bill tip is straight, so Trumpeters are sometimes

Adult Trumpeter Swan, AK, Jun (GLA) (left); adult Tundra Swan, VA, Feb (GLA) (right). The real identification issue is distinguishing Trumpeter from Tundra Swan, especially on lone birds. Structurally, Trumpeter typically shows a longer, straighter neck, while Tundra's neck is usually slimmer and curved.

Adult Trumpeter Swans, AK, Sep (GV) (left); adult Tundra Swans, AK, Jun (GLA). Note the general shape differences between these two swan pairs, and also the details of the facial skin. Tundra typically shows facial skin that is pinched in before the eye, with some yellow, but note the variation in yellow on these two breeding Tundras; some lack yellow altogether.

When both species occur together, size can be obvious, with Trumpeter being much larger. In the left-hand photo adult and juvenile Tundra Swans are flanked by adult Trumpeters, WA, Nov (BLS). In addition to size, note the thicker, longer neck on Trumpeter, and facial skin details. Adults of both species, WA, Nov (BLS).

Juvenile swans can be a challenge. Luckily, they are usually accompanied by adults, which are typically easier to identify. Juvenile bill color and pattern is highly variable, becoming more adultlike through early spring. On juveniles, note the extent of gray in the plumage by date, and note general bill shape and hints of adult bill pattern by midwinter. Adult and juvenile Trumpeter Swans, WA, Dec (SGM) (left); first-spring Trumpeter Swan, NY, Apr (TJ) (right).

Adult and juvenile Tundra Swans, WA, Feb (SGM) (left); juvenile Tundra Swan, NC, Dec (GLA) (right). In general, juvenile Tundra Swans become whiter earlier in fall than Trumpeters because of an earlier preformative molt.

Juvenile Trumpeter Swan, WA, Nov (SGM) (left) and juvenile Tundra Swan, WA, Nov (BLS) (right). These two photos underscore how similar these juveniles can be, especially in early fall, when both arrive and are largely grayish. Note also that mud can obscure the developing bill pattern, making identification even more difficult.

described as possessing a "Roman nose." Trumpeters have a more peaked (less rounded) rear crown, and also a more swollen mandible. The mandible flares out (broadens) a bit at the outer third, and there is both a more prominent nail at the end of the bill and, typically, a more prominent pinkish gape line. The feathering above the bill (best seen head-on with the bill slightly lowered) usually forms a distinct widow's peak (rounded in Tundra), though this is somewhat variable, and less obvious on immatures. The darker lores of Trumpeter are also broader than those of Tundra Swan, such that the eye is less isolated on the face. The border of the facial feathers (extending from eye to gape) averages straighter than on Tundra.

Adults: White with a large black bill, adults rarely show a small amount of pale yellowish in the lores, similar to Tundra. When present, however, the yellow is less rich (paler) and less distinct and seems farther from the eye (closer to the nostril) than is typical in Tundra. Most Trumpeters with yellow in the lores also have grayish or yellowish in the legs as well, while Tundra always has black legs (but be aware that dried mud on the legs can make them appear paler).[11] Any swan appearing as Trumpeter in shape with rich yellow in the lores may represent a hybrid Trumpeter × Tundra. *First-years:* From fall through winter, juveniles are a relatively even sooty to pale silvery gray (darker than Tundra, but becoming paler with age). In March–April they often start to show some white feathers in the scapulars on the back and then appear splotchy, with mixed white and gray. They remain mostly gray into late spring (April–June). They become white as adults (or nearly so; some second-year birds remain grayish), at about sixteen months of age.[3] Bill color is variable, with fresh juveniles in fall showing moderate to extensive pink in the middle of the bill, which has a blackish base and tip. By January some are entirely black billed, while others will remain pinkish into midwinter. First-year birds have yellowish legs that do not turn black until well into the spring, with some (many?) maintaining some yellow on their feet into their second winter; Tundra apparently always has black legs.[11] *Voice:* The common call is a coarse, nasal honking that sounds sort of like clumsy bugling on a trumpet. Trumpeter sounds much lower pitched and rougher than Tundra Swan.

Also Consider

Whooper Swan is a Eurasian species, closely related to Trumpeter Swan. It occurs as a vagrant rarely, if regularly, in western Alaska and is accidental on the Pacific Coast south to northern California, and in the northern Rockies. Records from eastern North America are believed to be largely escapees, but some may be wild vagrants. Whooper is most similar to Trumpeter in structure but shows a largely yellow bill, with just the outer third black. This makes confusion likely only with "Bewick's" Swan.

"Bewick's" Swan is the Eurasian form of Tundra Swan. Tundra Swan was formerly split into two species,[12] with the North American form known as "Whistling" Swan, a name that is still used to separate it from the Old World "Bewick's." Bewick's Swans occur annually as a vagrant in western North America as far east as western Montana, but there are very few reports from eastern North America, and none with adequate documentation.[13] Quite scarce in captivity in North America,[13] Bewick's seems to be increasing in overall population[14] and may be increasing as a vagrant to North America. It is similar to Whistling Swan in structure but differs in having more extensive yellow at the bill base. For Bewick's, typically at least 30 percent of the bill is yellow (minimally 23 percent),[9] but the darker-billed individuals are similar to the yellowest-billed Whistling Swans. Intergrades (perhaps from mixed pairs in the Russian Far East)[14] may further complicate identification. Calls of Bewick's are similar to those of Whistling Swan.[9] Compared to the larger Whooper Swan, Bewick's has less extensive yellow. On Whooper the yellow extends farther forward along the upper bill (maxilla), ending in a point below the nostril. The two differ in structure much as Trumpeter and Whistling do. Juvenile Bewick's shows pale pink in the bill, often with yellow near the eye, similar in shape to the yellow seen on adults.

Adult Trumpeter Swans, WA, Nov (BLS). Flight identification of swans is a challenge, as both species look very similar. Luckily they frequently vocalize in flight, and their calls are very different. Pay attention to the voice of any flying swans you encounter.

Adult Tundra Swan, OR, Feb (BLS). The same field marks used on land also hold up in flight, if birds are seen well. On this individual, the yellow bill patch is obvious. Tundra Swans are also a bit shorter necked in flight and in general have a smaller, slimmer build, which can be helpful once you have field experience.

Adult Tundra and Trumpeter swans, MO, Feb (BLS) Can you figure out which birds are Tundra Swans? In some cases, especially during interactions between the two, general size becomes less obvious. In this photo, the three birds at left are Tundra Swans. They perhaps look slightly smaller and shorter necked, but a good rule of thumb is to make sure you get the best views possible before attempting swan identification, and it is fine to record birds in the distance as "swan sp."

References

[1]Del Hoyo, J., A. Elliott, and J. Sargatal, eds. 1992. Handbook of the Birds of the World. Vol. 1. Barcelona: Lynx Edicions.

[2]Dewar, H. 2002. State devising plans to control local population of mute swans. Baltimore Sun. May 11, 2002. http://articles.baltimoresun.com/2002-05-11/news/0205110009_1_mute-swans-nests-birds

[3]Mitchell, C. D., and M. W. Eichholz. 2010. Trumpeter Swan (*Cygnus buccinator*). The Birds of North America Online. A. Poole, ed. Ithaca, NY: Cornell Lab of Ornithology. http://bna.birds.cornell.edu/bna/species/105

[4]Allin, C. C. 1981. Mute Swans in the Atlantic Flyway. Proceedings of the International Waterfowl Symposium 4:149–52.

[5]Howell, S.N.G. 2010. Molt in North American Birds. New York: Houghton Mifflin.

[6]Limpert, R. J., and S. L. Earnst. 1994. Tundra Swan (*Cygnus columbianus*). The Birds of North America Online. A. Poole, ed. Ithaca, NY: Cornell Lab of Ornithology. http://bna.birds.cornell.edu/bna/species/089

[7]Ciaranca, M. A., C. C. Allin, and G. S. Jones. 1997. Mute Swan (*Cygnus olor*). The Birds of North America Online. A. Poole, ed. Ithaca, NY: Cornell Lab of Ornithology. http://bna.birds.cornell.edu/bna/species/273

[8]Sibley, D. A. 2000. The Sibley Guide to Birds. New York: Alfred A. Knopf.

[9]Evans, M. E., and W.J.L. Sladen. 1980. A comparative analysis of the bill markings of Whistling and Bewick's Swans and out-of-range occurrences of the two taxa. Auk 97:697–703.

[10]Pieplow, N. 2011. Trumpeter and Tundra Swans. http://earbirding.com/blog/archives/2411

[11]Sibley, D. A. 2011. Trumpeter Swans with yellow loral spots. http://www.sibleyguides.com/2011/07/trumpeter-swans-with-yellow-loral-spots/

[12]American Ornithologists' Union. 1983. Check-list of North American Birds. 6th ed. Lawrence, KS: American Ornithologists' Union.

[13]Mlodinow, S. G., and M. T. Schwitters. 2010. The status of Bewick's Swan in western North America. North American Birds 64(1): 2–13.

[14]Rees, E. 2006. The Bewick's Swan. London: T. and A. D. Poyser.

Based on what you've learned in this chapter, can you figure out which one is the Whistling Swan? AK, Aug (DG).

Mallard and Monochromatic "Mallards"

Mallard (*Anas platyrhynchos*)

American Black Duck (*Anas rubripes*)

Mottled Duck (*Anas fulvigula*)

Mexican Duck (*Anas [platyrhynchos] diazi*)

First Breeding:	~1 year old
Breeding Strategy:	Seasonally monogamous (some extra-pair copulations); territorial
Lifespan:	Up to 30 years

Today, Mallards so overrun suburban community parks and ponds that it seems laughable that the species was once known in England as "the Wild Duck." Yet the core of the Mallard population still breeds across higher latitudes, staging spectacular and inspiring annual migrations. These flights of ducks are indeed wild, in every sense. As one of the most recognizable birds in the world, Mallard is among the Northern Hemisphere's most widespread species, and in many regions it is the default duck. For birders, the species is so common, so mundane, and so heavily manipulated by humans that it is met with indifference or even outright disdain. It is hard not to admire the species, however, for it is both remarkably adaptable and successful, and it also represents the stock from which nearly all domestic ducks originate (dating back to the twelfth century).[1]

A favorite among hunters, Mallards have been widely released for decades, and this has taken a toll on some other waterfowl populations.[2, 3, 4] Mallards are aggressive, often outcompeting their congeners, driving them to more marginal habitats. Mallards also interbreed with many other duck species, at times

affecting their population dynamics. Among those affected by the expanding range of Mallard are species of monochromatic "mallards" such as American Black Duck, Mottled Duck, and perhaps also "Mexican" Duck. The American Ornithologists' Union currently regards the latter taxon as a subspecies of Mallard, but some authorities consider it a distinct species (see Taxonomic Note and Natural History Note below). Compared to Mallard (note the capitalization), the monochromatic mallards (with a lowercase *m*) show little sexual dimorphism, with both males and females appearing essentially brownish overall. So they are grouped together under the term "monochromatic" (in some texts referred to as "hen-plumaged" mallards).

Mallard and these three monochromatic mallards are members of the widespread and diverse waterfowl family Anatidae. They are dabblers in the genus *Anas*, within which the mallard group consists of about fourteen species worldwide. The four dabblers included here are wetland species, preferring ponds or marshy habitats, eating plant matter, aquatic invertebrates, and occasionally small fish.[4, 5, 6]

These four ducks provide a good case study for birders interested in bird systematics (i.e., the relationship between species), as Mallard is found throughout the Northern Hemisphere, while the monochromatic species each occupy essentially identical niches, but in discrete regions of North America. Surely some vagrant monochromatics (American Black, Mottled, and Mexican ducks) go undetected because of their similarity to each other and to female Mallard, and also because of a general lack of interest in "brown ducks." Highlighted below are the field marks best used for separating them. Always consider range, but pay particular attention to the head and the pattern of the speculum (Latin for "mirror"), which is the colorful area at the rear of the wing in the secondaries.

Taxonomic Note:

Most authorities consider Mexican Duck a subspecies of Mallard,[7, 8] but it may deserve species status. Genetically it is actually most closely related to Mottled Duck.[9, 10] In fact, Mottled and Mexican ducks are both more closely related to American Black Duck than they are to Mallard, and the three are more closely related to Spot-billed Duck than any is to Mallard.[11] Mexican Duck and Mallard show little overlap in their natural ranges, with decreasingly few Mallards present in winter throughout the bulk of Mexican Duck's more limited range.[12] Introduced Mallards, however, complicate matters, and these barnyard or semidomestic ducks can be present year-round and potentially hybridize with Mexican Ducks.

Adult male Mallard, CA, Jan (BLS). This most distinctive species is immediately recognizable to birders and nonbirders alike, yet its close relatives present a highly complex identification challenge.

Focus on: *Range and habitat, Wing pattern, Head color/pattern, Bill color/pattern*

Unlike many birds, ducks wear breeding plumage during winter. Males molt into a female-like plumage briefly in summer, presumably to be more cryptic when nesting and tending young. In this sequence of photos, note the plumage progression followed by a male Mallard: top, CA, Jul (SNGH); middle, CA, Sep (BLS); bottom, CA, Jan (BLS).

Hints and Considerations

- Similar in structure and voice, these ducks are large and have white underwings. Beware of female or eclipse-plumaged male dabblers of other species, especially Gadwall, teal, Northern Pintail, and Northern Shoveler.
- American Black, Mottled, and Mexican ducks seldom overlap in range, but all three overlap with Mallard.
- The most common challenges in this group are: (1) distinguishing a female or eclipse-plumaged (see below) male Mallard from a monochromatic, and (2) distinguishing a pure monochromatic from a hybrid.
- The degree to which Mallard hybridizes with Mottled and Mexican ducks is unclear. It hybridizes often with American Black Duck.
- Upperwing pattern is useful. The speculum color varies somewhat in each species (with angle and light), but also note the presence or absence of a white border. Note whether the rest of the upperwings (shoulder area) are grayish brown or blackish brown.
- Note the color and darkness of the crown, and the degree to which the throat is streaked. Examine the flank pattern, the color and pattern of the tertials, and bill pattern and color.
- **Mallard-like characters that appear in hybrids include** broad white borders to either side of the speculum; probably most useful is white or extensive very pale buff in the tail. Male hybrids may show greenish in the crown, grayish tertials, and black in the rump or undertail. Female characters are less obvious and not so well studied, but they probably include an intermediate (orangish?) bill that is darkest at the midpoint, broad buff edges to the body feathers, and a paler belly and throat.

Identification

These dabblers fall mostly into three plumages—male, female, or juvenile—but male Mallards also occur in an eclipse plumage (see Natural History Note). In all four species, males are larger. Mallard is the only one to show marked sexual dimorphism. In the three monochromatics, males show more colorful bills, more contrast between the paler head and darker body, and darker bodies overall. The criteria for separating the monochromatics from female or eclipse male Mallards remain largely the same regardless of sex, though you must consider gender in the process of identification.

Natural History Note:

Many male ducks, including Mallard, enter a hen-like plumage in summer (June–September) called eclipse plumage (a term applied mostly to ducks but also to sunbirds and Red Junglefowl). Ducks are unusual in that males achieve their most striking plumage in the fall and then become more subdued in eclipse plumage in summer—the reverse of what most birds do. Ducks pair in winter, whereas most birds pair up on the breeding grounds, so their showy winter (basic) plumage is useful in displays that attract females. Ducks also undergo wing molt in summer, during which time they are flightless for a period of several weeks. The more subdued, camouflaged eclipse plumage helps them survive this dangerous stretch in their annual cycle. But it also makes them harder to identify during this time, as nearly all male dabblers become more similar in plumage to each other, and to female ducks.

Generally, among ducks, the female determines nesting location, as pairs return to her natal area.[13] This is a key factor in how duck populations evolve. Mottled Ducks (and probably Mexican Ducks) form pairs earlier (e.g., August) than Mallards, and this limits hybridization.[4, 5, 6] Also, pair bonds extending beyond one breeding season appear to be more common in sedentary Mallards than in migratory ones,[14] which might further limit it.

Molt remains poorly understood in many waterfowl,[15] but by the end of fall juveniles appear largely similar to adults, except with duskier bills. All seem to breed at one year old. Adult male Mallards enter eclipse plumage from June through September, when they appear more similar to a female mallard-type, or a hybrid (see below).

Typical individuals are described below, and most individuals are identifiable. Each species shows some variation. Voice is quite similar in all four species and is not a particularly useful point of separation between these ducks.

Hybridization (the dreaded *H* word) is common among waterfowl. It occurs between Mallard and the monochromatics but is rare among the monochromatics. Because the monochromatics segregate by range, hybrids are rare, and few if any are well documented. First-generation adult male hybrids with a Mallard as one parent are usually obvious, but other hybrids may be difficult or even impossible to identify since many backcrosses (hybrids × purebreds) appear similar to a purebred monochromatic. So really, birders probably

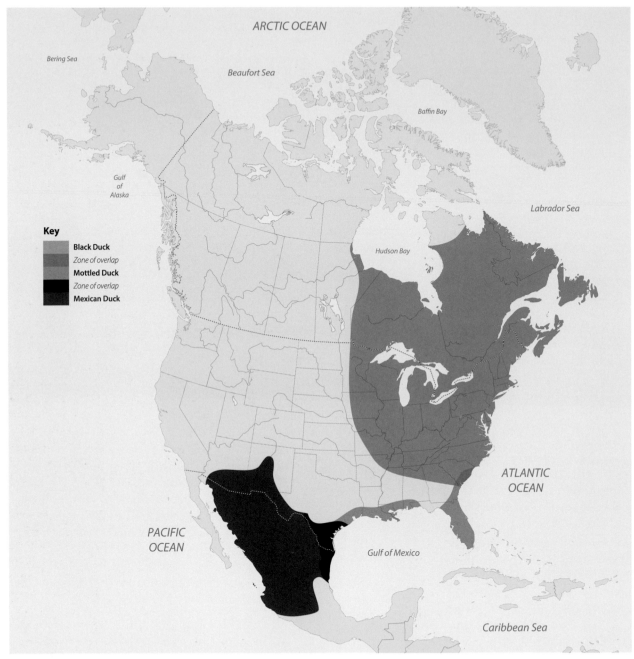

It is important to note that the ranges of these species of monochromatic ducks overlap very little, so range can be a useful identification clue as a starting point. Always rule out the expected species within range before assuming you've found a vagrant. In areas of overlap, caution is needed, and you must also consider the possibility of hybrids. This map is based on data collected in eBird (www.ebird.org).

shouldn't waste too much energy worrying about them. If a bird looks intermediate between Mallard and a monochromatic, then there's reason to suspect the bird is a hybrid. But if it looks good for a species of monochromatic, then you might as well treat it as one. To paraphrase the old adage, if it looks, swims, and quacks like a monochromatic, then it probably is one.

MALLARD: Common and widespread, this is probably the most familiar duck in the country, if not the world. From urban parks with ponds to remote island wetlands or desert oases, the adaptable Mallard can be found nearly anywhere there is water. *Breeding male:* Unmistakable in this plumage, the breeding male has a yellow bill, green head, gray body, white neck ring, and maroon chest. The white tail is bisected by blackish curly uppertail coverts, and the bright blue or purple speculum is boldly bordered with white. *Eclipse male:* From about June through October, the male appears more hen-like, being largely brown overall but with a yellow bill (less bright than in winter), some chestnut in the chest, grayish tertials, some white in the tail, and some black in the rump and vent. *Female:* The female is marbled brown, with a whitish tail. It is paler overall than the monochromatics, and often palest (at times whitish) on the throat, belly, and undertail. The tail is palest in the outer rectrices and may be a very pale buff, or more cinnamon. The bill varies in pattern and color but is typically orangish with a dark splotch in the middle.

AMERICAN BLACK DUCK: An eastern species, breeding from the Mississippi Valley east throughout much of the Northeast, Midwest, and eastern Canada, Black Ducks also winter throughout most of the Southeast. More migratory than other monochromatics, Black Ducks that breed in New England, the Great Lakes, and Canada move south for winter, and as a result this species is more prone to vagrancy. Pairs often form by December, and in some areas breeding may ensue as early as February.[5] Hybrids with Mallards are routinely encountered and in places outnumber Black Ducks.[3]

Inhabiting estuaries, impoundments, saltwater and freshwater marshes, Black Ducks are the darkest of the monochromatics. They are generally colder in color than the other species, with fewer warm buff tones, and the body feathers are solid dark brown, showing usually only thin grayish or cinnamon edges (usually more apparent on females). Black Duck averages a

duskier bill than the other monochromatics. Females show dull olive or blackish bills. Males have yellowish bills that range from an even yellow to olive yellow, but those showing rich school-bus-yellow bills should be examined for other Mallard-like characters that could indicate a hybrid. Compared to the others, Black Ducks also have darker, blackish crowns, and their faces and throats are grayish with fine streaking throughout. The tail is blackish brown.

In flying birds, the speculum is blue or purplish, with usually a thin white border along the trailing edge. In some Black Ducks this white trailing edge to the secondaries is absent. The shoulders are a solid dark brown. Underneath, since Black Ducks are darker than the others, they also show more contrast between the belly and the underwings, and the undertail and uppertail are darker as well.

MOTTLED DUCK: A species of the Southeastern United States, Mottled Duck replaces Black Duck along the coast in Florida (largely south of the panhandle), in the western Gulf Coast regions of Louisiana and Texas, and into Mexico. Despite being one of the few nonmigratory species of waterfowl in North America, Mottled Duck has on rare occasions strayed north of its normal range. It is generally less social than Mallard or Black Duck, typically found in pairs or small flocks. Pairs form usually by November, and breeding ensues in January.[4] Mottled Ducks are found in freshwater and brackish waters along the coastal plain, but they are seldom found in saltwater areas.

There are two populations, with the birds in Florida isolated from those in Louisiana and Texas (the latter population is sometimes considered a subspecies, *A. f. maculosa*).[4] The two populations differ in their genetics but appear largely similar in plumage, though some claim that Mottled Ducks in the western Gulf average darker.[10] The species was introduced to South Carolina in 1975, using stock from the western Gulf,[4] and these South Carolina ducks have expanded into Georgia and dispersed into Florida, where they breed with Florida Mottled Ducks,[4] and hybrids with Mallard occur to an unknown degree. In some areas of Florida, hybridization is not known to occur, but in other parts of the state up to 24 percent have been found to share Mallard genes.[16] Released Mallards may thus pose a real threat to Mottled Duck populations.

Mottled is overall intermediate in appearance between a female Mallard and a Black Duck. It is

Female Mallards: NY, Mar (BLS) (left); WA, Feb (BLS) (right). Female Mallards are the palest of the "monochromatics," averaging buffier below and usually showing an extensively white or buff tail. Bill color is usually orange with a dark central splotch, the extent of which is highly variable.

Male Black Duck, ME, Sep (SNGH) (left); female Black Duck, VA, Feb (GLA) (right). Black Ducks are the darkest of the "monochromatics," and the most widespread after Mallard. Black Ducks have blackish bodies with limited pale fringes below. Males have yellowish-green bills and females have dull olive bills, though some birds are difficult to sex in the field.

Composite image of female Mallards (right two birds) and American Black Duck pair (female top middle, male lower left) (BLS, GLA). Note the overall pale ventral color of the Mallard, and the broad white borders on both sides of the speculum. Black Duck is darker below, contrasting more strongly with white underwings, and has a limited white trailing edge to the speculum.

Male (left) and female Mottled Ducks, FL, Mar (BLS). Mottled Ducks have pale, skinny necks and pale heads in general. Males have bright yellow to yellow-green bills, and females have mostly orange bills; all show a dark gape spot, unlike any of the other "monochromatics." Also note dark body with strong neck contrast, and broad cinnamon fringes below.

Male Mexican Duck, CO, Jan (left), and female Mexican Duck, AZ, Feb (SGM). Male similar to Mottled Duck but lacks dark gape spot and has darker overall head and neck; female similar to Mallard but has darker body and stronger neck contrast. Both sexes show white borders on both sides of speculum, similar to Mallard. Note brownish mottled tail, usually darker than in Mallard.

Composite image of Mexican Ducks (right two birds; SGM) and Mottled Ducks (left two birds; BLS). They are similar overall, but note darker head and crown of Mexican, broader white borders to speculum, and slightly paler tail. Mexican shows stronger neck/body contrast than female Mallard, and usually slightly narrower white borders to the speculum.

smaller than the other monochromatics or Mallard, showing a pale buffy crown and a noticeably skinny neck. The face is buffy, with a broad buffy supercilium and a relatively indistinct eye line, and the cheeks and throat are unstreaked and buff. Males have bright yellow bills, fairly similar to those of a male Mallard. Females have yellow or orangish bills, and some show a hint of a black patch at the midpoint, similar to that on a female Mallard. Nearly all Mottled Ducks show an oblong black patch at the gape, a character seldom if ever observed in the other species. The body feathers show obvious buff or cinnamon fringes, cinnamon chevrons within the feathers, and a brown tail that is darker in the middle and paler cinnamon toward the outer edge. In a flying or standing Mottled, note how the belly is darker brown than on a female Mallard. Like Black Duck, Mottled shows dark blackish-brown upperwings/shoulders. The green or blue speculum is bordered narrowly and often indistinctly with white, typically only along the trailing edge, but occasionally also on the leading edge.

MEXICAN DUCK: This relatively little-studied taxon seems to deserve species status.[10, 12] It inhabits freshwater wetlands in the inland plateaus of Mexico and the southwestern United States, ranging from southeast Arizona east through southern New Mexico to west Texas, and south into the central Mexican highlands. It also occurs sparsely along the Rio Grande Valley of Texas and is increasingly detected north of its range to central Colorado, and rarely farther north. It is largely resident, but some seasonal movements are detected as birds move from smaller ephemeral wetlands for nesting to larger bodies of water in winter.[12, 16]

The degree to which hybridization occurs with Mallard is not well understood. At least in Arizona, hybridization seems limited[12, 17] in the wilder areas toward the southeast, but it is locally more frequent in urban settings toward the northwest. Relatively few Mallards overwinter (when pair formation occurs) in areas inhabited by Mexican Ducks, and not only do Mexican Ducks pair earlier, but they also maintain pair bonds longer. These aspects should limit the opportunity for mixed pairs to form with migrant Mallards. But some Mexican Ducks may still pair with domestic-type or released Mallards, especially in cities where neither occurred historically (e.g., Tucson). Second- and third-generation hybrids may

well be indistinguishable from typical Mexican Ducks. Within the range of Mexican Duck, however, it seems reasonable to assume that any bird appearing to be a Mexican Duck probably is one.

Agreement on just how a "typical" Mexican Duck should appear is elusive. Its features and identification require more study. Individuals at the northern end of the species' range seem to show more Mallard-like features than those farther south in Mexico, despite no obvious hybrid zone being known historically.[12, 18] One study found no morphological features separating northern and southern populations, but many birds in the northern part of the range showed Mallard-like features such as a slight green sheen to the head, rufous in the chest, brighter yellow bills, whitish feathers in the tail, and paler grayish tertials.[19] Whether these characters simply vary between individuals, are evidence of hybridization, or are retained characters of a shared ancestry (or some combination of these) remains unclear.

In appearance (and genetics) Mexican Duck is closest to Mottled Duck, but it is intermediate between it and a female Mallard. Separation from Mallard is the most common problem, but in south Texas it could overlap with Mottled, and both could occur as vagrants to the western Great Plains. Note that in flight Mexican shows gray-brown shoulders, and a blue or green speculum narrowly bordered with white at both ends; it is rather similar to Mallard's but with a less purplish speculum that has narrower borders on average. Mexican Duck averages slightly smaller than Mallard and is darker overall, with a darker brown belly, undertail, and tail. Males are darker in the face, with more heavily streaked cheeks than Mallard or Mottled. The back and tertials are darker brown as well. Males have yellow bills, and females have dull yellow, dusky orange, or olive bills. Distinguishing a female Mallard from a female Mexican Duck is difficult, and their separation remains in need of clarification. Female Mexican Ducks should appear darker overall, with richer dark brown chests (contrasting more with the paler head), generally dark underparts (not the whitish belly of a female Mallard), darker brown undertail coverts, a more cinnamon (less pale buffy) tail, and possibly more streaking on the face. Compared to Mottled Duck, Mexican Duck shows a darker and more extensively dark brown crown (especially males), the eye line is darker brown, and the face averages streakier. Mexican lacks the black gape spot present on Mottled.

Adult male Mallard × American Black Duck hybrid, VA, Feb (GLA) (left); and Mallard × American Black Duck hybrid, ME, Sep (SNGH) (right). Hybrids between these species are common. Most show obvious signs of mixed genes, such as the male at left. The bird at right is subtler, but note a much paler body than is typical of Black Duck.

Adult male Mallard × Mottled Duck hybrids, TX, Nov (SNGH). Hybrids between these two species can look intermediate, with obvious signs of male Mallard genes, or they can appear more like Mottled Ducks, as is the case in these two birds. Note the darker crown, face, and neck than is typical for Mottled Duck; also, the bill lacks a black gape spot on both, and each shows a whitish tail with curled coverts like male Mallard. Also note the narrow white-bordered speculum on the bird at right.

Mexican × Mallard hybrids, AZ, Feb (SGM). Hybrids between these two species can show obvious signs, such as the bird at left, or be subtler, such as the bird at right. Determining exactly where variation in one species ends and another begins is very difficult, especially in the case of Mexican Duck, which show more Mallard-like characters in the northern parts of its range.

References

[1]Clayton, G. A. 1984. Common Duck. In Evolution of Domesticated Animals, edited by I. L. Mason, 334–39. London: Longman.

[2]Merendino, M. T., C. D. Ankney, and D. G. Dennis. 1993. Increasing Mallards, decreasing American Black Ducks: More evidence for cause and effect. Journal of Wildlife Management 57(2): 199–208.

[3]Merendino, M. T., and C. D. Ankney. 1994. Habitat use by Mallards and American Black Ducks breeding in central Ontario. Condor 96:411–21.

[4]Bielefeld, R. R., M. G. Brasher, T. E. Moorman, and P. N. Gray. 2010. Mottled Duck (*Anas fulvigula*). The Birds of North America Online. A. Poole, ed. Ithaca, NY: Cornell Lab of Ornithology. http://bna.birds.cornell.edu/bna/species/081

[5]Longcore, J. R., D. G. McAuley, G. R. Hepp, and J. M. Rhymer. 2000. American Black Duck (*Anas rubripes*). The Birds of North America Online. A. Poole, ed. Ithaca, NY: Cornell Lab of Ornithology. http://bna.birds.cornell.edu/bna/species/481

[6]Drilling, N., R. Titman, and F. McKinney. 2002. Mallard (*Anas platyrhynchos*). The Birds of North America Online. A. Poole, ed. Ithaca, NY: Cornell Lab of Ornithology. http://bna.birds.cornell.edu/bna/species/658

[7]Hubbard, J. P. 1977. The biological and taxonomic status of the Mexican Duck. Bulletin of the New Mexico Department of Game and Fish 16.

[8]American Ornithologists' Union. 1998. Check-list of North American Birds. 7th ed. Washington, DC: American Ornithologists' Union.

[9]Johnson, K. P., and M. D. Sorenson. 1999. Phylogeny and biogeography of dabbling ducks (Genus: *Anas*): A comparison of molecular and morphological evidence. Auk 116(3): 792–805.

[10]McCracken, K. G., W. P. Johnson, and F. H. Sheldon. 2001. Molecular population genetics, phylogeography, and conservation biology of the mottled duck (*Anas fulvigula*). Conservation Genetics 2:87–102.

[11]Kulikova, I. V., Y. N. Zhuravlev, and K .G. McCracken. 2004. Asymmetric hybridization and sex-biased gene flow between Eastern Spot-billed Ducks (*Anas zonorhyncha*) and Mallards (*A. platyrhynchos*) in the Russian Far East. Auk 121(3): 930–49.

[12]Webster, R. E. 2006. The status of Mottled Duck (*Anas fulvigula*) in Arizona. Arizona Birds 2:6–9.

[13]Rohwer, F. C., and M. G. Anderson. 1988. Female-biased philopatry, monogamy, and the timing of pair formation in migratory waterfowl. Current Ornithology 5:187–221.

[14]Mjerstad, H., and M. Saederstal. 1990. Reforming of resident Mallard pair (*Anas platyrhynchos*), rule rather than exception? Wildfowl 41:150–51.

[15]Howell, S.N.G. 2010. Molt in North American Birds. New York: Houghton Mifflin.

[16]Williams, C. L., R. C. Brust, T. T. Fendley, G. R. Tiller, and O. E. Rhodes. 2005. A comparison of hybridization between Mottled Ducks (*Anas fulvigula*) and Mallards (*A. platyrhynchos*) in Florida and South Carolina using microsatellite DNA analysis. Conservation Genetics 6(3): 445–53.

[17]Brown, D. E. 1985. Arizona Wetlands and Waterfowl. Tucson: University of Arizona Press.

[18]Scott, N. J., Jr., and R. P. Reynolds. 1984. Phenotypic variation of the Mexican Duck (*Anas platyrhynchos diazi*) in Mexico. Condor 86(3): 266–74.

[19]Aldrich, J. W., and K. P. Baer. 1970. Status and speciation in the Mexican Duck. Wilson Bulletin 82:63–73.

White Herons

Snowy Egret (*Egretta thula*)

Great Egret (*Ardea alba*)

Cattle Egret (*Bubulcus ibis*)

Little Blue Heron (*Egretta caerulea*)

Reddish Egret (*Egretta rufescens*)

"Great White" Heron (*Ardea herodias occidentalis*)

Also: Little Egret (*Egretta garzetta*)

First Breeding:	1–3 years old
Breeding Strategy:	Promiscuous or seasonally monogamous; colonial
Lifespan:	13–20 years

Statuesque, stately, and elegantly plumaged, with long necks and long legs, herons rank among our most conspicuous and beautiful birds. They use their long, sharp bills to stab at fish, frogs, or large insects while gracefully wading through estuarine shallows, ponds, marshes, and ditches. In the early 1900s herons were hunted extensively for their flamboyant plumes, or "aigrettes," which were used to adorn ladies' hats. Their protection became a rallying point for the early conservation era, and today the Great Egret remains the symbol of the National Audubon Society. Familiar to all, herons provide many new birders with their first identification challenges and triumphs. All are in the diverse cosmopolitan heron family Ardeidae, which encompasses over sixty species globally, including the tiger-herons, bitterns, night-herons, and the more typical "day herons";[1] the latter include the species treated here. In North America thirteen species of heron breed, and hybridization between species is rare. The terms "heron" and "egret" do not correspond with a specific set of traits, and in fact all members of the family are often collectively referred to as "herons."

Herons are generally quite social, but some species are more so than others. All these species typically nest in colonies, and larger colonies may number in the hundreds, often containing multiple species. Mixed-species feeding flocks develop in areas with abundant small fish, and such situations allow for great comparative studies. White herons are conspicuous

Natural History Note:

Little Blue Heron is unique among these species in that the immature differs in color from the adult, appearing almost wholly white in plumage for its first year of life.[2] The white plumage appears to be an advantage in several ways. Foraging Snowy Egrets attract other herons, including Little Blues, and Little Blue Herons' feeding success increases when they hunt in association with Snowies.[3] But the Snowies and other herons often drive off the dark Little Blue adults while ignoring the white youngsters. The white immatures are thus given time to master fishing techniques[3] amid more abundant prey. They are also afforded a measure of safety as part of a flock. Immatures are less experienced and more vulnerable, and since white herons are preyed on more than dark ones, as part of a flock they benefit from the increased predator detection and safety in numbers.[4]

Along with tinamous, bustards, and parrots, herons are one of few groups of birds to produce "powder down." Powder down is used to enhance plumage in the same way that oil from the uropygial gland (a.k.a. the preen gland, which is much reduced in herons) helps fortify feathers against weather and abrasion.[5] Powder down comes from small specialized feathers that grow constantly on a bird (and never molt), but the tips continually disintegrate into a pale powder. This powder sticks to the plumage, protecting it somewhat from the sun while absorbing moisture and mud. It flakes away as it dries out, or it is preened away as it becomes dirty.[6]

and quite confiding, and beginners find it fun to distinguish between Snowy, Great, and Cattle egrets. They may eventually enjoy the challenge of aging these birds, and distinguishing them from white-morph Reddish Egrets and immature Little Blue Herons. Florida is a great place to study these species, as well as the enigmatic "Great White" Heron, which occurs fairly commonly in only the southern half of that state.

Most white herons are easily identified, yet others puzzle even the most expert among us. Learning the structural differences is key to identification, but habitat and behavior are also important. Habitat preferences, foraging techniques, and feeding postures differ among these birds, and being aware of these helps narrow the possibilities considerably. Learning to age herons is also important, as critical field marks change with age.

How many heron species can you find in this image? In this fairly typical scene, various species of white herons feed together in a Florida ditch. In this chapter we'll learn how to focus on more than plumage. Key elements of structure and behavior will quickly help you sort out these birds (BLS).

Focus on: *Structure, Behavior/habitat, Age/plumage, Bare parts*

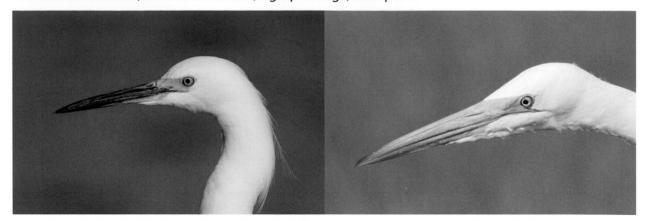

Snowy Egret, CA, Dec (BLS) (left); Great Egret, CA, Feb (BLS) (right). On this plate, focus on the different bill shapes and colors. Birds here are in nonbreeding condition, as they are during much of the year. Note the slim dark bill of Snowy Egret compared with the mostly yellow, heavier bill of Great Egret.

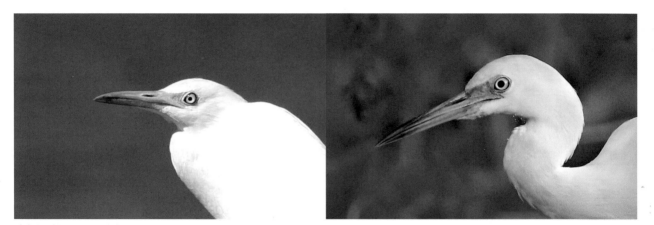

Cattle Egret, NC, Oct (GLA) (left); Little Blue Heron, FL, Jan (KK) (right). Cattle Egrets have short, stout bills, unlike those of any of the other herons. Little Blue Heron is slightly stouter and droopier than Snowy Egret, and usually bicolored.

Reddish Egret, Bahamas, Nov (BLS) (left); Great White Heron, FL, Mar (BLS) (right). Immature Reddish Egrets have dark bills and lores and can be confused with other herons. Note the rather long bill that has hints of pink at the base; over two years, the bill becomes drastically bicolored, with a pink base and dark tip. Great White Herons have the largest, heaviest bills of this group, unmistakably hefty and yellow; compare especially with the slimmer-billed Great Egret.

Hints and Considerations

- Rarely are these herons mistaken for anything but one another. Beware of distant Wood Storks, immature spoonbills, White Ibis, or Whooping Cranes that might cause confusion. Herons usually fly with their necks retracted (coiled, unlike ibis, storks, and cranes) but occasionally extend their necks during shorter flights.
- Each white heron has a distinctive "GISS." Habitat can be telling, but pay special attention to feeding postures and technique, and the manner of movement. Appreciating these, along with range, helps narrow the choices.
- In nearly all cases, determining age is an important step. Note the color and pattern of the legs, feet, bill, and lores. Breeding adults have showy plumes and colorful bare parts. Winter adults and juveniles lack plumes and have duller, less distinctive bare parts.
- Juvenile Little Blue Herons are white, similar to the egrets.
- Herons in late summer/autumn provide challenges to birders, as adults are in nonbreeding plumage and juveniles abound.
- Two of these herons are restricted in range and are unfamiliar to many birders. Reddish Egret is coastal, is almost never seen away from the Gulf Coast or north of South Carolina, and is rare in extreme southern California. Many birders are unfamiliar with the white morph of this species. Also, "Great White" Heron (currently considered a form of Great Blue Heron) is restricted to peninsular Florida and is rare north of there.
- Little Egret is a rare vagrant that may be overlooked by the unwary or misidentified by the overeager. Great care must be taken to distinguish it from Snowy Egret. Get photos!

Identification

Sexes are similar, but plumages differ with respect to age, so determining age is important in identification. Coloration of bare parts differs with age, as well as with season. Voice is infrequently useful in identification and is not treated below.

Information on when these species first attempt breeding and how often adults breed is sparse or incomplete, and consequently the molt/plumage progression of several species remains imperfectly understood. Adult plumage is apparently attained at

Taxonomic Note:

Great White Heron is a taxon of considerable confusion. Authorities today regard it as a subspecies of Great Blue Heron, but Great White averages larger and heavier billed, differs dramatically from Great Blue in plumage (color, plume structure), overlaps little with it in breeding range, and breeds mostly assortatively where overlap occurs.[16] In its genetics Great White is similar only to Great Blue of extreme south Florida[16] (where hybridization occurs perhaps just enough to prevent more divergence). "Wurdemann's" Herons are the products of pairings between Great Blues and Great Whites. Behavioral differences between Great White and Great Blue herons[19] appear weak, but Great Whites pair up and breed earlier[16] and are possibly more tied to saltwater and mangroves. Given all the above, Great White Heron merits reconsideration as a species.

The taxonomy of Little Egret (*Egretta garzetta*) is likewise vexed, and this confounds our understanding of its status in North America. All North American records of Little Egret are presumed to originate from western European or North African populations, represented by the nominate form *E. garzetta garzetta*. Apart from these, there are several records of dark egrets from the northeastern United States and Newfoundland, which have been identified as Western Reef-Herons (*E. gularis gularis*). But research suggests that *E. gularis gularis* is actually a subspecies of Little Egret in which dark morphs predominate[20, 21] (fide N. Haass).

two or three years old,[8] and breeding adults are usually easily identified by their showy nuptial plumes on the head and back, and by their richly colored bare parts. Herons undergo a prebasic molt that takes place in late summer/fall, and it is this molt that produces their nuptial plumes,[7] though these do not become apparent until spring (occasionally first-year birds may show variable plumes by spring).[8]

Nonbreeding adults lack long plumes and show more subdued coloration of bare parts, so they can be difficult to distinguish from immatures. The lores and bill in particular are less rich from August through mid-February, and then they begin to intensify in color (though some species breeding in the south may breed year-round). A second-year plumage in herons requires further study, and most are so similar to nonbreeding adults that they are not field identifiable. Juveniles have dull-colored lores, bills, and legs and are most conspicuous in later summer and early fall. They provide the most regular identification challenges.

Nonbreeding Snowy Egret, CA, Dec (BLS) (left); first-fall Snowy Egret, NJ, Oct (GLA) (right). Note long, thin, mostly dark bill, yellow lores, and blackish, bicolored legs (black and yellow). Immatures are variable and can have paler bills than are shown here, as well as mostly yellowish legs in summer. By late fall and first winter, they are more adultlike.

Nonbreeding Great Egret, CA, Oct (BLS) (left); nonbreeding Great Egret, CA, Feb (BLS) (right). Determining the age of Great Egrets is very difficult, as nonbreeding adults are nearly identical to immatures from late summer through late fall. Fortunately, age determination in this species is not critical for identification, because all share black legs year-round, as well as a long, moderately heavy, yellow bill; and importantly, all lack head plumes. Breeding adults show bright green lores briefly in spring.

Breeding Cattle Egret, CA, Apr (BLS) (left); nonbreeding Cattle Egret, CA, Feb (right) (BLS). Adult Cattle Egrets change drastically from the colorful breeding plumage to all white in winter. Yet Cattle Egret in any plumage is scarcely confusable with the others if seen reasonably well. Note stocky build, short, stout bill; forages in grassy habitat. Juveniles have black bills and legs for the first few months of life but are structurally similar to adults; bill color changes to yellow in first fall.

By spring it seems most first-year birds possess bare parts similar in color and pattern to those of adults.

SNOWY EGRET: This slender, medium-sized heron is for many birders the "classic" egret. Habitat choice varies, and Snowy is at home in fresh, brackish, or salt water but seems to favor estuarine shallows most of all. Great Egrets and other herons at times flock around them. Their hunting strategy varies more than that of the others. Often Snowy performs animated pursuits after prey, but at times it also holds still in crouching vigils with its neck coiled before stabbing its prey with its straight bill. Rarely, aerial foraging occurs (e.g., diving, hover-and-stab, flycatching, etc.).[9] Widespread and common on all coasts of the United States and along the Mississippi Valley, they are less abundant in scattered inland areas. In the northern part of their range they are migratory, and migrants are regular to parts of the US-Canadian border (only rarely breeding in Canada)[10] but become scarce north of there. Compare it with Little Egret and immature Little Blue Heron. Snowy nearly always shows a black or blackish bill with yellow lores. Its molt and plumage progression require further study.

Adults: Adult plumage aspect appears to be attained in the second fall following prebasic molt. Nonbreeding adults have relatively dull lores and bills and show yellow green along the back of the legs. In breeding plumage (March–August), adults exhibit black bills and nearly wholly black legs, which contrast (respectively) with their bright yellow lores and yellow feet ("slippers"). The lores may become reddish pink on some birds at the height of breeding. The nuptial plumes on the head form a short-moderate shaggy crest behind the nape (becoming spiky when erect). Plumes also extend off the chest and curl up ("recurve") off the back. *Immatures:* The bare parts of juveniles are less saturated than those of adults and appear to become similar to those of adults by the first spring. Juveniles have a dark-tipped bill with a greenish or grayish base, and they have greenish legs that become blackish at the front and darken as they age. In spring first-year birds develop some rudimentary plumes.[11]

GREAT EGRET: Second in size, smaller only than Great White Heron, the Great Egret is consistent in appearance across all ages. It is easily identified by the combination of its large size, black legs, and stout orange-yellow bill, but some show a black-tipped bill.

Slender, long necked, tall, and graceful in bearing, it is deliberate in its movements, frequently foraging with its bill held horizontal or tilted skyward. Great Egrets inhabit saltwater or freshwater, attend mixed heron flocks, and often associate with Snowy Egrets. But they will also form moderately large homogeneous flocks, and sometimes they frequent drier pastoral habitats. A widespread species, Great Egret is common along most coastlines and even inland in many places, as well as north into southern Canada.

Adults: Great Egret lacks head plumes. During breeding, the lores become rich green, and the long back (scapular) plumes become evident; the latter at times are stained buffy or brownish. Nonbreeders are similar but lack back plumes, the lores are duskier yellow, and the legs are duskier and less richly black. *Immatures:* These are similar to nonbreeding adults, but with even duskier bare parts. Compare this species with Great White Heron. Old World breeding Great Egrets have black bills and are accidental in North America, and it is unclear which subspecies has occurred here (*A. a. melanorhynchos* of sub-Saharan Africa or *A. a. alba* of Eurasia, North Africa, and the Middle East).[12]

CATTLE EGRET: This smallest white heron has a compact shape because of its short neck and relatively short legs, both of which suit its terrestrial feeding habits. The bill is short too, only just longer than the length of the head. A bird of farm fields, pastures, and grassy roadsides, it takes grasshoppers, crickets, and frogs and sometimes follows grazing cattle or tractors to feed on the displaced prey. It is the only species in its genus in the world, and the only North American heron in which the color of the plumage changes seasonally.[8] Prior to 1950, Cattle Egrets were unknown in North America, but today they are quite widespread across the Lower 48 and into southern Canada. Their colonization of North America was perhaps initially fed by east winds carrying these birds from North Africa across the Atlantic to the southern Caribbean (Barbados is often the first point of land encountered by such birds,[13] and from there they could have spread north).

Adults: Breeding adults are distinctive, white overall but with rich buff orange on the head, neck, and scapulars, and orange bare parts. How these orange areas become orange is mysterious (perhaps it is topically administered), but the coloration is not a result of molt.[8] Rarely, richly colored aberrant birds occur with extensive orange, blue-gray, or even blackish

Juvenile Little Blue Heron, Mexico, Sep (SNGH) (left); juvenile Little Blue Heron, CT, Oct (MS) (right). Note mostly white plumage with dusky wing tips, yellowish legs, greenish lores, and bicolored bill. Compare mainly with juvenile Snowy Egret.

Immature Reddish Egret, Bahamas, Nov (BLS) (left); presumed second-year Reddish Egret, TX, Aug (GP) (right). Determining the age of Reddish Egrets can be difficult. Bill color changes from all dark on fresh juveniles to bicolored on adults. By fall juveniles usually have some hints of pale in the base of the bill. Nonbreeding adults have pale-based bills (pale pink), but the demarcation between the base and the dark tip can be blurred compared with the high breeding bill pattern. Note moderate size, long neck, and bill structure.

Breeding adult Great White Heron, FL, Dec (MM) (left); immature Great White Heron, FL, Mar (TJ) (right). Difficult to age without the presence of plumes. Note head plumes on breeding bird, which help distinguish it from Great Egret. Also note general large size (like Great Blue Heron), long neck, heavy yellow bill, and pale legs.

First-spring Little Blue Heron, TX, Apr (BS). Little Blue Herons transition from their white immature plumage to the blue plumage of adults over the first spring/summer.

areas instead of the normal peach buff. Nonbreeding adults are wholly white, lack the orange patches, have yellower (less orange) bills, and have blackish legs. *Immatures:* Juveniles are like nonbreeding adults, with blackish legs but darker bills. (Compare the blackish-billed juveniles with the much larger, longer Great Egret). The bill seems to become yellowish by winter.

LITTLE BLUE HERON: Only first-year birds are white or mostly white. Adults are a distinctive inky gray blue or purplish blue. The white first-year birds remain white through the first winter but then become dappled with slate blue–gray feathers as they transition to adult plumage in their first summer (S. Howell, pers. comm.). These dappled birds are called "calicos" and are quite distinctive, though usually visible for only a few months in summer as birds complete their second prebasic molt.

Birds mostly of the Gulf Coast, the Mississippi Valley, and the Southeast, Little Blues occur widely if uncommonly inland and are scarce or rare in the Southwest and in California. In their normal range, they are generally less numerous, and more solitary than other herons and egrets, but they will take advantage of abundant food and join mixed heron flocks.

It is the white juveniles that are most confusing for birders. Similar in size to Snowy Egrets, juvenile Little Blues are slightly heavier, with thicker necks and a heavier, droopier, usually two-toned bill that is paler at the base. The lores are grayish or yellowish (never bright yellow) and blend into the gray-based bill, which becomes darker toward the tip. Note their structure and generally sluggish movements. When they forage, the bill is usually pointed down (not horizontally). The white juveniles usually show dusky tips to the primaries, and these are especially noticeable in flight. Leg color varies somewhat but is nearly always greenish, often becoming darker toward the first spring.

REDDISH EGRET: The white morph of this uncommon species occurs only in the Gulf of Mexico and along the Southeast coast north to South Carolina. The species also occurs sparingly in southern California

Snowy Egret (left) with Great Egret, CA, Oct (SNGH). In this direct comparison, note the much larger size and more elongated structure of Great, with bold yellow bill.

Breeding adult Reddish Egret (right) with Snowy Egrets, TX, Apr (KK). Note larger size of Reddish, and striking bicolored bill. Reddish is primarily a saltwater bird, whereas the other herons are also found inland.

Immature Little Blue Heron (right) with Snowy Egret, NJ, Sep (TJ). Roughly the same size, but note Little Blue's stouter, bicolored bill and greenish legs.

This composite shows four heron species in flight: Great Egret (left); Snowy Egret (lower middle); Little Blue Heron (lower right); and Cattle Egret (upper right, and trio of smaller birds) (BLS, GLA). The same structural differences generally apply to these species whether they are in flight or perched. Note Great Egret's larger size and longer legs, and note Cattle Egret's compact overall structure. The same bill and leg color differences can be seen in flight as well. These four species are the most likely to be seen in transit, flying singly or in small to large groups (Cattle Egret sometimes travels by the hundreds).

(and south along the Pacific Coast of Mexico), but all individuals there are dark morphs. The total US population is believed to be only about two thousand pairs,[14] and white morphs make up just 2–7 percent of the Gulf Coast population.[15] In part because dark morphs predominate, the white morphs are subject to neglect by unwary birders, especially vagrants away from the Gulf region. Vagrants are known north along the Atlantic Coast to New England. Inland records are exceptional. Nearly all (perhaps all?) vagrant records, however, pertain to dark morphs.

Reddish Egrets are intermediate in size between Great and Snowy egrets. They are slender, long legged, and long necked and have a fairly thick, straight bill and long, dark gray legs. Usually they are solitary, and they feed almost exclusively in open saltwater shallows, preferring salt lagoons, and less commonly coastal ponds. They hunt in an animated, acrobatic fashion, engaging in dashes, leaps, jogs, and sprints, raising their wings for balance or to startle or detect prey. An actively foraging Reddish Egret, with all of its antics, can scarcely go unnoticed. They also commonly employ the technique of "canopy-feeding," in which they raise their wings in a circle to shade the water and attract their prey.[14] They will also raise and flick their wings to startle prey.[14]

Compare the white-morph Reddish Egret to the smaller yellow-footed Snowy, or the sluggish immature Little Blue Heron. Sometimes individuals with a mix of white and dark feathers occur. They somewhat resemble "calico" Little Blues, appearing as dark-morph adults with some white feathers mixed in. Behavior, habitat, bare part coloration, and structure are the keys to identification. Reddish Egret attains full adult plumage in its third fall, and immatures can cause confusion when unfamiliar.

Adults: On breeding adults the back and scapulars are adorned with stringy plumes, and the bill is distinctively pink based and bicolored. The bill and the shaggy mane of plumes on the head and neck are the adult's most distinctive features, but these are less noticeable in late summer to winter, when the bill color is muted, though still bicolored. *Immatures:* Juveniles lack plumes and may show yellowish in the lores and a mostly dark bill. They may appear similar to Snowy Egrets, but note that Reddish Egrets are larger and sturdier and have bigger, stronger, grayish legs. Second-year birds have dark gray bills, and note how the dark lores offset the pale eye. Most second-years show some shagginess about the head and neck.

Wurdemann's Heron, FL, Mar (TJ). Wurdemann's Heron is a hybrid between typical Great Blue Heron and Great White Heron. Most look bluish on the body like a Great Blue but have a whiter neck, and especially head, indicating Great White Heron influence.

GREAT WHITE HERON: The largest heron in North America, Great White is very rare outside central and southern Florida (and quite rare elsewhere in its range; confined to the Caribbean). Though they are regular throughout most of the southern half of the state, Florida Bay holds the majority of known Great White Herons, with about 850 breeding pairs.[16] Very few are known to breed anywhere else in the world. Given their apparently small population, Great Whites exhibit a rather strong tendency to stray, with vagrant records west to Texas, north to maritime Canada, and inland to the Great Lakes.[17] Along with their large size, a most prominent feature is the very heavy and mostly yellow bill. Compared to the superficially similar Great Egret, the Great White is heavier overall and not as bright white, and the legs are dusky pale to grayish yellow. The Great White prefers saltwater, inhabiting mangroves, tidal shallows, or coastal ponds. It is mostly solitary, usually moving slowly and deliberately.

Adults: Breeding adults have medium-long slender head plumes that extend off the nape. The back plumes are short compared to those of Great Egret. The lores are grayish, becoming bluish during the breeding season. *Immatures:* These lack plumes and have less richly colored bare parts, and usually darker bills, with a darker maxilla and mostly yellow mandible.

The "Wurdemann's" Heron of the Florida Keys is the product of mixed pairings between Great Blue and Great White herons. It is intermediate in size and plumage, showing a Great Blue–like body but usually with a variably whitish head and neck.

Vagrants

Little Egret is an Old World species and an accidental vagrant to eastern North America, with records scattered between Newfoundland and Virginia. The nominate form (*E. g. garzetta*) breeds in Eurasia and parts of Africa and has recently nested in small numbers as close as Barbados.[13] It is very similar in habits to Snowy Egret, but generally, Little is slightly less animated when feeding. Though structurally they are very similar, Little Egret is more slender, with a slightly longer, more daggerlike bill. It is also slightly taller and longer necked, often appearing flatter headed. All differences are subtle, though, and require comparative experience to discern, and even then they may be difficult to note. But in breeding plumage Little Egrets have two to three long nape plumes that are a distinctive character. Briefly in the spring (~April–June), they have yellow lores, but for most of the year they show grayish or grayish-green lores. Birds with grayish lores that lack the distinctive head plumes are easily confused with juvenile Snowies. On adults the feet (especially the soles) tend to be greener and less rich yellow than those of Snowies; the legs perhaps average more extensively dark. Odd egrets showing characters intermediate between those of Snowy and Little (Snowy-like birds with long head plumes) have appeared in the Northeast and could be hybrids, or aberrant Snowies.[18] Some individuals may not be safely identified.

Breeding adult Little Egret, Ethiopia, May (GLA); nonbreeding Little Egret, Oman, Dec (GLA). Little Egret is strictly a vagrant to North America and is most similar to Snowy Egret. Little Egret averages slightly larger, longer necked, and generally bulkier. Adults (left) have two elongated head plumes, very different from the shaggy plumes of Snowy. In Little's nonbreeding plumage (right), note the all-black legs and grayish (not yellow) lores. Beware of hybrids between these two, which appear similar to Snowy Egret and have yellow lores, but usually show head plumes like those of Little Egret.

References

[1] Sheldon, F. H. 1987. Phylogeny of herons estimated from DNA-DNA hybridization data. Auk 104:97–108.

[2] Rodgers, J. A., Jr., and H. T. Smith. 1995. Little Blue Heron (*Egretta caerulea*). The Birds of North America Online. A. Poole, ed. Ithaca, NY: Cornell Lab of Ornithology. http://bna.birds.cornell.edu/bna/species/145

[3] Caldwell, G. S. 1981. Attraction to tropical mixed-species heron flocks: Proximate mechanism and consequences. Behavioral Ecology and Sociobiology 8:99–103.

[4] Caldwell, G. S. 1986. Predation as a selective force on foraging herons: Effects of plumage color and flocking. Auk 103:494–505.

[5] Wetmore, A. 1920. The function of powder downs in herons. Condor 22(5) (September–October): 168–70.

[6] Sibley, D. A. 2011. Powder down and the Black-crowned Night-Heron. http://www.sibleyguides.com/2011/06/powder-down-and-the-black-crowned-night-heron/

[7] Pyle, P., and S.N.G. Howell. 2004. Ornamental plume development and "prealternate molts" of herons and egrets. Wilson Bulletin 116:287–92.

[8] Howell, S.N.G. 2010. Molt in North American Birds. New York: Houghton Mifflin.

[9] Elphick, C., J. B. Dunning Jr., and D. A. Sibley. 2001. The Sibley Guide to Bird Life and Behavior. New York: Alfred A. Knopf.

[10] Manitoba Breeding Bird Atlas Newsletter. 2011. Vol. 2, Issue 2–3 (Summer and Fall). Manitoba Breeding Bird Atlas.

[11] Parsons, K. C., and T. L. Master. 2000. Snowy Egret (*Egretta thula*). The Birds of North America Online. A. Poole, ed. Ithaca, NY: Cornell Lab of Ornithology. http://bna.birds.cornell.edu/bna/species/489

[12] McCrimmon, D. A., Jr., J. C. Ogden, and G. T. Bancroft. 2001. Great Egret (*Ardea alba*). The Birds of North America Online. A. Poole, ed. Ithaca, NY: Cornell Lab of Ornithology. http://bna.birds.cornell.edu/bna/species/570

[13] Murphy, W. L. 1992. Notes on the occurrence of the Little Egret (*Egretta garzetta*) in the Americas, with reference to other palearctic vagrants. Colonial Waterbirds 15(1): 113–23.

[14] Lowther, P. E., and R. T. Paul. 2002. Reddish Egret (*Egretta rufescens*). The Birds of North America Online. A. Poole, ed. Ithaca, NY: Cornell Lab of Ornithology. http://bna.birds.cornell.edu/bna/species/633

[15] Sibley, D. A. 2000. The Sibley Guide to Birds. New York: Alfred A. Knopf.

[16] McGuire, H. L. 2002. Taxonomic status of the Great White Heron (*Ardea herodias occidentalis*): An analysis of behavioral, genetic, and morphometric evidence. Final report. Tallahassee: Florida Fish and Wildlife Conservation Commission.

[17] Sibley, D. A. 2007. "Great White" Heron - Not just a color morph. Great White Heron *Ardea herodias occidentalis*. http://sibleyguides.blogspot.com/2007/11/great-white-heron-not-just-color-morph.html

[18] Sibley, D. A. 2011. Possible hybrid Little × Snowy Egrets. http://www.sibleyguides.com/2011/08/possible-hybrid-little-x-snowy-egrets/

[19] Curry-Lindahl, K. 1971. Systematic relationships of herons (Ardeidae), based on comparative studies of behaviour and ecology: A preliminary account. Ostrich: Journal of African Ornithology 42 (supplement 1): 53–70.

[20] Bauer, H. G., E. Bezzel, and W. Fiedler. 2005. Das Kompendium der Vögel Mitteleuropas. Wiebelsheim, Germany: Aula-Verlag.

[21] Sibley, D. A. 2011. Little Egret *Egretta garzetta*. http://www.sibleyguides.com/bird-info/little-egret/

Coastal Birds

Eiders

Brachyramphus Murrelets

Pacific Cormorants

Though very different from one another, these three groups are similar in that they mostly hug the coast and are not seen away from nearshore waters very often. Each group provides regular identification challenges. Birders must often contend with wind, precipitation, distance, or difficult lighting when birding in coastal areas, and these factors, combined with the relatively similar plumages among each group, mean that even expert birders will find their skills tested by these birds. Breeding male eiders are easily identified, but otherwise all species within each group require study and experience to identify, and some species' ranges are not easily reached.

Birders often refer to a particular bird's "jizz." This slang term may have evolved from (and is synonymous with) the German word *gestalt*. Or it may be a corruption of the old air force acronym GISS, for "general impression, size, and shape," used in identifying distant aircraft. GISS is useful in bird identification, but only once you are familiar with a species and understand its shape, the space it occupies, and the way it moves in various situations. GISS is how you quickly recognize a close friend when you enter a crowded room, or how you identify that same friend in the hazy distance as he jogs toward you on the road.

Coastal birds in general (including winter loons, and many herons and seabirds, among others) are good entry points with which to begin thinking about GISS. GISS can help you identify birds that you already know, but it can also help you identify birds you don't yet know. When you see an unfamiliar species, the fact that it is is noticeably different but still similar to something you know very well is instructive. Knowing female Common Eider really well, for example, is helpful when you are suddenly confronted with a female King Eider for the first time.

Eiders

Common Eider (*Somateria mollissima*)

King Eider (*Somateria spectabilis*)

Spectacled Eider (*Somateria fischeri*)

Steller's Eider (*Polysticta stelleri*)

First Breeding:	2–4 years old
Breeding Strategy:	Seasonally monogamous. Solitary, but Atlantic Common Eiders are semicolonial.
Lifespan:	Up to 21 years

Eiders are large and sturdy seaducks, and male eiders rank among the most handsome of waterfowl, elegantly attired in black and white with colorful heads and bills. For birders, few if any other ducks possess such allure. Females and juveniles are more modestly patterned in browns, gray browns, or rust. These distinctive ducks inhabit harsh marine environments where they dive in search of mollusks (mussels and clams), crustaceans, and sea urchins. The females are famous for producing soft, downy feathers with superior insulating properties, and this "eiderdown" is popularly used in pillows and winter coats. Eiders are members of the waterfowl family Anatidae and are related to mergansers, goldeneyes, Harlequin Duck, Labrador Duck (extinct since the 1870s), and the scoters.[1] Like the scoters, eiders are less vocal than other waterfowl, and few recordings of their vocalizations exist. All four of the world's eiders are found in North America, and these include the three larger *Somateria* species, and also Steller's Eider. Steller's differs structurally and behaviorally and is in the monotypic genus *Polysticta*. Only Common Eider is polytypic, with several discrete populations scattered across the northern Holarctic region.

Eiders breed around small lakes or tundra pools, and sometimes in rocky areas, almost always nesting fairly near the coast; these ducks are surely the most marine of all waterfowl. Eiders winter at sea, at times forming large flocks, and they also flock when molting or feeding. They prefer mostly rocky shorelines near open ocean (but see Spectacled) and are occasionally seen

Male eiders are spectacular, and all species are easily identified if you have a reasonable view. This Pacific Common Eider is hard to confuse with any other bird—and it's the last pretty picture of a male eider you'll see in this chapter! Instead, we'll focus on brown eiders, either females or first fall/winter birds (GV).

Focus on: *Head and bill structure/pattern, Range, Wing pattern*

It's important to understand plumage progression in eiders. Females look similar year-round, but males are brown in the first fall (upper), and by late in the first fall/early winter they start to molt into a plumage with male characters. The top bird was photographed 28 December (GLA), whereas the one in the upper middle was photographed 18 December (BLS). These birds are the same age, but the upper bird is molting more slowly. The lower middle bird is from 5 March, when most first-winter males have a white breast, mixed back, and black sides (GV). The bottom bird is a second-winter, taken on 7 November (BH). Most second-winter birds show some signs of immaturity. This bird will molt into clean adult male plumage by the next fall/winter.

Natural History Note:

Eiders rank among the world's most striking examples of sexual dimorphism. Perhaps because males are so ornate and distinctive in plumage, hybridization appears very rare in eiders compared to other ducks, such as pochards (*Aythya*), goldeneyes, and dabblers.

Ducks are unusual in that males enter a cryptic (female-like) plumage called eclipse plumage. This plumage occurs during the breeding season, usually beginning in July, and is molted in mid to late fall, when it is replaced by the breeding plumage. That their summer plumage is less colorful than their winter plumage is unusual. This is quite the opposite of most other birds, which acquire their most colorful plumage in spring. The difference for waterfowl is that they pair up on the wintering grounds, whereas most other birds pair at breeding sites in spring. Also, July is just before ducks begin wing molt, during which they may become flightless for a period of several weeks, so they benefit from having a more cryptic plumage at this most vulnerable time.[7]

migrating in mixed flocks with other seaducks. Rarely, migrant Common and King eiders are found at inland lakes, sometimes forced down by inclement weather. Eiders enjoy turbulent waters and often keep company with Harlequin Ducks and scoters. Foraging eiders may spend over a minute underwater, sometimes reaching depths of one hundred feet or more.[2] Like other seaducks, they can process saltwater using their nasal salt glands.[3]

Because these birds are unfamiliar to many birders, the problem is often not identifying a duck as an eider, but determining which eider species it is. Breeding males are easy, but brown birds are challenging. When presented with a brown seaduck of unknown identity, be sure to consider nonbreeding Harlequin Ducks and the three scoter species. Eiders hybridize only exceptionally,[2, 4, 5, 6] so hybrids do not confound identification as they do with some other ducks. Perhaps more than anything, distance, heaving seas, and buffeting winds are the main obstacles to proper identification. When observed closely, these dapper ducks are usually fairly easily identified. Always focus on size and on the structure of the head and bill. Identifying males is straightforward, though flying males and those in eclipse plumage are more challenging. Females are always brown, but males, depending on their age and the season, may be brown, ornately plumaged, or somewhere in between. But

the structural cues most useful in separating the eider species are useful across all ages and sexes.

Hints and Considerations

- Compared to female and immature scoters or Harlequin Ducks, eiders are larger and more heavily built. Brown-plumaged *Somateria* eiders, such as eclipse males, females, or juveniles, show dark barring on the flanks and chest and are whitish in the axillaries. Harlequin Duck is much smaller, with a short, triangular bill. Scoters average more charcoal colored, usually show some whitish or pale grayish about the head, and lack barring.
- The three larger *Somateria* species are roughly similar in structure, yet each is distinct. Steller's Eider is a unique seaduck in its own genus, with a unique compact structure.
- Only Common and King eiders are seen with regularity outside Alaska. Distinguishing brown Kings from brown Commons is the most regular identification challenge within this group, particularly with vagrants.
- On the Pacific Coast all eiders are rare south of Alaska, but on the Atlantic Coast both Kings and Commons occur south to the Mid-Atlantic States in winter.
- Head and bill features are the keys in separation. Always note bill structure, and the shape and pattern of feathering where the head meets the bill. Also examine wing pattern. Structural differences hold up across all plumages regardless of age or sex.

Identification

Determining age and sex is not critical in eider identification, but it can be helpful. Eiders are mostly easy to sex as adults, but determing the sex of young birds is more complicated. All four species require two to three years to reach full breeding plumage, and they undergo several molts beforehand.[7] The plumage progression is most visible in males, as males are brown as juveniles, patchy or pied (brown/black/white) as immatures, brown again in eclipse plumage, and then distinctively ornate when breeding. First-year males begin to acquire some new adultlike feathers in their first fall and so may be "patchwork" brown, black, and white, with variable hints of their associated bill color and pattern. Second-year males are mostly

Brown eider comparison. The brown female and juvenile eiders are best identified by examining the head and bill details, but always consider size, too. Common Eider (top) has a steep forehead and a long, pale-tipped bill with long lobes that extend up the forehead. Also note the dark-barred flanks, compared with the black chevrons of female King. King (upper middle) has a more sloping forehead and a smaller black bill that imparts a smirking expression. Spectacled (lower middle) shows a shadow pattern of the spectacles so obvious on the breeding male and also has a more extensively feathered forehead. Steller's (bottom) is smaller, darker, and more compact, with a gray bill, a whitish eye ring, and broad white borders to the speculum (not always visible on sitting birds) (Common and King photos, GV; Spectacled, GLA; Steller's, SNGH).

adultlike in winter but retain a few signs of immaturity such as dusky shading on otherwise white plumage, and reduced head and bill coloration. Females change little over the course of their life, essentially always remaining brown. Juveniles resemble adult females. In *Somateria* (especially Common and King), brown birds vary somewhat in appearance with respect to range, but all show a shadow of the breeding male's head pattern. Voice is seldom of use in identification or detection.

COMMON EIDER: The most widespread eider, this is the largest duck in the Northern Hemisphere. It breeds farther south than other eiders, nesting as far south as Massachusetts, and winters annually from Atlantic Canada south along the Atlantic Coast to Virginia. A few immatures oversummer on the Mid-Atlantic Coast. In the Pacific, Common Eider is a vagrant south of Cook Inlet, Alaska. Vagrant migrants occur rarely inland, most often around the Great Lakes and the Northeast, and much more rarely elsewhere. Compared to other eiders, Common is large and has a longish neck; a long, heavy, wedge-shaped head; and a long, sloping bill profile. The head peaks above and in front of the eye. Note that the feathering of the face (loral region) extends far forward, sometimes beyond (below) the exposed nostril. The facial lobes (the exposed skin on the bill and forehead) extend up the bill toward the eyes (compare female Spectacled). From a distance the black cap on a breeding male may approximate the head pattern of a Spectacled Eider, but Common shows a white chest (sometimes buff white or rosy white). Compared to King, breeding male Common looks very white backed. It is more variable than other eiders. The bare parts vary regionally, and females range in overall color from pale grayish (Hudson Bay breeders, *S. m. sedentaria*) to reddish brown (Atlantic Canada to Massachusetts breeders, *S. m. dresseri*).[2] Pacific birds (*S. m. v-nigrum*) are split as the species "Pacific Eider" by some authorities.[1] Compared to other Commons, Pacific birds are larger, and females are dark brown, while males have rich yellow-orange bills with narrow, pointed lobes, and a small black *v* under the chin. Birds breeding in Arctic

Common Eider exhibits substantial geographic variation, with four generally recognized subspecies in North America, some of which may be elevated to full species in the future. Careful birders can distinguish females by using a combination of general body plumage color and detailed assessment of bill characters. The bilateral frontal processes (lobes) extending up toward the forehead vary in shape among subspecies, as does the extent and shape of the malar feathering that extends (or doesn't) under the nares. Along the Atlantic Coast birders encounter mostly the richly colored subspecies *S. m. dresseri*, which breeds farthest south along the Atlantic Coast and whose females are almost invariably a rich rufous coloration (see brown eider comparison). The frontal processes are long and rounded at their tips. Among the flocks of *dresseri* Common Eiders, careful birders might find a "Northern" Common Eider (*S. m. borealis*) (above, MA, Mar, CLW). Northern females average buffier in general plumage tone and have very pointed tips on the frontal processes. The malar feathering generally does not extend under the nares.

Common Eider

King Eider

Eiders in flight. Common (left, CLW) and King eiders (right, GLA) are the two species most frequently encountered by birders, and they are often seen in flight at migration points. Structurally, Common Eider is larger and more heavily built, with a bigger head that is distinctly sloped. King Eider is more compact and likely to be brushed off as a scoter. The distant flock on this page shows a typical view of migrating Common Eiders, with adult males sticking out like a sore thumb among the females and immatures (BLS).

Spectacled (left, SNGH) and Steller's eiders (right, CLW) are true Alaska specialties. Birders typically see these species on breeding grounds, but at a few places, such as Gambell, these eiders can be seen on migration. Spectacled is large and robust, like Common Eider. Males are unmistakable, while females usually show enough of the "spectacle" pattern to be obvious. Steller's Eider is smaller and more compact. Males are striking, but females are more likely to be confused. Look for the overall dark coloration, and the bold white borders on the speculum. The Surf Scoter flock above the horizon is meant to provide a comparison between the eiders and a species more familiar to most birders (BLS).

Canada (*S. m. borealis*) average smallest and may show more pronounced "scapular sails" than other forms.[2] Atlantic Common Eiders are much more social than other eiders; they are found in large flocks and even breed colonially.

KING EIDER: This is the most distinctive and smallest of the *Somateria*. Compared to other *Somateria* it has a smaller, rounded head, and a smallish bill. King Eider winters in small numbers from Atlantic Canada south along the coast, rarely but regularly to Virginia. Rarely, immatures oversummer along the coasts of New England and southeast Canada. In the Pacific it is a vagrant south of the Gulf of Alaska. Vagrant migrants occur very rarely inland, most often around the Great Lakes, the Midwest, and the Northeast, and exceptionally elsewhere. Breeding males are unmistakable, with a blue hood, orange frontal lobe, red bill, and long, black scapular feathers (terminating in hornlike "sails"). Males, compared to other male *Somateria*, are blacker above (mostly black backed at rest), with isolated white ovate shoulder patches in flight. Note that sometimes, male Common Eiders may also appear rosy chested, but Kings are smaller and stockier, with a shorter, thicker neck, a smaller head, and a shorter bill. Even first-year males show orangish bills. On females, note the somewhat smirking expression (curled gape) and the small, relatively dark bill contrasting with the paler face and bill base. Compared to other *Somateria*, they are less barred below, but more scaly or chevroned; also note the shorter, sloping head profile. The lobes on female King Eiders are shorter, broader, and concolorous with the blackish bill.

SPECTACLED EIDER: Among the most sought after of North American birds, this species virtually never strays from its range in Alaska and northeast Russia. A large eider, with a long, sloping forehead, it is most similar in shape and pattern to Common Eider. Though close in overall mass to King Eider, Spectacled often appears larger, yet it is noticeably smaller than Common ("Pacific") Eider. Most often it is seen in small flocks or singly. Even at some distance, breeding males are identified in flight by their dark underparts, with the black extending up onto the chest. The male's green head can become quite dark, almost olive brown, and sharply contrasts with the outline of the white spectacles. The yellow-orange bill is also visible at some distance. Brown-plumaged Spectacleds might be mistaken for either Kings or Commons, but note the lack of lobes and the consequent extensive feathering of the bill. Most of the culmen is covered in feathers. Females average duller gray than other *Somateria* but show a "ghost pattern" of the spectacles as well. The area above the bill and forecrown is dark and so offsets the paler spectacles. Spectacled Eider's wintering range was unknown until recently. Virtually the entire population (~350,000 individuals according to US Fish and Wildlife Service surveys in 1997) spends the winter on the Bering Sea amid polynyas (large openings in sea ice created by ocean currents) south of St. Lawrence Island.[8, 9]

STELLER'S EIDER: A unique seaduck that is a vagrant outside Alaska in North America. Note the dabbling duck–like appearance, with gray bill and white axillaries. Compared to *Somateria*, Steller's prefers calmer waters of protected bays or lagoons. Away from breeding areas, it forms tight flocks that often dive in unison. Alaskan breeders winter in the Bering Sea and the Gulf of Alaska and rarely stray south (accidental to California). It is accidental in New England, where strays may come from the population that typically winters in the Baltic and Barents seas. Steller's is smaller than the *Somateria* and differs in bill structure, head structure, and plumage. This compact species has a square, flat-crowned head, often appearing rather sharply angled down at the forecrown and nape. In flight it shows bright whitish axillaries. As in *Somateria*, females show white stripes on either side of the blue speculum, but these are broader and more striking on adult female Steller's (though at times absent on immature females). Adult males show a dark neck collar and dark chin, and eclipse males and immature males often show a shadow pattern of these markings, which contrasts with the paler face. Female Steller's is uniformly dark, with nearly no barring at all, and also shows a small whitish eye ring. Brown-plumaged Steller's is perhaps more often confused with female *Aythya* (e.g., scaup), scoters, or a Harlequin Duck than with *Somateria*. Steller's breeding success appears to be tied to brown lemming numbers.[10] In years when lemmings are abundant, Snowy Owls thrive because of the abundance of their primary prey. Eiders nesting near owl nests may reap the benefits of being inadvertently defended from predators by the owls.

References

[1]Livezey, B. C. 1995. Phylogeny and evolutionary ecology of modern seaducks (Anatidae: Mergini). Condor 97:233–55.

[2]Goudie, R. I., G. J. Robertson, and A. Reed. 2000. Common Eider (*Somateria mollissima*). The Birds of North America Online. A. Poole, ed. Ithaca, NY: Cornell Lab of Ornithology. http://bna.birds.cornell.edu/bna/species/546

[3]Nehls, G. 1996. Low costs of salt turnover in Common Eiders *Somateria mollissima*. Ardea 84:23–30.

[4]Pettingill, O. S., Jr. 1959. King Eiders mated with Common Eiders in Iceland. Wilson Bulletin 71:205–7.

[5]Forsman, D. 1995. A presumed hybrid of Steller's Eider × Common Eider in Norway. Birding World 8:138.

[6]Trefry, S. A., D. L. Dickson, and A. K. Hoover. 2007. A Common Eider × King Eider hybrid captured on the Kent Peninsula, Nunavut. Arctic 60(3) (September): 251–54.

[7]Howell, S.N.G. 2010. Molt in North American Birds. New York: Houghton Mifflin.

[8]Petersen, M. R., D. C. Douglas, and D. M. Mulcahy. 1995. Use of implanted satellite transmitters to locate Spectacled Eiders at-sea. Condor 97:276–78.

[9]Petersen, M. R., W. W. Larned, and D. C. Douglas. 1999. At-sea distributions of Spectacled Eiders (*Somateria fischeri*): A 120-year-old mystery resolved. Auk 116:1009–20.

[10]Fredrickson, L. H. 2001. Steller's Eider (*Polysticta stelleri*). The Birds of North America Online. A. Poole, ed. Ithaca, NY: Cornell Lab of Ornithology. http://bna.birds.cornell.edu/bna/species/571

Brachyramphus **Murrelets**

Marbled Murrelet (*Brachramphus marmoratus*)

Kittlitz's Murrelet (*Brachyramphus brevirostris*)

Long-billed Murrelet (*Brachyramphus perdix*)

First Breeding:	~3 years old
Breeding Strategy:	Seasonally monogamous; solitary
Lifespan:	< 10 years

Dwelling in the cold waters of the nearshore Pacific, these small, fast-flying marine species are enigmatic and intriguing. Known among some fisherman as "fogbirds," "fog larks," or even "Australian bumblebees,"[1] these seabirds feed mostly on small fish such as sand lance and capelin.[1, 2] Capturing their prey in pursuit dives and propelling themselves using their wings, they essentially fly underwater (much like a penguin or a feeding shearwater). Nesting relatively far inland, they situate their nests at remote sites, and this habit rendered their life histories mysterious for decades. Their unique nesting habits, including never nesting in colonies, distinguish them from other species in the auk family.

Along with puffins, auklets, guillemots, and murres, the murrelets are members of the auk family, Alcidae. Collectively referred to as "auks" or "alcids," they somewhat resemble penguins and occupy a similar ecological niche, and though the two families are not closely related, they are a good example of convergent evolution. Alcids are strong fliers, swimmers, and divers but are awkward on land, essentially making land only to nest. Exclusive to the Northern Hemisphere, alcids seldom occupy warm waters (some *Synthliboramphus* murrelets are exceptions), reaching their peak diversity in the North Pacific, particularly in the Bering Sea region. The three murrelet species in this chapter make up the genus *Brachyramphus*, which is Greek for "short beaked." Birds in the genus *Synthliboramphus* are also called "murrelets" but are more closely related to "typical auks" such as the murres, Razorbill, and Dovekie.[3, 4] Until 1997, Marbled and Long-billed murrelets were considered the same species[5] but have since been recognized as separate species. In fact, Marbled and Kittlitz's are more closely related.[3] Hybridization seems

Natural History Note:

The breeding habits of these species remained little known until recently; the first nests were described only in recent decades. The first Marbled Murrelet nest was discovered in 1974.[1] The first Kittlitz's nest was discovered in the early 1930s at Katmai by Father Bernard Hubbard, "the Glacier Priest,"[7] and about a hundred have been documented since, most in just the past two decades. Long-billed and Marbled murrelets are the only alcids that nest in trees. Kittlitz's nests on the ground amid treeless, unvegetated landscapes such as glacial cirques, rocky faces, or scree slopes, sometimes up to fifty miles from the ocean.[2] Unlike many other alcids, *Brachyramphus* murrelets possess a cryptic breeding plumage and a striking black-and-white nonbreeding plumage; the latter is similar to that found year-round on most other alcids. Because *Brachyramphus* are solitary nesters and build their nests on the ground or in trees (as opposed to on a remote island cliff face), they are more prone to predation, so a camouflaged breeding plumage helps them go unseen. Courtship has been observed in winter months, and specimens of Marbled Murrelets collected in winter have often been of one male and one female together, suggesting that pair bonds may last throughout the year.

Population declines over recent decades in Marbled and Kittlitz's murrelets have alarmed conservationists, and all three species are of conservation concern. Kittlitz's Murrelet has shown an 80–90 percent decline in its total population in recent years.[8] Though not recognized by the US government as an endangered species, it is deemed "critically endangered" by Birdlife International,[9] the highest risk category it assigns. Closely tied to glacial waters, Kittlitz's could be fatally victimized by global warming. Long-billed Murrelet is considered "near threatened,"[10] while Marbled is categorized as "threatened" by the US government, and "endangered" by Birdlife International.[11]

Steller's Jays routinely prey on Marbled Murrelet eggs, so conservationists have started placing decoy eggs in close proximity to murrelet nests. The decoy eggs are chicken eggs dyed the same blue green as the murrelets' and laced with carbachol, which causes the jays to vomit. The jays learn to avoid eating eggs of this size and shape, thus sparing the murrelet eggs.[12]

Breeding-plumage Marbled Murrelet, AK, May (BLS). In North America most birders are familiar with Marbled Murrelet, which breeds along the Pacific Coast from Alaska to California, but the species is so enigmatic that its nesting sites weren't discovered until the 1970s. Given views like this, the Murrelets are easily identified, but you will often see them at a distance, and seasonal plumage variation, molt, and a rare vagrant complicate matters.

Focus on: *Range, Head and Tail patterns, Habitat*

Breeding Marbled Murrelet, AK, May (BLS) (left); nonbreeding Marbled Murrelet, AK, May (BLS) (right). These two photos, taken the same day, show the variable appearance of Marbled Murrelet from the rusty-brown breeding plumage to the stark black-and-white nonbreeding plumage. In breeding, note the paler throat that is still heavily marbled with brown, and the strong rusty tones above. In nonbreeding, note the striking dark mask and broad white collar.

Molting adult Marbled Murrelet, BC, Jul (GB) (left); molting Marbled Murrelets, AK, May (BLS) (right). In late summer through fall, adults transition from breeding to nonbreeding plumage. At this time, beware of possible confusion with Long-billed Murrelet, as Marbled's throat turns white. On the bird at left, note the transitioning white throat, but also the broad pale collar that is forming; this area would be dark on Long-billed. By May (right photo) many birds are already back in full breeding plumage, but some are still in nonbreeding plumage, or beginning the transition, such as the bird at right. First-summer plumage is highly variable, with some attaining near breeding plumage while others remain mostly in nonbreeding black and white.

Breeding Marbled Murrelet, AK, May (BLS) (left); nonbreeding/juvenile Marbled Murrelet, WA, Aug (TJ) (right). On breeding-plumage birds in flight, note all-dark tail and dark trailing edge to wings; cf. Kittlitz's in flight. On nonbreeding birds, note broad pale collar and white bar at the base of the wings formed by the white scapulars. On this juvenile, note the dusky feather edges in the white underparts, but otherwise the plumage is similar to that of a nonbreeding adult. Over the course of the fall, juveniles molt into an adultlike nonbreeding plumage, so that by midwinter all are similar.

Breeding Kittlitz's Murrelet, AK, Aug (RC) (left); nonbreeding Kittlitz's Murrelet, AK, May (AJ) (right). Breeding Kittlitz's Murrelets vary in general appearance but usually lack the rusty tones of Marbled. Some are grayer, such as this bird, while some are spangled golden above. Nonbreeding birds are similar to Marbled though usually grayer above. Note the bold white face and very broad collar. Kittlitz's can always be distinguished from Marbled based on its very short, thick bill, which appears to be stuck onto its fluffy white face.

Kittlitz's Murrelets transitioning to breeding plumage, AK, May (TJ, left; BLS, right). Many birders' first experience with Kittlitz's Murrelets is searching for them on a nearshore pelagic trip in Alaska. Often they are seen in the company of Marbled, and usually the first key to finding Kittlitz's is that they are overall strikingly paler than Marbled and usually appear smaller. On these transitioning birds, note the tiny bill, how the prominent eye contrasts with the pale, stippled face, and how the paler gray upperparts are beginning to become spangled with golden brown.

Nonbreeding/juvenile Kittlitz's Murrelet, AK, Aug (RC). In flight, Kittlitz's Murrelet differs from Marbled in having white outer tail feathers (very hard to see in the field) and a white trailing edge to the secondaries (easier to see!). Also note the nearly complete dusky collar typical of Kittlitz's in flight. Juvenile plumage is highly variable, and some birds can be darkish faced. Compared with juvenile Marbled, Kittlitz's usually has some infusion of white above and behind the eye. By late fall, the dark flecks on the throat, face, and collar are replaced by a more adultlike white plumage, resulting in most birds looking similar by early winter.

to occur rarely in the family and appears unknown within *Brachyramphus*.[6] Though their cryptic habits have been resolved somewhat in recent years, much remains to be learned, and opportunities to study these enigmatic and charming seabirds are to be savored.

Compared to other alcids, these murrelets are quite small. Birders typically find them at rest on the sea, some distance from shore, or spot them buzzing along low over the water in speedy flight. They are usually in pairs or solitary but occasionally form small flocks. Murrelets prefer to dive or swim from a threat rather than fly, and though they are somewhat shy of boats, birders often obtain their best studies of murrelets during pelagic boat trips. When actively feeding, murrelets dive repeatedly, surfacing just briefly between dives. Identification problems arise particularly in Alaskan waters, but also south along the Pacific Coast. Long-billed Murrelet is an Asian species, and a rare vagrant to North America. Interestingly, though, despite its far-flung breeding areas, Long-billed Murrelet is the most likely of these three to be found inland in North America, including in the East and on the Atlantic Coast. Marbled and Kittlitz's murrelets breed along the north Pacific Coast, but their winter quarters remain poorly known, especially for Kittlitz's. Both are exceedingly rare on inland waters of any kind. Often it is sea conditions or distance that causes identification issues, and these same factors limit a birder's to ability to achieve familiarity with these birds. Close and extended views are unusual, and some patience and luck are required to get the studies needed for identification. These species are confused mostly with one another, but other alcids at times cause confusion, especially the *Synthliboramphus* murrelets. In all cases, consider range, head and neck pattern, and to a lesser extent habitat.

Hints and Considerations

- Craveri's, Guadalupe, Scripps's, and Ancient murrelets resemble nonbreeding *Brachyramphus* and are similar in structure, but they lack white scapular patches, instead having solidly dark upperparts. Ancient has a bluish-gray mantle. Beware of juvenile and nonbreeding Black and especially Pigeon guillemots, which are larger and structurally different, with longer necks and broader and more rounded wings. Lone juvenile or female Long-tailed Ducks may provide confusion when flying and distant.

- Beware of confusion with juvenile Common Murre, which is much smaller than the adult and has a black-and-white plumage similar to that of nonbreeding murrelets. Usually, adults closely attend juvenile murres at this stage.

- Marbled is the most familiar and widespread *Brachyramphus*, providing a good basis for comparison against the other species.

- Kittlitz's is strictly a vagrant south of Alaska.

- Long-billed is exceptionally rare in North America. Vagrants are rarely found along the Pacific Coast, but just as often the species is found at inland lakes. It is the only one to make regular use of freshwater, so any *Brachyramphus* found at a lake is likely a Long-billed.

- Generally, in both breeding and nonbreeding plumages, Long-billed Murrelet averages darkest, Kittlitz's is palest, and Marbled is intermediate.

- On swimming murrelets, pay attention to the pattern of the head, neck, and chest. On flying individuals, attempt to note the tail and undertail patterns, and whether the secondaries are white tipped. Obtaining photos often allows you to see characters later that were not apparent at the time.

- Despite assertions in some references, underwing pattern is not a useful point for separating species, but it may be helpful in determining age.

Identification

For these marine species that molt at sea, the plumage progression remains relatively poorly understood. Adults are categorized as being in either breeding or nonbreeding plumage, but transitioning individuals are frequently encountered that appear intermediate. Breeding (alternate) plumage is acquired through a prealternate molt of the body feathers in spring (March–May), while nonbreeding (basic) plumage is acquired via a complete prebasic molt that occurs after breeding (~September–October, sometimes earlier).[1, 2]

In contrast to most birds, these murrelets have a cryptic breeding plumage in which they appear marbled or dark sooty overall, with paler highlights in the scapulars. The nonbreeding plumage is more similar to that of other alcids, a contrasting black and white. Flight feathers are dropped (molted) all at once (usually in September), rendering the birds flightless for about eight weeks as they replace remiges.[13, 14, 15] Juveniles fledge around August and September, looking like fresh, shorter-tailed (often shorter-billed) versions of nonbreeding adults. Unlike some other alcids, these murrelets, once they fledge, are not found accompanied by parents at sea.[2, 16]

Sexes are similar in all plumages, though males average slightly larger. In breeding pairs one bird is often noticeably paler than the other, so more sexual dimorphism may exist than is currently appreciated. Possibly, one sex attains breeding plumage earlier in the year than the other; more study is needed. Seldom is voice a necessary component in identification, but you might occasionally first detect a member of this group by voice. Researchers survey for these species by listening for birds in the predawn hours commuting from feeding areas to nest sites farther inland. Opportunities to appreciate the vocalizations are few and far between.

MARBLED MURRELET: Famous for its elusive breeding habits, nesting in treetops of old-growth forests of the Pacific Northwest, this bird was the last in North America to have its nest described.[17] Not all, however, are arboreal nesters, and in Alaska (where roughly 75 percent of the population breeds), about 3 percent nest on the ground.[18] Breeding from the Aleutians south to the central coast of California, and wintering from the Bering Sea south to Baja California, this species is by far the most commonly encountered *Brachyramphus*. Less migratory than Long-billed, Marbled remains in waters near breeding areas or undertakes moderate southward migration.[1] Few, if any, vagrant records exist outside its typical range. Though many individuals breed miles from the coast (some at sites forty miles inland), it is otherwise unknown from the interior of the continent.

Among the three *Brachyramphus*, Marbled is intermediate in overall size, bill length, and plumage. Structure is seldom of much use, but Marbled is slightly heavier than Kittlitz's, and slightly smaller than Long-billed. (See those species for differences from Marbled). *Breeding:* Adults are largely blackish brown overall but show a paler and variably marbled throat and chest, with whitish in the scapulars and on the rear flanks, and white undertail coverts. The mantle and shoulders are at times suffused with flecks of rust orange. In flight they appear nearly entirely dark sooty brown. *Nonbreeding:* These have striking black-and-white plumage, with typical alcid countershading, largely black above and white below. The upperparts are black save the white scapulars and an incomplete, but bold,

white hind collar. The dark cap connects at the nape to the blackish mantle. The black cap extends down below and in front of the eye, thus surrounding it in black. In flight, the blackish upperparts extend downward onto the sides of the upper chest, forming an incomplete dark collar, which is broken in the middle by the white of the chest and throat. The tail is mostly black, but short, and so is sometimes surrounded by the white flank feathers.

Voice: At times Marbled Murrelets are vocal, especially near nest sites, giving a distinctive shrill, piping "kleeah" or "peeuh." This somewhat gull-like sound is given in flight, and when given in rapid succession it may recall a raptor; when agitated it becomes a sharper "kee-er!" At sea, Marbled gives a rapid and sometimes repeated "wee-doo," which when sped up in excitement or agitation may become "quipp" or "wheoo."

KITTLITZ'S MURRELET: Named for German zoologist Heinrich von Kittlitz, this dapper little alcid breeds only in Alaska and adjacent Russia. Winter sightings are rare, and wintering areas are poorly understood but are believed to include parts of the Gulf of Alaska, the Bering Sea, and perhaps polynyas (patches of open water amid pack ice) in the Bering Sea, or farther north.[19] Few vagrant records exist, and Kittlitz's has been recorded only a few times south of Alaska, always in coastal waters.

Kittlitz's differs from its congeners in its nesting habits, and in being tied to glacial waters. It is also smaller and paler overall than the others. Both the genus and species name refer to the short bill, and indeed Kittlitz's has a shorter and finer bill than the others. Though it frequently overlaps with Marbled, Kittlitz's feeds on smaller prey[20, 21] and perhaps favors nearshore waters for feeding more than Marbled.[2]

Arguably the most distinctive of the *Brachyramphus*, Kittlitz's is paler and shorter tailed than the others (appearing almost tailless at times), and in all plumages the eye is usually more pronounced, standing out well against the white face (lending it a sort of surprised expression). *Breeding:* Compared to Marbled, Kittlitz's is paler and more marbled gray, buff, and gold, with more fine whitish markings (but beware Marbleds in transition). The undertail coverts are cleaner and more extensively white as well. Even in the more cryptically patterned breeding plumage, the eye is usually visible, failing to blend in the way it does on Marbled. The scapulars are marked with whitish buff. In flying birds,

Breeding (left) and transitioning Long-billed Murrelets, CA, Aug (KR). Most records of Long-billed Murrelets come from either July–August (breeding-plumage adults) or late fall/early winter (nonbreeding adults/juveniles). In the July–August window, look for Long-billed Murrelets in the nearshore waters of the Pacific Coast. At this time, they differ from Marbled in having more starkly contrasting white throats; a clean demarcation between the dark cheek, neck and throat; and on transitioning birds, two pale ovals on the nape (Marbled should be developing a broader pale collar). The "long bill" is difficult to distinguish under field conditions.

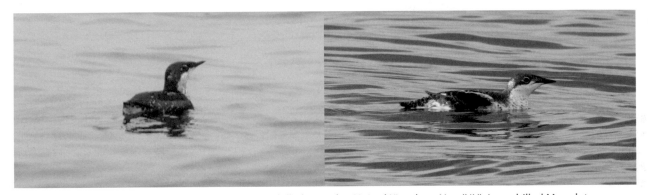

Long-billed Murrelet, WA, Jul (RM) (left); juvenile Long-billed Murrelet, United Kingdom, Nov (NH). Long-billed Murrelets occurring along the Pacific Coast in July–August may represent failed breeders or first-summer birds and thus could look like breeding adults, transitioning adults (like the bird at left), or even nonbreeding adults. Juveniles (right) have dark flecks mixed into the white underparts that should be replaced by wholly white feathers during a preformative molt in fall. Note that compared with that of Marbled, the dark neck is cleanly demarcated from the white throat and the two pale ovals on the nape.

Adult Long-billed Murrelet, CA, Aug (KR) (left); adult Long-billed Murrelet, WA, Jul (RM) (right). In flying birds note the dark belly contrasting with the whitish throat and dark underwings. For birds in nonbreeding plumage, you should rule out the superficially similar Scripps's Murrelet, which is completely dark backed and has whitish underwings.

Kittlitz's Murrelets feeding on glacial outflow, Kachemak Bay, AK, May (BLS). For birders, a trip to Alaska is required to see Kittlitz's Murrelet, as few have ever been recorded south of there. It is a truly enigmatic species, and biologists are still learning about its natural history requirements, but it seems closely tied to glaciers and is perhaps in danger of being heavily impacted by climate change.

note the significant white in the tail, the pattern almost recalling that of a meadowlark. Also, the rear flanks are white, and the secondaries are all tipped with white, standing out as a bold white trailing edge on the inner wing. Diving birds captured on camera often show extensive white on the belly. *Nonbreeding*: These are very white faced overall, with almost completely white lores, and a black eye surrounded with white (some show a small crescent of dark just outside the orbital ring). On the head, only the crown and nape are dark. In flying birds, note how the collar appears closer to being complete compared to that of Marbled, plus the tail is mostly white, with only some black at the center.

Voice: Kittlitz's is usually quiet, and not as vocal as Marbled; the common call is a one- or two-syllabled "ow," "auwh," "au-wa," or "a-rah,"[22] with the second syllable often somewhat abbreviated (ML Cat# 72777). The quality somewhat resembles the sound of a Long-tailed Duck, or when farther away, that of a meowing cat.

LONG-BILLED MURRELET: An Asian species with a breeding range centered around the Sea of Okhotsk and along the Kamchatka Peninsula of Russia, this is the most migratory of the *Brachyramphus*, so it is more prone to vagrancy than the others. It sometimes migrates five hundred miles or more from breeding areas[6] to winter along the coast in bays and harbors,

and unlike the other two, even on inland lakes. It was unknown in North America prior to 1979.[23] Since then it is found to stray rarely yet regularly to the ABA Area. Records are known from the Pacific Coast from Alaska south to California, and also at scattered inland lakes, as well as along the Eastern Seaboard. The dynamics of its vagrancy continue to emerge, but thus far most occur between late July and January, with a peak in mid-July to early August (presumably postbreeding adults), and then another peak from late October to early December (perhaps a combination of adults and juveniles).[24]

Long-billed is the largest and darkest *Brachyramphus* and, as the name suggests, the longest billed (the bill averages 15–30 percent longer than in Marbled).[25] It is quite similar in appearance to Marbled Murrelet, but in all plumages, note that Long-billed has thin but noticeable white eye arcs, a heavier build, and no pale collar. The paleness of the underwing coverts relates to age and appears to be unhelpful in separating Long-billed from Marbled, with both species typically showing some white in the underwings until their second prebasic molt at about one year old, after which they both show dark underwings.[6] Though both Long-billed and Marbled can show entirely dark tails, Long-billed occasionally shows some white or pale buff in the outer rectrices,[6] though only exceptional views or photographs confirm this field mark. In the field, some care and skill are required to distinguish the white flanks or undertail covert feathers from the tail feathers. *Breeding:* Identifying Long-billed in breeding plumage is difficult. Most of those found in North America are perhaps not coincidentally birds in nonbreeding plumage. Even in breeding plumage, however, adults often show a shadow pattern of the nonbreeding plumage. Long-billed shows a more extensively pale throat than Marbled Murrelet in breeding plumage. It is also darker overall, especially around the nape, and perhaps also on the undertail coverts. *Nonbreeding:* Distinguishing the two in nonbreeding plumage is easier, when Long-billed shows an entirely dark nape and lacks the blackish spur often present on Marbled, which extends from the mantle down onto the sides of the upper breast (this is perhaps most noticeable in flight). Lacking Marbled's nearly complete pale hind collar, Long-billed instead shows strong contrast between the entirely and extensively dark nape and the white of the lower cheeks and throat, thus more recalling a Guadalupe or Scripps's murrelet in pattern (both of which lack pale scapulars).

Voice: Sounds for this species are not well known. No recordings are present on Xeno-Canto or at the Macaulay Library, but the birds are described as giving a thin, whistled "fii fii." [26]

References

[1]Nelson, S. K. 1997. Marbled Murrelet (*Brachyramphus marmoratus*). The Birds of North America Online. A. Poole, ed. Ithaca, NY: Cornell Lab of Ornithology. http://bna.birds.cornell.edu/bna/species/276

[2]Day, R. H., K. J. Kuletz, and D. A. Nigro. 1999. Kittlitz's Murrelet (*Brachyramphus brevirostris*). The Birds of North America Online. A. Poole, ed. Ithaca, NY: Cornell Lab of Ornithology. http://bna.birds.cornell.edu/bna/species/435

[3]Friesen, V. L., J. F. Piatt, and A. J. Baker. 1996. Evidence from cytochrome b sequences and allozymes for a "new" species of alcid: The Long-billed Murrelet (*Brachyramphus perdix*). Condor 98:681–90.

[4]Moum, T., U. Árnason, and E. Árnason. 2002. Mitochondrial DNA sequence evolution and phylogeny of the Atlantic Alcidae, including the extinct Great Auk (*Pinguinus impennis*). Molecular Biology and Evolution 19(9): 1434–39.

[5]American Ornithologists' Union. 1997. Forty-first supplement to the American Ornithologists' Union Check-list of North American Birds. Auk 114:542–52.

[6]Thompson, C. W., K. J. Pullen, R. E. Johnson, and E. B. Cummins. 2003. Specimen record of a Long-billed Murrelet from eastern Washington, with notes on plumage and morphometric differences between Long-billed and Marbled Murrelets. Western Birds 34(3): 157–68.

[7]US Geological Survey. 2003. Kittlitz's Murrelet. http://alaska.usgs.gov/science/biology/seabirds_foragefish/photogallery/Picture_of_Month/pom.php?pomid=66

[8]Piatt, J. F., and K. Kuletz. 2005. Farewell to the Glacier Murrelet? Arctic Warbler 11(1): 1–3.

[9]BirdLife International. 2012. Species factsheet: *Brachyramphus brevirostris*. http://www.birdlife.org

[10]BirdLife International. 2010. *Brachyramphus perdix*. IUCN Red List of Threatened Species. Version 2011.2. www.iucnredlist.org

[11]BirdLife International. 2010. *Brachyramphus marmoratus*. IUCN Red List of Threatened Species. Version 2011.2. www.iucnredlist.org

[12] Oskin, B. 2013. Science on NBC News. May 20. Fighting to save an endangered bird – with vomit. http://www.livescience.com/32092-saving-marbled-murrelet-with-vomit-eggs.html

[13]Bent, A. C. 1919. Life histories of North American diving birds. US National Museum Bulletin 107.

[14]Kozlova, E. V. 1961. Fauna of the USSR: Birds, Charadriiformes, Suborder Alcae. Academy of Sciences USSR New Series 2(65): 1–14. Translated by R. Ettinger. Jerusalem: Israel Program for Scientific Translations.

[15]Carter, H. R., M.L.C. McAllister, and M.E.P. Isleib. 1995. Mortality of Marbled Murrelets in gill nets in North America. In Ecology and Conservation of the Marbled Murrelet, edited by C. J. Ralph, G. L. Hunt Jr., M. G. Raphael, and J. F. Piatt, 271–84. Albany, CA: USDA Forest Service General Technical Report PNW-152.

[16]Singer, S. W., D. L. Suddjian, and S. A. Singer. 1995. Fledging behavior, flight patterns and habitat characteristics of Marbled Murrelets tree nests in California. In Biology of the Marbled Murrelet: Inland and at Sea, edited by S. K. Nelson and S. G. Sealy. Special issue, Northwestern Naturalist 76:54–62.

[17]Binford, L. C., B. G. Elliott, and S. W. Singer. 1975. Discovery of a nest and the downy young of the Marbled Murrelet. Wilson Bulletin 87:303–19.

[18]Piatt, J. F., and R. G. Ford. 1993. Distribution and abundance of Marbled Murrelets in Alaska. Condor 95:662–69.

[19]Artukhin, Y. B., P. S. Vyatkin, A. V. Andreev, N. B. Konyukhov, and T. I. Van Pelt. 2011. Status of the Kittlitz's Murrelet in Russia. Marine Ornithology 39:23–33.

[20]Kishchinskii, A. A. 1968. O biologii Korotkoklyuvogo i Dlinnoklyuvogo pizhikov [The biology of Short-billed and Long-billed murrelets]. Ornitologiya 9:208–13.

[21]Bédard, J. 1969. Adaptive radiation in Alcidae. Ibis 111:189–98.

[22]Van Pelt, T. I., J. F. Piatt, and G. B. van Vliet. 1999. Vocalizations of the Kittlitz's Murrelet. Condor 101(2): 395–98.

[23]Sealy, S. G., H. R. Carter, and D. Alison. 1982. Occurrences of the Asiatic Marbled Murrelet (*Brachyramphus marmoratus perdix*) in North America. Auk 99:778–81.

[24]Mlodinow, S. G. 1997. The Long-billed Murrelet (*Brachyramphus perdix*) in North America. Birding 29(6): 460–75.

[25]Pitocchelli, J., J. F. Piatt, and M. A. Cronin. 1995. Morphological and genetic divergence among Alaskan populations of *Brachyramphus* murrelets. Wilson Bulletin 107:235–50.

[26]Brazil, M. 2009. Birds of East Asia. London: A & C Black Publishers.

Pacific Cormorants

Brandt's Cormorant (*Phalacrocorax penicillatus*)

Pelagic Cormorant (*Phalacrocorax pelagicus*)

Red-faced Cormorant (*Phalacrocorax urile*)

Also: Double-crested Cormorant
(*Phalacrocorax auritus*)

Neotropic Cormorant (*Phalacrocorax brasilianus*)

First Breeding:	2–3 years old
Breeding Strategy:	Seasonally monogamous; colonial
Lifespan:	< 20 years

For many people, there is something off-putting about cormorants. They seem sneaky, craftily snaking through the water in search of fish, recalling a loon yet lacking a loon's elegant appeal. A cormorant's plumage isn't terribly inspiring, and on land they really make a mess—a cormorant colony is no place for a first date! Indeed, cormorants are not the most popular birds, and fishermen the world over look at them with disdain, laboring under the misconception that fish-eating cormorants steal their livelihoods.[1, 2] But even among birders cormorants are frequently ignored or even frowned upon, and usually relegated to an afterthought when compiling a species list. It would seem that these birds, more than most, suffer from a public image crisis.

Cormorants are large, dark, long-necked, aquatic birds. They fly in loose *V*-shaped flocks or "skeins." As pursuit divers they are often seen swimming, sometimes with just the head, neck, and upper back exposed, and other times are seen resting on prominent perches such as cliffs, posts, or snags. Cormorants often face away from the sun or into the wind, with their wings spread open to dry. Unlike those of ducks or loons, cormorant feathers are permeable, and so they need to be dried regularly.[3] In the family Phalacrocoracidae, there are about forty species of cormorants and shags worldwide, most of which are in the Southern Hemisphere. The terms "shag" and "cormorant" are usually interchangeable, but some use "shag" to refer to the slender, marine, cliff-nesting species. In North America six species breed, all in the genus *Phalacrocorax*.

Natural History Note:

The Spectacled Cormorant (*Phalacrocorax perspicillatus*, a.k.a. Pallas's Cormorant) recently became extinct in the North Pacific. Discovered by George Steller in November 1741, it was a large, nearly flightless resident of the western Bering Sea, found on Bering Island of the Commandorski (Commander) Islands in Russia, at the extreme west end of the Aleutian chain.[5] Steller (for whom a jay, sea-eagle, sea lion, and sea cow are named) was a naturalist onboard the *St. Peter*, captained by Danish explorer Vitus Bering on an exploratory expedition to the North Pacific. After surviving a shipwreck on Bering Island, the crew reported the bounty of wildlife there, which led hunters to exterminate much of it. Like the Spectacled Cormorant, the Steller's sea cow is extinct. The cormorant is thought to be most closely related to Brandt's Cormorant, along with Bank, Black-faced, and Flightless cormorants.[6] Steller was the only ornithologist to see the cormorant alive, and his description of it, a few museum specimens, and a few skeletons are all that remain today of this enigmatic species.

Depending on conditions and behavior, loons, geese, and ibis may be mistaken for cormorants. In flight cormorants are often confused with geese or ibis, but cormorants have longer tails, often fly close to the water, and don't maintain their flock integrity very well. Individuals in flying flocks often break away, and the skeins seem always shifting and reshaping. On the water, swimming loons are frequently confused with cormorants, but they differ in bill shape and plumage pattern. Vagrant Anhingas, especially when soaring, can be confused with cormorants, but Anhingas have a longer tail with a narrow base, a thin neck, a tiny head, and a long, pointed bill.

These Pacific cormorants provide an example of the identification issues that arise when birders give common birds short shrift. Surprisingly few birders think of cormorants as an identification challenge; however, even very good birders frequently misidentify these species. At times Pacific cormorants are easily identified from a great distance, but conditions can obscure critical field marks, making even close birds difficult to identify. Because they are not particularly charismatic, cormorants are overlooked, but they do indeed merit careful scrutiny and cautious identification. Brandt's,

When breeding, cormorants have elaborate plumes and bold displays. This adult Brandt's Cormorant, CA, May (BLS) would pose little identification challenge to a birder in a close-up view, but nonbreeding and immature cormorants are much harder to identify. Couple that with the fact that these birds are often seen at a distance on the water or in flight, and you've got real potential for misidentification!

Focus on: *Structure (especially of the head and bill), Range, Behavior*

Juvenile Double-crested Cormorants, NJ, Oct (GLA) (left); CA, Dec (SNGH) (right). Juvenile cormorants are brownish, lacking the glossy iridescence and bright bare parts of adults; eyes are brownish, changing to blue green over the first two years. Juveniles of all species have uniformly fresh plumage, especially the upperwing coverts and flight feathers. Double-crested shows remarkable juvenile plumage variation, ranging from buffy to dark brown below, and from pale fringed to more adultlike above.

First-summer Double-crested Cormorant, CA, Aug (BLS) (left); second-winter Double-crested Cormorant, CA, Oct (BLS) (right). General plumage progression is from brown to glossy black over three years. First-summers are variable, some being more splotchy black below. By their second winter most are mottled blackish on the neck and breast; the age of this bird is determined by its retained juvenile outer primaries, and two waves of active wing molt.

Second-winter Double-crested Cormorant, CA, Nov (BLS) (left); breeding adult Double-crested Cormorant, CA, Mar (BLS) (right). Second-winter birds are usually obviously intermediate between juveniles (first-winters) and adults. Note the bright orange facial skin, pale bill, and greenish eye. Adults are completely glossy black, and for a short period in spring they show ornamental plumes, which are highly variable even within nesting colonies, ranging from white to black to salt-and-pepper.

Pelagic, and Red-faced cormorants inhabit marine environments such as coastal estuaries and rocky islands or cliffs. They forage mainly in nearshore ocean waters and essentially never wander far from the coast. At times they overlap and are confused with Double-crested Cormorant, which uses a wide variety of brackish and freshwater habitats and is the common cormorant seen inland over much of the continent. All along the Pacific Coast, from the Gulf of Alaska to southern California, more than one species of cormorant occurs, and in most places three (or even four) are possible. And on rare occasions, wanderers are recorded out of range. Structure is key, but also pay attention to habitat and behavior. Since several cormorant species may occur at a single location, these birds provide a good opportunity to practice distinguishing species using GISS.

Hints and Considerations

- Double-crested Cormorant is common and widespread and routinely makes use of both marine and inland waters. It is large and can be distinguished from the others at all ages by its orange-yellow throat (gular skin) and face.
- From coastal southern California north into British Columbia, the ranges of Pelagic, Brandt's, and Double-crested overlap. In the Bering Sea and in parts of the Gulf of Alaska, Pelagic, Red-faced, and Double-crested ranges overlap. Brandt's breeds only sparingly into southeast Alaska and is very rare north of there.
- Pelagic and Red-faced are smaller, cliff-nesting cormorants that typically forage in small groups or alone. Adults show white flank patches when breeding. Immatures are entirely dark brownish black.
- Brandt's is larger, and most similar in structure to Double-crested. It nests on top of flat rocky areas and is often seen in large aggregations. Immatures are tannish brown on the chest and upper belly.
- Red-faced is poorly known overall, and accidental outside its limited range in Alaska. It seldom wanders.
- On flying cormorants, concentrate on the size of the head relative to the thickness of the neck. Also consider the relative length and depth of the neck compared to the body.

Identification

Males and females appear similar, though males average slightly larger. Determining age can be important in identification. Cormorants are usually categorized as either adults or juveniles, but some individuals are identifiable as second-cycles. (Cormorant molt/plumage progression remains in need of clarification.) Adult plumage is attained at two to three years of age.[4] Breeding adults (March–June) have iridescent green, blue, or purple tones visible in their black plumage (on the back, neck, and head) when in good light. They also show small tufted crests and/or brightly colored bare parts, with the gular and facial skin becoming rich in color on breeding adults. Nonbreeding adults are similar but typically lack crests and have reduced color in the gular and facial skin. Juvenile cormorants show little or no iridescence in their plumage and have duller bare parts. They are browner than adults but become glossier and blacker with age. Juveniles vary more in appearance (especially Double-crested). Pay attention to chest pattern and overall color to separate juveniles; structure and behavior are most important. Second-cycle cormorants are over one year old and show a mix of brown feathers in their otherwise largely black plumage that may show some iridescence, and in summer they show some color on the bare parts of the face. In each species, eyes are brown in juveniles, becoming greenish or pale blue in adults.

BRANDT'S CORMORANT: This species is distinctive in its social behavior and its structure, and it is virtually never seen inland. It is the largest and most robust of these three marine cormorants. It is actually more similar in shape to Double-crested Cormorant than the others, but because of its habits it is most often confused with Pelagic. Compared to the latter, Brandt's has a heavier head, and it is short tailed and long necked. It often has a shallow, kink-necked appearance in flight, and it seems front heavy because of its long neck, big head, and relatively short tail. At all ages it may be readily identifiable by the buffy feathering around its throat, though this is often less noticeable on juveniles. Brandt's shows a brownish juvenile plumage.

A lone foraging Pelagic Cormorant may cause some confusion; in that case, try to assess size, look at the chin and chest, and note the head and bill structure. Brandt's and Pelagic feed in the same nearshore areas, but Brandt's favors shallower waters and typically occurs in groups. To separate Brandt's from Double-crested, note the smaller, more rounded head and the reduced pale throat patch that is pale grayish or buff (not yellow orange). The bill is black and seems relatively long and

Breeding adult Brandt's Cormorant, CA, Mar (BLS) (left); nonbreeding adult Brandt's Cormorant, CA, Dec (BLS) (right). Note buffy patch around base of mandible, a key field mark for Brandt's. Ornamental head plumes kept for a short time in spring.

First-summer Brandt's Cormorant, CA, Jun (BLS) (left); juvenile Brandt's Cormorant, CA, Oct (BLS) (right). Immature Brandt's often show mixed body plumage; by first summer most have blackish feathers mixed in below. Second-years are generally darker than this yet still lack the glossy iridescence of adults. Juveniles are brownish, palest on the belly, lacking gloss and showing uniform flight feathers and buff-tipped upperwing coverts. Note messy buffy throat patch of juveniles, sometimes nearly lacking and very difficult to see. Juveniles have brown eyes that turn dark bluish in the first winter and get progressively paler blue as they age.

Fishing Brandt's Cormorants, CA, Sep (BLS) (left); nesting Brandt's Cormorants, CA, Jul (BLS) (right). Habitat and behavior can be very helpful when identifying cormorants. Marauding packs of fishing birds, sometimes numbering in the hundreds, are a common sight near shore along the Pacific Coast. Pelagic Cormorant is more solitary. Nesting habits also differ: Brandt's favors flatter areas and Pelagic steeper sea cliffs. This dilapidated pier is typical Brandt's nesting habitat.

Breeding Pelagic Cormorants, AK, May (BLS) (left); nonbreeding adult Pelagic Cormorant, CA, Sep (BLS) (right). Outside Alaska, breeding adult Pelagic Cormorants are unlikely to be confused. Note bright red facial skin, big white flank patches, and short head tufts. Nonbreeding adults are overall glossy black, with purplish-green iridescence and duller red facial skin. Adults have greenish eyes that are duller than Brandt's.

Nonbreeding adult Pelagic Cormorant, CA, Dec (BLS) (left); first-winter Pelagic Cormorant, CA, Nov (BLS) (right). Note the overall glossy black plumage of the nonbreeding adult compared with the plain blackish plumage of the first-winter, which lacks iridescence altogether. Pelagic Cormorants are difficult to age because juveniles are blackish overall, so basic adults and juveniles are more similar than in other species. Also note the dark eye and lack of red facial skin on the juvenile.

First-winter Pelagic Cormorant, CA, Nov (BLS) (left); Pelagic Cormorant at nest cliff, CA, Mar (BLS) (right). On this flying juvenile, note overall black plumage lacking iridescent gloss of adult, and uniform-age flight feathers and upperwing coverts. This adult (right) is prospecting for nest sites on a typical steep rock cliff used by this species. Nests are placed on short open ledges.

slender. Especially noticeable in flight is that the tail is shorter than that of Double-crested, and this contributes to a slightly front-heavy appearance. Brandt's flies low to the sea, showing a shallow kink in the neck, and feeds in the open ocean. Brandt's virtually always occurs in flocks, but rarely a single vagrant turns up.

Adults: By their third spring Brandt's appear in adult plumage aspect, acquiring the white facial plumes and bright blue gular (throat) pouch. Adults are black with a greenish sheen, and an obvious buff throat below the gular area. Breeders have variable filamentous whitish head plumes on the neck and back and, in proper light, show a bright blue gular pouch. *Immatures:* Juveniles have a pale throat patch, but it is smaller (sometimes not visible) and less noticeable. First-year birds have brownish heads, necks, and chests (palest on the chest), with pale-fringed back feathers and upperwing coverts. First-years undergo a partial molt in their first fall/early winter, whereby some of the faded pale-fringed back feathers are replaced by more adultlike glossy black ones. First-years remain rather drab brownish and mottled overall through winter, and by late spring they often become quite bleached. When they begin their body molt, the dark brown new feathers are clearly visible among the old bleached whitish-brown ones. Two-year-olds (second-cycles) are still brownish overall and do not acquire the white breeding plumes of adults. By late spring of year two their body feathers are slowly being replaced by blackish semiglossy ones, and their eyes have changed color from brownish to pale blue.

PELAGIC CORMORANT: The smallest and skinniest cormorant, Pelagic Cormorant is potbellied and long tailed, possessing a very skinny neck and an equally small, fine head. The bill is also small and fine, and dark blackish gray in all plumages—a good distinction from Red-faced Cormorant (but beware of how it may reflect light and look paler). On the water Pelagic sits very low, often with just the neck, head, and top of the back visible above the water. When it dives it propels its entire body from the water in an arcing manner. It is poorly named because while it is an exclusively marine species, it does not venture far from shore and much prefers littoral over pelagic waters.

Structurally, this is a distinctive species, but at times Brandt's can appear nearly as slender, and similarly dark faced. Prolonged study should reveal Brandt's heavier, sturdier frame. Pelagic may feed among Brandt's Cormorant flocks but dives to greater depths and so may remain underwater longer. Compared to others, Pelagic Cormorant, even at the height of the breeding season, shows almost no gular skin (gular area is feathered black) but does show some facial skin. In Alaska, distinguishing Pelagic from Red-faced is a regular problem in much of the Bering Sea and in some parts of the Gulf of Alaska. Pelagic is smaller, has a skinnier head and neck, and always shows a dark bill. In flight the small head of Pelagic appears as an extension of the straight, thin neck, and it often seems that the neck is only slightly longer than the tail. Pelagic is usually found singly or in small groups, and it feeds near rocky areas.

Adults: In breeding plumage adults are glossy black overall, with a purplish sheen and white flank patches (January–May), and show a small amount of red facial skin surrounding the eye. The red facial skin is typically visible only at close range and does not extend broadly across the forehead as on Red-faced Cormorant, and Pelagic usually shows some red in the gape area (largely blue in Red-faced). Frequently, though, Pelagic appears dark faced when seen briefly or at a moderate distance or farther, and in winter the red facial skin disappears nearly entirely. In flight, Pelagic lacks the contrasting brownish wings evident on Red-faced. *Immatures:* First-year birds are brownish black overall, paler on the belly, with all-dark bill and facial skin (Red-faced has yellowish bill and face at this age). The aging sequence is similar to that described above for Brandt's Cormorant. One-year-old birds in spring fade to pale brown on the breast, with a mix of newer darker brown feathers coming in. Two-year-olds in spring have a darker brown breast, with variable glossy black mottling. By the third year they appear as adults. Eye color starts off dark brown in first-years but changes to pale greenish yellow before becoming bright greenish yellow in adults.

RED-FACED CORMORANT: Red-faced Cormorant is like a larger, more colorful version of Pelagic Cormorant. Red-faced is attractively marked and is a major target for birders visiting Alaska, as it is essentially never seen south of there. Seldom do they number more than a few dozen at any specific location. Red-faced Cormorants in all plumages show extensive pale yellowish or horn color on the mandible (the basal two-thirds), often with bluish at the gape, which is a distinctive feature. The species is similar in proportions to Pelagic Cormorant but is heavier overall, with a larger head and thicker neck, and the bill is slightly thicker, too. Nonbreeding adults and immatures are more difficult to distinguish

Breeding Red-faced Cormorant, AK, May (BLS) (left); adult and chick Red-faced Cormorant, AK, Aug (SS) (right). In high breeding plumage, note bright and extensive reddish facial skin including forehead, yellowish mandible, and bluish bill base. By late summer (right) these colors have become less intense, but the overall pattern is similar. Winter records are few, but adults likely look similar to this, with perhaps duller facial skin.

First-summer Red-faced Cormorant, AK, June (DG) (left); juvenile Red-faced Cormorant, AK, Aug (DG) (right). First-summers are brownish black, lacking the gloss of adults, and have muted facial skin and bill coloration. Compared with Pelagic, note yellow bill base with hints of blue around the gular pouch, and usually some dull reddish skin around the eye. Juveniles are dusky blackish; note dusky bill with some yellow along the cutting edges, and the pinkish-blue facial skin.

Pelagic and Red-faced cormorants, AK, May (BLS). Breeding Pelagic Cormorant (left bird in left photo) can have a surprisingly pale bill and extensive red facial skin (a red face). Do not be fooled by this! Red-faced (right) has a brighter yellow bill with a blue base, and brighter red facial skin. It's easy to convince yourself you're seeing a Red-faced when you're not; it's unmistakable when you actually see one! Size differences are not obvious when the two are perched together (right photo), but note the shorter, thicker neck on Red-faced (center bird).

Pelagic (top left) and Brandt's cormorants, CA, Dec (BLS) (left); Pelagic (left) and Double-crested cormorants, CA, Oct (SNGH) (right). In these two images, notice how size isn't very helpful when you compare perched cormorants. Even though Pelagic is smaller and slimmer than the others, this isn't always obvious. Pelagic is generally blackish. Note the buffy throat patches on Brandt's, and the prominent yellow-orange facial skin on Double-crested of all ages.

Juvenile Double-crested (top) and Brandt's cormorants, CA, Sep (BLS) (left); juvenile Brandt's (top) and adult Pelagic cormorants, CA, Oct (BLS) (right). Structurally, Double-crested is larger and heavier, with an obvious kink in the neck in flight. Brandt's and Pelagic are slimmer, usually with less obvious kinked necks. Pelagic is potbellied and long tailed, with a slim neck and head.

Breeding Pelagic Cormorant, CA, Feb (BLS) (left); breeding Red-faced Cormorant, AK, Jun (RO) (right). In flight these two species differ structurally, with Pelagic being slimmer overall, especially in the wings, neck, and head. Every year in California there are false reports of Red-faced Cormorants when Pelagic is in high breeding condition. Beware!

from Pelagic Cormorant, and care is needed to separate them. In flight, the depth of the head is slightly greater than that of the neck, and the neck is held straight or slightly kinked. Compared to Pelagic, a flying Red-faced Cormorant has broader wings, at times almost recalling a Double-crested in GISS.

Adults: In breeding plumage adults are unmistakable, having extensive bright red facial skin that surrounds the eyes and extends across the forehead. They have brightly colored bills that are largely yellow with a bright blue base. Breeding adults have glossy black bodies with dark brown wings and a bold white flank patch. Nonbreeding adults have reduced red facial skin, but it is still apparent in the lores, and some still show some bluish around the gape. *Immatures:* First-year Red-faced Cormorants are dark blackish brown overall and slightly paler below, with a pale whitish-gray mandible that is dull bluish at the base. Their foreheads are feathered, unlike those of breeding adults, and their facial skin is reduced and a pale pinkish yellow.

Also:

Double-crested Cormorant: This familiar cormorant is large and conspicuous, with an orange face, large blocky head, and a moderately stout, hooked bill. An adaptable species, Double-crested is found in almost any area of open water, be it fresh or salt. In North America it is the default cormorant in most inland areas. Double-crested usually flies higher than most other cormorants, shows a more prominent kink in the neck, and has a tail shorter than the head/neck projection. Bill color varies somewhat with season. The maxilla is often blackish or dark gray and the mandible is horn or orangish. On breeding adults the bill is mostly black but variably marbled with gunmetal gray. Adults are black overall, with an extensive orange gular patch and pale orangish lores. The eponymous crests are present only on breeding birds and are seldom useful in identification. Crest color varies, being whitish on the West Coast and blacker in the East. Immatures are variably pale brown or whitish brown on the breast, neck, and head but have darker brownish bellies. Juveniles are notoriously variable in plumage, and some are dusky brownish overall, whereas others have distinctly paler breasts and necks. Double-crested Cormorants of all ages can be distinguished from the three Pacific cormorants by the bright orange facial skin and lores. Inland in the West, Double-crested is likely to be confused only with a vagrant Neotropic.

Neotropic Cormorant is increasing in the United States. It is common in parts of Texas and southwest Louisiana, and regular in southern Arizona and New Mexico. Vagrants occur in southern California, and increasingly it strays elsewhere. It is small, smaller even than Pelagic, but is most similar to Double-crested. Neotropic prefers freshwater (lakes, ponds) or brackish estuaries. In addition to being smaller than Double-crested, it is longer tailed and shorter billed. Adults show a thin white border to the yellow-orange throat. Identification can be tricky, especially on lone immatures, and having photos to scrutinize after a sighting will help considerably.

Immature Neotropic Cormorant, LA, Apr (BLS). Neotropic Cormorant is quickly expanding its range in the West, now breeding regularly as far west as the Salton Sea in California. Vagrants are likely in the Pacific Coast region but could be more easily picked up at inland lakes where cormorants are more likely to be scrutinized. Neotropic is similar to Double-crested but is smaller, slimmer, and longer tailed. A key field mark is the shape of the feathering around the gape, which is typically more pointed in Neotropic. Also note the dark lores (orange in Double-crested), and white feathering around the bill base.

References

[1] Weseloh, D.V.C., and J. Casselman. 1992. Calculated fish consumption by Double-crested Cormorants in eastern Lake Ontario. Colonial Waterbird Society Bulletin 16(2): 63–64.

[2] Hatch, J. J., and D. V. Weseloh. 1999. Double-crested Cormorant (*Phalacrocorax auritus*). In The Birds of North America, No. 441, edited by A. Poole and F. Gill. Philadelphia: Birds of North America.

[3] Rijke, A. M. 1968. The water repellency and feather structure of cormorants, Phalacrocoracidae. Journal of Experimental Biology 48:185–89.

[4] Howell, S.N.G. 2010. Molt in North American Birds. New York: Houghton Mifflin.

[5] Johnsgard, P. A. 1993. Cormorants, Darters, and Pelicans of the World. Washington, DC: Smithsonian Institution Press.

[6] Siegel-Causey, D. 1988. Phylogeny of the Phalacrocoracidae. Condor 90:885–905.

Seabirds

Sulids

Tropical Terns

Atlantic Gadflies

Pelagic birding the hardest kind there is. The boat is moving, the ocean is moving, the birds are moving, and wind and lighting conditions are variable and ever changing. It is the ultimate in GISS birding. Color is less useful than structure, broad plumage patterns, flight style, and foraging techniques. Pelagic birding is similar to hawk watching in that you are often seeing birds at a distance and in flight. But unlike hawks, most seabirds species are unfamiliar to a majority of birders, and using GISS is tough, at least initially.

With the exception of some sulids, these birds are seen largely offshore. While any of the groups treated in this volume can provide identification challenges, these three groups probably provide more than their fair share. Again, pay attention to shape, size, and behavior, and if possible take some pictures.

Sulids: Northern Gannet and Boobies

Northern Gannet (*Morus bassanus*)

Masked Booby (*Sula dactylatra*)

Blue-footed Booby (*Sula nebouxii*)

Brown Booby (*Sula leucogaster*)

Red-footed Booby (*Sula sula*)

Also: Nazca Booby

First Breeding:	3–5 years old
Breeding Strategy:	Monogamous; colonial
Lifespan:	Up to 25 years

The family Sulidae comprises the gannets and boobies. A cosmopolitan family, absent only from polar seas, its members are large, streamlined seabirds with tapered bills and long, pointed wings and tails. There are ten species worldwide; the gannets are placed in the genus *Morus* and the boobies in the genus *Sula*. In gannets the sexes are similar, whereas in boobies the sexes differ slightly. Gannets differ from boobies in certain head features, too, but both have evolved unique nostrils on the sides of the bill (near the gape) with flaps that automatically close when they dive into the water.[1] Indeed, sulids are probably the world's most accomplished plunge divers, and watching a feeding flock torpedo into the water in pursuit of fish and squid is an unforgettable spectacle. On land sulids are considerably less graceful, walking awkwardly on large webbed feet. Both the genus name *Sula* and the word "booby" originate from words meaning "stupid," a reference to how clumsy and easily caught these birds are at colonies.[2] Famously colonial in their nesting habits, sulid colonies represent some of the world's largest concentrations of birds.

Natural History Note:

Northern Gannet is well known for its huge "gannetries," including those at St. Bonaventure Island (~70,000 birds),[3] and at St. Kilda, Scotland; the latter site is believed to have exceeded 100,000 birds. Apparently there is no exchange between breeders in North America and the colonies in Europe.[3] Most impressive, though, are Peruvian Booby colonies, some of which contain roughly 1.5 million birds.[1]

Hybridization is rare in sulids,[1] for at least two reasons: courtship is a complex process (a result of the considerable commitment required of both pair members to successfully bring off young); and in boobies the brightly colored bare parts not only signal fitness for breeding but also likely evolved in response to selective pressures on species recognition, as two or more species frequently nest at the same colony.[4] Northern Gannets form long-term pair bonds, but because boobies nest in more stable climatic conditions, their breeding is more spontaneous and usually occurs in response to food availability, so individuals show less fidelity from season to season. Sulids that are more pelagic, such as Masked and Red-footed boobies, may also feed nocturnally, while those feeding in littoral or shallow waters are mainly diurnal.

Adult Blue-footed Booby, Bahia Los Angeles, Mexico, Sep (BLS). Adult Boobies and Gannets are generally easily identified—check out the blue feet on this one! But immatures and juveniles are more challenging, especially when seen at a distance. Sulids represent a good opportunity to study age-related plumage progression, shape, and behavior differences.

Focus on: *Size/structure, Plumage, Behavior, Rump/tail pattern, Bare parts*

Sulids attain adult plumage in 2–3 years. Adults and juveniles are readily aged, but immatures are more difficult; they are best aged by assessing the number of molt waves in the primaries—often not easily accomplished in the field, at least without photos. Unlike many large birds, sulids exhibit an accelerated stepwise replacement of flight feathers, with the first wing molt beginning about 6–8 months after fledging; the second wave of wing molt begins before the first one finishes, usually at about 11–12 months of age (SNGH, unpublished data). Immatures may molt flight feathers almost constantly for their first 2–3 years, thus setting up a complete replacement of flight feathers (via 2–3 waves of molt) in a single molting event in adulthood. Howell[8] provides an excellent overview of this topic. Here we use Northern Gannet to illustrate plumage progression over 4 cycles. Adults (top left, NC, Dec, GLA) have clean white secondaries, tails, and upperwing coverts. Immatures (top right and middle row, NC, Feb, SNGH) are variable. Second-cycle birds in winter generally show darker wings and tails, whereas third-cycles appear more adultlike, with black feathers mixed in. First-summer or early second-cycle birds (lower left, ME, Sep, SNGH) look similar to juveniles but are generally tattered, retaining a few juvenile outer primaries while new inner primaries are molting in. Juveniles (lower right, Morocco, Sep, GLA) are overall brown and uniformly crisp, with same-age flight feathers and wing coverts.

Sulids are nearly always encountered on the ocean, in some cases far from land (with those wandering to the Salton Sea among the notable exceptions). All sulids feed in flocks, but they are also seen singly, as well as following fishing vessels in mixed-species feeding flocks. Sometimes they are seen resting on the sea, standing on flotsam, or perched on channel markers, rocky shores, or even boats. Northern Gannet is probably the most familiar sulid to North American birders. It is an Atlantic seabird that breeds in large colonies in Quebec and Atlantic Canada and winters along the coast abundantly from New England south to North Carolina, and more sparingly into the Gulf of Mexico. The boobies, on the other hand, only barely reach North America. They breed mostly on remote tropical islands outside the region but regularly reach the shores of southern California and southern Florida, only occasionally straying farther north along the coasts.

The orientation of their eyes provides sulids binocular vision and also a rather benign, companionable expression. Several species are named for their brightly colored bare parts, and the feet especially are used in courtship displays. Often, however, sulids are seen at some distance, so these features are less obvious. This can complicate identification, as can birders' lack of familiarity with the species. Being unfamiliar, they require some study and preparation to identify. They are confusable mostly only with each other (though distant sulids can be taken for tubenoses or pelicans), but structural and behavioral cues (e.g., flight style) help separate them. Five or six sulid species have occurred in North America (the status of Nazca Booby remains unclear; see below). Though adults are typically easily identified, distant birds and immatures are challenging. Diving and roosting behavior can be helpful in identification. Gannets do not visit land except to nest, whereas boobies often roost on shore or on human-made structures. Perhaps even more than plumage, a sense of each species' structure and habits is the best avenue toward accurate identification.

Hints and Considerations

- It is important to gain a sense of sulids' structure, and to observe behavior. Soak in their GISS from a wide-angle perspective, noting their heftiness, their surroundings, their diving and roosting behavior, and their flight style. Then zero in on plumage pattern.

- Most difficult is distinguishing Masked Booby from Northern Gannet, and also distinguishing immature Brown Booby from similarly plumaged (dark-morph and immature) Red-footed Booby. Foot color is useful on perched adults, but many vagrants are immatures or are seen at some distance, often in flight.
- On the Atlantic Coast, Northern Gannet is common and is the most familiar and regularly encountered sulid. It is rare on the Great Lakes, being found mainly in fall, and is a vagrant in the Pacific.
- On the East Coast, boobies are rare away from Florida, and exceptional north of North Carolina. In Florida's Dry Tortugas National Park, Masked and Brown boobies are regular, but Red-footed is rare.
- On the Pacific Coast, boobies occur rarely or sparsely off southern California, becoming increasingly rare north of there, and exceptional north of central California. Brown Booby is the most frequently encountered species, whereas the others are rare.
- Inland records of sulids are extremely rare. Blue-footed strays inland more than the others, especially at the Salton Sea.

Identification

Gannets show little sexual dimorphism, but in boobies, females are larger than males (and no, we did not omit any possessive apostrophes in that sentence, but yes, giggling is permitted). Adult female boobies have darker bare parts than males, and in some species (Masked, Nazca, and Blue-footed) the dark pupils are larger (personal observation).

Sulids require roughly two to four years to reach adult plumage, but the plumage progressions in these species remain imperfectly understood. Because each plumage does not neatly correspond to a year of the bird's life, sulid plumages are better described in plumage "cycles." The smaller species, including Brown, Red-footed, and Blue-footed boobies, acquire adult plumage in about their second year.[1, 5, 6] Any individual in those species is considered to be in either juvenile or adult plumage, but some may be identifiable as second-cycles. The larger Masked Booby usually attains adult plumage in its third year,[7] and Northern Gannet requires at least four years.[3] These two larger sulids are identifiable in juvenile, second-cycle, third-cycle (in gannets, and maybe some Masked Boobies), and adult plumages.

Adults are neatly marked, but juveniles are mostly dark and have duskier bills. Immatures (second- and third-

Adult Northern Gannet, NC, Dec (GLA) (left); juvenile Northern Gannet, Morocco, Sep (GLA) (right). Note that on the water Northern Gannet has a heavy build, with a large bill. There is little seasonal or sexual variation in adult plumage, but the yellowish cowl can fade in worn plumage. Juveniles have uniformly fresh plumage, essentially brownish at a distance, but spangled with white when close.

Third-cycle Northern Gannet, NC, Feb (SNGH) (left); third-cycle Northern Gannet, NL, Jun (BLS) (right). Third-cycle Northern Gannets are essentially adultlike, with obvious signs of immaturity. The seconadaries are usually mixed black and white, as is the tail. Some adultlike birds with one or a few black secondaries may be advanced third-cycle birds, or fourth-cycle or older. Third-cycle birds have three waves of primary molt.

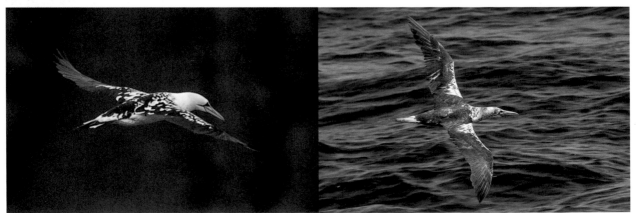

Second-cycle Northern Gannet, NL, Jun (BLS) (left); early second-cycle Northern Gannet, Morocco, Sep (GLA) (right). Gannets molt mainly from late summer through winter, so second-fall birds (right) look similar to worn juveniles, but they become more adultlike over the course of the fall. By their second summer (left) they are obviously different from adults, usually with all-dark flight feathers and spangled white upperparts.

cycles) are intermediate in plumage between juveniles and adults, with an odd mix of white and dark feathers in light morphs. As with many seabirds, sulids molt gradually, replacing flight feathers in staggered waves, (i.e., "stepwise molt" or "staffelmauser"),[8] allowing them to maintain the dynamic flying abilities critical in their lives. They show an accelerated stepwise replacement of flight feathers, replacing inner primaries beginning in the first winter, or at about six months old.

NORTHERN GANNET: The plumage of Northern Gannet, our largest sulid, varies remarkably with age. Compared to boobies, Gannet always appears larger and heavier, with longer wings and heavier wingbeats. Gannet prefers cool littoral waters and is less pelagic than the similar Masked Booby; the latter prefers tropical waters. Gannet's dives are almost always vertical and sometimes begin at spectacular heights (sometimes from over one hundred feet up).

Adults and juveniles predominate, and these are the easiest ages to distinguish in the field. Birds in their second and third cycle are confidently aged only by assessing primary molt, but this is difficult under field conditions. There are general differences between the two (see below), but most of these birds should be classed simply as "immatures." Adults are distinctive, being nearly entirely white except for the black outer half of the wings (primaries and primary coverts). Adults often show a yellow-buff tinge on the back of the head, and importantly, their tails, secondaries, and secondary coverts are white (these are black in Masked Booby). Juveniles are nearly entirely dark gray brown, with obvious white only on the uppertail coverts (rump) and axillaries. At close range the upperwing coverts are neatly stippled with white. Juveniles have uniform-age flight feathers. Gannets in their second or third cycle vary more. A second-cycle typically attains more white in the underparts, becoming somewhat white bellied and white headed, yet remains nearly entirely dark dorsally. Third-cycles are whiter still, with mostly white coverts, but still show largely dark secondaries, a variably dark tail, and an irregular mix of dark and white feathers on the upperwing coverts. These third-cycle birds are most easily confused with Masked Booby. At close range, compared to boobies, notice Gannet's feathered forecrown (feathered in front of the eye) and chin, and the distinct black gape and throat lines. Gannets essentially do not come to land except to nest, or when sick or injured.

MASKED BOOBY: This medium-sized sulid is a rare vagrant along the Gulf Coast and north along the Atlantic to North Carolina, and accidental north of there. It is rare in southern California, and a rare vagrant north to the Bay Area. It is always black tailed and has a mostly horn-colored bill. In all plumages, Masked Booby is mostly pale below and mostly dark above. It is less social than other sulids, preferring to feed in warm pelagic waters, though many North American birders see this species for the first time on the white sands of Hospital Key in the Dry Tortugas. Compared with other boobies, Masked is shorter tailed. Adults have entirely blackish flight feathers (wings and tail) and facial skin but are otherwise an immaculate white. Unlike the adult Gannet, Masked Booby shows black secondaries and secondary coverts and an entirely dark tail. But beware of similar immature (e.g., third-cycle) Gannets. Gannets of this age usually show some odd white feathers in the tail, secondaries, and secondary coverts. Juvenile Masked Booby is mostly dark brownish above, but with a white patch on the upper rump and usually a whitish hind collar. The underwings are mostly pale, particularly along the leading edge (carpal area) and on the primary (and some secondary) coverts; these coverts are dark on most immature (second- and third-cycle) Gannets. Dives are usually from fairly high up and are not unlike those of Gannet. Masked Booby usually nests and roosts on the ground.

BLUE-FOOTED BOOBY: Rare in southern California, Blue-footed Booby periodically invades the region, usually in response to prey population crashes in the Gulf of California. Accidental elsewhere in North America, this distinctive booby is medium-small in size and brownish above, with distinct white patches on the nape, back, and midtail. It roosts on rocks and prefers warm, nearshore waters for feeding. Dives are usually from fairly low heights (six to sixty feet) and are often diagonal, not vertical like those of Masked Booby or Gannet. Note that the tail pattern shows a whitish midsection and a darker outer tail, which is unique among boobies. The underwings are mostly dark, but note the contrasting white armpits (axillaries), which are concolorous with the belly. Adults are more neatly marked than juveniles. Adults have gray-brown heads streaked with rather bright white, as well as grayish bills and bright blue feet. Nonadults (some individuals are identifiable as second-cycle) have grayer feet and

Nesting Masked Boobies, FL, Mar (GV) (left); adult Masked Booby, FL, Apr (GLA) (right). Adult Masked Booby is unlikely to be confused if seen reasonably well. Note the black mask, yellowish bill, black flight feathers and black tail. When at rest note the extensive black upperwing coverts compared with similarly plumaged Red-footed Booby.

Second-cycle Masked Booby, CA, Dec (TB) (left); early second-cycle (second-spring) Masked Booby, NC, May (SNGH) (right). Masked Booby takes three years to attain adult plumage. Many vagrants are immatures, and second-cycle birds such as these appear intermediate between juveniles and adults.

First-spring Masked Booby, NC, May (SNGH) (left); juvenile Masked Booby, HI, Sep (CR) (right). Juvenile Masked Booby usually shows a broad white collar, a horn-colored bill, and a dark eye. Juveniles are best identified by their uniformly crisp plumage. By first spring (left), look for signs of white on the head and upperparts, as well as the first wave of primary molt visible out through the middle primaries.

Adult (left) and juvenile (right) Blue-footed Boobies, Galápagos, Jul (GLA). Blue-footed Booby is typically easy to identify in any plumage. Adults have striking blue feet that can be hard to see on flying birds, but easy to see when perched. Juveniles are distinguished from other similar immature boobies by messy demarcation between dark breast and white belly, white nape and back patches, and white-based tail with mostly white central tail feathers.

Adult Blue-footed Boobies, Baja California, Mexico, Sep (BLS). On adults note mainly white head and tail, staring yellow eye, and broadly white-tipped scapulars. See frontispiece for a study of the underwing pattern of this species.

Second-cycle Blue-footed Booby, Galápagos, Aug (GLA) (left); juvenile Blue-footed Booby, Mexico, Jan (SNGH) (right). Blue-footed Booby takes 3–4 cycles to attain full adult plumage. In the second cycle, note 2 waves of primary molt, and generally duller plumage than on adults, especially the duskier head and back. First-winter birds (right) show duller plumage still, with minimal white on the nape and back, but still show a mostly white tail.

Adult female Brown Booby, Costa Rica, Nov (BLS) (left); juvenile Brown Booby, FL, Apr (GLA) (right). Adult Brown Booby is distinguished from other boobies by its clean brown upperparts and strong demarcation between brown neck and white belly. Juvenile Brown Booby is overall brown, with a subtly paler belly. Juvenile foot color is variable; most show yellowish feet, but some can be reddish or pink. Beware of confusion with juvenile Red-footed Booby!

Adult male Brown Booby, Eastern Pacific ssp., Baja California, Mexico, Sep (BLS) (left); adult female Brown Booby, Baja California, Mexico, Sep (BLS) (right). Breeding adult females are yellow faced, while males are dark faced. In eastern Pacific breeding *brewsteri,* males have whitish heads. Note strong pattern below, and neat underwing pattern with blackish outer "hand."

Second-cycle Brown Booby, CA, Mar (BLS). Brown Booby takes 3–4 cycles to attain full adult plumage. Second-cycle birds, such as this one, show 2 waves of primary molt, and the beginnings of the adult pattern below. This bird (same bird in both images) is early in its second cycle, just beginning the second wave of primary molt.

Breeding adult white-morph Red-footed Booby, HI, Mar (TB) (left); adult dark-morph Red-footed Booby, Galápagos, Jul (GLA) (right). White morph is generally similar to Masked Booby, but note white tail and different face pattern. Dark morph is the only wholly dark sulid, with completely dark underwings.

Probable second-cycle white-morph Red-footed Booby, Galápagos, Jul (GLA) (left); juvenile Red-footed Booby, Galápagos, Aug (GLA) (right). Juvenile Red-footed Booby is brown with a gray bill and face; the underwings are dark. During the first year they begin to show signs of the respective adult plumage, with late first-cycle birds becoming whitish on the head and belly. In the second cycle, white morphs are similar to adult white morphs but have mottled wings; note brightening bill and foot color as age progresses.

First-cycle dark-morph Red-footed Booby, Costa Rica, Nov (BLS) (left); juvenile Red-footed Booby, Galápagos, Aug (GLA) (right). Note uniformly fresh plumage of juvenile (right) compared with a similar bird that is halfway through the first wing molt. The bird at left is ~6–9 months old and has started to show pinkish facial skin and bill.

darker backs and are dark hooded, with blackish bills and a dark brown face, throat, and neck. Inland sulid records are extremely rare, but when they occur, they often pertain to this species.

BROWN BOOBY: A small sulid with a long tail, this species is entirely chocolate brown above in all ages. It is more adaptable in feeding habits than the others, but it is often encountered near shore, amid mixed flocks of other boobies, terns, and pelicans. A few dozen pairs of Brown Boobies now nest on Islas Coronados, Mexico, just a few miles south of the California border, and this species is now regular on San Diego pelagic trips. In the Atlantic it is very rare away from south Florida, but there are isolated records scattered north to Canada, and along the Gulf Coast. Brown Booby dives are diagonal, usually from lower heights (less than fifty feet), and it roosts in trees or on cliffs or posts. In flight Brown Booby appears more agile than other boobies and has deeper wingbeats compared to larger sulids. Adults have bright, contrasting white bellies, axillaries, and vents, bright yellow feet, and horn or yellow-green bills. Breeding adults show colorful facial skin (blue in males, yellow in females). Males breeding in the eastern Pacific (*S. l. brewsteri*; at times afforded species status) are regularly seen off California; they are paler headed than those in the Atlantic (*S. l. leucogaster*) and also have duller yellow bills. Juveniles of all populations are always entirely chocolate brown, save a few axillaries and underwing coverts, and they have blackish-gray bills. Juveniles often show a shadow pattern of adult plumage, with the underparts paler than the rest of the body. Juveniles may have pinkish feet, similar to dark-morph or immature Red-footed, so pay attention to differences in plumage and structure (see Red-footed below). Brown Booby in its second cycle is similar to an adult but the bare parts are more muted in color, and the plumage patterns are more subdued and less crisp.

Boats are a part of our ecosystem now, and boobies are not shy about taking advantage of them when the opportunity arises. This fishing boat in Costa Rica is covered with Brown Boobies and frigatebirds looking for an easy meal (BLS). In some cases, boobies have ridden boats into US waters, such as a Red-footed Booby that landed on a boat in Mexico and ended up in San Diego harbor!

RED-FOOTED BOOBY: This small sulid occurs only very rarely in North American waters but shows up about every other year at the Dry Tortugas. Records away from there number very few. It is distinct from the others in several respects: it is more pelagic, it is the only polymorphic sulid, and it is the only one that nests in bushes or trees. Red-footed feeds over deep water, at times with other pelagic species, taking mostly flying fish and squid. It dives vertically from lower elevations (about thirty feet) and usually roosts in trees. Red-footed regularly lands on and rides in boats, and its relatively slender build suits its more pelagic habits, allowing for a more agile and buoyant flight than that of the others. Note also the smaller, more slender bill and notably rounder head with a steeper forehead, which combine to give this species a unique expression. Being polymorphic, Red-footed Booby is highly variable in adult plumage, with some appearing almost entirely brown (similar to immature Brown Booby) and others appearing mostly bright white with black primaries and secondaries (similar to Masked Booby). Many found in the United States are brown birds (and often immatures), but both white and brown morphs are possible and have occurred on both coasts.[9, 10] Adults (both light and brown morphs) from the Caribbean show white tails, but those in the Pacific vary, having brown or white tails. Florida records are mainly immatures, and those birds are usually entirely brown. Occasionally immature (apparent second-cycle) Red-footeds show dappled upperparts. Adults have bright red feet, bluish-gray bills, and pinkish facial skin. Confusion is most likely with immature Brown Booby, but note the difference in head shape, body proportions, and chest and underwing patterns. Compared to Brown Booby, Red-footed has more slender and more pointed wings, and brown-plumaged Red-footeds are also wholly dark on the underwings. Most juvenile Brown Boobies show a shadow pattern

Breeding adult white-morph Red-footed Booby, HI, Mar (BH). Red-footed Booby has the most colorful facial skin of any of the sulids, and it is the only species that is polymorphic, occurring in brown and white morphs. There is variation even among brown and white morphs, however, with Caribbean birds being white tailed, and eastern Pacific birds being both light and dark, though most are dark tailed. Note Red-footed Booby's more delicate build, lighter bill, and steeper forehead.

Juvenile Red-footed Booby perched on researcher's head, HI, Sep (CR) (left); presumed second-cycle Red-footed Booby, FL, Jan (TJ) (right). Boobies got their common name for being "stupid" on land, and easily caught. Young birds can be particularly confiding! Vagrants, such as this FL bird, are often dark morphs in the Atlantic. Note duller bill than on adult, but obvious red feet. Caribbean dark morphs have white tails, which can barely be seen in this photo.

Roosting Blue-footed Boobies, Mexico, Sep (BLS) (left); and Mexico, Jan (SNGH). Boobies often roost on offshore rocks and in rare cases gather in numbers—as in during a recent invasion off California. More often in the ABA Area, a single booby is found roosting among pelicans, gulls, and cormorants on offshore rocks or jetties.

Presumed juvenile Nazca Booby (right) with adult Brown Booby, Mexico, Oct (SNGH) (left photo); juvenile Nazca Booby, Galápagos, Jul (GLA) (right). Nazca Booby's status in US waters remains unclear but this species should be considered in any case of vagrant Masked Booby on the Pacific Coast. Similar overall to Masked Booby, but juvenile Nazca typically lacks the broad white hind collar. By second cycle the orange bill coloration characteristic of this species should be apparent. Adults are similar to Masked Booby but have orange (not yellow) bills.

of adult plumage, with a slight contrast between the solid dark chocolate brown of the head, back, and chest and the paler brown underparts. Similarly plumaged brownish Red-footeds show a paler brown "collar" around the neck, bordered below by a darker brown chest band. Juvenile Red-footed in flight may show a pale dorsal wrist patch. In its second cycle, it is similar to an adult but the bare parts are more muted in color, and the plumage patterns are more subdued.

Nazca Booby was recently split from Masked Booby,[11,12] and its status in North America is muddled by its similarity to Masked. The Nazca is a Pacific species that breeds as near to California as the Revillagigedo Islands and Clipperton Island off Mexico. Birders should be conscious of this species when identifying any Masked Booby on the Pacific Coast, as there is now at least one documented record of an adult for California. Adults are fairly easily separated, as Nazca usually shows an orange-pink bill (difficult to see from a distance), and sometimes two white central rectrices. But immatures are so similar that they may not be separated safely. The second- and third-cycle plumages in Nazca Booby especially are poorly known. It appears that juvenile Nazca usually lacks a white hind collar, but more study is needed to see whether this is a consistent character.

References

[1]Del Hoyo, J., A. Elliott, and J. Sargatal, eds. 1992. Handbook of the Birds of the World. Vol. 1. Barcelona: Lynx Edicions.

[2]Holloway, J. E. 2003. Dictionary of Bird Names of the United States. Portland, OR: Timber Press.

[3]Mowbray, T. B. 2002. Northern Gannet (*Morus bassanus*). The Birds of North America Online. A. Poole, ed. Ithaca, NY: Cornell Lab of Ornithology. http://bna.birds.cornell.edu/bna/species/693

[4]Kricher, J. 2006. Galápagos: A Natural History. Princeton, NJ: Princeton University Press.

[5]Schreiber, E. A., R. W. Schreiber, and G. A. Schenk. 1996. Red-footed Booby (*Sula sula*). The Birds of North America Online. A. Poole, ed. Ithaca, NY: Cornell Lab of Ornithology. http://bna.birds.cornell.edu/bna/species/241

[6]Schreiber, E. A., and R. L. Norton. 2002. Brown Booby (*Sula leucogaster*). The Birds of North America Online. A. Poole, ed. Ithaca, NY: Cornell Lab of Ornithology. http://bna.birds.cornell.edu/bna/species/649

[7]Grace, J., and D. J. Anderson. 2009. Masked Booby (*Sula dactylatra*). The Birds of North America Online. A. Poole, ed. Ithaca, NY: Cornell Lab of Ornithology. http://bna.birds.cornell.edu/bna/species/073

[8]Howell, S.N.G. 2010. Molt in North American Birds. New York: Houghton Mifflin.

[9]Stevenson, H. M., and B. H. Anderson. 1994. The Birdlife of Florida. Gainesville: University Press of Florida.

[10]California Bird Records Committee. 2007. Rare Birds of California. Edited by R. A. Hamilton, M. A. Patten, and R. A. Ericson. Camarillo, CA: Western Field Ornithologists.

[11]Pitman, R. L., and J. R. Jehl. 1998. Geographic variation and reassessment of species limits in the "Masked" Boobies of the eastern Pacific Ocean. Wilson Bulletin 110(2): 155–70.

[12]American Ornithologists' Union. 2000. Forty-second supplement to the American Ornithologists' Union Check-list of North American Birds. Auk 117:847–58.

[13]Roberson, D. 1998. Sulids unmasked: Which large booby reaches California? Field Notes 52:276–87.

Sooty Tern
breeding

Long-tailed Jaeger
juvenile

Sooty Tern
juvenile

Bridled Tern
nonbreeding

Brown
Noddy

Black Tern

juvenile

breeding

Tropical Terns

Sooty Tern (*Onychoprion fuscata*)

Bridled Tern (*Onychoprion anaethetus*)

Brown Noddy (*Anous stolidus*)

Black Noddy (*Anous minutus*)

First Breeding:	3–7 years old
Breeding Strategy:	Monogamous; colonial
Lifespan:	Up to 34 years

Elegantly patterned in black, gray, white, or hues of soft chocolate, and feeding on small fish, squid, crustaceans, and marine insects, these medium-sized seabirds prefer warm, tropical or subtropical seas and are often collectively referred to as "tropical terns." They only just reach the southern fringes of North America, breeding mostly on remote islands outside our region. The cosmopolitan family Sternidae comprises just over forty species, including these four species, though studies suggest that noddies are more primitive than other terns and are perhaps more closely related to gulls.[1,2] Formerly, Bridled and Sooty terns were placed in the genus *Sterna*, but they are now placed in *Onychoprion*, along with Aleutian and Gray-backed terns. Sooty Tern differs from the others in downy[3] and juvenile plumages and is perhaps less closely related to the other *Onychoprion* terns. In this text we use "terns" to collectively refer to Bridled and Sooty terns, and "noddies" to collectively refer to Brown and Black noddies.

For many North American birders, tropical terns are sought-after and seldom-seen species. At sea they swoop and dip, hovering and picking prey from the ocean's surface. Noddies roost in trees, but at sea they may rest (sit) on the water; terns are quickly waterlogged and so remain in the air or perch on flotsam. At times tropical terns are displaced inland by tropical storms and hurricanes. More often, however, birders see their first ones on a pilgrimage to Dry Tortugas National Park. There, about seventy miles west of Key West, Florida, you have the chance to see all four species. The Sooty Tern colony at Bush Key hosts about forty thousand pairs, and the sound

Natural History Note:

Sooty Terns are expert aerialists, spending the great majority of their lives on the wing. Adults frequently forage sixty miles or more from nesting colonies, and immatures may not make land for seven years or more before their first breeding attempt, instead spending their time at sea; young from the Dry Tortugas often spend five years at sea (some as far away as the Gulf of Guinea) before returning to breed.[3]

An active colony of Sooty Terns can be one of the world's greatest bird spectacles. These colonies are so staggeringly dense (occasionally numbering near two million birds) that taking in the volume of birds can be overwhelming. A result of such densely occupied colonies is that parents and young evolved the ability to locate one another by voice,[3] although they all sound the same to human ears. The species remains one of the world's most abundant birds, with a world population estimated at about eighty million.[3] As with almost all other seabirds, pair bonds are strong (sometimes lasting more than a season) and are reinforced through stereotyped courtship displays.

The word "noddy" and various parts of these species' scientific names (*Anous, stolidus, anaethetus*) derive from words that mean "stupid" or "mindless,"[4] as humans have found tropical terns easy to capture, kill, and eat.

is deafening as thousands cry "wide-awake" (a local nickname). Around them are roughly four thousand pairs of nesting Brown Noddies, which nest in bushes but ascend skyward in paired courtship flights, flapping synchronously with rapid, snappy wingbeats.

Away from the Tortugas these four species are much harder to find. Sooty and Bridled terns are regular in summer on pelagic trips to warm Gulf Stream waters off Cape Hatteras, North Carolina, as well as off other ports along the Southeast and Florida coasts. But noddies are scarce away from the Tortugas, with Brown Noddy occasionally wandering north into the Gulf Stream, while Black is strictly accidental away from the Tortugas. In California, Sooty and Bridled terns are rare vagrants, and neither species of noddy has been recorded from the Pacific Coast. Tropical terns are seldom seen from shore, except during tropical storms,

Tropical terns are sometimes confused with other seagoing birds. In this composite, find two typical confusion species: Black Tern and immature jaegers. Sooty and Bridled terns are sometimes confused with basic and juvenile Black Terns, but note Black Tern's smaller size, compact build, and blackish breast patch. Brown Noddy and juvenile Sooty Tern are sometimes confused with immature jaegers. Note this juvenile Long-tailed Jaeger's broader wings, white primary bases, and barred underwing coverts, characters shard by all juvenile jaegers (all photos, BLS, GLA).

but in rare instances, wayward Sooty and Bridled terns show up at tern colonies, perhaps prospecting potential breeding sites.

Because of their seagoing habits, it is generally difficult to achieve a familiarity with tropical terns, and even experienced birders may struggle to distinguish Bridled Tern from Sooty Tern, or Black Noddy from Brown Noddy. Some birders confuse these species with nonbreeding Black Terns, especially during stormy conditions when overcast skies make Black Terns look darker backed. But usually it is easy to know when you have happened upon one of these species—deciding which one is the challenge! Pay close attention to structure, head pattern, general plumage patterns, feeding habits, and flight style.

Hints and Considerations

- In the ABA Area, Dry Tortugas National Park is the only place where Black Noddy is somewhat regular (and nearly annual), and Brown Noddy is very rare away from there.
- The two terns are regular in Atlantic Gulf Stream waters north to Cape Hatteras during summer and are sometimes found on pelagic trips in the Gulf of Mexico or off the southeastern United States.
- Structure is key, and noddies have a distinctive tail shape. When folded, a noddy's tail appears long and pointed (but broad compared to those of terns); when fanned slightly it is rounded, with a shallow notch at the center.
- Note that juvenile Sooty Terns are nearly entirely dark and are often confused with Black Tern, noddies, and jaegers.
- Black Tern (or vagrant White-winged Tern) can cause confusion. Breeding at freshwater marshes but wintering and often migrating at sea, Black Tern is smaller and more agile, has a short, square, grayish tail, and is more compact and broader winged.
- On the ocean, dark jaegers may cause confusion, especially when soaring like a Sooty Tern.
- Perching on flotsam is a behavior far more common in Bridled than Sooty Tern (perhaps 90 percent of such birds are Bridled); Sooty Tern is more aerial (often soaring), and more social.
- Unlike most other terns (but similar to Black Tern), tropical terns seldom plunge dive. Noddies patter at the surface, and the terns usually dip and peck, or snatch prey from the surface.

Identification

Residing in a relatively stable climate, adult tropical terns molt gradually, more or less continuously, suspending molt only for breeding,[5] though Bridled Tern differs, as some populations molt and breed simultaneously.[2] Age-related plumage differences need study but are most striking in Sooty Tern. Sexes are similar in all four species, but plumage varies with respect to age in the two terns, and to a lesser extent in noddies. Among noddies, juveniles and adults differ in crown pattern, with adults showing more extensive white crowns, especially in Brown Noddy; the extent of the crown patch is harder to determine on flying birds. Adult noddies are overall more evenly plumaged, showing less contrast between the wing coverts and the body. The identification text below concerns mainly birds at sea, where voice is seldom useful, but Sooties are vocal and sometimes first detected by call.

SOOTY TERN: Sturdy and broad winged, Sooty Tern is blackish dorsally with a mostly black tail. It is the most pelagic tropical tern and frequently occurs in feeding aggregations, especially over schools of tuna. Foraging flocks are loose, with some birds high and others closer to the sea. They attain great heights, often soaring while waiting for tuna schools to regroup, and then descend to feed when the tuna have driven the smaller baitfish to the surface, within striking distance. Distant, high-flying tropical tern flocks are likely Sooties, and they are easily identified as such if they contain some all-dark juveniles.

Sooty Tern is most often confused with Bridled Tern, but Sooty is heavier, with a more substantial head, thicker bill, broader shoulders, and shorter tail. The white forehead patch on adults is short yet thick, and restricted to the area between the eyes and the bill. The upperparts are blacker, and the nape and tail are more extensively dark. Only the outermost rectrices are white in Sooty Tern. The underside of the primaries is dark and contrasts strongly with white underwing coverts, imparting a strong two-toned appearance on the underwing.

The mostly dark juvenile Sooty Tern is often confused with the noddies or with Black Tern. Sooty is heavier, though (especially compared to Black Tern), with a narrow, pointed tail (when folded), and the contrasting whitish lower belly and vent help separate it from a noddy. Also, the back is not solid brown, as the upperpart feathers are finely whitish tipped, creating a more scaled or stippled appearance. Virtually all Sooties in North

America appear in either juvenile or adult plumage (J. B. Patteson, pers. comm.) More study is needed on the molt and classification of immature plumages, but it seems that most Sooties are indistinguishable from adults after their second summer. First-summer Sooty Terns are mottled dark below, intermediate in plumage between the mostly brownish juvenile plumage and the whiter-bodied adult plumage. Second-winter Sooty Terns are adultlike but often retain dusky smudges below and have a less distinct face pattern, sometimes with dark flecking on the forehead.[5]

At times Sooty Tern may recall a jaeger, but jaegers average heavier bodied, show a more bulbous head, and have darker underwings, often with white at the base of the primaries. Jaegers typically fly with palpable purpose. And unlike Bridled Tern, Sooties rarely perch on flotsam and don't rest on the water like noddies. They essentially live on the wing, basically landing only to nest.[3]

Perhaps more than any other bird, this species is associated with tropical storm systems. Because of their aerial nature and light wing loading, Sooty Terns are more susceptible to being swept inland by hurricanes than other seabirds (at times by the dozens, even hundreds), with records north to the Great Lakes region and Atlantic Canada, and west as far as Colorado! Even relatively weak systems can displace a few Sooty Terns.

BRIDLED TERN: This is a buoyant, delicate tern, usually seen singly but sometimes feeding in small groups of three or four, especially along "weed lines" where temperature breaks concentrate sargassum in the Gulf Stream. Though they have bred a few times in the United States (in the Florida Keys), they are nearly always encountered flying at sea or resting atop flotsam—a habit of this species. When perched on flotsam, they often allow close approach. In summer and fall, Bridled Terns are regular offshore in the Gulf and in the Atlantic Gulf Stream waters north to North Carolina, becoming rarer north of there, but still probably annual to waters off New York and Massachusetts. Those seen off the United States are presumed to breed in the Bahamas or farther south in the Caribbean.[2] Unlike Sooty Tern, storm-driven vagrants are rare and are usually encountered on the immediate coast instead of well inland.

Bridled Terns are often drawn to areas with feeding shearwaters, storm-petrels, or phalaropes, but they are much less social than Sooty Terns and less pelagic, seldom found far from a perch (i.e., flotsam). Preferring somewhat shallower, continental shelf waters or those at the shelf break, they are almost never seen from shore. In the South Atlantic Bight (seas between Cape Canaveral and Cape Hatteras), they are strongly associated with the seaweed sargassum, which is found in lines along salinity and temperature changes (often called "breaks"), in places forming large "mats." These mats serve as nursery habitat for sea turtles, fish, invertebrates, and crustaceans and also attract predatory fish and birds. Bridled Terns patrol sargassum lines and temperature breaks and tend to feed lower to the water than the more high-flying Sooty Terns. Rarely, Bridled Terns will soar, but this habit is common among Sooty Terns. Occasionally, where food is abundant, a Bridled or two may join Sooty Tern groups, even soaring among them (J. B. Patteson, pers. comm.).

Routinely confused with Sooty, Bridled is smaller and slimmer, has a longer and whiter tail, and is more agile in the air. It may at times recall a more slender *Sterna* species, such as Common Tern, and is less likely to be confused with a jaeger. Other structural differences from Sooty are more subtle but include a relatively narrow waist (tail base), a more lightly built head and neck, and a slightly finer bill. Breeding adults have smart black caps with a thin white "eyebrow" that extends well behind the eye. Nonbreeding adults show more extensive white in the forecrown, but all adults have a dark gray-brown mantle, paler than that of Sooty Tern. The mantle contrasts with a noticeably extensive whitish hind collar. The rump is paler than in Sooty's, and the tail shows more extensive white in the outer tail feathers. Bridled is also paler on the underparts, particularly on the underside of the primaries, which contrast less with the white underwing coverts. Juveniles roughly resemble adults but are paler headed with a dark eye line, paler backed with white fringes (scales) on their upperparts, and shorter tailed. Unlike first-year Sooties, first-year Bridleds do not molt wing feathers until their first spring.[6] They look adultlike by their second fall.

BROWN NODDY: Medium sized and chocolate brown with a pale cap, this species is rarely seen away from the Dry Tortugas. They stray north along the Gulf Stream up to North Carolina, and the few records north of there are almost all associated with tropical storm systems. Typically noddies fly low to the water (less than thirty feet high), moving with steady, shallow, rowing wingbeats. Sometimes they flock over schools of tuna. Adults have a silvery-whitish crown and an even-toned, overall chocolate-brown plumage. Juveniles are similar

Focus on: *Structure, Habits, Head/neck pattern, Tail shape and pattern*

Sooty Tern (left column) and Bridled Tern (right column). Adult Sooty differs from Bridled in being darker backed, showing little to no pale collar, a shorter and thicker white eye line, and more contrasting blackish flight feathers with stark white underwing coverts. Adult Sooty looks the same year-round, but Bridled has a clean breeding plumage (top) and a distinctive nonbreeding plumage. Nonbreeding Bridled has a reduced black cap often streaked with white, but the upperwings and back lack the pale fringes shown by juveniles (lower right). On first-summer Bridled (lower middle) note mixed adult and juvenile wing feathers with primaries in active molt, or adultlike wings with a variably pale-fringed back. (ventral adult Sooty Tern, GV; dorsal adult Bridled, TB; ventral small juvenile Bridled, CS; all other Bridled Terns, SNGH).

first-summer

Juvenile Sooty Tern (left column) is strikingly different from the adult. It is overall brownish with pale-fringed upperparts, and whitish underwings and belly. At a distance it can appear all dark, inviting confusion with a host of species, including Brown Noddy (right column), Black Tern, and immature jaegers (see frontispiece) (all photos SNGH, except going away, CS). Brown Noddy is dark bellied in all plumages, and the underwings are darker than in Sooty Tern. Adult Brown Noddy has a distinctive white crown, but juveniles and first-summers (lower right) have only limited white in the forecrown. Brown Noddy has a rounded tail that when fanned appears very broad and unusual for a tern (top, MA; dorsal adult, GV; dorsal first-summer, RG; other, GLA).

but have darker brown crowns and often show bleached or worn wing coverts that contrast with the darker body feathers. The tail is long and entirely dark brown, and the bill is moderately long and stout compared to that of the others. Compared to Black Noddy, Brown is heavier (similar in size to Sooty Tern) and bull headed, has a more sloping forehead and a heavier (deeper) and slightly more drooping bill, and is more brown and less black overall. Lone birds are difficult (especially in flight), even with comparative experience, but good views that allow accurate assessments of size, structure, overall color, and pattern should permit identification.

BLACK NODDY: Similar to Brown Noddy but smaller, more delicate, blacker, and somehow more dapper, this species also shows a longer, thinner, and straighter bill. It has a skinnier neck, a smaller, rounder head, and often a neater white cap. It is essentially only ever observed at the Dry Tortugas (where nearly annual) and is accidental elsewhere in North America (very few records for the Texas coast). At the Dry Tortugas it is most often found perched among the roosting Brown Noddies on the old coaling docks or amid the nesting colony, perched up in the bushes. Unlike for Brown Noddy, there are no storm-associated records of this species in North America.

When Black and Brown noddies are seen together and can be compared, distinguishing them is fairly straightforward. Flying or solitary birds, though, are quite difficult, and just as often, lack of experience with any noddy species is a problem. The two behave similarly, but Black's smaller proportions result in snappier wingbeats and more agile movements. It is slightly blacker overall than Brown Noddy and has shorter legs. Some Pacific

Taxonomic Note:

The provenance of the Black Noddies at the Dry Tortugas is uncertain. Some have identified the birds there as *A. m. atlanticus* (breeding in the tropical Atlantic off Brazil, St. Helena, Ascension Island, Gulf of Guinea), based on a specimen taken at the park in 1960.[7] Surely *A. m. americanus* would be more expected, but it is an enigmatic taxon. The subspecific name was first applied to birds breeding at Glover's Reef, Belize, discovered in 1862, but Black Noddies haven't been recorded breeding there since 1907.[8] Colonies on Los Roques, Venezuela,[9] appear to be the only known regular breeding birds in the Caribbean today and are presumed to be *A. m. americanus*. Breeding has occurred or is suspected to occur elsewhere (Las Aves off Venezuela, Aruba, Bonaire, Hato Island in the Lesser Antilles, and off the coast of Caribbean Central America; D. T. Shoch, pers. comm.) but is only sparsely documented. The subspecies are in need of review, but *A. m. atlanticus* is said to be larger, longer winged, heavier billed, and blacker tailed, and to have a more restricted white cap, compared to *A. m. americanus*.[10, 11]

populations show a grayer tail that contrasts with the darker back. This character needs study but it doesn't seem to be a routinely reliable mark (at least in the Caribbean). The more distinct pale cap of Black Noddy is especially noticeable in first-year birds in spring/summer (the cap of Brown is more obvious on adults, less so on first-years). Some first-year Black Noddies have rather brownish wing coverts, which can cause confusion, and they usually show worn and faded retained juvenile outer primaries contrasting with fresher inner primaries. Many (all?) birds seen at the Tortugas are in this plumage.

References

[1]Hackett, S. J. 1989. Effects of varied electrophoretic conditions on detection of evolutionary patterns in the Laridae. Condor 91:73–90.

[2]Haney, J. C., D. S. Lee, and R. D. Morris. 1999. Bridled Tern (*Sterna anaethetus*). The Birds of North America Online. A. Poole, ed. Ithaca, NY: Cornell Lab of Ornithology. http://bna.birds.cornell.edu/bna/species/468

[3]Schreiber, E. A., C. J. Feare, B. A. Harrington, B. G. Murray Jr., W. B. Robertson Jr., M. J. Robertson, and G. E. Woolfenden. 2002. Sooty Tern (*Sterna fuscata*). The Birds of North America Online. A. Poole, ed. Ithaca, NY: Cornell Lab of Ornithology. http://bna.birds.cornell.edu/bna/species/665

[4]Holloway, J. E. 2003. Dictionary of Bird Names of the United States. Portland, OR: Timber Press.

[5]Pyle, P. 2008. Identification Guide to North American Birds: Part II. Bolinas, CA: Slate Creek Press.

[6]Howell, S.N.G. 2010. Molt in North American Birds. New York: Houghton Mifflin.

[7]Robertson, W. B., Jr., D. R. Paulson, and C. R. Mason. 1961. A tern new to the United States. Auk 78:423–25.

[8]Howell, S.N.G., and S. Webb. 1995. A Guide to the Birds of Mexico and Northern Central America. New York: Oxford University Press.

[9]Bond, J., and S. D. Ripley. 1960. The Black Noddy at Los Roques, Venezuela. Auk 77:473–74.

[10]Mathews, G. M. 1912. The Birds of Australia. Vol. 2. London: Witherby.

[11]Gauger, V. H. 1999. Black Noddy (*Anous minutus*). The Birds of North America Online. A. Poole, ed. Ithaca, NY: Cornell Lab of Ornithology. http://bna.birds.cornell.edu/bna/species/412

Adult (back) and juvenile Bridled Terns, NC, Aug (SNGH) (left); adult Sooty Terns, TX, Apr (BLS) (right). Note uniformly fresh, scaly back and upperwing coverts on juvenile Bridled Tern. Sooty Terns are unusual on shore in North America away from the Tortugas, but occasionally a bird prospects for a nesting site among other terns or Black Skimmers, and rarely a pair nests along the Gulf Coast.

Adult (right) and first-summer Brown Noddy, FL, Apr (GLA) (left); first-summer Black Noddy (top) with adult Brown Noddy, FL, Apr (LM) (right). Unlike Black Noddy, juvenile and first-summer Brown Noddy has only limited white in the forecrown. Note retained tattered juvenile primaries on the first-summer as well. In direct comparison with Brown Noddy, note Black's smaller size and slimmer build, its bill is thinner and straighter, and there is a more distinct demarcation between the white cap and blackish nape. Most Black Noddies encountered in North America are first-summers: note very worn upperwing coverts and retained juvenile outer primaries.

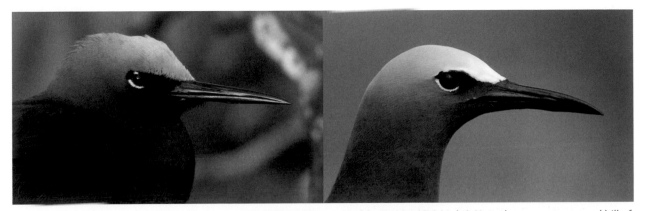

9.5. Head and bill detail of Black Noddy, HI, Jun (CR) (left) and Brown Noddy, FL, Mar (GV) (right). Note deeper, more curved bill of Brown Noddy. Photos of Caribbean Black Noddy are hard to find; this Black Noddy is from Hawaii. While much work remains to be done on differentiating the taxa of Black Noddy (some forms may represent different species), the bill shape differences of all subspecies of Black Noddy consistently help distinguish them from Brown Noddy.

Atlantic Gadflies

Black-capped Petrel (*Pterodroma hasitata*)

Bermuda Petrel (*Pterodroma cahow*)

Fea's Petrel
(*Pterodroma feae feae / Pterodroma feae desertae*)

Trindade (Herald) Petrel
(*Pterodroma arminjoniana arminjoniana*)

Also: Zino's Petrel (*Pterodroma madeira*)

First Breeding:	4–5 years old
Breeding Strategy:	Monogamous; pairs are often together for multiple seasons
Lifespan:	20+ years

For many birders, the sleek, smart "gadfly" petrels are the Ferraris of the bird world, ranking among the most sought-after birds one can see from our continent. Superb aerialists, most at home in the brisk winds of the open ocean, these seabirds need only a little breeze to spin dramatic arcs across the horizon, stooping and ascending in dashing fashion. In many ways, they are the quintessential seabirds. Subsisting largely on squid and fish, they visit land only when breeding, or exceptionally when driven inshore by hurricanes or tropical storms. They nest on remote islands away from North America, only barely reaching our offshore waters.

The family Procellaridae includes the petrels and shearwaters, and together with the storm-petrels, albatrosses, and diving-petrels, they form the order Procellariformes, also known as "tubenoses." Breeding species of these seabirds are poorly represented in the United States and Canada, with only Manx Shearwater, Northern Fulmar, and Ashy, Leach's, and Fork-tailed storm-petrels known to nest. About thirty species reach our continental waters, mostly as nonbreeding visitors or vagrants. Such is the case with these gadfly petrels, all of which breed on remote islands in the tropical or subtropical Atlantic. A fascinating, compelling group of birds, these petrels are all in the genus *Pterodroma* (meaning "winged runner") and evolved to breed in burrows on islands devoid of terrestrial predators, today suffering declines from the introduction of rats, cats, and other animals at nesting areas.

The Gulf Stream waters off North Carolina are the best place in North America to see the Atlantic *Pterodroma*. There, the continental shelf-edge and warm Gulf Stream waters reach closer to land than at any other point along the East Coast. The petrels are seen primarily between May and September, but the waters remain little explored in other months. For most birders, merely reaching Gulf Stream waters is itself a challenge, and achieving a familiarity with these gadfly petrels is tougher still.

Gadflies are highly mobile and sparsely distributed, and they usually only briefly approach boats. When at rest on the water they typically flush while at a considerable distance. Often they are solitary, but sometimes they aggregate in small groups, at times associating with storm-petrels, shearwaters, gulls, and terns, which may attract jaegers or skuas. Quality sightings of gadflies are infrequent and thrilling, but with time, repeated sightings will allow you to achieve comparative experience. Understanding the different appearances that a *Pterodroma* can assume will allow you to identify them from some distance. GISS is critical, but also pay attention to plumage pattern, especially of the underwings and uppertail.

Hints and Considerations

- In moderate to strong winds, a characteristic roller-coaster flight style often helps identify a *Pterodroma* to genus, but in lighter winds they fly differently, hugging the sea surface and becoming more easily confused with shearwaters and even jaegers.
- The Gulf Stream waters off Cape Hatteras are the best place to see these five species, mainly during spring and summer, and only exceptionally is one seen elsewhere.
- Black-capped Petrel occurs year-round in the Gulf Stream and is fairly common. Use it as a basis for comparison, as the others are rare and irregular.
- Habitat, behavior, and season offer few clues for separating these petrels, so GISS is important. Black-capped is large and heavy, while the others are smaller and slimmer.
- Keep an eye on sea conditions. Wind, lighting, and molt, as well as other factors (e.g., presence of food, or jaegers and skuas) can affect a bird's appearance and behavior, in turn affecting its GISS.

Black-capped Petrel over the Gulf Stream off Cape Hatteras, NC, May (BLS). Speedy, powerful, and dynamic, Black-capped Petrel is the target of many birders taking their first pelagic trips off the Mid-Atlantic. While still relatively common there, this species faces many threats. Two possible taxa include dark-faced and white-faced variants, with this bird being a good example of a darker-faced individual.

Focus on: *Structure, Plumage pattern of the uppertail and underwing*

Black-capped Petrel

Black-capped Petrel variation. Black-capped Petrel typically shows a distinctly white-based tail, and usually a distinct pale collar. But head pattern is variable, with white-faced and dark-faced types as well as some intermediates: these likely represent distinct taxa, but more study is needed. White-faced birds usually have white extending up in front of the eye and also usually have a distinct capped appearance. Dark-faced types can appear more hooded and occasionally have dusky collars (all photos, BLS).

Black-capped Petrel

Great Shearwater

Bermuda Petrel

Compare the dark-faced Black-cappeds on this page (center left; bottom left) with the Bermuda Petrel (center). Look for the heavier build and bigger bill of Black-capped, and also note Bermuda Petrel's more cowled appearance. Also compare Black-capped with the Great Shearwaters on the right. Great Shearwater has a long, slim bill, stiffer, straighter wings, a scaly back pattern, dusky belly, and less white in the upper tail (all photos BLS, except Black-capped Petrel bottom left, GLA; and Bermuda Petrel, CS).

Identification

In gadfly petrels (and indeed in most tubenoses), males, females, and juveniles all appear essentially the same. Males average slightly larger and have heavier bills, but otherwise the sexes are similar. Age is at times possible to determine via molt, but age is usually not important in the identification of these birds.

Pterodroma have long undertail coverts covering their relatively short tails below, so tail pattern (including the uppertail coverts) is best assessed from above. In the discussion of wing patterns, the term "dorsal" denotes the upper side of the wing, and "ventral" the underwing.

When seabirds are molting their flight feathers, white patches are apparent at the center of the wings and rump. These pale areas are the exposed white bases of the primaries, secondaries, and rectrices and may cause confusion for birders.

Voice is distinctive but seldom if ever heard at sea.

BLACK-CAPPED PETREL: The most common Gulf Stream gadfly, this species is a stocky, heavily-built *Pterodroma*. Known as "Diablotin" (meaning "little devil," for its eerie nocturnal calls) on its breeding grounds, Black-capped Petrel nests (November–May) primarily on Hispaniola (mostly Haiti) but may also persist in the Lesser Antilles (Dominica, possibly Guadeloupe, and/or Martinique).[4] Breeding is also suspected in Jamaica[11] and Cuba.[12] The population on Hispaniola is estimated at about six hundred to two thousand pairs,[13] with perhaps a total population of about five thousand birds.[3] Black-capped seems in decline overall,[14] and numbers seem to have declined off North Carolina over the last two decades (J. B. Patteson, pers. comm.), but spring and summer trips continue to record daily totals of about ten to seventy birds.[15]

Black-capped Petrel's plumage pattern is highly distinctive, but lighting and sea conditions occasionally obscure these markings. In optimal viewing conditions the extensive white rump is visible even at a distance, which contrasts remarkably with the black to gray-black back and wings. The tail is entirely black but is hard to discern at a distance, leaving the impression that the bird is white tailed and dark backed. The eponymous cap is visible at a moderate distance or closer. Some show an obvious white collar, while others are duskier on the nape. Black-capped is largely white ventrally, except for a broad black ulnar bar extending from the wrists to the axillaries.

Taxonomic Note:

As with many *Pterodroma*, the taxonomy of these species is complex. Bermuda Petrel is monotypic, but Black-capped, Fea's, and Trindade petrels share vexed taxonomies.

Black-capped Petrel is historically treated as monotypic, but two groups have been identified that may represent separate taxa. One group is larger and whiter faced, molts earlier, and is more common off North Carolina in spring, while the other is smaller and darker faced, molts later, and predominates in summer.[1] The presumed-extinct **"Jamaican" Petrel** (*P. (h.) caribbaea*) is considered a subspecies of Black-capped Petrel,[2] but more modern authorities consider it a separate species.[3, 4] It has not been documented alive since the 1890s. It differs dramatically in appearance from Black-capped, being smaller and sooty brown overall, with a paler rump and at times a dusky pale collar.[4, 5, 6]

Fea's Petrel, named for Italian zoologist Leonardo Fea, is split by most authorities[4, 7] into three species: Fea's Petrel (pronounced "Fay-uhs"; a.k.a. "Cape Verde")[4] (*P. feae*), Desertas Petrel (*P. desertae*), and Zino's Petrel (*P. madeira*; see below). Fea's and Desertas Petrel are most closely related[8] and are nearly identical in appearance. But they nest on separate archipelagos (Cape Verde and Bugio, respectively) and differ in timing of nesting as well as in voice, bill size, and genetics.[7, 8] Both likely occur off North Carolina,[4] but because of their similarity we treat them together as "Fea's Petrel." Zino's Petrel breeds only on the island of Madeira, and it differs very slightly from Fea's/Desertas in appearance. It has been documented once off North Carolina.[4] Until recently all three (Fea's, Desertas, and Zino's) were considered the same species as Soft-plumaged Petrel of the Southern Ocean.[9, 10]

Trindade Petrel is often regarded as a subspecies of Herald Petrel (*P. heraldica*), but more modern authorities treat it as a species in its own right.[3, 4] It breeds off Brazil on Trindade and Martim Vaz islands. Unlike the other petrels in this chapter, Trindade Petrel is polymorphic. Light morphs and dark morphs both occur off North Carolina. In addition to their physical differences, the light and dark morphs seem to breed at different seasons and at different sites,[4] indicating that they too are perhaps different species. Occasionally individuals are seen (including off North Carolina) that appear intermediate in plumage between the two morphs, and whether they represent individual variation (possibly pale examples of dark morphs), hybrids, or a completely separate taxon is unclear.[10]

Compared to the other gadflies, Black-capped is set apart by its heavy structure and obvious white rump, but the bill is heavier than in the other species, as well. Black-capped is also rather black dorsally, seldom showing much of an *M* pattern above. At rest on the water, Black-capped is remarkably white, as the white neck, chest, and flanks are obvious, even when distant (at times almost recalling a tropicbird). It is most commonly confused with Bermuda Petrel, but the latter is smaller and more agile ("zippy"), has a smaller bill, and is darker overall. Bermuda Petrel shows more dark feathering on the rump and around the head, often appearing cowled, but beware of dark-faced Black-capped Petrels.

BERMUDA PETREL: Frequently called by its local name on Bermuda, the "Cahow" is truly one of a kind. Though it was presumed extinct for centuries, its rediscovery and continuing recovery make it the great protagonist at the center of a wonderful conservation success story. With a current population of about 250 individuals, Bermuda Petrel remains one of the world's rarest birds, and it breeds on but a few islets around Bermuda (January–June).[4] First detected off North Carolina only in 1993,[16] the species is now almost annual in the Gulf Stream waters there. Usually solitary, it is sometimes found among a group of Black-capped Petrels.

A smallish, lightweight, and agile gadfly, Bermuda Petrel shows a small bill and a relatively long gray tail. Perhaps as a result of the longer tail, it seems to have a relatively narrow "waist." Dorsally, it is black or grayish brown. Compared to Black-capped, in addition to being more delicate, the rump pattern differs in being more extensively gray, with only a relatively narrow band of whitish across the rump (extensive on Black-capped). All but the most worn individuals show a similar rump/tail pattern, and a dark "cowl" that wraps around the sides of the neck and down onto the chest, imparting a hooded appearance. Rarely it shows a distinct white hind collar similar to that of Black-capped. Ventrally, the black ulnar bar averages broader than in Black-capped. Overall, it differs from Black-capped in having a slimmer build, and it is less distinctly marked or contrasting, instead appearing darker, duskier, and more muted in pattern.

Bermuda Petrel is also confused with its close relative,[8] Fea's Petrel, and the two are similar in size, shape, and movements. In fresh plumage Bermuda appears grayer and less blackish than it does when worn, making it yet more similar to Fea's, and fresh Bermudas may show a hint of an *M* pattern above, too. Notice that Bermuda has a darker tail, considerable white on the underwing with an obvious ulnar bar, a darker head, and a smallish bill.

FEA'S PETREL: (Includes *P. (f.) feae*, *P. (f.) desertae*; see Taxonomic Note.) Perhaps the most dapper of these gadflies, this petrel breeds on islands in Macaronesia but disperses west to reach North American seas. It was first recorded off North Carolina in 1981 but is now annual, if rare.[4] As with the others treated in this chapter, most sightings are between May and mid-September, but likely it occurs in other months, and it has been detected elsewhere off the Atlantic Coast a few times as well.[4, 17, 18]

An attractive, medium-sized *Pterodroma*, noticeably more delicate than a Black-capped, but similar in structure to a Bermuda Petrel, the Fea's is agile and speedy in the air, with a relatively slim build. Often making sharper turns closer to the water than would a Black-capped, Fea's has a pale gray tail and mostly dark underwings that are a distinctive combination; both features are striking even at some distance. The underwings are mostly dark charcoal, but the inner part of the leading edge and some of the upper axillaries are white, like the body, and these contrast sharply with the rest of the underwing. In good light, the dorsal wings show a blackish *M* pattern, in which the hand area, the rump, and a band of feathers from the inner secondaries to the wrist are all the same dark blackish gray, while the mantle, inner shoulder, and secondaries are paler gray. From above, the tail is the palest part of the bird. Some Fea's show a mostly dark crown, while others have a gray crown with only a dark eyespot. In poor light, the plumage pattern is difficult to see, and it also gives the bird good camouflage, aiding its ability to disappear quickly into the wavy background as it glides away.

TRINDADE PETREL: The most variable of these gadflies, this long-winged species breeds on islands off the coast of Brazil (not Trinidad off Venezuela) but disperses north to reach North American waters semiroutinely. First recorded off North Carolina in 1978,[4] the species is now annual but scarce in the state's offshore waters. There are a few records at sea elsewhere in the ABA Area, and storm-blown individuals have turned up in far-flung places a few times. A controversial bird that flew past

Light *Pterodroma* comparison. Black-capped Petrel (left column) is the largest and most heavily built; all have a bold white tail base (all photos, BLS). Bermuda Petrel (left middle column) is similar in size and shape to Fea's, but patterned more like Black-capped (all photos, MD, except center SNGH). Compared to Black-capped note the darker tail base, slimmer structure (including bill), and usually dark hind neck that produces a cowled appearance.

Fea's Petrel

Trindade Petrel
light morph

Fea's Petrel (right middle column) is small, slim, and agile, with blackish underwings, a pale tail, and a pearl-gray back with a darker M pattern (all photos SNGH, except center, BLS). Trindade Petrel light morph (right column) is brownish above with a dusky head and neck. The underwings show strongly contrasting dark coverts and light flight feathers (all photos, SNGH).

Trindade Petrel
dark morph

Trindade Petrel (dark morph) comparison. Very different from the other Atlantic gadflies, the dark-morph Trindade Petrel is more likely to be confused with Sooty Shearwater and immature jaegers. Trindade Petrel has blackish underwing coverts with pale-based flight feathers; rarely the underwings appear mostly dark. Dark morph Trindade gives the impression of having a longer, more pointed tail than light morph Trindade; perhaps two taxa are involved here, but more study is needed.

Sooty Shearwater

Sooty Shearwater

Sooty Shearwater is paler overall, with a different underwing pattern; the pale areas are confined mostly to the middle of the underwing, and the ulnar area contrasts less than it does on Trindade Petrel. Structurally the two differ rather dramatically, as Sooty has straighter wings, a shorter tail, and a noticeably longer bill. Immature jaegers (far right) show a fair amount of checkering and barring below, with white confined to the base of the primaries; they also have longer bills than Trindade Petrel and are more gull-like in structure (all photos, BLS, GLA).

Hawk Mountain, Pennsylvania, in October 1959 may have been this species or possibly a Kermadec Petrel;[19] the latter was recently proven to occur in the Atlantic.[20] At least two morphs occur (see Taxonomic Note). Dark morphs comprise roughly 80 percent of the individuals encountered off North Carolina.[4] Sooty Shearwater and jaegers are confused often with Trindade Petrel.

Trindade is unique among these four petrels in possessing uniformly brown upperparts. In both morphs, the head, nape, rump, and tail are all an even chocolaty brown. Distinct from the other petrels in shape, Trindade has a slender body, and narrow wings that make it appear long winged. Both morphs show a white base to the primaries on the underside of the hands. Sometimes this bleeds into the middle of the wing along the secondaries, making for a fairly extensive patch of white on the underwing. The axillaries and leading edge of the underwing are the darkest area of the underwing.

Dark morphs are chocolate brown above, sometimes mixed with steely gray. Some dark morphs are chocolate brown throughout, while others show slightly paler underparts from the midchest through the belly that contrast slightly with the darker axillaries. Otherwise, only the white underwing patch disrupts the dark pattern. They resemble Sooty Shearwater in general appearance, and Sooties engage in arcing and rolling flights akin to those of *Pterodroma*. A fleeting view of a Sooty may fool even the most expert seabirder, but prolonged views should show the *Pterodroma* shape of Trindade and the underwing pattern. The white in the underwing of Sooty Shearwater is not at the base of the primaries, but more toward the interior of the wing, amid the coverts.

Light morphs appear like dark morphs dorsally, with a similar underwing pattern (including a noticeable dark ulnar bar), but they have a white belly, and often some white on the chin. The head is at times paler brown than on a dark morph, and the face is sometimes flecked with white. The undertail coverts are brownish, which can be a helpful mark in separating them from other Atlantic gadflies, especially when they are flying directly away.

Zino's Petrel (a.k.a. Madeira Petrel), documented only once off North Carolina,[4] is extremely rare and endangered, with just sixty-five to eighty breeding pairs known (all along the central massif of Madeira).[21] Named for conservationist Paul Alexander Zino, the species

Natural History Note:

There are about thirty *Pterodroma* species worldwide, and the genus is home to some of the rarest and least-known birds on the planet. Pelagic birds that breed on remote islands, nest in well-hidden burrows, and feed mostly nocturnally are typically difficult to study. Nests are self-excavated (or human-made) burrows, and petrels visit them nocturnally to avoid diurnal predators (e.g., gulls). Virtually all tubenoses evolved to breed in areas free of terrestrial predators, so introduced rats, cats, mongooses, and other such animals can quickly wipe out eggs and chicks at breeding colonies. Luckily, Procellariiformes are among the longest-lived birds, allowing endangered species such as Bermuda and Zino's petrels to persist for a long time at sea, despite years of failed breeding attempts on land.

Certainly the rediscovery of the "Cahow" in 1935[22] and the subsequent finding of its nesting area by David Wingate, Louis Mowbray, and Robert Cushman Murphy on several small islands in Castle Harbour on Bermuda[23] was one of the great stories of the twentieth century. Wingate's herculean efforts to protect the Bermuda Petrel paid dividends, and the population has since climbed from about three dozen in 1951 to 250 or more birds today.[24] In 2003 several nestlings were moved to Nonsuch Island in the hopes that they would imprint on that site and return there to breed, where there is great potential for expansion and growth. In 2008 those birds reached breeding age and nested there for the first time in four hundred years. A Bermuda Petrel captured over multiple seasons at a burrow in the Azores[25, 26] indicates that they may breed away from Bermuda occasionally, and skeletal remains from the Bahamas[27] indicate that Cahows were once more widespread.

is extremely similar in appearance to Fea's/Desertas petrel, and at-sea identification criteria are still evolving. Currently, it is extremely difficult or impossible to distinguish most birds from Fea's/Desertas. In addition to being smaller and finer billed, Zino's has a more delicate head (it's more "dove-headed")[10] and slightly shorter and rounder wings. The dark eye patch averages darker than in Fea's.[4] Some Zino's show a white bar in the middle of the underwing that offsets the darker ulnar bar. "Fea's-type" Petrels that are molting flight feathers in the fall or winter,[4] or that appear relatively small and fine billed, should be photographed extensively and scrutinized for other characters consistent with Zino's.

References

[1] Howell, S.N.G., and J. B. Patteson. 2008. Variation in the Black-capped Petrel: One species or more? Alula 14:70–83.

[2] American Ornithologists' Union. 1998. Check-list of North American Birds. 7th ed. Washington, DC: American Ornithologists' Union.

[3] Brooke, M. De L. 2004. Albatrosses and Petrels across the World. Oxford: Oxford University Press.

[4] Howell, S.N.G. 2011. Petrels, Albatrosses and Storm-Petrels of North America: A Photographic Guide. Princeton, NJ: Princeton University Press.

[5] Collar, N. J., L. P. Gonzaga, N. Krabbe, A. Madroño Nieto, L. G. Naranjo, T. A. Parker III, and D. C. Wege. 1992. Threatened Birds of the Americas: The ICBP/IUCN Red Data Book. Cambridge, UK: International Council for Bird Preservation.

[6] Douglas, L. 2000. Status of the Jamaican Petrel in the West Indies. In Status and Conservation of West Indian Seabirds, edited by E. A. Schreiber and D. S. Lee, 19–24. Society of Caribbean Ornithology, special publication 1.

[7] Robb, M., K. Mullarney, and The Sound Approach. 2008. Petrels Night and Day. Dorset, UK: The Sound Approach.

[8] Jesus, J., D. Menezes, S. Gomes, P. Oliveira, M. Nogales, and A. Brehm. 2009. Phylogenetic relationships of gadfly petrels Pterodroma spp. from the northeastern Atlantic Ocean: Molecular evidence for specific status of Bugio and Cape Verde petrels and implications for conservation. Bird Conservation International 19:199–214.

[9] Harrop, A.H.J. 2004. The "Soft-plumaged Petrel" complex: A review of the literature on taxonomy, identification, and distribution. British Birds 97:6–15.

[10] Patteson, J. P., and E. S. Brinkley. 2004. A petrel primer: Gadflies of North Carolina. Birding 36:586–96.

[11] Shirihai, H., M. San Roman, V. Bretagnolle, and D. Wege. 2010. Petrels of the Caribbean: The Jamaican Petrel pelagic expedition. Unpublished report for the Tubenoses Project and Birdlife's Preventing Extinctions Programme. http://www.birdlife.org/news/news/2010/05/jamaica-petrel-search.html

[12] Farnsworth, A., D. F. Stotz, and I. O. Melian. 2005. Birds. In Cuba: Parque Nacional La Bayamesa, edited by D. Maceira F., A. Fong G., W. S. Alverson, and T. Wachter, 76–81, 143–47, 232–37. Rapid Biological Inventory Report 13. Chicago: Field Museum.

[13] Lee, D. S. 2000. Status and conservation priorities for Black-capped Petrel in the West Indies. In Status and Conservation of West Indian Seabirds, edited by E. A. Schreiber and D. S. Lee, 11–18. Los Angeles: Society for Caribbean Ornithology (special publication).

[14] BirdLife International. 2012. Species factsheet: Pterodroma hasitata. http://www.birdlife.org

[15] Patteson, B., and K. Sutherland. Seabirding Pelagic Trips. http://www.seabirding.com/

[16] Wingate, D. B., T. Hass, E. S. Brinkley, and J. B. Patteson. 1998. Identification of Bermuda Petrel. Birding 30:18–36.

[17] Haney, J. C., C. A. Faanes, and W.R.P. Bourne. 1993. An observation of Fea's Petrel, Pterodroma feae, (Procellariiformes: Procellariidae) off the southeastern United States, with comments on the taxonomy and conservation of the Soft-plumaged Petrel and related petrels in the Atlantic Ocean. Brimleyana 18:115–23.

[18] Hooker, S. K., and R. W. Baird. 1997. A Fea's Petrel off Nova Scotia: The first record for Canada. Birder's Journal 6:245–48.

[19] Hess, P. 1997. The "Hawk Mountain Petrel": First Pennsylvania record, but which species? Pennsylvania Birds 11(1):2–5.

[20] Imber, M. J. 2008. Kermadec petrels (Pterodroma neglecta) off the Azores, North Atlantic Ocean. Notornis 55:106–8.

[21] Menezes, D., F. Zino, P. Oliveira, and A. Buckle. 2005. Conservation of Madeira's Petrel Pterodroma madeira through restoration of its habitat. Abstract of poster presented to the Second International Manx Shearwater Workshop, Belfast, Northern Ireland, August 2–4.

[22] Beebe, W. 1935. Rediscovery of the Bermuda Cahow. Bulletin of the New York Zoological Society 38:187–90.

[23] Murphy, R. C., and L. S. Mowbray. 1951. New Light on the Cahow, Pterodroma cahow. Auk 68(3) (July–September): 266–80.

[24] BirdLife International. 2012. Species factsheet: Pterodroma cahow. http://www.birdlife.org

[25] Bried, J., and M. C. Magalhães. 2004. First Palearctic record of the endangered Bermuda Petrel Pterodroma cahow. Bulletin of the British Ornithological Club 124(3): 202–6.

[26] Gantlett, S. 2007. The western Palearctic year. Birding World 20:26–43.

[27] Nichols, J. T., and L. L. Mowbray. 1916. Two new forms of petrels from the Bermudas. Auk 33:194–95.

Large Shorebirds

Curlews

Godwits

These two groups represent the largest of the shorebirds (or waders, as they are called in Europe), each containing familiar ABA Area species, scarce or isolated ABA Area breeders, and also Eurasian taxa that turn up here as rare vagrants. Because curlews and godwits are migratory (some species spectacularly so), vagrants occur on occasion, and regularly in certain regions (especially along the coasts) of the United States and Canada. While GISS is helpful with these birds, plumage patterns on the head, and particularly on the wings, rump, and tail, are keys, too.

Curlews

Whimbrel (*Numenius phaeopus***)**

Bristle-thighed Curlew (*Numenius tahitiensis***)**

Long-billed Curlew (*Numenius americanus***)**

First Breeding:	~3 years old
Breeding Strategy:	Monogamous; territorial
Lifespan:	Up to 24 years

The largest shorebirds, dressed in buff and brown, and adorned with long, slender, decurved bills, curlews feed on tidal mudflats, beaches, rocky shores, prairie, tundra, or at the margins of marshes. Using their exceptional bills, they extract crabs, worms, and other invertebrates from these various substrates. Curlews are in the diverse and cosmopolitan sandpiper family Scolopacidae, which contains about one hundred species varying in size from the tiny Least Sandpiper (*Calidris minutilla*) to the rangy Far Eastern Curlew (*Numenius madagascariensis*). All eight of the world's curlews are in the genus *Numenius*, and they are closely related to Upland Sandpiper (*Bartramia longicauda*).[1] Within *Numenius*, the medium-large Whimbrel and the Bristle-thighed and Slender-billed curlews are closely related, and the larger curlews (which lack head stripes), such as Long-billed, Eurasian, and Far

Eastern, are similarly closely related.[2, 3]

Though juveniles generally resemble adults, curlews usually require about three years before reaching adulthood and first breeding, though some females may breed earlier.[4, 5, 6] When breeding, territorial males hover and glide high overhead, vocalizing repeatedly in aerial display. Curlews are long-lived birds; they have reached over twenty years of age, and one Bristle-thighed reached nearly twenty-four years—the oldest known scolopacid from North America.[7] Hybridization appears unproven in *Numenius*, but a bird from Easter Island could be a Whimbrel × Bristle-thighed Curlew hybrid (A. Jaramillo, pers. comm.).

All eight curlews have occurred in North America, but only Whimbrel and the Bristle-thighed and Long-billed curlews are regular. Eskimo Curlew was once a common Arctic breeder and migrant across eastern and central North America, but like the Slender-billed Curlew of Eurasia, it now appears likely extinct. Long-billed Curlew breeds on the northern Great Plains and winters along the Pacific and Gulf coasts, and also inland in parts of California and the Southwest. Whimbrel and Bristle-thighed Curlew are tundra breeders, but Whimbrel is widespread, wintering along all coasts and occurring throughout much of the continent in migration. Bristle-thighed has a restricted range, breeding only in a small area of western Alaska and wintering in Oceania (including Hawaii), but occurring rarely as a vagrant along the Pacific Coast. All curlews are migratory, and Whimbrel[8] and especially Bristle-thighed Curlew perform incredible feats of flight. From their staging grounds in Alaska (where they fatten up prior to migration) to their wintering grounds in French Polynesia, Bristle-thigheds travel over six thousand miles in only seven to eight days.[9]

As a group, curlews are distinctive and seldom confused with anything else, but because of their migratory nature, strays do occur. Little Curlew, Far Eastern Curlew, and Eurasian Curlew are all extremely rare vagrants to North America. Distinguishing between curlews can be challenging, but in most places only one or two species are likely. Understanding range and voice helps narrow the possibilities. On silent birds, structure and plumage patterns are important keys to identification.

Whimbrel, CA, Oct (BLS). Whimbrel is the most familiar and widespread of the curlews, occurring across most of North America during migration, and especially along the coast. Curlews use their long, down-curved bills to probe deep into the sand and soil to extract invertebrates, though Whimbrel does less deep probing than the others on average and more surface picking.

Focus on: *Voice, Uppertail/rump pattern, Head pattern, Underwing pattern, Back pattern*

Breeding adult Whimbrel, AK, Jun (GLA) (left); worn adult Whimbrel, CA, Sep (BLS) (right). Whimbrel is characterized by its generally drab brownish plumage that lacks strong contrasts, except for the bold head stripes. Breeding adults have black bills; nonbreeding adults have a pinkish base on the mandible.

Nonbreeding adult Whimbrel, CA, Oct (BLS) (left); nonbreeding adult Whimbrel, CA, Oct (BLS) (right). Whimbrels molt on the nonbreeding grounds, often arriving on southern beaches in very worn plumage by midsummer. They quickly initiate a complete prebasic molt, which puts them in fresh plumage by fall. Distinguishing these fresh-plumaged adults from juveniles can be tricky. On fresh birds look for retained worn outer primaries (left), or any sign of active wing molt (right), which indicates an adult.

Juvenile Whimbrel, CA, Sep (BLS) (left); worn adult or first-summer Whimbrel, CA, Jun (BLS) (right). Juvenile Whimbrels appear on nonbreeding grounds in August, and at this time they are markedly uniform and crisp compared with worn and molting adults. By midfall these distinctions are harder to note because of adults completing their prebasic molt, and distinguishing first-winter birds from winter adults is very difficult. On juveniles note the uniform, dark-centered pale coverts that contrast with darker scapulars; adults are more uniformly drab overall. Failed breeders can arrive in late June on southern beaches (right).

Hints and Considerations

- Ibis might conceivably be mistaken for curlews, but more often curlews are confused with flying or sleeping godwits, when bill features are hard to assess. Marbled or female/nonbreeding godwits can be especially tough to distinguish in these instances. Note that godwits have darker, blackish legs. Usually after some time, these large shorebirds reveal their bills, and/or their distinctive underwing, upperwing, and rump/tail patterns. Also, Upland Sandpiper is essentially a small curlew itself, yet it has a shorter, straighter bill and a large dark eye, and it lacks head stripes.
- *Listen up!* Curlews are vocal, frequently calling in flight (including nocturnal migrants). The quality of calls is similar across species: they emit shrill, piping whistles that run together. But the cadence and tones differ noticeably between species.
- Breeding birds are usually easily separated by range, habitat, and voice. Elsewhere, however, curlews may overlap in habitat. When flying, or standing with wings raised, they reveal distinctive rump/tail and underwing patterns. When they are at rest, note the back and flank patterns and assess the overall size and color of the bird, and the presence or absence of head striping.
- Whimbrel and Bristle-thighed are similar in structure but differ in plumage pattern. Long-billed is larger and longer billed (!) and lacks head stripes.

Identification

Plumages are roughly similar across the ages and sexes, so the same identification criteria are applied regardless of age or sex. In fall, juveniles are fresher and uniformly plumaged, with neatly marked paler coverts that contrast with darker scapulars, and have shorter bills and often warmer peach tones. Adults are more uniform above but worn in fall, with the pale notches and fringes of the back feathers appearing smaller and less obviously pale. Females are larger and longer billed than males in all species. When breeding, Whimbrel and Bristle-thighed Curlew have black bills, while juveniles and nonbreeders usually show a pale, pinkish base to the mandible. All species in all plumages and ages show obvious white outer primary shafts and grayish legs. Here we treat the North American subspecies of Whimbrel as separate from the Eurasian forms, calling it "Hudsonian" Whimbrel, while we group the Eurasian forms under the name "Eurasian" Whimbrel. Generally, we emphasize differences most useful in identifying migrant or vagrant curlews, since those on the breeding grounds are usually easily identified.

"HUDSONIAN" WHIMBREL: This is a medium-large curlew with a moderately long bill, similar in structure to both Eurasian Whimbrel and Bristle-thighed Curlew. Hudsonian Whimbrel is the most widely encountered curlew in North America, found in a greater variety of habitats than the others. Nonbreeders often use tidal flats, but migrants are less choosy, and inclement weather may force them down into less ideal habitats. The overall ground color of Hudsonian Whimbrel varies somewhat, with some approaching warm buff brown (especially juveniles) while many are cold gray brown. Hudsonian usually appears warmer in color than Eurasian Whimbrel and is darker than both Eurasian Whimbrel and Bristle-thighed Curlew, showing an entirely darkish brown rump and tail when its wings are raised. It always shows obvious head stripes (i.e., dark eye line and lores, pale supercilium, dark lateral crown stripes with a pale median crown stripe). Compared to Bristle-thighed it

Taxonomic Note:

Whimbrel may consist of more than one species. There appear to be no significant vocal differences between any Whimbrel subspecies, but they do differ in appearance and segregate by range. In addition, genetic data indicate that North American populations (*N. p. hudsonicus*), sometimes referred to as "Hudsonian" Whimbrel, are best treated as a separate species from the Eurasian whimbrels.[10] There are three Eurasian subspecies,[11] all of which show varying amounts of white on the back, rump, and tail. Two subspecies stray rarely to North America: "Eurasian" Whimbrel (*N. p. phaeopus*) breeds in northern Europe and western Siberia, winters on African coasts, and is rare yet probably annual on the East Coast of North America; "Siberian" Whimbrel (*N. p. variegatus*) breeds in eastern Siberia, winters from the Bay of Bengal through Australasia and the western tropical Pacific, and is rare but regular in western Alaska, and rarer still south along the Pacific Coast.[6] The third Eurasian subspecies, the "Steppe" or "Southern" Whimbrel (*N. p. alboaxillaris*) is unknown from North America. Poorly known, it breeds in very small numbers in the Ural Mountains, farther south than other forms,[12] and apparently winters along the western Indian Ocean.[11]

"Hudsonian" Whimbrel, CA, Oct (BLS) (left); CA, Jun (BLS) (right). Three subspecies of Whimbrel have occurred in North America. The widespread *N. p. hudsonicus* subspecies breeds here and is overall brownish, with a brown back and rump, whereas the two Old World forms have white backs.

"Eurasian" Whimbrel, United Kingdom, Jun (IHL); "Eurasian" Whimbrel, Gambia, Dec (JWS). Distinguishing the Old World forms takes some care, as both have white backs. The European subspecies *N. p. phaeopus* averages whitest overall, with whitish underwing coverts and belly, and a white-based tail.

"Siberian" Whimbrel, Asia, Sep (KL) (left); "Siberian" Whimbrel, Asia, Aug (KKH) (right). The Asian subspecies *N. p. variegatus* is overall similar to *hudsonicus* but has a distinct white back, often barred black. It differs from "Eurasian" in having a brown tail lacking white at the base, but these differences can be subtle. In North America, any Whimbrel with a white back represents a rarity.

Breeding adult Bristle-thighed Curlew, AK, Jun (GV). Most North American birders find their lifer Bristle-thighed Curlew on a targeted trip for the species in Alaska. Note that compared with Whimbrel, Bristle-thighed has bolder buffy-spotted upperparts, a streaked neck and breast contrasting with plain belly and flanks, and a characteristic cinnamon or buffy rump and tail.

Adult Bristle-thighed Curlew, HI, Feb (CR) (left); juvenile Bristle-thighed Curlew, Tahiti, Sep (SNGH) (right). Adults undergo a complete prebasic molt after arriving on wintering grounds, and their age can be safely determined from their worn plumage and wing molt only in fall. By winter, they are in fresh plumage and are very similar to juveniles (right). Juveniles arrive in fresh plumage but have slightly more worn flight feathers in winter. Age determination is difficult. Note variation in bill length and curvature.

Spring adult Bristle-thighed Curlew, AK, May (GV) (left); worn adult Bristle-thighed Curlew, Tahiti, Sep (SNHG) (right). Birders seeking vagrant Bristle-thighed Curlews on the West Coast should be prepared to identify fresher spring adults that may be blown off course during the trans-Pacific crossing in May, or worn adults and juveniles off course in fall. Worn adults are perhaps most challenging and most similar to worn Whimbrels, but note breast/belly contrast, and always look for the cinnamon-buff rump and tail, most easily seen in flight. Also pay attention to voice; calls differ greatly!

Curlews are often seen in flight during migration and transit around feeding areas. In this composite we compare the three primary species. "Hudsonian" Whimbrel (left group of four) is overall the drabbest and brownest in flight, with little notable contrast or color. Note the relatively narrow barring on the underwings and plain breast. Bristle-thighed Curlew (middle group of four) is more colorful, with richer plumage tones in general, heavily barred underwings, darker breast contrasting with buff belly, and cinnamon-buff rump and tail. Long-billed Curlew (right group of three) is largest and most colorful, washed with buff all over. Note the plain cinnamon-buff underwing coverts and the long bill, even longer than the others in juveniles (right) (all images BLS, GLA except Bristle-thighed Curlew top, CR; middle top, DG; bottom, ID).

is less buffy, especially on the back, underwings, and underparts, and is much darker backed, darker tailed, and more heavily and extensively marked on the flanks and chest with dark streaking or barring. Compared to Long-billed, it is smaller and shorter billed, has a more elongate body, shows obvious head stripes, and lacks rich orange-cinnamon tones. *Voice:* Call is a shrill, staccato, hollow, piping set of whistles nearly all on the same pitch, "pi-pi-pi" or "hwih-whi-wi-wi-weep-weep" or "bi-bi-bi-beh-beh," usually five or more notes strung together, but sometimes only three (ML Cat# 136145).

"EURASIAN" WHIMBREL: (Includes *N. p. phaeopus*, *N. p. variegatus*.) Similar to Hudsonian Whimbrel, Eurasian averages colder brown and has a distinctly white rump/lower back. Habitat preferences appear similar to those of Hudsonian, and it is found rarely but regularly in spring along the Atlantic Coast among migrant flocks of Hudsonians. Most records of Eurasian Whimbrel are coastal, and East Coast birds are thought to be the nominate subspecies, while West Coast records likely pertain to "Siberian" Whimbrel. Generally, separating nominate birds from (Siberian) *N. p. variegatus* is extremely difficult or impossible. The tail of Eurasian Whimbrel varies from mostly pale whitish (in nominate *phaeopus*) to largely gray brown (in *variegatus*). Underwings vary similarly from mostly white (nominate) to more heavily marked (*variegatus*) but are always whiter than those of Hudsonian. At rest, a Eurasian Whimbrel might easily be overlooked as a Hudsonian until the white rump/lower back is exposed when the bird raises its wings or takes flight. *Voice:* This is roughly similar to that of Hudsonian, but perhaps some differences exist in repertoire on the breeding grounds.[13]

BRISTLE-THIGHED CURLEW: In North America, this species is almost never seen outside its breeding grounds in western Alaska. It winters in Oceania, where it prefers coastal meadows, dune habitats, salt pans, and lagoon beaches, but vagrants occur rarely during migration along the Pacific Coast (mostly in spring). On average it is perhaps a more upland species than Whimbrel, but there is overlap. Structurally, Bristle-thighed is similar to Whimbrel but often appears a little warmer toned overall, and its distinctive voice and peach-buff rump and tail set it apart. On resting birds, note the pattern of the back with pale markings in the coverts that tend to be larger and buffier than on Whimbrel; thus Bristle-thighed appears more spangled on its upperparts. Also

Breeding adult Long-billed Curlew, UT, May (JL) (left); juvenile Long-billed Curlew, UT, Jul (JL) (right). Long-billed Curlew is big, long billed, and buffy cinnamon below, and it lacks crown stripes. Adults are similar year-round, and juveniles become adultlike over the first fall/winter. Age determination can be difficult and is best accomplished by focusing on the wing coverts: juveniles have dark-centered coverts with broad pale fringes, and adults have dark-barred coverts with a narrow central streak. Juveniles often tend to be whiter faced and shorter billed than adults.

Fresh adult Long-billed Curlew, CA, Oct (GV) (left); adult Long-billed Curlew, CA, Dec (BLS) (right). Adults arrive on wintering grounds in midsummer and quickly begin a complete prebasic molt; the bird at left has two ages of adult wing coverts. Note very long bill with a pink-based mandible (darker when breeding). Long-billed Curlew tends to wade in deeper water, unlike other curlews, and deftly extracts crustaceans with its long bill.

Foraging Long-billed Curlew, CA, Dec (BLS) (left); molting adult Long-billed Curlew, CA, Aug (TB) (right). Long-billed Curlew is highly versatile, feeding on sandy beaches, mudflats, and upland fields. When a bird is sleeping or feeding, the bill can be hidden. Note the grayish legs compared with the black legs on Marbled Godwit. Any Long-billed Curlew molting flight feathers (right) can be safely identified as an adult on the wintering grounds.

Long-billed Curlew flock, CA, Jul (BLS). Long-billed Curlews are unusual among curlews in spending much of their time in upland habitat. While some winter on coastal beaches and mudflats among Whimbrels and other shorebirds, many spend the nonbreeding season in agricultural areas and grasslands. This scene is typical of a foraging flock of Long-billed Curlews in a flooded alfalfa field.

Bristle-thighed Curlew on breeding grounds, AK, Jun (GLA). Enigmatic and spectacular, the Bristle-thighed Curlew not only undergoes one of the longest transoceanic migrations in the world, it breeds in spectacular rolling tundra in remote western Alaska. This is a much-sought-after species for most birders, but is it overlooked as a vagrant on the Pacific Coast because of its similarity to Whimbrel?

Vagrant Bristle-thighed Curlew with "Hudsonian" Whimbrel, AK, May (DG). Can you tell which one is the Bristle-thighed? Study this image, as this is likely what you'll encounter when you search for a vagrant Bristle-thighed on the Pacific Coast.

note the relatively fine streaking on the chest (most obvious in spring), which is sharply demarcated from the cleaner-looking belly and underparts (somewhat recalling the pattern of Pectoral Sandpiper). The flanks are less heavily marked compared to those of Whimbrel, contributing to the overall cleaner appearance. Even on birds at rest, you can often see the alternating orange and brown bands on the tail, but these are more easily seen when the wings are raised. In the air, the obvious distinctive clean orange-buff rump and upper tail become obvious, so you need only a good angle on a flying bird to easily identify a Bristle-thighed. The eponymous feathers around the legs have lustrous, elongated shafts, which, though diagnostic, are not easily seen. *Voice:* The call is a highly distinctive, two- to three-syllable "tEEw-WHEEt" or "tEE-Ow-EEt," almost like a wolf whistle, usually repeated, and rapidly so when a bird is agitated (ML Cat# 137534).

LONG-BILLED CURLEW: The largest breeding shorebird in North America, it is one of the few breeding endemics to the Great Plains. Its absurd bill and rather potbellied appearance give it a distinctive GISS. Away from the breeding grounds, it is also more of a wading curlew than others,[14] preferring tidal flats and saltmarshes but also upland fields and beaches.[4] Overall, it is more richly buff orange than the others, with extensive cinnamon peach in the wings and tail, though these become less rich in color with wear and bleaching. Lacking head stripes, it shows a relatively pale head, with darker lores and a more obvious eye. It is most similar in plumage to Marbled Godwit, but note the decurved bill (upturned in Godwits), the gray legs, the heavier structure, and the more deliberate movements. Always, Long-billed shows a pinkish-pale base to the mandible. Juveniles may show bills only slightly longer than those of female Whimbrel, so focus on head pattern, wing pattern, overall color, and voice. *Voice:* Calls are shrill, including a somewhat explosive "plur-ee," "wee-pweep," "pwee-pwep," "we-hee weee," or a more tremulous and rapid "kwee-wee-wee-ee, kwee-wee," building to a descending wail (ML Cat# 172109).

Vagrant Curlews

Little Curlew (*N. minutus*) is accidental on the Pacific Coast. Within its typical range, it prefers coastal grassy areas. Closely related to Eskimo Curlew and similar to it in structure, it differs in having plain gray-brown

Natural History Note:

Eskimo Curlew appears to be extinct. It was once an abundant migrant, breeding in the Northwest Territory and wintering in Argentina. Large numbers were seen in migration in the eastern United States and maritime Canada during fall, and also along the Gulf Coast and in the Great Plains in spring (a similar migration to that of Hudsonian Godwit and Upland Sandpiper). The last documented records are from Texas in 1962, and from Barbados in 1963, but undocumented reports continue to fuel speculation that it might yet survive. Similar in structure to Little Curlew, it might also be confused with Whimbrel or Upland Sandpiper. Compared to Whimbrel, it is smaller and has cinnamon axillaries, and at rest the wing tips extend beyond the tail.

Slender-billed Curlew may also be extinct. It occurred once in North America, in Ontario in "about 1925."[15] Documented reports in the Mediterranean and Middle East extended into the late 1990s, and more recent sighting reports are cause for grim hope.

Bristle-thighed Curlew is unique among shorebirds in several respects, which include being the only shorebird to molt all its primaries simultaneously, and using tools.[16]

underwings. The dark rump/tail and underwing pattern is similar to that of Hudsonian Whimbrel, but Little is only about half as big, the tail projects beyond the wing tips, and the eye is more prominent.

Far Eastern Curlew (*N. madagascariensis*, a.k.a. Eastern Curlew) is the *largest shorebird* in the world. It breeds in Siberia and winters in Australia. In North America it is a vagrant to western Alaska and is accidental to British Columbia. Similar to Long-billed in structure, it is even larger and longer billed and lacks peach-cinnamon tones in the wings and tail. The common call is a plaintive "kur-ree" or "cue-ree," which may be repeated.

Eurasian Curlew (*N. arquata*, a.k.a. Curlew) is a widespread breeder in Eurasia, wintering coastally from Iceland south into Africa and east to Japan and Indonesia. It has occurred as a rare vagrant from Newfoundland to New York, Nunavut, and Greenland (and once to Argentina!). Compared to Long-billed it differs in its mostly white underwings, white rump and back, whiter belly, and paler tail. Common calls include a full-throated, whistled "kooour-ee," with the first note rather drawn out and the emphasis on the second syllable.

Juvenile Little Curlew, Asia, Oct (KL) (left); adult Little Curlew, CA, Sep (MD). Little Curlew is an Asian species that has occurred a few times on the Pacific Coast. You should be aware of this possibility and scrutinize any short-billed curlew with head stripes.

Eurasian Curlew, Japan, Dec (ID) (left); Far Eastern Curlew, Asia, Oct (KL). These two big, long-billed species occur as vagrants; Eurasian Curlew on the Atlantic Coast, and Far Eastern on the Pacific Coast. Note streaked overall plumage, and plain face and crown on both, but also note that Eurasian has a bold white rump and back, a white belly, and bright white underwings. Far Eastern is most similar to Long-billed Curlew, but it is browner overall, with heavily barred underwings, and lacks the cinnamon buff of Long-billed.

Eurasian Curlew in flight, Belgium, Dec (BLS) (left); Far Eastern Curlew in flight, China, May (KKH). The similarities between these two large curlews disappear in flight, as Eurasian shows bold white on the back, underwings, and belly, while Far Eastern is overall drab brown; and note its barred underwings compared to Long-billed.

References

[1] Piersma, T. 1996. Family Scolopacidae. In Handbook of the Birds of the World. Vol. 3, Hoatzin to Auks, edited by J. del Hoyo, A. Elliott, and J. Sargatal, 444–87. Barcelona: Lynx Edicions.

[2] Larson, S. 1957. The suborder Charadrii in Arctic and boreal areas during the Tertiary and Pleistocene. Acta Vertebratica 1:1–84.

[3] Mayr, E., and L. L. Short. 1970. Species taxa of North American birds. Publications of the Nuttall Ornithological Club 9.

[4] Dugger, B. D., and K. M. Dugger. 2002. Long-billed Curlew (*Numenius americanus*). The Birds of North America Online. A. Poole, ed. Ithaca, NY: Cornell Lab of Ornithology. http://bna.birds.cornell.edu/bna/species/628

[5] Marks, J. S., T. L. Tibbitts, R. E. Gill, and B. J. McCaffery. 2002. Bristle-thighed Curlew (*Numenius tahitiensis*). In The Birds of North America, No. 705, edited by A. Poole and F. Gill. Philadelphia: Birds of North America.

[6] Skeel, M. A., and E. P. Mallory. 1996. Whimbrel (*Numenius phaeopus*). In The Birds of North America, No. 219, edited by A. Poole and F. Gill. Philadelphia: Academy of Natural Sciences.

[7] Marks, J. S. 1992. Longevity record for the bristle-thighed curlew: An extension. Journal of Field Ornithology 63(3): 309–10.

[8] Watts, B. D., B. R. Truitt, F. M. Smith, E. K. Mojica, B. J. Paxton, A. L. Wilke, and A. E. Duerr. 2008. Short Communications: Whimbrel tracked with satellite transmitter on migratory flight across North America. Wader Study Group Bulletin 115:55–57.

[9] McCaffery, B. J. 2008. On scimitar wings: Long-distance migration by the Bar-tailed Godwit and the Bristle-thighed Curlew. Birding 40(5): 50–59.

[10] Zink, R. M., S. Rohwer, A. V. Andreev, and D. Dittman. 1995. Trans-Beringia comparisons of mitochondrial DNA differentiation in birds. Condor 97:639–49.

[11] Cramp, S., and K. E. L. Simmons. 1983. The Birds of the Western Palearctic. Vol. 3. Oxford: Oxford University Press.

[12] Morozov, V. V. 2000. Current status of the southern subspecies of the Whimbrel (*Numenius phaeopus alboaxillaris*) (Lowe 1921) in Russia and Kazakhstan. Wader Study Group Bulletin 92 (August): 30–37.

[13] O'Brien, M., R. Crossley, and K. Karlson. 2006. The Shorebird Guide. New York: Houghton Mifflin.

[14] Sibley, D. A. 2000. The Sibley Guide to Birds. New York: Alfred A. Knopf.

[15] Dunn, J., and J. Alderfer. 2006. National Geographic Guide to the Birds of North America. Washington, DC: National Geographic.

[16] Howell, S.N.G. 2014. Varia: Bristle-thighed Curlew and Tuamotu Sandpiper: Two endangered shorebirds from the South Pacific. Dutch Birding 36:178–87.

Godwits

Marbled Godwit (*Limosa fedoa*)

Hudsonian Godwit (*Limosa haemastica*)

Bar-tailed Godwit (*Limosa lapponica*)

Black-tailed Godwit (*Limosa limosa*)

First Breeding:	2–4 years old
Breeding Strategy:	Seasonally monogamous
Lifespan:	Up to 30 years

Elegant in shape and pleasingly patterned, godwits, unlike most birds, have unusual "recurved" bills, a character that contributes to their stately appeal. Rare visitors in many areas of North America and much sought after among birders, these tall and long-legged shorebirds inhabit wetlands, mudflats, marsh edges, or freshwater shallows, where they probe the soil for mollusks, crustaceans, annelids (worms), insects, and other invertebrates. They are members of the sandpiper family Scolopacidae, but their proper placement within the family is debated; many believe the curlews are their closest relatives.[1,2] All four of the world's godwits are in the genus *Limosa*, large waders that possess long bills and legs and are strongly migratory. Each species performs impressive seasonal migrations, but those undertaken by the Bar-tailed Godwits breeding in Alaska are simply incredible. Their migration and that of the Hudsonian Godwit have put these large shorebirds at the forefront of the rapidly evolving field of avian migration research.

Three godwit species breed in North America, but Black-tailed Godwit occurs only as a rare vagrant, breeding in Eurasia. Bar-tailed breeds in Arctic Eurasia and Alaska, while Marbled and Hudsonian godwits are endemic breeders to North America. On the breeding grounds the godwit species rarely overlap, segregating by both range and habitat, and so in their breeding plumage they are seldom confused with one another. Migrants, however, turn up widely, sometimes in areas where they are rare or even accidental, and godwits are often unfamiliar to birders and appear in places where several godwit species are possible. Away from

Natural History Note:

Given that so few birds possess recurved bills, you might wonder what advantage there is in having one. One study determined that curved bills (decurved or recurved) are more maneuverable and better for grasping in confined spaces like cavities under rocks or fiddler crab tunnels.[3]

In shorebirds, such as godwits, curlews, knots, and phalaropes, males are smaller than females and assume a greater share of the parental care of their young; just the opposite of lekking, promiscuous species like Ruff, Buff-breasted, Pectoral, and Sharp-tailed sandpipers. Smaller body size is thought to translate to less energy required for self-maintenance, allowing for a greater concentration on parental care, and shorter bills make for better feeding in the shorter vegetation most suitable for foraging with the precocial nestlings.[4]

Marbled Godwit shows less pronounced sexual dimorphism in plumage than the other godwits, perhaps as a result of its affiliation with grasslands and marshes. Shorebirds that frequent such upland habitats (e.g., curlews, snipe) show little seasonal or age-related plumage differences.[5]

the breeding grounds godwits are often less confiding, and even when they are reasonably close and provide lengthy studies, they can be difficult to identify, even for experienced birders. Patience is key, as identification may require not only perched views but also in-flight views.

Migrants are most commonly encountered along the coast in habitats such as sheltered lagoons and estuaries, coastal impoundments or pools, mudflats, and beaches. Inland, migrants are found in marshy habitats, on lakeshores, or in flooded fields. There is considerable overlap in habitat among the godwit species, but each has tendencies that are useful to understand. Godwits feed prominently, often on mudflats, but also stride about in water too deep for many other shorebirds, periodically exposing their long, distinctive bill. But they are frequently inconspicuous when at rest with their bill tucked in, or when sitting concealed amid a group of roosting shorebirds. Many times a "mystery godwit" is first noticed, and best identified, as it takes

Godwits are widespread around the globe, and all four species occur in North America. The most familiar to birders is Marbled Godwit (above, CA, Sep, BLS), which spends the nonbreeding season conspicuously foraging along beaches and mudflats, often in the company of other shorebirds. During the breeding season all four godwit species are rather easily identified, but during migration and winter they are trickier, and two sought-after vagrant species should be considered whenever an out-of-range godwit is detected. This chapter will focus on identifying godwits that might cause confusion.

Focus on: *Wing pattern, Uppertail pattern, Structure, Range, Voice*

Breeding adult Marbled Godwit, AB, May (GV) (left); breeding adult Marbled Godwit, ND, Jun (BLS) (right). Unlike other godwits, Marbled Godwit has little seasonal, sexual, or age-related variation in plumage. Breeders are lightly barred with black on the underparts; nonbreeders are plain buffy below. Breeds in interior grasslands and prairies, winters widely along both coasts.

Worn adult Marbled Godwit, CA, Jul (BLS) (left); fresh adult Marbled Godwit, CA, Oct (BLS) (right). Adults arrive during July on wintering grounds, usually in tattered condition; note worn coverts (left). They immediately initiate a complete prebasic molt, and by midfall most are in fresh plumage (right), which is more colorful and crisp. All show uniform buffy underparts, plain head pattern with faint supercilium ending above the eye, and complex cinnamon-buff and blackish barred pattern above.

Worn juvenile Marbled Godwit, CA, Oct (BLS) (left); fresh juvenile Marbled Godwit, CA, Aug (BLS) (right). Occasionally, worn birds approach the overall plumage of Bar-tailed Godwit. Note the short supercilium, though, which would be bolder and continue behind the eye in Bar-tailed. Birds like this are best identified in flight, when underwing and tail/rump pattern differences can be more easily assessed. Fresh juveniles (right) have uniformly crisp plumage with pale coverts contrasting with darker back. Note that the bill is completely covered in mud, obscuring the pink base.

flight or when it raises its wings, as the striking wing and tail patterns are revealed. Beware of other large, similarly patterned shorebirds such as Willet or curlews. And when any shorebird takes flight, listen up for vocalizations, as bill features become harder to assess on moving birds. Focus on the rump and underwing patterns, try to assess structure, and make comparisons to any other birds present.

Hints and Considerations

- Godwits often keep company with other large shorebirds and are at times confused with curlews, willets, yellowlegs, or dowitchers. Only curlews average larger, and they cause identification problems only when their bill shape isn't obvious. Note that curlews have paler gray legs.
- Willet (*Tringa semipalmata*) is often confused with Hudsonian Godwit.
- Outside Alaska and away from the central flyway (i.e., the western Gulf Coast, Great Plains) in spring, Marbled is the most regularly encountered species. It is also essentially the only species encountered in North America in winter.
- Standing or foraging godwits can be a challenge. Flying godwits reveal distinctive patterns in their wings and tail. When they take flight, take pictures, and listen for calls.
- Godwit species differ from each other in structure: Hudsonian and Bar-tailed are more dowitcher-like; Marbled and Black-tailed are rangier, with longer legs and bills.
- Marbled Godwit appears quite similar across all ages and seasons (worn birds often appear darker backed and washed out below). In the other godwits, juveniles differ dramatically from adults in plumage, so determining their age and sex is important in identification.
- Season, bill pattern, habitat, and voice may offer additional clues, but nonbreeding godwits are less vocal than many shorebirds.

Identification

The information provided here is oriented toward the identification of migrant or vagrant godwits, rather than those on the breeding grounds, where identification is usually straightforward. Female godwits are larger and longer billed than males. Marbled Godwit appears

fairly similar year-round, but the other three godwit species have distinct breeding, nonbreeding, and juvenile plumages, and the sexes differ somewhat in breeding plumage, too.

Usually by April adults are in breeding plumage. Nearly all the Hudsonians and Bar-taileds seen in spring in North America are breeding-plumage adults, as typically, first-year birds remain on the wintering grounds or migrate only a short distance away.[5] Fall adults typically look somewhat patchy, with mostly new gray feathers (nonbreeding or basic plumage), but they also retain some worn breeding-plumage feathers, even into late fall. Among the non-Marbled godwits, the prebasic molt is usually completed on the wintering grounds,[5] so that seldom is an adult seen in North America showing no trace of breeding plumage. Juveniles have fresher feathers, are more evenly grayish or buffy, and show more finely patterned backs (so compare them with Marbled Godwit). Determining the sex of juveniles is more difficult, but differences in bill size are helpful.

All four species show dark gray or blackish legs (unless coated in pale mud), but there is variation in the richness of their plumage color (see Taxonomic Note on subspecific variation). Worn late-summer adults may be especially hard to identify. Some godwits show brownish staining on the face.

MARBLED GODWIT: The most familiar godwit to most North American birders, Marbled breeds in the Prairie Pothole grasslands of the northern Great Plains and Great Basin, and it winters along both coasts of the United States. It is found widely in migration, but migrants are sparse or rare inland, and it generally avoids mountainous areas. Approximate migration peaks for inland migrants are April–May and August–September. From November to March they are almost never seen away from the coast, then making use of beaches, tidal flats, coastal lagoons, shorelines, and shallow ponds during winter and migration.

Marbled is a large godwit that is marbled black against buff, with colorful buff-orange wings. The wings are nearly entirely peach orange below but have a dark leading edge above (blackish on the outer primaries and primary coverts). Marbled has a bicolored bill with an extensive pinkish base (one-third to one-half) and a blackish outer half. Generally it is more similar in plumage to Long-billed Curlew than to the other godwits, but beware of juveniles of other *Limosa*. In particular, juvenile Bar-tailed or Black-tailed godwits can appear buffy, especially when they are foraging or at rest (and not exposing their wing and tail patterns). In flight, Hudsonian and Black-tailed have contrasting black-and-white wing and tail patterns, but the North American breeding subspecies of Bar-tailed Godwit (*baueri*) is more evenly patterned and thus more similar to Marbled. Distinguishing worn adult Bar-tailed Godwits from worn Marbled Godwits can be a real challenge. Pay attention to structure and voice and note that all Marbled Godwits show a rather plain buff rump, peachy axillaries (armpits), and long legs (especially a longer tibia than in other godwits).

Breeding: Adults in spring are pale buff overall, showing not only obvious blackish marbling above on the back, but also variable marbling below on the chest and flanks. *Nonbreeding:* These are similar to breeding-plumage adults but often appear buffier or even peachy orange overall, usually showing cleaner chests. *Juvenile:* These are similar to the adults but with fresh, nicely contoured flight feathers, and the chest and belly are unmarked, appearing clean and creamier in color. The back feathers are less marbled compared to those of adults and are dark centered with pale fringes.

HUDSONIAN GODWIT: This relatively small godwit has distinctive black wing linings, which are its best field mark. A long-distance migrant, undertaking a nonstop flight from its wintering grounds in southern South America to staging areas in the United States, it then picks up again for another nonstop flight to its Arctic breeding grounds. Nesting in several disjunct populations in Alaska and Arctic Canada, it is absent from North America in winter, gone by December and not returning until April. Migrants are encountered as flybys, or as visitors to freshwater ponds, coastal pools, impoundments, and less frequently tidal mudflats (their primary habitat in South America). West of the Rockies, Hudsonian Godwit is very rare, with the majority of records from the West Coast. Like other migrant shorebirds, they are at times grounded by inclement weather and sometimes appear in unexpected areas. In April and May the species migrates primarily west of the Mississippi Valley, through the Great Plains and the western Great Lakes north to the breeding areas, but heading south in the fall, they take a more easterly route. Between August and mid-October, they move from the breeding areas through the Great Lakes to the coasts of Atlantic Canada, New England, and the Mid-Atlantic States before heading offshore and flying nonstop to South America.

In all plumages the most distinctive feature is the black underwing, and the combination of the tail and wing pattern is diagnostic. The black underwings are bordered by a narrow white wing stripe. Compare this pattern to that found on Willet; birders often confuse these species. Willet has a paler tail, a thicker, grayer bill, and more rounded wings. Hudsonian has a black tail and white rump, and a dark eye line with a noticeable white supercilium, which is most prominently pale in front of the eye. Hudsonian is rather similar in overall pattern to Black-tailed Godwit when seen from above, especially in the upperwing and tail. Note the underwing differences (Black-tailed has white underwings), and also Black-tailed's larger size, longer and straighter bill, and long legs. Breeding adult Hudsonians have bicolored bills with an orange or pinkish-orange base and a blackish outer half, while nonbreeding adults and juveniles have more extensively blackish bills, with a reduced pinkish base.

Breeding male: With the grayish head, the whitish lores contrasting with the darker crown, the rufous underparts, and the blackish upperparts flecked with buff, a breeding male Hudsonian Godwit is unlikely to be confused with other shorebirds. A richly colored Long-billed Dowitcher, however, with its bill tucked or submerged, might present a pitfall. Note the godwit's long primaries and black legs. *Breeding female:* Similar to the breeding male in pattern, females are more subdued in plumage, with reduced rufous below, and they appear generally grayer than males, with a more pinkish (less orange) bill base. *Nonbreeding:* Seldom is an adult Hudsonian Godwit found in North America that shows no trace of breeding plumage, but especially in late fall, adults are seen that are largely in nonbreeding plumage. They appear sort of like an oversized dowitcher (but are heftier, with a pinkish bill base and dark legs) and are mostly gray, with gray upperparts and a gray hood and neck, but a whitish belly, and they still show a noticeable white supercilium. Many fall migrants appear this way but show a smattering of breeding-plumage feathers, with flecks of the rufous on the underparts, and/or often hints of the darker barring below the legs and on the undertail. *Juvenile:* These are similar to nonbreeding adults but are dingier and grayer, and the white underparts are more gray and so contrast less with the chest than they do in adults. Juveniles are quite gray

Breeding male Hudsonian Godwit, MB, Jun (TJ) (left); breeding female Hudsonian Godwit, MB, Jun (TJ) (right). Hudsonian Godwit has distinctive breeding, nonbreeding, and juvenile plumages, as well as difference between the sexes in breeding plumage. Males are more richly rusty colored below, whereas females are more coarsely barred below. Females of all godwit species average longer billed than males.

Juvenile Hudsonian Godwit, CA, Sep (BLS) (left); fall adult Hudsonian Godwit, MA, Jul (JT) (right). Juvenile Hudsonian Godwits lack the bright colors of breeding adults and more resemble nonbreeding adults. Note uniformly fresh plumage with scaly upperparts, unlike the plain gray upperparts of nonbreeding adults. During fall migration, which begins in July for adult Hudsonian Godwits, many birds either have worn breeding plumage (right) or are transitioning to adult nonbreeding plumage.

Adult Hudsonian Godwit, MA, Aug (JT) (left); adult Hudsonian Godwit, MA, Aug (ID) (right). By August, many adults have transitioned partly into basic plumage, so most have a mix of fresh gray nonbreeding plumage and remnants of worn adult plumage. There is considerable variation, but almost all birds show traces of breeding plumage as they are encountered in fall migration in North America.

Taxonomic Note:

Among shorebirds, migration strategy seems an inherited trait, influenced by genetics.[7] Each godwit species has multiple discrete breeding populations, and genetic differences[8] or morphological differences have evolved between some subspecies,[1, 9] causing some uncertainty about their taxonomy.

- Marbled Godwit comprises two subspecies;[10] the Alaskan population is heavier than other populations and has shorter wings and a shorter tail, but the genetics remain in need of study.[11]
- Hudsonian Godwit is monotypic,[12] and individuals appear essentially the same regardless of where they breed, but each population is distinct genetically.[8] Recent tracking studies have shown that birds from different breeding areas also winter in different parts of South America (N. Senner, unpublished data).
- Bar-tailed Godwits vary in appearance throughout their range. Those breeding in Alaska and eastern Siberia are distinctly larger and darker than those breeding in Scandinavia.[1] These two extremes of the population are clearly different in appearance and possess different migration strategies. Bar-taileds breeding between them in central Eurasia are intermediate in size and plumage, however, so these differences appear to be clinal.[1]
- Black-tailed and Hudsonian godwits were once considered the same species[13] but are now treated as separate species.[14] Some authorities today split Black-tailed Godwit into more than one species,[15] but genetics between the three described subspecies appear to differ only slightly.[14] The nominate form, *L. l. limosa* (breeds from western Europe to Russia), averages larger overall and shows intermediate brightness below in breeding plumage; *L. l. islandica* (breeds in Iceland, Scotland, and Norway) averages smaller and shorter billed, with the brightest rufous underparts of any subspecies; and *L. l. melanuroides* (breeds from Siberia to Mongolia) averages smallest and dullest in breeding plumage, with a finer-tipped bill than in the other subspecies.[16, 17] While typical breeding individuals may be identified to subspecies, many birds are intermediate and cannot be safely assigned.

above also, with some darker, roughly anchor-shaped shaft streaks on the back feathers. Hudsonian is grayer in juvenile plumage than the other godwits.

BAR-TAILED GODWIT: This migration champion is rarely seen outside Alaska in North America. Two subspecies occur, and they differ in plumage. *L. l. baueri* breeds in Alaska (and eastern Siberia), is a rare vagrant on the Pacific Coast, and is accidental along the East Coast. This subspecies winters largely in New Zealand, and during the journey there from Alaska, it performs the longest known nonstop migration of any bird, covering over seven thousand miles in eight days while averaging about thirty-five miles per hour![6] Nearly all West Coast records for the Lower 48 occur between August and November; most are juveniles, but vagrants early in that window can be adults. *L. l. lapponica* breeds in western Europe and is a very rare vagrant along the Atlantic Coast. It has a white rump (dowitcher-like pattern) and pale, whitish underwings (see photos). Virtually all sightings of Bar-tailed Godwit in North America are from along the coast.

The remaining text in this species' account refers to *L. l. baueri*. (For *L. l. lapponica* see photos.) In all plumages, Bar-tailed shows a barred rump, tail, and underwings, which at a distance make these areas appear sort of grayish. When foraging they keep their back flat and parallel to the ground, which combined with their short legs gives them a different GISS than the others. And note how the supercilium is rather broad behind the eye, and the wing pattern (or rather the lack of one) differs from that of other godwits, as Bar-tailed's wings are evenly gray, with essentially no wing stripe, and plain grayish underwings. Closest in shape to Hudsonian, Bar-tailed nearly always feeds on beaches and mudflats.

Breeding male: Males are rich rufous below from the face through the chest to the undertail coverts, with an all-blackish bill. Often they show some dark brown streaks on the sides of the neck, but the belly is usually clean rufous with no barring. The upperparts are blackish brown and flecked with buff and orange. *Breeding female:* Largely straw buff in overall color, and so somewhat similar to Marbled, Godwit, sleeping females with their bills tucked in may be mistaken for curlews. More often, separation from Marbled Godwit is the issue, however, so note the size of the bird and the wing and tail pattern, and be aware that Bar-tailed has a darker back and bill than Marbled. Bar-taileds are brown above, most show some orangish in the face and chest, and some have variable rufous barring on the chest. Bill color varies, as some show a largely dark bill and others show a rather extensive pink base (~one-third of the bill). *Nonbreeding:* Gray brown overall, this species is streakier than other godwits in nonbreeding plumage,

Breeding male Bar-tailed Godwit, subspecies *baueri*, AK, Jun (GV) (left); breeding male Bar-tailed Godwit, Portugal, May (AG) (right). Bar-tailed Godwits breeding in Alaska are of the subspecies *baueri*, which averages less richly colored below than its Old World counterparts. Even within *baueri* there is variation, with birds breeding in the Yukon-Kuskokwim Delta (left) averaging paler than those from farther north. The European form, *lapponica* (right), is very richly colored and has whitish underwings, rump, and back. West Coast Bar-tailed Godwits have been mostly *baueri*, whereas East Coast ones have been mainly *lapponica*. A third intermediate subspecies is sometimes recognized, *menzbieri* of Siberia, and it is most similar to *baueri* but has a paler rump, lower back, and underwings.

Breeding male Bar-tailed Godwit, subspecies *baueri* or *menzbieri*, China, May (GV) (left); breeding female Bar-tailed Godwit, subspecies *baueri* or *menzbieri*, China, May (GV) (right). In high breeding condition, males attain mostly blackish bills. Some females show more rust below but note how this typical female differs remarkably from the male, being much paler below and longer-billed. Subspecies is difficult to determine on perched birds, but in flight note the tail, rump, and underwing patterns.

Juvenile Bar-tailed Godwit, Pribilof Islands, AK, Sep (DG) (left); juvenile Bar-tailed Godwit, China, Oct (GV). Fall juveniles have uniform plumage that is largely fresh, as well as patterned upperparts. Note bold supercilium extending past the eye, and uniformly pale buffy underparts (cf. Marbled Godwit).

Breeding male Black-tailed Godwit, subspecies *islandica*, NL, May (MT) (left); transitioning adult female Bar-tailed Godwit, Ireland, Apr (DD) (right). Black-tailed has distinctive breeding, nonbreeding, and juvenile plumages, and breeding adults differ by sex. Males average more richly colored with shorter bills. Most eastern North American records are thought to be of the *islandica* subspecies, which breeds in Iceland, though some birds are not safely distinguished from the European form *limosa*.

Nonbreeding Black-tailed Godwit, Gambia, Nov (JWS) (left); juvenile Black-tailed Godwit, subspecies *islandica*, Portugal, Sep (AAG) (right). Winter adults are easily separated from Hudsonian in flight by white underwings. At rest, Black-tailed also shows fewer primary tips visible past the tertials (typically 3 or fewer; Hudsonian typically shows 4). Juvenile *islandica* averages more richly colored than juveniles of other subspecies; cf. juvenile Hudsonian Godwit, which is much drabber overall.

Juvenile Black-tailed Godwit, subspecies *melanuroides*, China, Sep (KKH) (left); breeding adult Black-tailed Godwits, subspecies *melanuroides*, China, Mar (KKH) (right). Birders in Alaska and on the West Coast should be on the lookout for the Asian subspecies *melanuroides*, which averages smaller, shorter billed, and shorter legged and has duller breeding plumage (adults) than European birds. On juveniles (left) note drab coloration similar to juvenile Hudsonian Godwit, and fresh scaly upperparts. Note underwing pattern in flight.

Vagrant Bar-tailed Godwits are often found with Marbled Godwits, such as this transitioning adult *baueri* from WA, Oct (RS) (left). Note Bar-tailed's more prominent supercilium extending behind the eye, darker upperparts with a few scattered basic feathers (gray), and plain brown wing coverts. This worn adult, CA, Aug (TB) (right) is typical of what birders should use as a search image for summer Bar-tailed Godwits on the Pacific Coast.

Juvenile Bar-tailed Godwit, subspecies *baueri/menzbieri*, with Marbled Godwits, WA, Oct (RS) (left); adult Bar-tailed Godwit with Willets, FL, Feb (MOB) (right). Juvenile Bar-tailed has neatly patterned wings and back, a bold supercilium, and creamy buff underparts. A number of birds have wintered in North America. This adult (right) was identified as one of the Siberian forms (*baueri/menzbieri*) because of its barred underwing coverts and darkish rump/back (not visible in this photo).

Adult Bar-tailed Godwit, subspecies *lapponica*, with Willet, FL, Oct (MJ) (left); probable first-summer Bar-tailed Godwit, subspecies *lapponica*, VA, Jul (TJ) (right). Note the streaky overall appearance to the upperparts of the adult (left), whitish-buff underparts, and relatively bold pale eyebrow. First-summers are variable, some appearing more like breeding adults, and others more like nonbreeders (right). Note retained outer primaries from juvenile plumage, white underwings and rump, indicating subspecies *lapponica*.

Hudsonian Godwit is the smallest and most inconspicuous of the godwits, especially in juvenile and nonbreeding plumage. Can you find the juvenile (left) among the wintering Willet and Greater Yellowlegs in this photo (Baja California, Mexico, Oct, SNGH)? Hudsonian Godwit often forages in deeper water with longer-legged shorebirds such as dowitchers. This juvenile (right) was not obvious among the dozens of nearby Long-billed Dowitchers (CA, Sep, BLS).

Worn juvenile Marbled Godwit (center) with typical Marbled Godwits and Willets, CA, Sep (BLS) (left); nonbreeding Black-tailed Godwit, VA, Mar (SG) (right). Occasionally, searching for a vagrant Bar-tailed Godwit leads you to an atypical Marbled Godwit. The bird in the middle is overall paler, with plain upperwing coverts, a darker back, and a fairly bold supercilium—all good marks for Bar-tailed. This bird was photographed and watched until it took flight, and it showed cinnamon underwings typical of Marbled, as well as uppertail and rump typical for Marbled. It pays to take time when working with any potential vagrant! Like Bar-tailed, a few Black-tailed Godwits have overwintered (right). Note this bird's plain gray upperparts, rusty-tinged neck, and worn tertials and wing coverts.

Black-tailed Godwit should be looked for from July through midwinter. July seems to be a good month for arrivals, perhaps failed breeding adults or wandering first-summers. This bird appeared in TX in July (MG) and could be a first-summer or an adult female. Note larger size than nearby breeding-plumage Hudsonian Godwits, and white, not black, underwings.

with a diffusely streaked head and neck and streakier gray upperparts. The basal third of the bill is pink. *Juvenile:* Being buffy overall and neatly checkered on the back, the juvenile is somewhat similar to a Marbled Godwit, but note the more compact structure, the extension of the supercilium behind the eye, the darker crown and nape, the whitish (less buffy) belly, and the duskier bill. The basal third of the bill is pinkish, as in Marbled, but in addition to the characters mentioned above, juvenile Marbleds have more tawny-colored underwings, whereas those of Bar-tailed are grayish.

BLACK-TAILED GODWIT: A very rare vagrant in North America, this species is a tall, long-legged godwit, fond of estuarine and marshy habitats. It is a Eurasian breeder and is extremely rare in western Alaska and along the Atlantic Coast. Most North American records are from spring or summer, and compared to other godwits, it has a straighter bill (less upcurved), and usually the basal half or more (often two-thirds) of the bill is pink or yellow orange. Black-tailed Godwit in all plumages shows immaculate white underwings, which combined with the bold white wing stripe, the

black tail, and white uppertail coverts, are distinctive. When foraging it frequently leans down, pointing its rear (wing tips and tail) skyward, keeping on average a less horizontal posture than Bar-tailed or Hudsonian. In flight the longer legs project more obviously beyond the tail than in the other species.

Breeding male: With their elegant structure, a brick or peachy orange face and neck, and gray upperparts flecked with orange and black, breeding males are quite distinctive. The underparts vary in pattern and color. Some are orange from the chest to the undertail, but others are white on the belly and vent. There is variable black barring between the chest and legs. *Breeding female:* Similar to the males in plumage, but females are paler, with less of the dark barring below. *Nonbreeding:* Solid brownish gray above, with a gray neck, nonbreeders have a darker brownish crown, and a white belly. The whitish supercilium narrows and disappears behind the eye. *Juvenile:* Quite buffy overall, juveniles have a rich buff neck, a white eyebrow, and a whitish vent. The upperparts are nicely patterned (~checkered), with the back feathers showing blackish at the center with pale buff tips.

References

[1] McCaffery, B., and R. Gill. 2001. Bar-tailed Godwit (*Limosa lapponica*). The Birds of North America Online. A. Poole, ed. Ithaca, NY: Cornell Lab of Ornithology. http://bna.birds.cornell.edu/bna/species/581

[2] Naish, J. 2007. The godwits' many bills. http://scienceblogs.com/tetrapodzoology/2007/01/the_godwits_many_bills.php

[3] Ferns, P. N., and H. Y. Siman. 1994. Utility of the curved bill of the Curlew Numenius arquata as a foraging tool. Bird Study 41:102–9.

[4] Del Hoyo, J., A. Elliot, and J. Sargatal. 1996. Handbook of Birds of the World. Vol. 3, Hoatzin to Auks. Barcelona: Lynx Edicions.

[5] Howell, S.N.G. 2010. Molt in North American Birds. New York: Houghton Mifflin.

[6] Stap, D. 2009. Flight of the Kuaka. Living Bird Magazine (Autumn 2009). Cornell University Press.

[7] Berthold, P. 1996. Control of Bird Migration. New York: Chapman and Hall.

[8] Haig, S., C. L. Gratto-Trevor, T. D. Mullins, and M. A. Colwell. 1997. Population identification of Western Hemisphere shorebirds throughout the annual cycle. Molecular Evolution 6:413–27.

[9] Gibson, D. D., and B. Kessel. 1989. Geographic variations in the Marbled Godwit and description of an Alaska subspecies. Condor 91:436–43.

[10] Gratto-Trevor, C. L. 2000. Marbled Godwit (*Limosa fedoa*). The Birds of North America Online. A. Poole, ed. Ithaca, NY: Cornell Lab of Ornithology. http://bna.birds.cornell.edu/bna/species/492

[11] Olson, B. E. 2011. The biogeography of Marbled Godwit (*Limosa fedoa*) populations in North America. Paper 1119. http://digitalcommons.usu.edu/etd/1119

[12] Walker, B. M., N. R. Senner, C. S. Elphick, and J. Klima. 2011. Hudsonian Godwit (*Limosa haemastica*). The Birds of North America Online. A. Poole, ed. Ithaca, NY: Cornell Lab of Ornithology. http://bna.birds.cornell.edu/bna/species/629

[13] Johnsgard, P. A. 1981. The Plovers, Sandpipers and Snipes of the World. Lincoln: University of Nebraska Press.

[14] Höglund, J., T. Johansson, A. Beintema, and H. Schekkerman. 2009. Phylogeography of the Black-tailed Godwit Limosa limosa: Substructuring revealed by mtDNA control region sequences. Journal of Ornithology 150(1): 45–53. doi:10.1007/s10336-008-0316-8

[15] Brazil, M. 2009. Birds of East Asia. London: A & C Black Publishers.

[16] O'Brien, M., R. Crossley, and K. Karlson. 2006. The Shorebird Guide. New York: Houghton Mifflin.

[17] Howell, S.N.G., I. Lewington, and W. Russell. 2014. Rare Birds of North America. Princeton, NJ: Princeton University Press.

Marbled Godwit (left column) and Bar-tailed Godwit (right column). While these two species can be similar when perched, they are usually obviously different in flight. Marbled is washed cinnamon buff in all plumages and has unmarked cinnamon underwings; Bar-tailed is whitish or barred darker. Marbled has uniform buff rump, back, and upperparts, whereas Bar-tailed has more contrasting gray or whitish markings in these areas. Alaska breeding Bar-taileds, subspecies *baueri* (top middle, bottom middle, and right), are darkest, with barred underwing coverts, dark backs, and rumps. The European subspecies of Bar-tailed, *lapponica* (middle center-right, middle right, middle lower-right) is palest in these areas, usually showing whitish underwings, a whitish rump, and white back. The enigmatic Siberian subspecies, *menzbieri* (top right), is intermediate, with a paler back and a darker-barred rump (all Marbled Godwit photos, BLS; all Bar-tailed Godwit photos, GV, except molting bird, JT; and juveniles, AG).

Hudsonian Godwit (left column), Willet (center bird), and Black-tailed Godwit (right column). Hudsonian Godwit is best identified in flight by the combination of black tail and black underwings contrasting with a fairly prominent white wing stripe. Adults are variably marked red below, and transitioning birds can have a range of plumages. High-flying flocks of migrating Hudsonians are sometimes encountered in fall along the East Coast or on offshore boat trips (top left); note reddish underparts and black wing coverts. Black-tailed Godwit is similar to Hudsonian in flight but has white underwings in all plumages and subspecies. Willet is often misidentified as a godwit, but note its shorter bill, wider, more rounded wings, whitish tail, and bolder white wing stripes (all Hudsonian Godwit photos, JT, except two overhead, TJ; Willet, BLS; Black-tailed Godwit flock, GV; dorsal and small ventral, GLA; middle right dorsal, JWS; middle right ventral, TJ; bottom right, MG).

Skulkers

Marsh Sparrows

Small Wrens

These two groups of skulking birds are probably more of a challenge to see than to identify. Glimpsing them is not uncommon, but obtaining lengthy enough studies to identify them is tougher. On the breeding grounds their identification is usually rather straightforward, as they are often territorial, vocal with distinctive sounds, and a bit more conspicuous in their behavior. In migration and in winter they are quieter and more furtive, but this is when they are most accessible for most birders. Flying rather weakly, they remain out of sight much of the day to avoid predation. The marsh sparrows and two wetland wren species are often active at night when breeding, and they also migrate at night. Range and habitat usually offer the first and best clues, but rarely individual birds break these rules. Confirm identification using a combination of GISS, sounds, and plumage.

Marsh Sparrows

Le Conte's Sparrow (*Ammodramus leconteii*)

Nelson's Sparrow (*Ammodramus nelsoni*)

Saltmarsh Sparrow (*Ammodramus caudacutus*)

Seaside Sparrow (*Ammodramus maritimus*)

First Breeding:	1 year old
Breeding Strategy:	Monogamous or polygynous
Lifespan:	Up to 10 years

Too often sparrows are relegated to the nefarious category of "LBJ." This unsatisfying acronym is not a reference to the thirty-sixth US president but rather is shorthand for "little brown job." For birders, "LBJ" is sort of like a storage locker where we stow stuff we don't really want to deal with. Indeed, when you conjure up an image of a generic "sparrow," you quickly envision a small, streaky brown bird that prefers to lurk in the shadows rather than sit out in the open. And a fleeting view of a bird such as Le Conte's Sparrow registers itself in a flash of drab gray brown, but a close inspection reveals a bounty of color, including hues of peach, ocher, silver, and a chestnut so rich it almost suggests burgundy. And who but birders indulge so commonly in terms such as rufous, fulvous, chestnut, buff, russet, ocher, straw, amber, sandy, clay, rusty, or auburn? Seldom are such colors so elegantly displayed as they are in the delicate markings of North American sparrows. In fact, the LBJs, as we call them, are exquisite tapestries of color.

The "marsh sparrows" are a group of closely related skulking species within the family Emberizidae. All are in the genus *Ammodramus*, which translates to "sand runner."[1] These sleuths are somewhat terrestrial, favoring dense grassy meadows or marsh habitat, and indeed prefer to scurry away mouse-like from a threat rather than take to the air. With relatively pointed bills, they crunch seeds, snag insects, and even probe mud for invertebrates, and with short, pointed tails and understated but beautifully cryptic plumages, they are well adapted to the thick ground cover they prefer.

On the breeding grounds, seldom are more than two species possible in a given area, and while they are not especially impressive songsters they do vocalize, sometimes conspicuously. The song of each species is distinctive, though in the prairie regions where Le Conte's and Nelson's both nest, it may require some practice and careful listening to distinguish them. During migration and in winter marsh sparrows become more furtive in their habits, and they also overlap in range and habitat with each other, thus providing a bigger challenge to birders. Winter along the Mid-Atlantic Coast provides opportunity for the most acute identification problems, as all four species are present in certain locations, including all three subspecies of the variable Nelson's Sparrow.

Marsh sparrows are challenging to see and to identify because of their shy nature, and because their habits render them unfamiliar to most birders. Even biologists actively studying them have found their identification, taxonomy, and population dynamics vexing. Seaside Sparrow's appearance varies geographically but is usually quite distinctive, whereas the others are more similar in general plumage pattern. When the young

This skulking group of birds can be difficult to see, much less identify. Because of their habit of staying low and running mouse-like across the ground, views like this are rare. Occasionally they will respond to pishing by sitting up briefly, when they miraculously transform from "Little Brown Jobs" into wonderful tapestries of color. This fresh-plumaged Le Conte's Sparrow is a good example of the subtle beauty of this group of birds (MS, Dec, BLS).

Focus on: *Structure, Head pattern, Habitat and season, Breast/throat pattern, Back/rump pattern*

Fresh basic Le Conte's Sparrow, MS, Dec (BLS). Adult Le Conte's Sparrows undergo a complete prebasic molt after breeding, so during fall migration and in early winter, they are in crisp colorful plumage. Note overall pale plumage and small bill, with finely streaked flanks and breast, white central crown stripe, rufous-streaked gray nape, and buffy underparts contrasting with a white belly.

Molting spring Le Conte's Sparrow, TX, Apr (BLS) (left); worn breeding adult Le Conte's Sparrow, WI, Jun (LE). By late spring most birds are in the throes of prealternate molt and look relatively disheveled (left). On breeding grounds Le Conte's is at its most "contrasty," as much of the characteristic buffy plumage has faded to white and the pale-fringed fresh feathers are worn away, revealing the darker colors beneath, especially on the upperparts.

Juvenile Le Conte's Sparrow, MA, Oct (ID) (left); Le Conte's Sparrow in typical winter habitat, MS, Dec (BLS) (right). Le Conte's Sparrow often retains its juvenile plumage through fall migration, so many vagrant Le Conte's are in full juvenile plumage or transitioning to adult basic plumage. Juveniles (left) have less contrast and color than adults, with weaker streaking below and buffy napes. Le Conte's Sparrow can be found in a variety of grassy habitats in migration and during winter, but it especially prefers rank, wet fields. In this typical view, note pale overall coloration with buffy breast, finely streaked sides, and bold eye line broadening behind the eye.

fledge in late summer and early fall, juveniles of each species cause considerable confusion, as they appear very different from their parents but can look quite similar to the adults of other marsh sparrow species.

Provided you can obtain decent views, most marsh sparrows are fairly easily identified. Pay particular attention to habitat, structure, head pattern, and the pattern of the throat/breast, and in late summer and early fall, beware of juveniles.

Hints and Considerations

- To separate marsh sparrows from other sparrows, consider behavior. Marsh sparrows prefer not to fly from a threat; instead they freeze and then scurry mouse-like into vegetation. They flush usually only when closely approached, appearing weak in flight, keeping low, and not going far before pitching back into the grass. They often respond with curiosity to pishing and squeaking but don't stay perched up high for long.
- Other birds confused with marsh sparrows include the variable Savannah Sparrow, which is a strong-flying bird of open country that usually flies many meters when flushed. Henslow's and Grasshopper sparrows occasionally overlap in habitat with Le Conte's and are similar in GISS, but they differ in plumage. If seen poorly, Marsh and especially Sedge wrens might be mistaken for Le Conte's.
- Nelson's and Le Conte's sparrows are accidental to the Pacific Coast, while Seaside and Saltmarsh are unrecorded west of the Rockies.
- During the breeding season marsh sparrows are typically easily identified, segregating somewhat by range, and being quite vocal and more conspicuous in behavior.
- In migration or in winter, in coastal areas of the Mid-Atlantic and Southeast, you may see several species together. Saltmarsh and Seaside, as their names suggest, seldom venture away from the coast. Le Conte's and Nelson's breed inland, so during migration they are the most likely marsh sparrow species to be found away from the coast.
- Seaside Sparrow is most distinctive, being the most vocal and the largest; it is also nearly entirely dark in plumage, with a contrasting white throat. But juvenile Seasides are confusing and are frequently misidentified as Saltmarsh or even Nelson's sparrows.

Identification

Marsh sparrows have distinct juvenile and adult plumages. They look particularly smart in the fall and early winter when their plumage is fresh after a complete prebasic molt. They also average paler at this time because of the pale-fringed feathers on the back. By spring these pale fringes have mostly worn away, leaving a darker dorsal plumage that contrasts more sharply with the pale areas (e.g., white mantle stripes are bolder on a blacker back). Juvenile plumage in late summer/fall is held only briefly. Most juveniles molt out of it quickly near their natal areas in August or September, but Le Conte's is an exception, often migrating and occurring as a vagrant in juvenile plumage (October–December).

Songs of marsh sparrows are insect-like. They can go unnoticed amid the din of a noisy marsh chorus. In addition to their typical songs, these species have "flight songs" as well, which are variations on their typical songs, given during low, fluttering flights. In migration and in winter, they are mostly quiet, but chip notes occasionally betray their presence. Their vocalizations are distinctive but not easily summarized, and they are often not of primary importance in identifying a wintering or migrant marsh sparrow (though spring migrants are at times detected by song). We do not describe the sounds here, as they are better learned in the field or by studying recordings.

LE CONTE'S SPARROW: A dainty and dapper species, Le Conte's is the smallest marsh sparrow and also the most skulking. Even on the breeding grounds it often sings from low perches or amid cover. It differs from the others in its habitat preferences, occupying a variety of habitats throughout the year, but individuals show little site fidelity from season to season (in both wintering and breeding areas).[12] Like other marsh sparrows, it makes use of moist meadows and marshes, but these are nearly always freshwater or occasionally brackish areas. They like rank grassy areas that often contain bluestem, sedges (*Carex* spp.), and broomsedges (*Andropogon* spp.).[13] But Le Conte's also inhabits drier upland grasslands, including fields of alfalfa and wheat,[13] where other marsh sparrows are essentially never found. In these dry areas, Le Conte's is more likely to be confused with Grasshopper and possibly other sparrows. Grasshopper Sparrow shows more straw-buff tones in the chest and face (rather than ocher), has a larger bill, typically lacks obvious flank streaking, and often shows a noticeable yellow loral spot.

Taxonomic Note:

Le Conte's Sparrow is monotypic, but the others contain two or more subspecies each. Until 1995,[2] Nelson's and Saltmarsh sparrows were considered the same species, and both contain subspecies that are still in need of clarification.

Nelson's Sparrow, named for American naturalist Edward William Nelson, has three disjunct breeding populations (some perhaps deserving species status):

(1) *A. n. nelsoni*, the most richly colored subspecies, breeds in the northern Great Plains and pothole prairies. It winters along the Gulf and Atlantic coasts.

(2) *A. n. alterus* is similar in appearance to the nominate form but is slightly duller, and it breeds along James Bay and lower Hudson Bay. It also winters along the Gulf and Atlantic coasts.

(3) *A. n. subvirgatus* is distinctive, appearing very washed out and gray, with blurry streaks below. It averages less well marked and larger compared to other Nelson's. It breeds in brackish marshes of southern Quebec and the Maritimes south into Maine, and sparingly into New Hampshire. It winters on the Atlantic Coast (rare in winter north to Massachusetts) south to Florida.

Saltmarsh Sparrow has two poorly defined subspecies that appear very similar, with the nominate *A. c. caudacutus* breeding from Maine to New Jersey, and *A. c. diversus* breeding from New Jersey south to North Carolina. The two subspecies differ subtly in back pattern and tertial pattern. *A. c. diversus* averages darker overall on the back with fewer olive tones, and the tertials are solidly blackish centered.[3]

Studies surveying Saltmarsh Sparrows breeding between New York and Maine have shown that about 8 percent of individuals are actually hybrids (between Nelson's *subvirgatus* and Saltmarsh *caudacutus*), though all appear very much like typical Saltmarsh Sparrows.[4, 5]

Seaside Sparrow exhibits considerable variation, and so not surprisingly it has a complicated taxonomic history. As many as nine subspecies are often placed into two or three groups:[6, 7, 8]

(1) The Atlantic Coast group (*A. m. maritimus*, *A. m. macgillivraii* [incl. *pelonota* of coastal northeast Florida]) is dull gray overall and indistinctly streaked, and it breeds from Maine south to northeast Florida. It is mostly resident, but northerly *A. m. maritimus* is partly migratory.[9]

(2) The "Dusky" group, resident in the marshes of central and south Florida, is more closely related to the Atlantic group.[8] It includes the now extinct "Dusky" Seaside Sparrow (*A. m. nigricans*; see Natural History Note), which was very blackish, and the dark olive "Cape Sable" Seaside Sparrow (*A. m. mirabilis*; threatened status). Both were formerly considered species,[10] and unlike other Seasides, these make (or made) use of freshwater. The "Cape Sable" Seaside Sparrow especially is exclusive to freshwater areas and differs in both appearance and voice from other Seasides, while occupying an isolated range in the Everglades.[9, 11] It could merit species status.

(3) The Gulf of Mexico group[8, 9] (*A. m. sennetti*, *A. m. fisheri*, *A. m. juncicola*, and *A. m. peninsulae*) is mostly resident and averages a bit more colorful than the Atlantic group, showing more warm chestnut tones in the wings and flanks, and more distinct streaking below.

Small and well camouflaged, Le Conte's easily avoids detection. To search for one is to search for a disappearing mouse that occasionally picks up and flies a few meters. It is a sneaky bird and very much resists flushing until practically underfoot, and then it flies away weakly and usually not very far before pitching back into cover. It's hard not to admire its stealthiness. In flight the buffy rump is often conspicuous, and sometimes the ocher face and the straw-on-black back are evident. Occasionally, after landing it perches or runs to an opening in the grass to observe an intruder, and there, confident in its camouflage, it may allow wonderful studies.

Le Conte's is likely to be confused only with Nelson's (especially *nelsoni* and *alterus*), but note its white central crown stripe; small, fine bill; and pale lores.

Also compared to Nelson's, Le Conte's is smaller and more delicate, smaller headed, and paler overall. Le Conte's typically lacks lateral throat stripes or shows only thin, weak ones. From September to about March, adults look particularly dapper, with a rich buff-ocher supercilium and malar that contrasts nicely with the grayish cheeks. The dark postocular line broadens at the rear, making the gray cheek patch more prominent. The throat, central breast, and belly are a paler buff, while the flanks are yet buffier, but with distinct dark streaks. On some, the streaking below may meet under the throat and become finer and paler there than on the rear flanks, where it is most obvious. The nape is gray but with small, fine, burgundy-brown streaks. The dark back feathers are fringed pale buff, often aligning to create straw-colored braces ("corn rows"), or giving a scaled appearance. From April to August they show the same general pattern, but the more worn plumage shows more contrast, and they appear blacker backed and whiter on the belly (which then contrasts more with the orangish chest), and the streaking below is more obvious.

Of the marsh sparrows, only Le Conte's is known to migrate in juvenile plumage. This may result from their fledging in natal areas that are prone to fires or flooding, and where sudden paucities of food present a real risk to less-mobile fledglings.[12, 14] Juvenile Le Conte's is buff tan overall. It lacks ocher but instead is pale buff in the face, and it still shows the triangular postocular stripe that broadens at the rear. It has faint streaking below that is most prominent at the sides of the chest. The back and crown patterns are similar to those of the adult, but all pale areas are a similar pale buff. As always, note the small bill.

NELSON'S SPARROW: This medium-sized marsh sparrow defies easy summary. It encompasses three disjunct breeding populations (see Taxonomic Note above), each differing somewhat in appearance and preferring varying levels of water salinity. The three forms can overlap in winter or in migration.

First, note that *A. n. subvirgatus*, the "Acadian" Nelson's Sparrow, is rather distinctive compared to other Nelson's. Though a fresh fall Acadian can appear similar to the "James Bay" Nelson's Sparrow (*A. n. alterus*), the Acadian both behaves and appears more similar to a Saltmarsh Sparrow than it does to other Nelson's. Like Saltmarsh and Seaside it is a coastal marsh sparrow, seldom if ever encountered inland, and it overlaps with these in winter and in migration along the Atlantic Coast (Massachusetts south to Florida). It is rare or accidental along the Gulf Coast. See the photos to appreciate its distinctly large-billed and blurry gray appearance. It is sort of intermediate in plumage between a Seaside and Saltmarsh, but smaller than either, yet larger than other Nelson's. The James Bay Nelson's and "Prairie" Nelson's (*A. n. nelsoni*) are close in appearance to one another, though Prairie Nelson's averages richer in color. The remainder of this account deals with separating the interior-breeding Nelson's (*nelsoni/alterus*) from Le Conte's and Saltmarsh sparrows.

Nelson's Sparrows breeding in the interior are found rather widely in migration but become essentially a coastal species in winter, when they occupy marshes (fresh, brackish, and sometimes salt) along the Gulf

and Atlantic coasts. To distinguish them from Le Conte's, note that Nelson's has a gray crown, heavier bill, darker lores, darker wings, darker plain gray nape, coarser streaking below, and often, white back "braces" that contrast with a darker back. The buffy ochraceous face and breast contrast more sharply with the more distinctly white belly. At inland breeding sites, where they overlap with Le Conte's, they often inhabit the same wet meadows, but Nelson's prefers slightly wetter habitat (Le Conte's preferring drier, higher marsh edges).

Compared to Saltmarsh, Nelson's is smaller, smaller billed, and more uniformly orange throughout the face, throat, and breast. Nelson's has a rounder crown and softer, blurrier streaks that are heavily concentrated on the breast sides and flanks, while Saltmarsh shows darker, crisper streaks on both the flanks and breast. Usually, if the breast shows dark, crisp streaks all the way across, it's a Saltmarsh Sparrow, not a Nelson's. Nelson's lacks streaks in the ocher supercilium behind the eye, while Saltmarsh has short, fine streaks there.

Juvenile Nelson's is distinctive, as it is extremely rich ochraceous buff overall (lacking a contrasting white belly as on adults) and has reduced flank streaking.

SALTMARSH SPARROW: This aptly named, rangy sparrow appears threatened by a variety of forces including rising sea levels,[15] marsh manipulation for mosquito control and development projects, and invasive plants.[16] Strictly coastal, it is also found in brackish marshes, but it is almost never found away from the coast or coastal bays. A moderate-sized, long-billed sparrow, it exhibits a whitish or pale buffy throat and whitish underparts, with distinct crisp streaks across the chest and down the flanks. Structurally it is intermediate between Nelson's and Seaside, but most often it is confused with Nelson's. To separate one from a Nelson's, consider the differences noted above, and note that Saltmarsh typically shows noticeable dark lateral throat stripes (which separate the orange malar from the pale throat). Saltmarsh also looks rather long bodied and potbellied, and the orange areas of the head are brightest on the face, particularly the supercilium and malar. The pale throat makes it seem more similar to a Seaside at times, and indeed in late spring/summer a Saltmarsh that is worn can appear darker, brown backed, and white breasted, with the buff confined to the face. In parts of Maine, breeding Saltmarsh Sparrows overlap with nesting Acadian Nelson's (hybridizing to some degree), and there

Fresh basic Nelson's Sparrow, MA, Sep (JT) (left); adult Nelson's Sparrow, TX, Apr (BS) (right). In fresh plumage note orange face, breast, and flanks, with broad orange supercilium that lacks streaking, and flanks with fine dark streaking usually not connecting across the breast (cf. Saltmarsh Sparrow). The gray central crown stripe helps distinguish it from Le Conte's, as does the plain gray nape and boldly streaked back. In late spring most are relatively fresh as a result of a prealternate molt.

Nelson's Sparrow, subspecies *alterus*, NY, Oct (PS) (left); Nelson's Sparrow, subspecies *subvirgatus*, ME, Jun (BS) (right). Nelson's Sparrow comprises three subspecies, two of which are distinctive. The widespread nominate subspecies *nelsoni* (top two birds) is brightest and most colorful overall, whereas the subspecies *subvirgatus* (right), breeding in coastal marshes of the Northeast and Atlantic Canada, is much drabber overall, washed grayish on the flanks and back, with muted streaking and dingier overall appearance. Subspecies *alterus* is rather poorly known and confusing; most look more like *nelsoni*, with grayish-washed upperparts and flanks (left).

Breeding Nelson's Sparrow, ND, Jun (BLS) (left); typical view of a wintering Nelson's Sparrow in coastal marsh, MD, May (BH). Breeding birds become very worn with "contrasty" upperparts; note broad buffy supercilium and gray crown and nape. In a typical distant view, note the buffy-orange face, flanks, and breast, and the lack of strong streaking across the breast.

Fresh basic Saltmarsh Sparrow, FL, Feb (DB) (left); breeding Saltmarsh Sparrow, ME, Jun (BS) (right). Note buffy-orange face contrasting with whiter flanks and breast; flanks are heavily streaked usually continuing across the breast, though in some cases it can be fine in the middle of the breast. Compared with that of Nelson's, the supercilium is usually more muddied, especially behind the eye, where dark streaking or grayish intrusions are often present. Saltmarsh averages longer billed than most Nelson's.

Worn breeding Saltmarsh Sparrow, subspecies *caudacutus*, CT, Jun (MS) (left); basic Saltmarsh Sparrow, subspecies *diversus*, FL, Dec (DB). Northern breeding Saltmarsh Sparrows, subspecies *caudacutus*, average paler on the back and tertials (see two photos above, and left here), whereas the more southern-breeding subspecies, *diversus* (right), averages darker dorsally and might be more easily confused with interior Nelson's. Note the wholly blackish tertial centers on this bird that confirm the subspecies ID, and the streaked rear supercilium that distinguishes it from Nelson's.

Fresh basic Saltmarsh Sparrow, MA, Feb (JT); typical view of a wintering Saltmarsh Sparrow, NC, Dec (BLS) (right). In fresh basic plumage, many Saltmarsh Sparrows can have some buff color on the flanks and breast, making them more similar to Nelson's. In a typical distant view, note colorful face with paler whitish-buff underparts, and distinct streaking extending across the breast.

Worn breeding Seaside Sparrow, MD, Jul (GLA) (left); fresh basic Seaside Sparrow, LA, Oct (GV) (right). Seaside Sparrow differs from the rest in being overall duskier grayish, with the most notable color in the bright yellow supraloral spot. It is also larger, longer tailed, and longer billed, and more conspicuous. Three main subspecies groups exist but there is plumage overlap. Gulf Coast breeders (right) average more colorful than Atlantic breeders (left), usually showing buffy streaking on the breast and a buffy auricular border.

Fresh basic "Atlantic" Seaside Sparrow, GA, Dec (ES) (left); worn alternate Seaside Sparrow, coastal FL, May (RG). These birds highlight how variable Seaside Sparrow can be. In fresh plumage, even Atlantic breeders can be quite colorful. In worn plumage, Gulf Coast breeders (right) can appear as drab as Atlantic birds. Species identification, however, is straightforward!

Cape Sable Seaside Sparrow, FL, Apr (BS); juvenile Seaside Sparrow, DE, Jul (GLA) (right). Cape Sable Seaside Sparrow is distinct in having strongly streaked underparts, different voice and breeding biology; breeds in freshwater marshes of interior Florida. Juvenile Seaside Sparrows are frequently confused with Saltmarsh and Nelson's sparrows. Juvenile Seaside is variable but averages paler below than juvenile Saltmarsh, with bold yellow supraloral contrasting with a grayer rear supercilium.

Natural History Note:

Male Saltmarsh Sparrows lack territories, instead patrolling a "home range" that overlaps with that of other males and females. Within that range, they sing from perches and search for females, and any female they encounter they try to mate with, whether she is interested or not. In some cases females are pursued by multiple males at the same time. With no territories to protect or offer, males compete to produce sperm and to increase mating frequency. As a result, the testes of male Saltmarsh Sparrows are much larger than those of their congeners,[17] and the flight song appears greatly suppressed.[18]

The story of the Dusky Seaside Sparrow is sad. In 1963, Merritt Island National Wildlife Refuge was created to protect around a thousand individuals resident there. But the bird's habitat requirements were poorly understood, and land management practices (e.g., mosquito control ditching) flooded the marshes there; after just a few unproductive breeding seasons, almost none remained.[17] By 1980 only six individuals were left, and all were males. Five were taken into a captive rearing program to see whether the subspecies could be propagated through pairing with adjacent peninsular Florida races, but that was unsuccessful, so the Dusky Seaside Sparrow was lost to extinction.

Today, the Cape Sable Seaside Sparrow is threatened and losing ground in the Florida Everglades, with only about three thousand birds remaining.[9, 19] It is unique among Seaside Sparrows in its use of freshwater marshes. Its vocalizations and appearance are unique also, suggesting that it may warrant further consideration as a species. It is declining because of changing water levels and fire regimes, which prevent it from breeding in historically suitable habitat.[9]

Saltmarsh prefers more saline marshes in coastal areas, while Nelson's occupies more upland brackish areas.

Juveniles often look fluffy and unkempt and show a hint of the yellowish gape. The face is not as rich orange compared to that of adults, and the supercilium shows some dark streaks. They show little contrast between the belly and breast but are more wholly buffy below, with shorter and fainter streaks across the chest and flanks.

SEASIDE SPARROW: This sparrow of salt and brackish marshes along the Atlantic and Gulf coasts is more conspicuous than the other marsh sparrows. It often gives its relatively loud song from more prominent perches and feeds almost shorebird like amid open soil, using its long bill to pick bugs and invertebrates. This is the largest and darkest marsh sparrow, and with its heavy bill, overzealous birders might easily mistake it for a Black Rail, especially when it is flying or darting across the mud and into the marsh. Notice the prominent white throat patch. The pale throat is bordered with broad, dark, lateral throat stripes, while the malar is cream or pale buff. The yellow supraloral spot above the eye varies in prominence but is usually noticeable.

While the above patterns hold up throughout its range, Seaside Sparrow varies in appearance regionally, with Gulf Coast birds averaging richer in color and having more distinct breast streaking. The "Cape Sable" Seaside Sparrow is distinctive, with white underparts and heavy blackish streaks. Generally, though, identification is not a problem even with the plumage variation, because no other sparrow combines the habits of this species with a dark overall plumage, large size, and white throat.

Juveniles are found from about June to September and are frequently misidentified, often as Saltmarsh Sparrows. Juvenile Seasides show paler underparts than the worn adults and may be buffy in places. Juvenile plumage is not seen away from the breeding grounds, so the adults that are present (both Seaside and Saltmarsh) usually appear quite worn. Also, compared to adult Saltmarsh, juvenile Seaside is duskier overall, with a whitish throat and malar, and it shows a hint of the supraloral yellow and maintains the long, heavy, mostly dark bill.

Nelson's Sparrow in breeding habitat, ND, Jun (BLS) (left); Saltmarsh Sparrow in breeding habitat, MD, Jun (BH) (right). Interior Nelson's and Le Conte's sparrows breed in similar habitat, usually wet meadows, fens, or rank fields. Saltmarsh Sparrow breeds and winters in salt marsh, but it shares that habitat during breeding with the Acadian Nelson's Sparrow, and in winter with Nelson's of all forms.

Le Conte's Sparrow winter habitat, MS, Dec (BLS). Le Conte's Sparrow typically winters well inland in more upland habitat than the others, usually steering clear of pure salt marsh. Across its winter range it uses wet, dank fields, usually with a good bit of residual grass matting the ground below. Le Conte's shares this habitat with both Grasshopper and Henslow's sparrows in winter, and Nelson's could be found in this habitat during migration but in winter uses mainly salt marsh.

Coastal salt marsh habitat used primarily by Saltmarsh and Nelson's sparrows in winter, MD, Oct (BH). If you hope to gain experience with the "marshland sparrows," you should key in on this type of habitat during migration and in winter, and you must exercise patience when trying to obtain views of these birds that will allow their identification.

References

[1] Holloway, J. E. 2003. Dictionary of Bird of the United States. Portland, OR: Timber Press.

[2] American Ornithologists' Union. 1995. Fortieth supplement to the American Ornithologists' Union Check-list of North American Birds. Auk 112:819–30.

[3] Smith, F. 2011. Photo essay: Subspecies of Saltmarsh Sparrow and Nelson's Sparrow. North American Birds: 65(2): 368–77.

[4] Shriver, W. G., J. P. Gibbs, P. D. Vickery, H. L. Gibbs, T. P. Hodgman, P. T. Jones, and C. N. Jacques. 2005. Concordance between morphological and molecular markers in assessing hybrdization between Sharp-tailed Sparrows in New England. Auk 122(1): 94–107.

[5] Walsh, J., A. I. Kovach, O. P. Lane, K. M. O'Brien, and K. J. Babbitt. 2011. Genetic barcode RFLP analysis of the Nelson's and Saltmarsh Sparrow hybrid zone. Wilson Journal of Ornithology 123(2): 316–22.

[6] McDonald, M. V. 1988. Status survey of two Florida Seaside Sparrows and taxonomic review of the Seaside Sparrow assemblage. Technical Report 32. Gainesville: Florida Cooperative Fish and Wildlife Research Unit, University of Florida. http://aquaticcommons.org/1133/

[7] Pyle, P. 1997. Identification Guide to North American birds: Part 1. Columbidae to Ploceidae. Bolinas, CA: Slate Creek Press.

[8] Nelson, W. S., T. Dean, and J. C. Avise. 2000. Matrilineal history of the endangered Cape Sable Seaside Sparrow inferred from mitochondrial DNA polymorphism. Molecular Ecology 9(6): 809–13.

[9] Post, W., W. Post, and J. S. Greenlaw. 2009. Seaside Sparrow (Ammodramus maritimus). The Birds of North America Online. A. Poole, ed. Ithaca, NY: Cornell Lab of Ornithology. http://bna.birds.cornell.edu/bna/species/127

[10] American Ornithologists' Union. 1957. Check-list of North American Birds. 5th ed. Washington, DC: American Ornithologists' Union.

[11] Post, W., and J. S. Greenlaw. 2000. The present and future of the Cape Sable Seaside Sparrow. Florida Field Naturalist 28(3): 93–110.

[12] Lorenz, S. 2013. Le Conte's Sparrow: A shy gnome of dense grassland. Bird-watcher's Digest 35(3) (January/February): 64–71.

[13] Lowther, P. E. 2005. Le Conte's Sparrow (Ammodramus leconteii). The Birds of North America Online. A. Poole, ed. Ithaca, NY: Cornell Lab of Ornithology. http://bna.birds.cornell.edu/bna/species/224

[14] Howell, S.N.G. 2010. Molt in North American Birds. New York: Houghton Mifflin.

[15] Bayard, T. S., and C. S. Elphick. 2011. Planning for sea level rise: Quantifying patterns of Saltmarsh Sparrow nest flooding under current sea level conditions. Auk 128:393–403.

[16] Shriver, G. 2000. Sharpen up on Sharp-tailed Sparrows: Sharp-tailed Sparrow Breeding Biology Project general information. http://virtualbirder.com/sts/research.html

[17] Elphick, C., J. B. Dunning Jr., and D. A. Sibley. 2001. The Sibley Guide to Bird Life and Behavior. New York: Alfred A. Knopf.

[18] Greenlaw, J. S., and J. D. Rising. 1994. Saltmarsh Sharp-tailed Sparrow (Ammodramus caudacutus). The Birds of North America Online. A. Poole, ed. Ithaca, NY: Cornell Lab of Ornithology. http://bna.birds.cornell.edu/bna/species/112

[19] Pimm, S. L., C. N. Jenkins, and S. Bass. 2007. Cape Sable Sparrow annual report 2007. Unpublished report. Homestead, FL: Everglades National Park.

Small Wrens
(*Troglodytes* **and** *Cistothorus*)

House Wren (*Troglodytes aedon*)

Winter Wren (*Troglodytes hiemalis*)

Pacific Wren (*Troglodytes pacificus*)

Sedge Wren (*Cistothorus platensis*)

Marsh Wren (*Cistothorus palustris*)

First Breeding:	1 year old
Breeding Strategy:	See Natural History Note
Lifespan:	Up to 9 years

Among the smallest of birds, wrens are like little brown, feathered mice, but what they lack in appearance they make up for with attitude and voice. Indeed, wrens are superlative songsters, and they possess a charming and fussy nature. Their intentions seem quite plain when they vocalize: scold notes are scratchy, curt, staccato expressions of indignation; songs are boisterous yet mechanical, chattering and chortling, proud declarations that warn rival males to come no closer, yet entice prospective females. Perpetually busy, wrens have a charm in seeming so overtly goal oriented, always achieving a purpose.

Wrens are members of the largely New World family Troglodytidae. Only the Eurasian Wren (*Troglodytes troglodytes*) is found outside the Americas, occurring across Eurasia and parts of North Africa. Just recently split from its North American relatives,[1] Eurasian Wren may yet represent multiple Old World species. Another eighty or so species are found in the Americas, and wrens reach their highest diversity in the tropics. The House Wren and the Sedge Wren are among the most widespread birds in the New World, ranging from Canada to Tierra del Fuego. All wrens have barred tails, a character unique to the family among the North American passerines. In North America, there are ten breeding wren species (but see Taxonomic Note). Here we focus on the five smaller species, in the genera *Troglodytes* and *Cistothorus*, which appear more closely related to one another than to other wrens. Unlike the others, they are migratory and share unsettled and interesting taxonomies.

Taxonomic Note:

Our understanding of wren taxonomy is evolving, but considering the expansive ranges of House Wren and Sedge Wren, it seems likely that each represents more than a single species. A dearth of information exists for some populations, and birders who record vocalizations and study the habits of these wrens can make real contributions to our collective understanding.

Marsh Wren also likely represents more than one species. There are vocally distinct eastern and western Marsh Wren groups, and where they overlap females choose males based on song type.[2,3] Though there are some average differences in appearance (see photos), the two are best separated using the introductory notes of their song (see voice). Interbreeding occurs along a band that runs north-south (about one hundred miles wide) in the northern Great Plains, from Nebraska north and west into Saskatchewan,[4] but the two segregate largely by range and song type. The two types employ different molt strategies, too. Both undergo a complete (prebasic) molt in the fall, but eastern Marsh Wren undergoes a substantial (at times complete) prealternate molt in the spring, while western Marsh Wren replaces few if any feathers in spring.[5,6]

Pacific Wren was split from Winter Wren in 2010, and both were simultaneously split from their Old World counterpart, Eurasian Wren.[1] The limits of contact between the breeding ranges of Winter and Pacific wrens, as well as the migration habits of Pacific Wren, remain poorly understood: it is largely resident, whereas Winter Wren is migratory. Also, given apparent differences between mainland and Bering Sea populations of Pacific Wren (including differences in song, size, bill length, and plumage), it seems possible that Bering Sea individuals represent yet another species. More study is needed.

Another question is whether the Eurasian Wren is more closely related to Winter Wren or to Pacific. Eurasian Wren's song is more similar to that of Winter Wren,[5] but Pacific Wren ranges fairly close to Eurasian, with many Pacifics breeding on the Bering Sea islands. Answers may lie in studying the call notes of these birds, which may be innate, rather than learned (as are their songs).[7]

Breeding Marsh Wren, WA, Apr (GV). If all of the small wrens were this conspicuous, we probably wouldn't be treating them here! Marsh Wren is less shy for a short while when breeding, perching prominently and bursting with song. But the others are more secretive, and birders tend to be less familiar with the small wrens during migration and winter, when they can be among the most skulking of birds. This chapter focuses on using a combination of plumage, sound, and habitat to help you identify these species.

Focus on: *Voice, Habitat and behavior, Structure, Plumage color and pattern*

Fresh basic House Wren, CA, Sep (BLS) (left); breeding House Wren, WA, May (GV) (right). The most widespread and familiar bird in this group, House Wrens are slim and relatively long tailed, and generally plain brownish gray overall with rusty brown tail, variable dark barring, and a paler throat with plain head and face. Western birds average paler and grayer than Eastern birds, but there is much overlap, and subspecies are not safely identified.

House Wren, eastern CA, Jun (BS) (left); House Wren, CT, May (MS) (right). Despite being photographed on opposite sides of the country, these two brownish examples of House Wren are very similar. Note slightly paler throat and more rusty-brown coloration toward the rear end, especially tail, vent, and rump. Some House Wrens show a very faint supercilium (left), but never as broad as in wren species that typically show bold eyebrows.

Worn breeding House Wren, CT, Jun (MS) (left); "Brown-throated" House Wren, AZ, Nov (LE) (right). In addition to being in worn breeding plumage, this eastern bird is much grayer overall, and hence more similar to typical western House Wrens. Arizona's "Brown-throated" House Wrens usually have more prominently barred underparts, warmer brown plumage including the throat, and a more prominent supercilium.

For all of their zeal and industry, wrens can be quite inconspicuous. Feeding on insects and spiders, they are usually near to the ground, amid thick vegetation, seldom venturing higher than a meter or two. House Wren is a backyard bird across much of the United States, and unlike the others it may sing from relatively high perches. Winter Wren is one of our most heralded songsters, but it becomes more mouse-like in its habits during migration and winter and is often confused with House Wren. Pacific Wren was only recently split from Winter Wren and the two are very similar in appearance, so its identification and distribution stands in need of clarification. Finally, despite being common in many areas, because of their secretive habits Sedge and Marsh wrens often remain unfamiliar to many birders.

Because it can be hard to get a good look at a wren, and because some species are unfamiliar, the wrens can present identification challenges. Voice, structure, and plumage characters usually easily separate these species, but wintering and migrating birds often do not allow extended study, and they can be silent for long periods. When you see a wren too briefly to identify it by sight alone, listen for distinctive call notes, note the general plumage and structure, and consider range, habitat, and behavior.

Hints and Considerations

- *Listen up!* Wrens are vocal. Even away from breeding areas, they frequently call, and their call notes are diagnostic and easily learned.
- Many times wrens are seen only briefly as they flit away into vegetation. Note the GISS and consider the habitat. Sedge Wren and Marsh Wren are strictly wetland species preferring marshes or wet meadows. *Troglodytes* wrens prefer wooded or brushy areas.
- Structurally, Winter Wrens and mainland Pacific Wrens are nearly identical in shape and size, but the other three species differ. Marsh and House wrens are chunkier, while Winter, Pacific, and Sedge are very small. All species cock their tails upward, especially when singing or agitated, and tail length is helpful in identification.
- Much remains to be learned about the status, distribution, and identification of Winter and Pacific wrens in the montane West and on the western Great Plains. Pay attention to their call notes—they differ!

Natural History Note:

The *Troglodytes* are seasonally monogamous (monogamous for a season), and nest duties are largely shared. House Wrens nest in cavities, and Winter and Pacific wrens nest in cavities too, as well as in cracks or crevices in stone or wood, or at the bases of them. Like a number of marsh passerines, *Cistothorus* wrens are typically polygynous, and the nest duties are performed mostly or entirely by the females, who select mates based on song and/or quality of their territory. Males in all wrens usually initiate nest building and may begin several nests before settling on one with a female.[5] Male wrens frequently build extra ("dummy") nests. These may function as a signal of fitness, aid in establishing territory, become nest sites in future years, or provide shelter for fledglings or adults in nonbreeding months.[5, 12] Sedge, Marsh, and House wrens are known to destroy the eggs, young, or nests of neighboring wrens or other birds in an attempt to improve their share of a site's available resources. This habit among House Wrens is thought to be one of the main causes for the massive decline of Bewick's Wren in the eastern United States.[13]

Identification

Though most species vary somewhat geographically, wrens appear the same year-round, regardless of age or sex, but because of their habits they can show considerable wear, especially in late summer. A prealternate molt is present among *Cistothorus* but absent in *Troglodytes*.[6]

HOUSE WREN: A common nester in suburban areas, backyards, and semiopen parks across the United States and southern Canada, the House Wren is conspicuous when breeding, as it sings frequently, at times from fairly high perches. It has less of an aversion to open spaces with sparse vegetation than the other wrens (though it overlaps with Bewick's Wren in these habitats in parts of the West). Breeders generally prefer open areas with scattered trees that border patches of dense cover (e.g., low bushes, hedges, brush, etc.). In the East, House Wren is often found in suburban yards near deciduous woods. In the West, it is more often in open woodlands. Most individuals migrate, and in winter House Wrens are less confiding and seldom sit out prominently, inhabiting low, brushy areas with thick, knee- to chest-high vegetation (behaving similarly to wintering Common Yellowthroat, and not so different from it in shape). The House Wren is adaptable, readily making use of bird houses and occurring in a wide variety of habitats.

Breeding Winter Wren, ME, Jun (BS) (left); fresh basic fall Winter Wren, ME, Oct (JT). Winter Wren looks similar year-round, though breeding birds can be a bit worn (left) compared with fresh fall birds (right). In general, Winter Wren is duskier and more compact overall than House Wren, with a bolder supercilium, and a shorter tail that is habitually cocked upward. Winter Wren is a champion skulker, and views like this require much patience.

Winter Wren, PA, Oct (GLA) (left); Winter Wren, ME, Oct (JT) (right). Winter Wren shows quite a bit of general plumage variation, ranging from paler, more contrastingly marked birds (left) to more rufescent-brown birds that are harder to distinguish from Pacific Wren (right and below).

Winter Wren, VA, Dec (GLA) (left); Winter Wren, AZ, Apr (TJ) (right). Birds such as this particularly rufescent example of a Winter Wren (left) must be identified by a combination of features. Confirmed records of Winter Wren in the West are relatively few but are increasing now because of the recent split and because more birders are paying attention to this identification issue. Always consider voice when attempting to identify an out-of-range Winter or Pacific wren.

Breeding Pacific Wren, BC, Mar (left) and Jun (right) (GB). Essentially identical in shape and structure to Winter Wren, Pacific Wren averages more rufescent overall, especially on the throat. Their songs differ along with their calls, and these are the best two features for definitive identification. Note stocky build with short tail typically cocked upward, rufous plumage, and relatively bold, but usually buffy, supercilium.

Fresh basic Pacific Wren, WA, Jan (BS) (left); Pacific Wren, CA, Sep (BLS) (right). Pacific Wrens breeding from southeast Alaska through California show relatively little plumage variation, and there is little seasonal change except through wear and molt. Fresh basic birds (left) may average more "contrasty" than worn birds, with dappled white spotting below and more prominent barring.

Pacific Wren, Bering Sea subspecies *alascensis*, Attu, AK, May (DG) (left); Pacific Wren in typical habitat, CA, Jul (BLS) (right). Pacific Wrens breeding on the Aleutians and Bering Sea islands average larger, longer billed, and paler than mainland forms. Can you find the Pacific Wren in this image (right)? Pacific Wren is a skulker, and birds typically don't stray far away from dense, rank undergrowth.

Breeding Sedge Wren, AB, Jun (GV). Sedge Wren is small and overall pale, with a rather colorful patterned appearance if seen well. It favors damp, grassy fields with scattered shrubs where it is more likely to be confused with a grassland sparrow than with another wren. Though it is superficially similar to Marsh Wren, note that Sedge Wren has more boldly patterned wings and a streaked crown.

Adult Sedge Wren, AB, Jun (GV) (left); adult Sedge Wren, ND, Jun (BS) (right). Sedge Wrens are active birds, flitting about grassy or reedy habitats, yet rarely showing themselves for any extended view. Note the expressive tail, frequently cocked above the back, particularly when excited.

Sedge Wren, VA, Dec (GLA) (left); Sedge Wren, MS, Dec (BLS) (right). During migration and winter, Sedge Wrens can be highly inconspicuous. A typical view consists of a small buffy bird with an orange rump shooting out from underfoot and dumping back into the grass 15 feet away. Remember, Sedge Wren rarely frequents salt marsh, and Marsh Wren rarely frequents grassy fields, so habitat is a useful clue in identification.

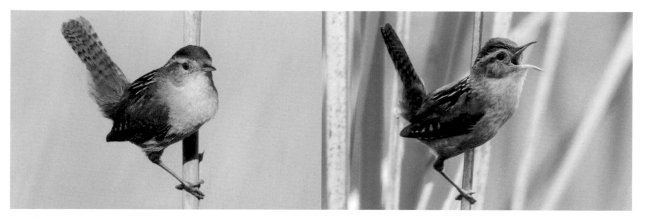

Breeding Marsh Wren, coastal WA, Apr (GV) (left); breeding Marsh Wren, interior CA, Feb (BS) (right). Marsh Wrens are larger, heavier billed, and more plainly patterned than Sedge Wrens. Eastern and Western Marsh Wrens differ greatly in voice, but less so in plumage. Coastal Pacific breeders (left) average darker and browner than interior West breeders, though identification to subspecies is based largely on range.

Western Marsh Wren, CO, Jul (TL); Eastern Marsh Wren, ON, May (AGa). When you compare Western (left) and Eastern (right) Marsh Wrens side by side, Western birds average paler overall and drabber, and they have pale tails with narrow barring. Eastern birds are darker tailed. Western birds apparently have little to no prealternate molt, which means they are in a more worn plumage state when breeding than Eastern birds. Western breeders sing much more complex and varied songs than Eastern breeders.

Breeding Eastern Marsh Wren, CT, Jun (MS) (left); "Worthington's" Marsh Wren, GA, Jun (ES) (right). These birds look quite different, right? Both are Marsh Wrens of the Eastern breeding group, but Marsh Wrens breeding locally along the Southeast coast, usually referred to as Worthington's Marsh Wren, are much drabber and dingier than surrounding populations. Might these also represent a distinct species? More study is needed.

Irresistible, amazing songsters, wrens have boisterous personalities and enigmatic habits. In some places, Marsh Wrens (here) nest in close proximity to Sedge Wrens, but Marsh Wrens are restricted to cattail marshes while Sedge Wrens occupy the surrounding wet meadows. Paying attention to these differences in habitat use will result in more rapid identifications (ND, Jun, BLS).

Compared to the other small wrens, House Wren is rather nondescript, with an even brown or gray-brown plumage lacking a bold head pattern, but it shows a relatively long tail, a moderately long bill, and often a whitish eye ring. Plumage varies somewhat, but all show fine dark barring on the wings and tail, and to a variable extent on the back as well. The legs are fleshy gray in color. The base of the mandible is usually pale horn or yellowish.

House Wren is most likely confused with Winter or Pacific wrens but differs from them in shape, being larger and longer with a longer tail, and it is more slender and less round. Its plumage is also paler brown and grayer, with less obvious barring on the rear flanks. Juvenile or worn adult Rock Wren might be confused with a House Wren, but Rock Wren is larger and heavier, with a longer and straighter bill, black legs, and buffy tail corners, and it usually perches upright on bare rocks. *Voice*: Song varies with range, but the quality and structure of song is recognizable everywhere. The song is a pleasing, distinctive, rapid, meandering warbling, mixed sometimes with a few warbling rattles. It often begins with several short warbles or chatters and ends with a couple of longer, shriller warbling trills (parts of it may recall the song of Lincoln's Sparrow). Calls include a muttered, stuttering chatter (similar to that of Ruby-crowned Kinglet; usually double noted) and a fussy rattling chatter.

WINTER WREN: A tiny brown golf ball of a bird, winter wren has a short, perpetually cocked tail and a fine black bill; there isn't a stubbier bird on our continent (except the similar Pacific Wren). This species prefers dense boreal forest, being especially fond of dark, dank, coniferous woods, and requires ample ground cover. It very much avoids open ground, moving mouse-like along overgrown logs, fallen branches, and brush piles, and is often found near drainages or low areas with water.

It is nearly identical in appearance to Pacific Wren, so you can't use GISS to separate the two, and voice alone is probably the one reliable means of separation—the call note in particular. In general, Pacific Wren is more uniformly ochraceous in color, lacking the plumage contrasts of Winter Wren, especially a notably pale throat. Like Pacific, Winter shows a distinct, short supercilium with a contrasting darker postocular stripe, but Winter averages whitish whereas Pacific Wren is a bit buffier. The dark barring on the rear flanks possibly averages more prominent and extensive in Winter Wren.[4] Both species may show variable tiny white spots in the shoulder area (tips of upperwing coverts), and whether there exists an average difference between the species on this character still needs study. Differences in plumage also require more study. *Voice*: Songs of Winter and Pacific wrens are similar in their superlative nature and are impressively robust, symphonic, and lengthy (sometimes ten seconds long). Both produce long songs containing many high-pitched trills mixed with a few odd, scattered, more singular notes. Though Pacific's song is more complex, this is difficult to appreciate in the field, and they differ most noticeably in the quality of their song. The trills in the song of Pacific Wren sound less rich and musical and more dry, buzzy, and thin, so the song is perhaps more twittering than warbling (more warbling in Winter Wren). Vocal differences are most apparent in the call notes. The common call of Winter Wren is a repeated "dip-dip," similar in quality to the familiar "chimp" call note of the Song Sparrow.

PACIFIC WREN: Best separated from Winter Wren by range and/or voice. The two overlap as breeders in northeastern British Columbia and western Alberta,[8] and the extent of their winter ranges still needs clarification. Generally, Pacific Wren is darker and richer reddish brown (especially below), but Bering Sea Pacific Wrens differ, being larger, longer billed, and more clay brown in color. In general, Pacific may average darker billed than Winter Wren but is similar in habits (though it frequents redwoods). Pacific is found in a wider variety of habitats. At the west end of its range, in the Bering Sea, it inhabits rocky cliff edges. In the Pacific Northwest, it breeds amid ground cover within old-growth forests, near streams, and in riparian areas.

Pacific Wren presents a combination of characters, the sum of which may be distinctive, but all require more study. Careful interpretation of field marks of a Pacific Wren should show a constellation of features that include a rufous-buff supercilium, with more russet throat and cheeks than in Winter, and a relatively clean chest and neck sides.[9] For extralimital claims of Pacific, the call note should be heard (or better yet, recorded) to confirm the identity. *Voice*: For song see Winter Wren, but note that the song varies considerably more than Winter Wren's does.[8] Male Pacifics may have many song variations. The distinctive call note is more abrupt, higher pitched, and often doubled. It is reminiscent of a Wilson's Warbler call note, a lip-smacking "tsik-tsik" or "chet . . . chit-chit."

SEDGE WREN: Uniquely small and straw buff, this species has an understated beauty. Because of the ephemeral nature of its breeding areas, Sedge Wren is unpredictable and nomadic in its occurrence, showing low fidelity to both sites and mates. It breeds mainly in the northern Great Plains, east through the Great Lakes region, and irregularly farther east. Sedge Wren winters along the Atlantic and Gulf coasts, as well as inland in wet fields along the coastal plain and piedmont. It is rare west of the Great Plains and in the Northeast. Generally it prefers moist grassy meadows or sedge marshes, and it is sometimes found in brackish or freshwater areas, but usually it avoids true saltmarsh (unlike Marsh Wren).

Sedge Wren is small, pale, and buffy, with a short bill and a medium-length tail. When seen well it is actually beautifully marked in buff and straw tones, with fine barring in the wings and tail. The crown is finely streaked with white, black, and brown. The bill is short and shows a mostly pale mandible (an old name is "Short-billed Marsh Wren"). The short, buffy supercilium is variably prominent but is offset by a darker, short, dusky-brown postocular stripe. In flight, Sedge Wren shows an orangish rump and so can be confused with the heavier, dumpier Le Conte's Sparrow, and the two overlap in habitat.

Sedge Wren is confused mainly with Marsh Wren, but Sedge is smaller and paler, has a shorter bill, and shows a finely streaked crown, as well as more patterned (checkered) wings. The back is also more boldly streaked with vertical black-and-white stripes. The scapulars and tertials are more patterned than in Marsh Wren, and Sedge shows little or no barring on the rear flanks. *Voice*: Song ensues with two or three dry introductory chips, followed by a rattle; the latter is similar in quality to that of a Common Yellowthroat. The common call (similar to the introductory notes of the song) recalls the chirping you hear under high-tension wires, an abrupt and understated "tsirt" or "tsit," sometimes doubled.

MARSH WREN: A small yet sturdy species, the Marsh Wren is set apart from the others by its whitish supercilium and longish bill, and its more conspicuous behavior when breeding. It is a widespread breeder in the northern half of the United States and in southern Canada, but most migrate to the southern United States or Mexico for the winter. Parts of the western United States, like much of the Atlantic and Gulf coasts, host Marsh Wrens year-round. Generally they prefer cattails or marshes with *Scirpus*, but they can be found in a variety of wetland habitats during migration.

Though some wrens vary in appearance with respect to range, Marsh Wren does so more than most (see photos and Taxonomic Note above). Regardless of the geographic variation, all Marsh Wrens show a medium-length tail, a solid black or brownish crown, and a pale supercilium that is offset by blackish lateral crown stripes. The mantle and rear crown are finely streaked, black with white. Note that the scapulars are unmarked brown (or gray brown) and contrast with the mostly black tertials. The crown, back, and tertials are usually similarly dark in color. The throat and belly are grayish white. The flanks are buffy or buff gray and sometimes show barring at the rear flanks and undertail. Confusion is most likely with Sedge Wren (see above). *Voice*: Song is introduced by one or several burbling or chirping notes, followed by a trilling rattle, perhaps transcribed "tuk-to, tee-eeh-eeh-eeh-eeh-eeh-eeh." Western-types begin their song with a couple of low "tuk" notes, the second of which is immediately followed by a mechanical trill. Eastern-types begin their song with buzzy and nasal "beer" or "bzt" notes and have a more musical trill.[10, 11] The common calls are a harsh, scolding "drrt, drrt . . . drrt, drrt, drrt," and so on, but they also give a blackbird-like "dek," which is at times repeated.

References

[1] American Ornithologists' Union. 2010. Fifty-first supplement to the American Ornithologists' Union Check-List of North American Birds. Auk 127(3): 726–44.

[2] Kroodsma, D. E., and J. Verner. 1987. Use of song repertoires among Marsh Wren populations. Auk 104:63–72.

[3] Kroodsma, D. E. 1989. Two North American song populations of the Marsh Wren reach distributional limits in the central Great Plains. Condor 91:332–40.

[4] Roberson, D. 2013. Monterrey Birds: Marsh Wren (*Cistothorus paludicus*). http://creagrus.home.montereybay.com/MTYbirdsMAWR.html

[5] Kroodsma, D. E., and J. Verner. 1997. Marsh Wren (*Cistothorus palustris*). The Birds of North America Online. A. Poole, ed. Ithaca, NY: Cornell Lab of Ornithology. http://bna.birds.cornell.edu/bna/species/308

[6] Howell, S.N.G. 2010. Molt in North American Birds. New York: Houghton Mifflin.

[7] Hejl, S. J., J. A. Holmes, and D. E. Kroodsma. 2002. Winter Wren (*Troglodytes troglodytes*). The Birds of North America Online. A. Poole, ed. Ithaca, NY: Cornell Lab of Ornithology. http://bna.birds.cornell.edu/bna/species/623

[8] Toews, D.P.L., and D. E. Irwin. 2008. Cryptic speciation in a Holarctic passerine revealed by genetic and bioacoustic analyses. Molecular Ecology 17(11): 2691–705.

[9] Sibley, D. A. 2011. Distinguishing Pacific and Winter Wrens. http://www.sibleyguides.com/2010/08/distinguishing-pacific-and-winter-wrens/

[10] Leukering, T., and N. Pieplow. 2010. Eastern and Western Marsh Wrens. Colorado Birds 44:61–66.

[11] Pieplow, N. 2010. Earbirding: Eastern and Western Marsh Wren. http://earbirding.com/blog/archives/1897

[12] Belles-Isles, J. C., and J. Picman. 1986. House Wren nest-destroying behavior. Condor 88:190–93.

[13] Kennedy, E. D., and D. W. White. 1997. Bewick's Wren (*Thryomanes bewickii*). The Birds of North America Online. A. Poole, ed. Ithaca, NY: Cornell Lab of Ornithology. http://bna.birds.cornell.edu/bna/species/315

Birds of Forest and Edge

Accipiters

American Rosefinches

These two very different groups share only a general preference for habitat, and each requires a different identification approach. Accipiters are most often seen in flight, when identification by GISS is most useful, but birders make many mistakes with identification when trying to identify these hawks when they are perched. The American rosefinches often offer good vocal clues and segregrate largely by habitat or range, but the species come into contact enough that misidentifications occur fairly regularly.

Accipiters

Sharp-shinned Hawk (*Accipiter striatus*)

Cooper's Hawk (*Accipiter cooperii*)

Northern Goshawk (*Accipiter gentilis*)

First Breeding:	Usually 2 years old
Breeding Strategy:	Monogamous; highly territorial
Lifespan:	Up to 20 years

Dynamic woodland hawks, accipiters are renowned for their agility and fierceness. With short, rounded wings they nimbly hunt land birds through dense forest, using their long tails to rudder around trees and branches. Their watchful, alert eyes are accentuated by the supraloral ridge and, combined with their overall sleek shape and hooked bill, create a stern, fierce, yet elegant impression. Surely it is these features along with this group's doggedness when pursuing prey that account for much of their immense popularity with birders. But despite being much loved, these three species are among the most frequently misidentified birds in North America! Indeed, the two smaller species, Sharp-shinned Hawk and Cooper's Hawk, are nearly identical in plumage at first glance, but subtle differences do exist. Goshawks are different, but generally scarce; they are on many birders' "most wanted" lists, and the two common accipiters are frequently misidentified as the

Natural History Note:

As in many predatory birds, female hawks are larger than males.[3] This is the opposite of most sexually dimorphic species. This disparity in size between smaller males and larger females is most noticeable in accipiters and may be correlated with an increased ability to hunt agile prey such as birds. The size differences are less striking in mammal-eating raptors, and nonexistent in carrion-eating vultures. Smaller land birds are more abundant than larger birds, and given that male hawks provision the female while she incubates, it stands to reason that females would favor smaller males who are more efficient hunters with a larger base of prey. And in places where breeding *Accipiter* species overlap, the differing sizes of the males may prevent them from competing with one another for prey.[4]

larger, more powerful Goshawk by overeager birders engaged in wishful thinking.

Accipiters are part of the large and diverse family Accipitridae, which also includes buteos, eagles, harriers, and kites. The genus *Accipiter* is the largest within the family, containing about fifty species worldwide,[1] with representatives on all continents except Antarctica, most of which are named "goshawks" or "sparrowhawks" (the latter not to be confused with the old American common name for the American Kestrel). Just three species of *Accipiter* reside in North America: Northern Goshawk is a Holarctic species; Cooper's Hawk is monotypic and confined to North America (Mexico and north); and Sharp-shinned Hawk is a more complex taxon, probably representing multiple species, found from Alaska south through Central America, the Greater Antilles, and into South America.

In North America, accipiters prefer woods or edge habitat. During the breeding season they become inconspicuous, but they are notoriously aggressive at nest sites, frequently driving humans or other predators away from nests through aerial attacks and alarming calls. Females are larger than males and perform virtually all the incubation, so they are seldom seen in summer; males provision the nest and are thus more visible while moving around hunting for prey. Early in the breeding season, adults (especially males) perform courtship flights in which they advertise their territory while slowly flapping their wings in an exaggerated manner,

Juvenile Cooper's Hawk, NV, Sep (BLS). Accipiters represent a bird identification challenge that ranks among the hardest in North America. Luckily, there are many places where you can compare them directly during migration. Practice makes perfect, and there's no substitute for spending time in the field watching these birds.

Focus on: *Structure, Flight style, Plumage, Tail pattern*

Perched accipiters present an especially vexing problem for birders, as the characters of wing shape and flight style are not apparent. On perched birds, a good study of the head can reveal a lot. In this image the species are purposefully not to scale, as judging size on a perched accipiter is often very difficult. Instead focus on the general differences in these juveniles. On Goshawk (left), note the broad white eyebrow flaring behind the eye, the big bill, peaked rear crown, and well-defined harrier-like facial disk. On Cooper's (middle), note the raised hackles, small-eyed appearance, and weak eyebrow. On Sharp-shinned (right), note the dove-headed appearance without a raised rear crown, big-eyed look, and messy eyebrow. Eye color can be helpful; Sharp-shinned usually has the yellowest eyes in early fall (all photos, JL).

usually flaring their bright white undertail coverts out at the base of the tail, and this courtship flight frequently confuses observers. Cooper's Hawks, especially, when performing these displays are misidentified as Goshawks because of their slow wingbeats.

Generally, accipiters are more obvious in winter, including when they perch quietly near bird feeders, waiting to ambush their prey. They become yet more conspicuous during migration, when passing hawk watches in large numbers. Juveniles tend to predominate at coastal passage sites, and they also tend to migrate earlier than adults in fall, when prey is more abundant.[2] It is at this season that observers can gain direct side-by-side comparative experience with all three species—something invaluable in learning to identify this group.

Hawks provide real identification challenges for beginners and experts alike. Frequently seen in flight or at a distance, hawks often represent a birders' first foray into learning how to identify birds by GISS, using a combination of shape and flight style. Mostly encountered in flight, when plumage details can be hard to discern, accipiters have relatively short, rounded wings and a long tail compared to falcons or other hawks, providing the genus with its unique shape. But learning the different shapes and flight styles of each *Accipiter* and understanding how these change under various weather and lighting conditions is key for species identification. When perched, accipiters can be surprisingly challenging to identify, and many are misidentified even by good

field birders. Building comparative experience takes time and effort but is essential for learning to distinguish these species. Fortunately, these hawks are seen together in numbers at many hawk migration points around the country, and hawk watches offer great opportunities to sharpen GISS birding skills, as you see dozens or even hundreds of hawks in a single day.

Hints and Considerations

- Distinguishing an accipiter from other types of hawk is an important first step. Appreciating structure and flight style are critical, both in distinguishing accipiters from other raptors and in separating accipters from each other.
  1. Small buteos (Red-shouldered and Broad-winged hawks) or perched buteos are confused with accipiters. Note breast pattern and structure.
  2. Falcons too provide confusion, and Merlin is close in size to smaller accipiters. Falcons are more streamlined and front heavy, have tapered, pointed wings, and typically fly with purpose and speed. Merlin is darker overall than accipiters and inhabits more open areas. It also has a proportionately bigger head, and large *dark* (not yellow or red!) eyes.
  3. Any raptor may intersperse bouts of flapping with gliding, but accipiters commonly fly this way. When hunting, they move more quickly and directly. They sometimes soar but do so less habitually than buteos.

- In the breeding season, usually just one accipiter is likely in a given area. In winter or in migration, Sharpies and Cooper's are widespread, overlap in habitat, and are common in suburban areas, where they hunt at feeders. Goshawks are scarce or rare across the continent and prefer larger birds or small mammals, and less disturbed habitats. They are reported disproportionately by overeager or casual birders, yet they are also occasionally overlooked because of their more furtive nature.

- Accipiters are often seen in flight, briefly and/or at a distance, so GISS is more important than general plumage pattern and is usually the first, best clue:

  1. Sharp-shinned Hawk is small and compact, with a slim, often squared tail, wings held pressed forward at the wrists, and snappy, rapid, powerless wingbeats.

  2. Cooper's is larger, lankier, and bigger headed, often has a broader, more rounded tail, and in the air offers a cross-like shape with wings held more straight out from the body, and powerful, stable flight.

  3. Goshawk is chesty and broad, with more tapered "hands" than the others; a long, broad tail, often with a graduated tip; and deep, powerful wingbeats. It is more of a chameleon than the others, at times appearing more like a buteo or even a large falcon.

- Remember, females are noticeably larger than males. Male Sharpies are tiny, but females are nearly the size of male Cooper's. Also, after eating, hawks show a full crop, and the "full-throated" appearance (somewhat recalling the coiled neck of a heron) can make the head appear larger.

- Though widespread and generally common, Sharp-shinned Hawks are in decline. They overlap with Cooper's in habitat but are even more strongly associated with dense forest and tend to breed in higher-elevation areas.

Identification

Females are larger in all species, and age is also important to consider. Accipiters have two plumage types: adult (blue gray/grayish above and barred below) and juvenile (brownish above and vertically streaked brownish below). Juvenile plumage is retained through the first year into the first summer, when accipiters molt into an adultlike plumage by the second fall. Goshawks may retain some juvenile flight feathers in the second year,

Taxonomic Note:

Sharp-shinned Hawk is a complex taxon comprising four groups (each perhaps a separate species), including Sharp-shinned Hawk (*A. s. striatus*) of North America, White-breasted Hawk (*A. s. chionogaster*) of Central America, Plain-breasted Hawk (*A. s. ventralis*) of northern and central South America, and Rufous-thighed Hawk (*A. s. erythronemius*) of eastern South America. A noteworthy form in North America is *A. s. perobscurus*, which apparently breeds only on the Queen Charlotte Islands of British Columbia and averages noticeably darker (especially as juveniles) than other forms.[5] *A s. venator* is endemic to Puerto Rico and is highly endangered (only ~150 individuals remain); it averages more rufous on the cheeks and flanks.

A subspecies of Northern Goshawk, *A. g. laingi*, breeds only on Queen Charlotte and Vancouver islands and north into southeast coastal Alaska. It averages darker, is smaller overall with smaller feet, has a more avian-based diet,[6] occurs in lower densities,[7] and differs somewhat genetically from surrounding populations of Goshawks.[6, 8, 9] The blackish-backed "Apache Goshawk," *A. g. apache*, of the montane Southwest is considered a valid subspecies by some authors, but its true status requires further study.

and Sharpies and Cooper's Hawks often retain a few brown upperwing or uppertail coverts into their second fall, but these can be hard to see in the field. Eye color changes from yellow in juveniles to orange red (adult females) or blood red (adult males). Second-year birds usually have intermediate orange eyes (both sexes). In adults, the sexes differ only marginally in plumage, as adult males are more richly colored with finer, more distinct markings. Voice is seldom useful when trying to distinguish species but is helpful in detection.

SHARP-SHINNED HAWK: Our smallest hawk, Sharpies are lightly built, with a smaller head and a shorter, slimmer, usually squarish tail tip. Males are particularly tiny, being nearly robin sized, usually with the slimmest tails that often show a square or notched tip. Females are obviously larger, with either a squared or slightly rounded tail tip, typically showing a narrow white terminal band, and thus more similar to Cooper's Hawk. Juveniles usually show more rusty fringes to their brown upperparts compared to the others and are buffy below, with fairly dense rufous-toned streaking that coalesces across the breast and belly, while the undertail coverts are typically white. *Flight:* Compact, light, and buoyant, Sharp-shinned is easily buffeted by strong wind. When gliding or soaring, it presses its shoulders forward, making the head appear small and on an even plane with the wrists. The tail appears short and narrow based, and the tip usually appears square tipped, but it can be slightly rounded or even notched. The wingbeats are rapid and stiff, given in the classic accipiter "flap-flap-glide" cadence. Sharpies seem to have to do a lot of flapping to get anywhere; the other two species are more powerful in flight. *Perched:* Sharpies are small, slim, and lightly built, with narrow shoulders and a shortish tail. The small, rounded head contributes to an often big-eyed expression, and it lacks the square-cut nape (caused by raised hackles) of Cooper's. The legs and feet are delicate, not thick and burly like those of the lankier Cooper's or the heavily built Goshawk. While leg size is useful in identification, the "sharp shins" are virtually useless as a field character for birders and are not especially noticeable even in the hand.

COOPER'S HAWK: Similar to Sharp-shinned Hawk in all plumages, this medium-large hawk has a larger-headed appearance and a longer, broader-based, more rounded tail on average. Cooper's is increasing across much of its range, especially on the northern periphery, often preferring slightly more open areas than Sharpie. It commonly frequents suburban areas and even takes up winter territories amid cities. Like Sharpie, Cooper's frequently perches in the branches of a tree but at times is more bold, also perching more conspicuously atop posts or poles.[10] Males are especially easy to confuse with larger female Sharpies and are best distinguished by shape, flight style, and subtle plumage differences. Adult males often show grayish cheeks, adult females usually orange cheeks.[11] Juveniles show buffy-rufous fringes to the brown upperparts, with a contrastingly tawny head and nape. They are white below, with sparse, narrow, dark-brown streaking that terminates above the undertail coverts. *Flight:* Compared to Sharpie, Cooper's generally appears heavier, more solidly built, and stable in flight, with longer and narrower wings, giving the bird a longer "hand." The tail is more substantial, long, and broad, and more rounded, often with a bold white tip (year-round, but less obvious on worn spring birds). Unlike Sharpie, Cooper's appears more stable in strong wind, rarely appearing buffeted or out of control. Cooper's larger head projects beyond

the wings noticeably, imparting a more cross-shaped appearance. In soaring birds, the wings are held nearly straight out from the body, with a straighter leading edge, emphasizing the big-headed appearance (head projection). Unlike the other two accipiters, Cooper's may show a slight dihedral when soaring (especially juveniles). Wingbeats are slightly heavier than those of Sharp-shinned but are still characterized as "snappy," with a similar overall cadence. *Perched:* Medium sized and more strongly built than Sharpie, Cooper's has broader shoulders, a longer and broader tail, thicker legs and toes, and a square-cut head with a small-eyed appearance. On adults note the blackish cap contrasting with the paler nape. (Sharpie is more concolorous, showing less contrast here). Juvenile Cooper's is more sparsely streaked below than Sharpie and has whiter underparts. The tail of a perched Cooper's is usually notably rounded, and some are strongly graduated, similar to that of Goshawk.

NORTHERN GOSHAWK: Very large, heavy, and chesty, Goshawk has broad shoulders, a bold, pale supercilium, and a thick tail base. This species is scarce, tolerating little human disturbance, and so inhabits mostly remote areas. In much of southern Canada and the United States this species occurs only in winter or during migration: peak migration is later in fall (October–November) and earlier in spring (February–March) than in the other accipiters. They periodically "invade" the Lower 48 in fall/winter in cycles that occur every ten years or so, when large numbers (sometimes hundreds in a day) are seen on migration at hawk watches around the Great Lakes, most notably at Hawk Ridge near Duluth, Minnesota. Such invasions are the result of a sudden crash in prey populations (especially snowshoe hare or grouse), forcing birds to move away from typical wintering areas. Despite their size, Goshawks are inconspicuous when roosting. They prefer mature forest with closed canopy[12] but in migration may be seen in more varied habitats. Always, Goshawks show a long, broad tail, which when closed tapers toward the tip (especially in adults), and the tail tip may be rounded or graduated and is usually a bold white. The powerful chest, big size, and broad shoulders result in a small-headed and short-tailed look, compared to Cooper's. The bold supercilium is whitish in adults and buffy in juveniles, and it widens behind the eye, often connecting across the nape. Other accipiters may show a smaller, less distinct supercilium. Among accipiters, adult Goshawks are uniquely plumaged,

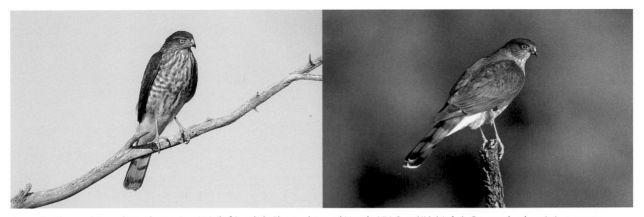

Juvenile Sharp-shinned Hawk, NJ, Oct (JL) (left); adult Sharp-shinned Hawk, NV, Sep (JL) (right). On perched accipiters, note overall shape, head and plumage details, and general size (if possible). Sharp-shinned Hawks are slim bodied, have skinny tails, usually with a squarish tip with little white, are round headed, and appear big eyed. They lack the raised hackles that create the square-headed look of Cooper's and Goshawk. Juveniles have distinctly rusty-toned streaking below.

Juvenile Cooper's Hawk, UT, Oct (JL) (left); adult Cooper's Hawk, UT, Oct (JL) (right). Cooper's Hawks are bulkier, with thicker legs and longer, broader tails that are usually rounded at the tip with bold white, are square headed (variable), and appear small eyed. Juveniles have finer, dark-brown streaking below, contrasting with a tawny head and pale belly. Adults have a distinct dark cap that contrasts with the paler nape (cf. adult Sharp-shinned).

Juvenile Northern Goshawk, OR, Feb (BLS) (left); adult Northern Goshawk, NV, Oct (JL) (right). Northern Goshawk is heavily built, with a broad chest and back, and a long, broad tail, usually with a strongly graduated tip; all have bold pale eyebrows. Juveniles have thick dark streaking below, usually including the undertail coverts, and upperparts that are spangled with buff. Adult males average bluer above and more finely vermiculated below.

Adults

Cooper's Hawk versus Sharp-shinned Hawk: Adults. On both pages of this plate, each pair of birds has a Cooper's on the left and a Sharp-shinned on the right. Note bluish upperparts and reddish-barred underparts of adults of both species. Females (left side of this page) are larger, bulkier, and drabber overall; males (right side of this page) are brighter colored and more compact. On Cooper's, note blackish cap contrasting with paler nape and back; longer, more rounded tail that is wider at the base; longer, narrower wings held straight out from the body; and big-headed appearance in flight (all photos BLS, except adult female Cooper's Hawk dorsal and Sharp-shinned Hawk in upper left pair, JL).

Juveniles

Cooper's Hawk versus Sharp-shinned Hawk: Juveniles. These juveniles share the same general structural differences as described for adults, though juveniles tend to be lankier overall than adults, especially females. Note longer, more rounded tail of Cooper's versus Sharp-shinned's narrow-based, usually more squarish-tipped tail. Sharp-shinneds push their wrists forward in all positions, masking the length of the head and making them appear smaller headed than Cooper's. Juvenile Cooper's are generally cleaner below, with more chocolate-toned streaking (rusty on Sharp-shinned), though there is much overlap. Also note the even more pronounced T-shaped flight profile of soaring juvenile Cooper's, with big head projecting past straight leading edge to wings (all photos BLS, except middle left juvenile dorsal Sharp-shinned Hawk, JL).

Northern Goshawk versus Cooper's and Sharp-shinned Hawks. Adult Northern Goshawks (top row this page) are so different that they are unlikely to be confused with other accipiters. But juveniles (middle and bottom left) share plumage similar to that of other juvenile accipiters and are more likely to be misidentified. On this plate, compare juvenile Goshawk with Cooper's (middle and lower middle) and Sharp-shinned (middle and bottom right). Goshawk averages more heavily streaked below, with dark chocolate streaking through the undertail coverts; it usually shows a broad white eyebrow, and the upperwing coverts are spangled with buffy, usually creating a buffy wing bar on the greater coverts. Also note Goshawk's broader-based, long tail with wavy pale highlights, wider secondaries, and tapered hands that create a more pointed-wing effect (all photos BLS, except juvenile dorsal Northern Goshawk, JL; adult dorsal and ventral Northern Goshawk, AH).

The bottom three pairs allow direct comparison of juvenile Goshawk with juvenile Cooper's (Goshawk on left in all pairs). Note heavier streaking below, broader secondaries, and more tapered hands, the latter especially notable when seen head-on (middle left). The trio at upper left shows two Goshawks and a juvenile Broad-winged Hawk (top right in that group). The foursome on the top right shows a juvenile Goshawk (left) with juvenile Cooper's (top), Red-tailed Hawk (bottom), and Red-shouldered Hawk (right). Note Goshawk's very large size for an accipiter compared with these buteos, its broad-based wings, and long tail, the length of which can be masked when fanned. Goshawks typically look small headed when soaring (all photos BLS, except top right, middle right, and lower left Northern Goshawk and lower left Cooper's Hawk, JL).

barred gray below and lacking rufous tones to the underparts. Adult males are bluish gray above and whitish below, with fine gray vermiculation. Adult females are slaty gray above and grayish below, with coarse gray vermiculation. Juveniles are brownish above, with gold and buff spangled spots, particularly on the upperwing coverts (forming a tawny wing bar) and on the nape. Juveniles show a fairly bold facial disk (unlike other accipiters), somewhat recalling the face of a Northern Harrier. Being scarce, Goshawks are also unfamiliar and so are confused with several hawks including the rare Gyrfalcon, and especially the small buteos. Shape is key. *Flight:* Unmistakably powerful, Goshawks often recall a small buteo, and because of their broad body Goshawks look shorter tailed than other accipiters (especially adults). Adults are more angular than other adult accipiters, with moderately pointed wings and a straight-cut trailing edge to the wings. Juveniles are lankier, with longer, tapered wing tips and more curved trailing edges to the wings. Juveniles have particularly long, broad tails. Goshawk's wingbeats are heavy and more labored than in the others; not as "snappy." Red-shouldered Hawk has square-cut (~rectangular) wing tips, whereas these are more tapered/pointed in Goshawk. Also on flying Red-shouldered, note the white crescents in the outer primaries, and how the wings are pressed forward, rather than held straight out from the body. Broad-winged Hawk can be more problematic, especially where the more angular adult Goshawks overlap with Broad-wingeds. When gliding, the two can be similar, but note that Broad-winged has a shorter tail and a slimmer build. *Perched:* Goshawks are large (about Red-shouldered Hawk–sized) and powerful, with broad shoulders and back and a wide tail base. The long, bold, pale supercilium is always a good field mark, and note the smallish head relative to the broad shoulders. Adults are distinctive with their unique plumage, but juveniles are more similar to other accipiters. Note the considerable gold-buff spangling above on juvenile Goshawks, especially on the greater upperwing coverts (other accipiters have variable but sparse whitish spotting above), and the nape and upper back are distinctly tawny on Goshawk. The underparts are buffy, with heavy, distinct dark-brown streaking that extends into and through the undertail coverts (typically unmarked white in the others). The dorsal tail pattern is distinctive, too, with wavy dark bands bordered boldly with buff. The tail is often graduated or wedge shaped on juveniles, with a bold white tip.

References

[1]Clements, J. F. 2007. The Clements Checklist of Birds of the World. Ithaca, NY: Cornell University Press.

[2]Delong, J. P., and S. W. Hoffman. 1999. Differential autumn migration of Sharp-shinned and Cooper's Hawks in western North America. Condor 101(3): 674–78.

[3]Smith, S. M. 1982. Raptor "reverse" dimorphism revisited: A new hypothesis. Oikos 39(1): 118–20.

[4]Reynolds, R. T. 1972. Sexual dimorphism in accipiter hawks: A new hypothesis. Condor 74:191–97.

[5]Bildstein, K. L., and K. Meyer. 2000. Sharp-shinned Hawk (*Accipiter striatus*). The Birds of North America Online. A. Poole, ed. Ithaca, NY: Cornell Lab of Ornithology. http://bna.birds.cornell.edu/bna/species/482

[6]McClaren, E. 2004. "Queen Charlotte" Goshawk *Accipiter gentilis laingi*. Accounts and Measures for Managing Identified Wildlife, version 2004. British Columbia Ministry of Water, Land and Air Protection. http://www.env.gov.bc.ca/wld/frpa/iwms/documents/Accounts_and_Measures_North.pdf

[7]US Fish and Wildlife Service. 2007. Queen Charlotte Goshawk: Status Review. Alaska Region, Juneau Fish and Wildlife Field Office, April 25.

[8]Gust, J. R., S. L. Talbot, G. K. Sage, S. A. Sonsthagen, T. Swem, D. Doyle, F. Doyle, P. Schempf, C. Flatten, and K. Titus. 2003. Genetic analysis of goshawks (*Accipiter gentilis*) of Alaska and British Columbia (abstract). In Raptor Research Foundation 2003 Annual Meeting—General Session. Anchorage, AK: Raptor Research Foundation.

[9]Talbot, S. L. 2006. Genetic characteristics of goshawks in northwest North America: Testing subspecies and Pleistocene refugium hypotheses (abstract). 4th North American Ornithological Conference, Veracruz, Mexico.

[10]Sibley, D. A. 2000. The Sibley Guide to Birds. New York: Alfred A. Knopf.

[11]Liguori, J. 2005. Hawks from Every Angle. Princeton, NJ: Princeton University Press.

[12]Squires, J. R., and R. T. Reynolds. 1997. Northern Goshawk (*Accipiter gentilis*). The Birds of North America Online. A. Poole, ed. Ithaca, NY: Cornell Lab of Ornithology. http://bna.birds.cornell.edu/bna/species/298

American Rosefinches

House Finch (*Haemorhous mexicanus*)

Purple Finch (*Haemorhous purpureus*)

Cassin's Finch (*Haemorhous cassinii*)

Also: Common Rosefinch **(*Carpodacus erythrinus*)**

First Breeding:	1–2 years old
Breeding Strategy:	Monogamous; territorial
Lifespan:	Up to 11 years

Charming, small, reddish or streaky brown finches of open woods or shrubby areas, these birds commonly visit feeders. With pleasant warbling songs they add lively melody and a splash of color to backyard settings across southern Canada and the Lower 48. Never far from trees or shrubs, they may feed on the ground and they use their stout, conical bills to wrestle fruit, buds, and seeds from shrubs and trees.

Until recently all were in the genus *Carpodacus*, but now the species breeding in North America are placed in the distinct New World genus *Haemorhous*.[1] Collectively, with the Old World genus *Carpodacus*, they are often referred to as "rosefinches," and all are part of the "true finch" family Fringillidae, a diverse and cosmopolitan family with members residing from remote oceanic islands (including the Hawaiian honeycreepers) to bleak deserts. As elsewhere in the world, many North American fringillids are alpine species, and several are nomadic or irruptive migrants. North American representatives include the *Haemorhous* and the related goldfinches, crossbills, and redpolls, among others. One *Carpodacus* from Eurasia, the Common Rosefinch, is a very rare vagrant to Alaska and California (see below).

American rosefinches are frequently found in pairs or small to medium-sized flocks; less commonly they are alone or in very large flocks (occasionally hundreds). All are strong fliers and move in typical undulating finch fashion, and some populations are migratory or nomadic, while others are more sedentary. They are often detected by their distinctive calls when flying high overhead, but these take practice to detect and learn. Rosefinches often feed unobtrusively in treetops, resting and preening there, but being expressive and vocal, they often let slip distinctive call notes. In fact, they are rabid songsters, and just a touch of sunshine at almost any time of year may be all the encouragement a male needs to begin chirping and warbling away. When taking to the air, especially, they call, declaring their identity with distinctive sounds.

All three *Haemorhous* are relatively common and easily encountered within the heart of their ranges, and during the breeding season identification is usually straightforward. Males sing persistently in spring and

Natural History Note:

The House Finch is native to western North America, breeding from southern British Columbia south through most of Mexico. But in 1940 it was introduced in New York, and its status has since changed rapidly. Caged bird traders released surpluses of "Hollywood Finches" on Long Island,[3] and they prospered. By 1990[4] the species was one of the most ubiquitous birds in the East, and it remains so today.

The decline of the eastern Purple Finch (by ~50 percent)[5] is eclipsed neatly by the ascension of the House Finch. House Finches are affected by mycoplasmal conjunctivitis, or "House Finch eye disease," a respiratory infection that causes inflammation around the eyes (especially the left eye),[6] which may swell to the point of blindness. Being social feeder birds, they easily spread the disease to other such birds at times, infecting also Purple Finch, American Goldfinch, Pine Grosbeak, and Evening Grosbeak. Keeping bird feeders clean helps limit the spread of this malady.[7]

Song is learned (not inherited) in these (cardueline) finches, and song mimicry occurs in many species. Lawrence's and Lesser goldfinches, Pine Grosbeak, Eurasian Greenfinch, and some *Haemorhous* finches incorporate elements of other species' songs into their own.[8, 9, 10] Cassin's and western Purple finches add pieces of song from other species too, including flickers, jays, Barn Swallow, towhees, Brown-headed Cowbird, American Goldfinch, and Pine Siskin.[11] Usually these sounds are part of a secondary ("whisper") song (A. Jaramillo, pers. comm.), not the primary song, and its function remains unclear.[10, 12] An understudied aspect among rosefinches is what appears to be a relatively high incidence of female song,[4, 11, 13] though first-spring males sing and resemble females, so it is difficult to tell whether a female-plumaged bird is actually a female.

Male House Finch, NM, Jan (RS) House Finch is the most widespread and familiar species in the North American group of "rosefinches," breeding across most of the Lower 48 and occurring frequently in the vicinity of human settlement. House Finches are emblematic of this group, with males showing a characteristic reddish plumage, and females showing a drabber, brownish-streaked plumage. This group is challenging primarily during migration and in winter, when the two other species wander, and the vagrant Common Rosefinch from Eurasia is also worthy of consideration.

Focus on: *Voice, Range, Habitat, Plumage (color and streaking), Bill shape*

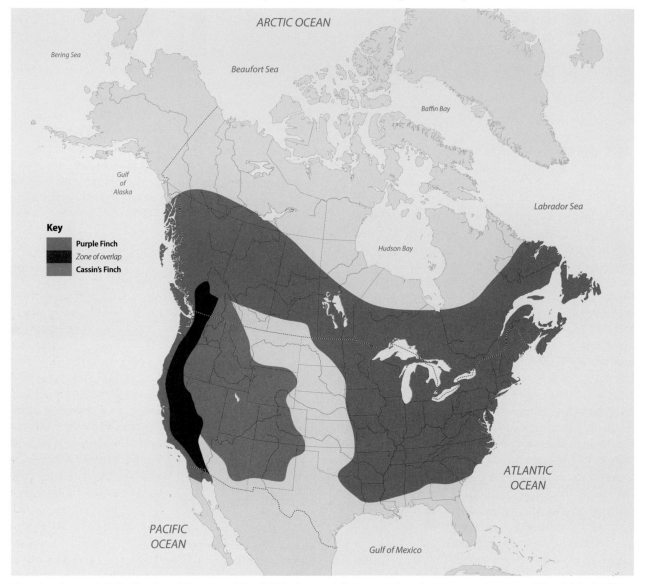

Map showing typical distribution of Purple and Cassin's finches, and the range of overlap between Purple and Cassin's in the West.

summer, and the species predictably segregate by range and somewhat by habitat as well. In fall and winter the lines become more blurred when they wander more, and there are also the drab, streaky brown juveniles to deal with. Some years, large autumn/winter "invasions" of Purple Finches occur in the East,[2] but even during noninvasion years, the separation of House and Purple finches is a regular challenge for birders there. In the West, all three species' ranges may overlap in certain areas, and there a combination of voice, plumage, and structure, along with an understanding of status and distribution, is key to distinguishing these finches.

Hints and Considerations

- *Listen up!* Vocalizations, especially flight calls, are a great tool for identification and detection.
- Aptly named, the House Finch is a common backyard bird, providing a good basis for comparison. Its range overlaps with that of the other two, but it prefers lower-elevation, more open suburban areas with scattered trees. Unlike the others, male House Finches vary widely in the color of head, breast, and back. So, male rosefinches appearing orange or yellow are likely to be House Finches.

- Cassin's and Purple finches are closely related, and both breed in the Sierras and Cascades and winter in the western Great Basin, but even in these areas of overlap they differ in habitat preferences. Occasionally during migration or invasions they may share habitat or join House Finches at feeders. Both have more deeply notched tails than House Finch.
- Cassin's is a high-elevation species (3,000–9,000 feet) of the interior West and prefers pine forest with some older trees.[13]
- Purple and Cassin's finches incorporate elements of other species' songs into their songs. Purple Finch has a particularly vireo-like call: winter or early spring reports of singing vireos often pertain to these finches.

Identification

Adult males of all species are variably reddish about the head, sometimes orange or yellow (especially in House Finch; only rarely in the others).[14] Females are brownish above and streaky brown and whitish below throughout the year, but their pattern becomes more faded and worn during spring and summer. Adults molt completely on the breeding grounds, a (prebasic) molt that results in a more subdued plumage on males, as red feathers are tipped buff brown. The buff wears away over winter, eventually revealing the familiar bright red coloration below by spring.

Juveniles of both sexes resemble adult females but show tawny-buff wing bars and loosely textured feathers throughout the underparts. First-year male plumage in *Haemorhous* appears variable and needs more study. First-year male Purple and Cassin's finches molt into a female-like plumage during their first fall and appear similar to females through their first spring (yet may sing vigorously and even breed).[15] Male Purple and Cassin's finches attain their red adult plumage in summer/fall of their second year, but first-year male House Finches seem to vary tremendously after their first molt, in both the extent and quality of red color attained. Some are similar to adult males, some show reduced red, some are marked in yellow or orange, and still others appear similar to females.[16] To identify a confusing first-year male rosefinch, focus on voice, structure, and plumage pattern.

HOUSE FINCH: Because of its affinity for suburban habitats, this species is the most familiar of the American rosefinches. Where its range overlaps with the others' it is usually absent in coniferous forests, dense woodlands, and at higher elevations (present up to ~6,000 feet).[4] Instead, House Finch prefers edge habitat and, true to its name, nests frequently in human-made structures, and so it is widespread and mainly resident (somewhat nomadic), showing considerable geographic and individual variation. Males vary in color and can appear yellow, orange, or red. The majority are red, but their color is determined by diet and is affected by the availability of carotenoid pigments when they are molting and growing new feathers.[17, 18] Male House Finch is the only rosefinch to regularly show such variable plumage color, and House is smaller and more slender than the others, with shorter wings (primary projection) and a longer, more shallowly notched tail. It is rounder headed than the others, with a short, stubby bill and a strongly decurved culmen. Many show wing bars, and when present these are pale buff, not reddish. *Male:* Variable but typically rose or orange red about the head and chest, males are brightest on the brow, malar, and throat. The red areas usually contrast quite sharply with the brown areas (especially the auriculars and back), and compared to the others, House Finch shows less red overall and has a browner back. The underparts are streaked along the flanks and belly with broad, diffuse brown streaks over off white or buff. *Female:* Nondescript, drab, and dingy gray brown overall, female House finches have an unmarked face (usually lacking any eye ring, pale supercilium, or much of a pale malar) and so show little contrast within the face. They have blurry brownish steaks below and are quite solidly brown backed, but they are overall paler dorsally compared to the other species. *Voice:* The call, often given in flight, is a rising, inquisitive "djip" or "fleep!" (abruptness varies). This may be combined with a longer, louder "djee-ip?" The song is drier and higher than in the others, beginning with rapid high, clear, chortled notes and then descending into more burry, jumbled phrases, usually ending with a longer slurred, burry note.

PURPLE FINCH: A chunky, bull-headed rosefinch with a short tail, Purple Finch comprises two subspecies with little range overlap. Compared to nominate eastern birds, the Pacific form (*H. p. californicus*) averages smaller and drabber (with less contrast between light and dark areas), shows more olive tones in the brown, has streaking on the undertail coverts, and shows shorter primary projection (being less migratory);

Breeding male House Finch, CA, May (BLS) (left); worn male House Finch, CA, Jul (BLS) (right). Male House Finches are typically brightest in color on the eyebrow, malar, and throat, and these reddish areas usually contrast with browner upperparts and ear coverts; some birds tending toward orange or yellow. Underparts are streaked brownish, usually with broad, diffuse streaks. The bill is stouter than that of the others, with a distinctly curved culmen.

Female House Finch, CT, Oct (MS) (left); female House Finch, CA, Jul (BLS) (right). On females note plain head pattern lacking strong contrast, rounded crown, weak eye ring, and diffusely streaked underparts. House Finches vary little seasonally, except through wear and fading.

Juvenile House Finch, CA, Jul (BLS) (left); immature male House Finch, CA, Sep (BLS) (right). Juveniles have loosely textured underparts and very fresh uniform coverts and tertials in late summer, when older birds are molting. Juveniles have rusty wing bars whereas fresh adults' are buff. Juveniles of both sexes are similar, but they quickly molt into formative plumage in early fall (right), when some males attain adultlike plumage, some look like females, and some are intermediate.

Male "Eastern" Purple Finch, CT, Oct (MS) (left); male "Pacific" Purple Finch, BC, Apr (GBe) (right). Note extensively reddish coloration extending to underparts, flanks, back, and rump, and peaked crown. Note browner ear coverts with pinkish-red supercilium, and larger bill than on House Finch. Underparts have blurry streaks. Pacific males average browner below and have shorter primary projection, though individual birds out of range should be identified to subspecies with care: pay attention to songs and calls!

Female "Eastern" Purple Finch, CT, Oct (MS) (left); female "Pacific" Purple Finch, CA, Dec (SNGH) (right). On females, note bolder head pattern than on House Finch, with prominent pale eyebrow and malar, longer wing tips, and shorter tail. The underparts are more distinctly streaked with dark brown. Pacific females average more muted in face pattern and underparts streaking.

First-winter "Eastern" Purple Finch, CT, Oct (MS) (left); juvenile "Pacific" Purple Finch, CA, Aug (SNGH) (right). Note uniformly fresh rusty wing bars; adult females have fainter buffy wing bars in fresh plumage. The bird at left has completed its preformative molt and is in first-winter plumage; the one at right is in full juvenile plumage. Unlike House Finch, Purple Finch molts into a female-like formative plumage that is kept through the first summer, so some first-spring males can breed (and sing!) in this female-like plumage.

the two differ vocally as well.[11, 19] Pacific females and immature males have drabber head patterns than eastern birds. Pacific adult males often have brownish-washed underparts, whereas eastern males are more overall reddish below. Aside from breeders in Canada or the occasional vagrant, Purple Finch is generally absent from the Rockies and the Great Plains. Western birds are largely sedentary, whereas eastern birds are migratory and irruptive. Purple Finch covers a greater elevational range than the others, however, and is found from the mountains to the coast.

Purple Finch overlaps infrequently with Cassin's and is more often confused with House Finch. Compared to House Finch, Purple is more robust and bull necked, and with its broader shoulders, it appears better built for the cold. It has a streakier back and looks more crested. The bill is short and thick, with only a slight curve to the culmen. It is a more retiring species, too, often taking cover in denser trees (e.g., conifer foliage). The migratory eastern Purple Finch shows relatively long primary projection compared to the mainly resident House Finch. *Male:* The adult male Purple is the most extensively colorful of the American rosefinches, with raspberry or pink rose (sometimes ~purple) on the head, breast, flanks, and rump. The wings and back are often suffused with pinkish red also. The head averages more extensively reddish down the nape and back than in the others. The flanks show only faint streaks and are usually mostly pinkish red (but Pacific birds can be washed brownish). *Female:* Eastern females appear more similar to Cassin's, whereas Pacific females are more similar to House Finch. Eastern females show a distinctive bold head pattern (more muted in Pacific birds). Dark auriculars are offset by a white supercilium and a pale malar, bordered by dark lateral throat streaking. Pacific birds appear similar in general structure to those in the East (but are slightly shorter winged) and can be separated from House Finch on structural characters. *Voice:* The flight call is a short, soft, dry "tik" or "pip," easily unnoticed if unfamiliar, but once learned it can be heard even at a considerable distance. The song is similar to that of Cassin's, a rising, fast, burbling, almost thrush-like ramble, occasionally with wren-like rattles. Eastern birds have a sing-song quality to their song, even-toned in a rambling way, perhaps similar to the song of eastern Warbling Vireo. But Pacific Purple Finch sounds more agitated, recalling a Bell's Vireo, being faster paced, shorter, and more jumbled, with a distinct rising and falling quality.

Both forms give a vireo-like phrase often transcribed as "teeeo." It is unclear whether eastern birds mimic to the extent that Pacific Purple Finches do.

CASSIN'S FINCH: The largest American rosefinch, with a heavy bill and a straight culmen, this species is confined to mountainous areas west of the Great Plains. Usually it stays in areas of middle to upper elevations (3,000–9,000 feet)[13] around pines, but it also nests in aspen, cottonwood, juniper, or even sagebrush.[20] Winter habitat is similar to that of nesting areas, but their movements are unpredictable and in need of further study;[13] periodic "irruptions" occur (presumably when food is scarce) when birds move south (even to central Mexico),[21] and some years this species is found widely and unpredictably in the West in fall/winter.[22] In general, birders in the West should be prepared to identify a vagrant Cassin's Finch just about anywhere, despite the relatively low likelihood of its occurrence outside the normal range.

Along with the heavy triangular bill and large size, note also the peaked crown, the crisp streaking (particularly on the back), the very long wings (suggesting that they likely move more often and farther than we know!), and the notably pale eye ring. Closer in structure to Purple Finch, Cassin's is heavier and larger billed and has finer, crisper streaking. *Male:* The red is usually confined to the crown, face, upper chest, and rump and so is less pervasive than in Purple, and Cassin's is less colorful in general. The distinct red cap is brighter than any other part of the bird, and it contrasts with the rest of the head. Streaking below is absent or sparse. If present it is usually confined to the rear flanks (many show it on the undertail coverts) and is finer and not as broad and blurry as in Purple (as if drawn by pencil rather than crayon). The back and wings show less color and are browner than Purple's, with distinct dark streaks. The flanks are often white but may be washed reddish. *Female:* Aside from the structural differences, compared to a female Pacific Purple, a female Cassin's shows crisper streaking overall, with finer streaking on the head and crown. The brown tones of Cassin's are often warmer and tawny, lacking the olive tones of Pacific Purple. Overall, Cassin's appears more colorful, streaky, and contrasting. *Voice:* The distinctive call is a whistled, upslurred "swi-sweee." Also a lower, modulated "te-deeoo" or "floo-eoo." The song is similar to Pacific Purple's but is drier, higher, less agitated, and often longer and more rambling.

Male Cassin's Finch, CA, Mar (BS) (left); male Cassin's Finch, OR, Jun (BS) (right). Cassin's Finch is larger and heavier than Purple Finch and has a bigger bill. Males are generally less reddish overall than Purple, with brightest red on the crown, and reddish pink extending onto the face, upper chest, and rump. The underparts are cleaner than on Purple Finch, with little to no streaking, except there is often distinct, very fine streaking on the undertail coverts. Cassin's bill has a triangular shape with a straight culmen; males average larger billed.

Male Cassin's Finch, OR, Aug (GB) (left); female Cassin's Finch, CA, Mar (BS) (right). Male Cassin's can have a distinctly pinkish quality to the plumage, and some are less colorful overall. Female Cassin's has a streaked overall appearance, with bold head pattern, notable white eye ring, and a distinctly golden tone to the darker ear covert patch.

Female Cassin's Finch, CA, Mar (BS) (left); female Cassin's Finch, OR, Jun (BS) (right). Like Purple Finches, male Cassin's Finches do not molt into a red adultlike plumage in the first fall; thus it is hard to say with certainty whether female-like birds are actually adult females, or immature males. Note the crisply streaked underparts, triangular bill with straight culmen, and golden-tinged ear covert patch.

Adult male Common Rosefinch, Siberia, May (OC) (left); female or immature male Common Rosefinch, AK, Aug (MT) (right). Common Rosefinch is highly unlikely outside western AK, and is very rare even there. However, given its similarity to other finches, could it be overlooked as a vagrant elsewhere? Note the adult male's head and chest are more evenly suffused with red. This species has a round head and a smallish, stubby bill with strongly curved culmen (a great field mark). Many show greenish tinged upperparts and greenish edges to the primaries and tail feathers.

Vagrants

Common Rosefinch (*C. erythrinus*) is a rare vagrant to western Alaska, where there are few records of any other type of rosefinch (and only Purple Finch is a rare vagrant). There is one fall record for California of Common Rosefinch, and the species could easily be overlooked in places where other rosefinches are numerous. Note the stubby bill with strongly decurved culmen in all ages and both sexes. Males are red, with a brown auricular patch. Females and first-year males are overall plain greenish brown and lack the broad blurry streaks of House Finch; they are instead marked more diffusely below, sometimes lacking streaking altogether. Note the very plain head pattern with a pale throat, lacking a contrasting supercilium or malar.

References

[1] Chesser, R. T., R. C. Banks, F. K. Barnes, C. Cicero, J. L. Dunn, A. W. Kratter, I. J. Lovette, P. C. Rasmussen, J. V. Remsen Jr., J. D. Rising, D. F. Stotz, and K. Winker. 2012. Fifty-third supplement to the American Ornithologists' Union Checklist of North American Birds. Auk 129(3): 573–88.

[2] Kennard, J. H. 1977. Biennial rhythm in Purple Finch migration. Bird-Banding 48:155–57.

[3] Elliot, J. J., and R. S. Arbib Jr. 1953. Origin and status of the House Finch in the eastern United States. Auk 70:31–37.

[4] Hill, G. E. 1993. House Finch (*Carpodacus mexicanus*). The Birds of North America Online. A. Poole, ed. Ithaca, NY: Cornell Lab of Ornithology. http://bna.birds.cornell.edu/bna/species/046

[5] Wootton, J. T. 1987. Interspecific competition between introduced House Finch populations and two associated passerine species. Oecologia 71:325–31.

[6] Davis, A. K. 2010. Mycoplasmal conjunctivitis in house finches (*Carpodacus mexicanus*) is more severe in left eyes than right. Avian Biology Research 3(4): 153–56.

[7] Cornell Lab of Ornithology. 2009. House Finch disease survey. http://www.birds.cornell.edu/hofi/hofifaqs.html

[8] Dawson, W. L. 1923. The Birds of California. Vol. 1. Los Angeles, CA: South Moulton.

[9] Guttinger, H. R. 1977. Variable and constant structures in greenfinch songs (*Chloris chloris*) in different locations. Behaviour 60:304–18.

[10] Watt, D. J., and E. J. Willoughby. 1999. Lesser Goldfinch (*Spinus psaltria*). The Birds of North America Online. A. Poole, ed. Ithaca, NY: Cornell Lab of Ornithology. http://bna.birds.cornell.edu/bna/species/392

[11] Wootton, J. T. 1996. Purple Finch (*Carpodacus purpureus*). The Birds of North America Online. A. Poole, ed. Ithaca, NY: Cornell Lab of Ornithology. http://bna.birds.cornell.edu/bna/species/208

[12] Goldwasser, S. 1987. Vocal appropriation in the Lesser Goldfinch. Master's thesis, University of Arizona, Tucson.

[13] Hahn, T. P. 1996. Cassin's Finch (*Carpodacus cassinii*). The Birds of North America Online. A. Poole, ed. Ithaca, NY: Cornell Lab of Ornithology. http://bna.birds.cornell.edu/bna/species/240

[14] Van Rossem, A. J. 1921. A yellow phase of the Cassin purple finch. Condor 23:163.

[15] Magee, M. J. 1924. Notes on the Purple Finch (*Carpodacus purpureus purpureus*). Auk 41:606–10.

[16] Howell, S.N.G. 2010. Molt in North American birds. New York: Houghton Mifflin.

[17] Brush, A. H., and D. M. Power. 1976. House Finch pigmentation: Carotenoid metabolism and the effect of diet. Auk 93:725–39.

[18] Hill, G. E. 1992. The proximate basis of variation in carotenoid pigmentation in male House Finches. Auk 109:1–12.

[19] Sibley, D. A. 2011. Sibley Guides. Identification of North American birds and trees. http://www.sibleyguides.com/2011/03/distinguishing-the-subspecies-of-purple-finch/

[20] Sullivan, S. L., W. H. Pyle, and S. G. Herman. 1986. Cassin's Finch nesting in big sagebrush. Condor 88.378–79.

[21] Howell, S.N.G., and S. Webb. 1995. A Guide to the Birds of Mexico and Northern Central America. New York: Oxford University Press.

[22] Willett, G. 1933. A revised list of the birds of southwestern California. Pacific Coast Avifauna 21.

Aerial Insectivores

Swifts

Superficially resembling swallows, swifts are more closely related to hummingbirds and are the lone group of aerial insectivores treated in this volume. Cryptically plumaged in black or charcoal brown, they hurtle through the air, usually high overhead, emitting characteristic vocalizations. Listen for their calls and pay attention to GISS, particularly their flight style. Nesting in areas difficult for humans to access, when away from breeding areas in winter North American swifts overlap in Central and South America with other nearly identical swift species. Combine these factors with their extremely aerial habits, and much remains to be learned about this fascinating group of birds.

Swifts

Chimney Swift (*Chaetura pelagica*)

Vaux's Swift (*Chaetura vauxi*)

White-throated Swift (*Aeronautes saxatalis*)

Black Swift (*Cypseloides niger*)

First Breeding:	1 year old
Breeding Strategy:	Monogamous; solitary or semicolonial
Lifespan:	Up to 16 years

Aptly named, swifts are fleet, consummate aerialists, sleek, dark birds with long, narrow wings and a plumage patterned in gray, black, and white. Foraging during the day at great heights, they nimbly hawk aerial plankton (e.g., winged ants, beetles, leafhoppers, bees, aphids, mayflies, spiders, etc.) with their small bills and wide mouths. Swifts comprise the family Apodidae, which contains some one hundred species worldwide,[1] among them some of the most enigmatic birds on the planet. Indeed, many species are poorly known because of their cryptic nesting habits and long-distance migrations, so swift taxonomy and identification remains unsettled in many areas. Many species comprise multiple subspecies, and future studies will likely reveal several of those as cryptic species.

Natural History Note:

Swifts nest in areas all but inaccessible to humans. The *Chaetura* species nest, often in nearly complete darkness, in large hollowed-out tree trunks, chimneys, or similar structures. They build nests from small twigs, moss, and their saliva and attach them to vertical surfaces. Bird's nest soup, a delicacy in China, is made from the nests of swiftlet (*Aerodramus*) species breeding in Southeast Asia, and these nests are made entirely from the bird's saliva.

Chimney Swifts prospered in eastern North America as chimneys became available, but they are now in decline as most modern chimneys preclude nesting, and as their prey base is also declining (especially beetles, perhaps a result of pesticide use).[15]

Black Swift is one of North America's most mysterious birds. Its population appears limited by the small number of suitable nesting areas.[8, 16] In 2009 biologists at the Rocky Mountain Bird Observatory retrieved geolocator devices placed on Black Swifts breeding in Colorado and were able to determine for the first time that these birds winter in the Amazon Basin of western Brazil.[17]

In North America nine species have occurred, but only four breed, and within them all three swift subfamilies are represented: Black Swift in the New World group Cypseloidinae; Chimney and Vaux's swifts in the spine-tailed group Chaeturinae; and White-throated Swift in Apodinae,[2] which all share a common unique foot structure with lateral grasping toes (similar to those of a koala or a chameleon).[3] Swifts are almost always seen in flight, and they may sleep and can even mate (!) while on the wing.[4, 5, 6] Breeding adults may cover one hundred miles a day on routine foraging flights,[7] and migrants travel farther still. Swifts land only at roosts or nest sites and cannot perch horizontally, instead clinging with their feet to sheer surfaces (e.g., chimneys, hollow trees, cliffs). Swifts show strong site fidelity, and pairs often return to the same nest site year after year, with nesting duties shared by both members of the pair.[6, 8]

In some places swifts are obvious, yet because of their habits seeing them well is difficult. They are best sought out during early morning, late afternoon, or in light rain, when they fly relatively low, joining flocks of swallows. Most North American swifts are highly migratory, vacating the ABA Area after breeding (October–March).

Distinguishing swifts from swallows and martins can be difficult, especially when they are flying high overhead. Can you pick out the three species of swifts among the swallows and martins shown here? See answers at the end of the chapter (all photos, BLS).

Focus on: *Structure, Voice, Dark/light patterns, Flight style, Tail shape*

White-throated Swift (left column) is easily distinguished by its white throat and belly, the white trailing edge to its secondaries, its large size, and its tail that is pointed when closed, or forked when spread. Black Swift (right column) is the largest, and wholly blackish overall. Tail shape varies from notched in males to squared or rounded in females and immatures; juveniles are scaled white below, at least into the first summer.

Chimney Swift

Vaux's Swift

Chimney (left column) and Vaux's (right column) are very difficult to distinguish in the field, except in the rare cases when they are seen together. Vaux's is smaller and slimmer and averages paler, especially on the rump, though there is great variation. Chimney is larger and has a slightly broader, more swollen-looking hand area (inner primaries), and though this is tough to see in the field, it can be captured in photos. These two species are best distinguished by voice; Vaux's has a higher-pitched, insect-like call (all photos, BLS).

Taxonomic Note:

Swifts, together with hummingbirds, comprise the order Apodiformes. The two families share a similar wing structure,[2] and during times of extreme cold both can assume a reduced metabolic state called torpor, which saves energy.[10]

Black Swift comprises three subspecies,[8] but only *C. n. borealis* is known from the ABA Area, though the smaller *C. n. niger* of the Caribbean could occur as a vagrant (and likely has). Given the disjunct breeding ranges of each, it seems likely that more than one species is involved, and the same is true for the polytypic Vaux's Swift. The winter range of the North American breeding form of Vaux's, *C. v. vauxi*, remains poorly understood, as it overlaps with similar congeners in Central America.

The names of certain swifts are cause for some confusion. Vaux's Swift is named for William S. Vaux, a mineralogist at the Academy of Natural Sciences of Philadelphia, and his name is pronounced "vawks." The origin of the species name of Chimney Swift, *pelagicus*, may be a misspelling by Linnaeus of the Greek word *pelasgi*, a nomadic tribe from ancient Greece. The word *pelagicus* means "of the sea," which seems odd for this species, while a word attributing a nomadic and migratory nature makes more sense.[11]

But the movements of White-throated Swifts are less clear cut, and many commonly winter in the breeding range, especially the southern parts of California, Nevada, Arizona, New Mexico, and west Texas. During fall migration, Chimney and Vaux's swifts gather at nocturnal roost sites where large flocks (sometimes in the thousands) appear in spectacular huge vortices, towering above big chimneys before funneling into them with great speed, disappearing nearly all at once as the sun sets. Because of their highly aerial nature, major storms can carry swifts far off course. Hurricanes in the fall have displaced hundreds of Chimney Swifts to Atlantic Canada and occasionally even farther, to Greenland, Britain, and western Europe.[9]

With good views most swifts are readily identified, but Chimney and Vaux's (often referred to as "flying cigars") are extremely similar and even in ideal conditions are difficult to distinguish between. In less ideal conditions, all four species are potentially confused, and vagrants are possible too (though very rare) and could occur almost anywhere, especially along the coast during migration. Pay attention to structure, flight style, and voice. Except for the White-throated Swifts wintering in the Southwest, any swift seen in late fall or winter in the ABA Area merits scrutiny, and if possible thorough documentation. Surely, more so than other birds, some vagrant swifts go undetected because of their cryptic plumage and remote and mobile habits.

Hints and Considerations

- Superficially resembling swallows, swifts are faster, often fly higher and more directly, and have stiffer wingbeats and narrower wings (especially at the wing base).
- In most areas only one swift species is likely. In the East, Chimney Swift is the only species (vagrants are exceptional), and in the West, species overlap at times but usually segregate by habitat. Distinguishing between the two *Chaetura* is most problematic, but try to note any pale versus dark areas on the throat and rump, and note Chimney Swift's slightly broader inner wing (bulging at the inner primaries).[12]
- Black Swifts are scarce and rarely seen in the ABA Area away from known nesting areas. Unlike the other swifts, Black Swifts are essentially unknown on migration, with the only visible migration occurring along coastal southern California in May. In fall they simply disappear without a trace!
- From mid-October to mid-April, Chimney, Vaux's, and Black Swifts rarely occur in North America. Vaux's winters in small numbers in southern California (sometimes in concentrations nearing one hundred birds), but the other two species would be accidental during this season in North America.
- On the California coast in May, Vaux's Swifts feed in large flocks. Amid these flocks a few White-throated Swifts are often present, and sometimes there is a Black Swift or two as well. Such flocks present great opportunities to compare all three genera.
- Voice is most helpful, and often the point of first detection. Flocking birds are most vocal. At first swift voices may seem similar, but with a little practice you can tell that their hyper chattering calls differ significantly by species.
- To get a sense of a swift's structure, pay attention to the tail length, the presence or degree of a fork in the tail, and the length and breadth of the wings.

Identification

Sexes and ages are mostly similar, but juveniles show more distinct pale fringing, though this is often difficult to see in the field. Juvenile *Chaetura* have pale-fringed primaries, but fringes wear away soon after fledging. Juvenile Black Swifts have pale white fringes on the underparts, and White-throateds have pale fringes on the forehead and undertail coverts. Black Swifts molt on the nonbreeding grounds after migration; the others molt during the breeding season.[13]

CHIMNEY SWIFT: A small, dark "flying cigar," very similar to Vaux's Swift but larger and sturdier in flight, this species is widespread from the Great Plains eastward. Within its range it is typically the only swift around, but it strays regularly if rarely to southern California, even breeding there and into central California in very small numbers. Rarely seen in the ABA Area before March or after October, the species is a trans-Gulf migrant, wintering in the Upper Amazon Basin but breeding in urban and suburban areas (near chimneys), foraging widely, including over lakes and rivers. Appropriately, Chimney Swifts are sooty gray brown overall and show little plumage contrast, but they are palest ventrally on the throat, usually becoming increasingly dark blackish toward the vent. Dorsally they are palest on the rump (though not as pale as Vaux's). No subspecies are described, but those breeding on the Great Plains average paler, and this further complicates separating them from any Vaux's that might reach the region. Chimney Swift's large head and short, rounded tail give the impression of equal weight distribution in front of and behind the wings. The wings are short and bladelike, with a short "arm" (section of the wing between the body and the wrist). Typical flight is quick, with fast, snappy wingbeats, at times appearing spring loaded. They tend to soar more frequently than Vaux's, especially when breeding. Indeed, when Chimney is seen together with Vaux's, it appears distinctly larger and darker, at times almost recalling a Black Swift. Chimney Swifts seem to wander more widely and stray more often than Vaux's, but their similarities obscure a clear extralimital pattern. At close range, like Vaux's, they show short, stiff spines extending off the tail-feather shafts, which help provide support when at rest. *Voice:* Chimney Swifts produce distinctive twittering that is fast paced and moderately high pitched. Multiple calling birds can create a lilting, almost musically rhythmic series (ML Cat#: 134092).

VAUX'S SWIFT: Our tiniest swift, on average smaller and paler than Chimney Swift, Vaux's is a fairly common breeder in old-growth forests of the northern Rockies, Pacific Northwest, and south-central British Columbia. Generally present from April to October, it is exceptionally rare east of the Rockies (accidental to the Gulf Coast) and it is more dependent on forest, preferring hollow trees to chimneys, making it less urban than the Chimney Swift. But during migration large roosts do gather in chimneys. It averages darker backed and paler rumped than Chimney, and the paler gray rump contrasts more noticeably with the upperparts. Also, the dark belly/vent usually contrasts a little more with the throat, which averages slightly paler than in Chimney Swift. Overall, the plumage

Seeing a perched swift is always a treat, as these species are most at home in the air. On this Chimney Swift, note the very long wings, and the spiked tail typical of the genus *Chaetura*. OH, Jul (GLA).

pattern is similar but a little more contrasting than Chimney Swift's, with the lighter areas a bit more strongly demarcated (especially the rump). While it is slightly shorter tailed than Chimney, this is difficult or impossible to note in the field. *Voice:* Calls are similar in quality and cadence to those of Chimney, but higher pitched and quieter. It tends to be less vocal yet perhaps owns a more varied repertoire. The voice is often described as "insect-like."[12] (ML Cat#: 63130).

WHITE-THROATED SWIFT: A midsized slender swift with an elegant shape, contrasting plumage, and a long, forked tail, the White-throated prefers rocky cliffs in mountains and canyons, and it sometimes nests under bridges in surprisingly urban areas. Less territorial than *Chaetura*, it often nests semicolonially, and nonbreeders are yet more social, with winter roosts numbering at times in the hundreds.[14] Good views reveal extensive white patches from the chin to the belly, and also along the sides of the rump into the secondaries. These distinctive white areas can be hard to see at a distance or in bad light, and note that the vent is black, as is the middle of the rump. Larger than the two *Chaetura*, White-throated is more slender and buoyant on the wing. It has long wings and a slim body and appears slightly front heavy compared to the others. The long tail often appears pointed (so the bird looks pin tailed), but when fanned it is notched with a moderate fork. White-throated is the only swift in North America with a clear white breast and central belly, or with white-tipped secondaries, and the only species expected across much of the Southwest during winter. *Voice:* It is often easily detected by ear, even when high overhead. The gremlin-like calls are a distinctive, scratchy cascade, often agitated in tone. The moderately high-pitched, shrill twitter song usually descends in pitch and volume, becoming scratchier as it proceeds (ML Cat#: 164121).

BLACK SWIFT: Black Swift is uncommon and enigmatic, with a patchy distribution west of the Rockies. Present in the ABA Area mainly from May to September, even within its range it is never numerous and is rarely encountered away from known nesting sites. Linked closely to wet microclimates, Black Swifts nest mostly in remote, montane habitats behind waterfalls (!), or on rocky caves in sea cliffs. The limits of its nonbreeding range remain in need of clarification. Black Swifts winter in tropical South America (see

Natural History Note below), where the presence of other resident *Cypseloides* species (some nearly identical to Black Swift) obfuscate the boundaries of its nonbreeding distribution.

Compared to other swifts, Black Swift is more robust, as well as large, long winged, and dark. It generally flaps less hurriedly, with slower, more controlled wingbeats. But Black Swift is a chameleon, changing its shape with varying conditions, behavior, age, and sex. At times it can recall a Chimney Swift in structure; females and immatures especially have squared tails that can appear short. But adult males can appear very long tailed, and they frequently show a notably notched tail that sometimes appears quite forked. Determining age or sex in normal field conditions is often impossible, though.

Three forms of flight are observed: slow cruising with measured but flicking constant wingbeats, very fast pursuit flight with rapid wingbeats, and soaring and gliding on set wings. Black Swifts possess an amazing ability to quickly change direction, rocking back and forth and turning on a dime. They are blackish overall, but when they are seen well, a pale whitish brow is visible, and fresh birds (especially juveniles) show white fringing or even spotting on the belly, and sometimes on the entire underparts and neck. Unlike the other swifts, Black Swift has never been seen actively molting in North America,[7] so any species showing wing molt in summer is certainly not this species (compare Common Swift). *Voice:* Black Swifts are often quiet, but at times quite vocal, especially when in small groups or pairs. A sharp, evenly spaced "chip-chip-chip" when cruising accelerates into a Chimney Swift–like twitter during frequent aggressive encounters (ML Cat#: 164200).

Vagrant Swifts

Finding a vagrant swift is exceptionally thrilling, but documenting one is very difficult because of their speedy flight at high elevations. Moreover, even when they are documented well, our lack of knowledge about possible confusion species from South America and elsewhere makes coming to a firm identification difficult. At times, a vagrant swift is not identifiable to species. But chance favors the prepared observer. Knowing the migration timing of the expected swift species in your area will help you recognize a potential vagrant. For example, any swift seen in November across

White-collared Swifts are very large and have a prominent white collar. They are an exceptional vagrant to North America. Costa Rica, Nov (BLS).

Common Swift is distinctive in its large size, mainly black plumage with white throat, and long, forked tail. England, Aug (BLS).

White-throated Needletail, Australia, March (BLS). Big and strikingly patterned, this Asian swift occurs as a spring vagrant mainly in western Alaska.

the East should be documented carefully, as Chimney Swifts have largely left the ABA Area by this time, and vagrant swifts often occur in late autumn. In addition to the four regularly occurring North American species, the following five species have occurred as vagrants to the ABA Area (mostly in western Alaska, but they seem possible elsewhere). Always remember, extraordinary claims require extraordinary evidence, so be prepared to back up claims of any vagrant swift with photo or audio documentation.

White-collared Swift (*Streptoprocne zonaris*) is a large swift from Central and South America. Larger than Black Swift, it has a white collar that is usually visible but is less obvious on immatures. It is long tailed and often soars. Records exist for Florida, Texas, California, and Michigan.

White-throated Needletail (*Hirundapus caudacutus caudacutus*) is a gorgeous, large, Asian swift with several spring records from western Alaska. Stocky and marked with a bold white throat and a white *U*-shaped patch around the vent and flanks, it is otherwise dark brownish black, with a paler gray-brown mantle.

Common Swift (*Apus apus*) is a large, pale-throated, dark swift of Eurasia. Records exist for Alaska and Atlantic Canada (Miquelon Island, off Newfoundland). Sightings of large, all-dark swifts from the Atlantic Seaboard may pertain to this, or to vagrant Black Swifts. Compared to Black Swift, Common has a deeply forked tail and a pale throat.

Fork-tailed Swift (*Apus pacificus*) is an Asian species, and the most regular vagrant swift to western Alaska. It is large and dark, with a long, forked tail (pointed when closed), a paler throat, and a bold white rump patch.

Antillean Palm-Swift (*Tachornis phoenicobia*) is a small, well-marked Caribbean species with one Florida record. It is a distinctive blackish swift with a whitish throat and belly, a white rump, and a dark blackish cap. It flies low, with looser, bat-like wingbeats. The tail is long with a shallow notch.

References

[1] Clements, J. F. 2007. The Clements Checklist of Birds of the World. Ithaca, NY: Cornell University Press.

[2] Elphick, C., J. B. Dunning Jr., and D. A. Sibley. 2001. The Sibley Guide to Bird Life and Behavior. New York: Alfred A. Knopf.

[3] Collins, C. T. 1983. A reinterpretation of pamprodactyly in swifts: A convergent grasping mechanism in vertebrates. Auk 100:735–37.

[4] Chantler, P., and G. Drieseens. 1995. Swifts: A Guide to the Swifts and Treeswifts of the World. East Sussex: Pica Press.

[5] Cink, C. L., and C. T. Collins. 2002. Chimney Swift (*Chaetura pelagica*). The Birds of North America Online. A. Poole, ed. Ithaca, NY: Cornell Lab of Ornithology. http://bna.birds.cornell.edu/bna/species/646

[6] Bull, E. L., and C. T. Collins. 2007. Vaux's Swift (*Chaetura vauxi*). The Birds of North America Online. A. Poole, ed. Ithaca, NY: Cornell Lab of Ornithology. http://bna.birds.cornell.edu/bna/species/077

[7] Howell, S.N.G. 2010. Molt in North American Birds. New York: Houghton Mifflin.

[8] Lowther, P. E., and C. T. Collins. 2002. Black Swift (*Cypseloides niger*). The Birds of North America Online. A. Poole, ed. Ithaca, NY: Cornell Lab of Ornithology. http://bna.birds.cornell.edu/bna/species/676

[9] Alström, P., and P. Colston. 1991. A Field Guide to the Rare Birds of Britain and Europe. London: HarperCollins.

[10] Ramsey, J. J. 1970. Temperature changes in Chimney Swifts (*Chaetura pelagica*) at lowered environmental temperatures. Condor 72:225–29.

[11] Holloway, J. E. 2003. Dictionary of Birds of the United States. Portland, OR: Timber Press.

[12] Sibley, D. A. 2010. Identification challenge: Vaux's vs. Chimney Swift. http://www.sibleyguides.com/bird-info/vauxs-swift/

[13] Pyle, P. 1997. Identification Guide to North American Birds. Part I. Columbidae to Ploceidae. Bolinas, CA: Slate Creek Press.

[14] Ryan, T. P., and C. T. Collins. 2000. White-throated Swift (*Aeronautes saxatalis*). The Birds of North America Online. A. Poole, ed. Ithaca, NY: Cornell Lab of Ornithology. http://bna.birds.cornell.edu/bna/species/526

[15] Finity, L., J. P. Smol, T. K. Kyser, M. W. Reudink, J. M. Blais, C. Grooms, and J. J. Nocera. 2010. COS 26-5: Historical declines in Chimney Swift populations are associated with dramatic changes in insect prey consumption. http://eco.confex.com/eco/2010/techprogram/P26280.HTM

[16] Hess, P. 2009. News and notes: Black Swift nests. Birding Magazine 41(1): 27–28.

[17] Beason, J. P., C. Gunn, K. M. Potter, R. A. Sparks, and J. W. Fox. 2012. The northern Black Swift: Migration path and wintering area revealed. Wilson Journal of Ornithology 124:1–8.

Quiz photo answers: top row (left to right): Purple Martin, Vaux's Swift, Tree Swallow, Vaux's Swift. Upper middle: Purple Martin, Black Swift. Lower middle: White-throated Swift, Black Swift, Barn Swallow. Bottom: Vaux's Swift.

Night Birds

Screech-Owls

Nighthawks

Given their nocturnal habits, it is often difficult to see birds such as owls and nightjars, but hearing them is not uncommon. Owls hoot or make rolling whistled sounds that penetrate the dark hours, and they are strictly nocturnal in their movements. Nighthawks are in the nightjar family but differ from other nightjars in their more crepuscular nature, and they are even somewhat active during the day. The species within each group have unique voices, so when one is heard it is easily identified. Silent birds, though (when seen on day roosts, for example), represent real identification challenges. In these cases subtle plumage characters and structural features will aid identification, but there are other considerations as well.

Screech-Owls: An *"Otus"* and the *Megascops*

Eastern Screech-Owl (*Megascops asio*)

Western Screech-Owl (*Megascops kennicottii*)

Whiskered Screech-Owl (*Megascops trichopsis*)

Flammulated Owl (*Otus flammeolus*)

First Breeding:	1–2 years old
Breeding Strategy:	Monogamous; solitary nesters
Lifespan:	Up to 13 years (20 in captivity); 8 in Flammulated

These small, charming owls provide birders only infrequent and much-treasured sightings. Cryptically colored with patterns that provide camouflage amid the bark of their favorite trees, they roost in tree cavities, becoming active at night when they hunt for insects or small rodents. Members of the large worldwide family Strigidae, which contains roughly two hundred species, night-hunting owls like these have asymmetrical ear openings, useful in pinpointing prey. They also possess modified flight feathers with serrated edges that reduce drag, allowing them to fly noiselessly in the still night air. The screech-owls (*Megascops*) are a strictly New World group, reaching their highest diversity in the Neotropics. Because of their retiring nature, and the prevalence of polymorphism and geographic variation, much remains to be learned of them, and it is likely that cryptic species remain unrecognized. Flammulated Owl is different from the Screech-Owls and for the time being remains in the otherwise Old World genus *Otus* (the scops-owls). All four species treated here share unsettled taxonomies, but song is a good genetic marker because it is an inherited trait in owls.[1, 2] Some argue that vocalizations are so critical in the speciation of screech-owls that any variation in song indicates a species-level difference,[3] but more study is needed.

All four of these owls are quite similar in habits, spending the daylight hours at roosts, usually alone or in pairs, and they tend to prefer south-facing tree cavities or evergreens. Occasionally they are seen sunbathing in broad daylight while wedged against a tree trunk, or peering unobtrusively from cracks in trees, nest boxes, or old woodpecker holes. Pellets (indigestible masses of bones, fur, and/or cartilaginous material) indicate an owl roosting spot, and similarly, "whitewash" (droppings) in branches or on the ground can reveal a roosting owl. Sunbathing birds affect a fluffy, pudgy posture, with sleepy-looking eyes, but when a threat is perceived they assume a "snag posture" in which they elongate their bodies, narrow their eyes, and raise their ear tufts to mimic a broken branch and camouflage themselves. At night they take on a more relaxed, rotund posture, with eyes wide open and ear tufts flattened. Both males and females call, mostly at night, but occasionally also during the day, and males' voices are typically lower pitched. Often they opt to breed in nest boxes, so setting one up in your yard may prove rewarding for both you and the owls.

Despite their perceived scarcity, these owls are all quite common within their ranges. The three screech-owls are mostly resident, but some in northern populations may migrate short distances, and perhaps some elevational migration occurs as well (the extent of migration is clouded by a dispersal of juveniles away

The mysterious "McCall's" Eastern Screech-Owl, TX, Mar (GV). This fascinating group of small owls is a favorite among birders, and it's always a treat to happen across a day-roosting owl in a tree cavity. The species in this group are best distinguished by voice; silent day-roosting birds can be challenging. Mostly they segregate by range, but in certain areas several species occur together, making identification more challenging. Add to this the ongoing taxonomic uncertainties about some forms, such as the "McCall's" Screech-Owl of south Texas pictured here, and you have a very interesting group of birds indeed.

Focus on: *Voice, Range, Habitat, Bill color, Eye color, Underparts pattern*

Gray-morph Eastern Screech-Owl, WY, May (SB) (left); Gray-morph Eastern Screech-Owl, NY, Nov (GV) (right). All Eastern Screech-Owls have greenish bills and yellow eyes, but note how hard it can be to determine eye color on these day-roosting birds. The birds on this page are organized roughly from northwest to southeast in order to represent the geographic variation across this species' range. Gray morphs occur across the entire species' range (right), but average more common in the North and West. The palest birds, subspecies *M. a. maxwelliae* (left), occur on the Great Plains.

Rufous-morph Eastern Screech-Owl, OH, Mar (DBe) (left); gray-morph Eastern Screech-Owl, MD, Nov (BH) (right). Rufous-morph Eastern Screech-Owl is distinctive, with fox-red upperparts and ventral streaking. It is common in the East (~40 percent of birds), but rare on the Great Plains. In general, Eastern is more coarsely patterned below than Western, with stronger horizontal cross bars, but occasional eastern gray morphs are quite pale below (right).

"McCall's" Eastern Screech-Owl, south TX, Nov (GLA) (left); brown-morph Eastern Screech-Owl, FL, Jan (JG) (right). In south Texas, "McCall's" Eastern Screech-Owl occurs only in a gray morph, and its song apparently lacks the characteristic "whinny" of Eastern Screech-Owl heard across the rest of its range. In the Southeast and across Florida, brown morphs are more common. Note boldly marked underparts (right), with the thick cross bars typical of Eastern Screech-Owl.

Brown-morph Western Screech-Owl, BC, Jan (TS) (left); gray-morph Western Screech-Owl, MT, Jun (DC) (right). Bill color is generally blackish in Western, but in some birds the bill can be grayish with a pale tip. The birds on this page are organized roughly from northwest to southeast in order to represent the geographic variation across this species' range. Western Screech-Owl shows less marked polymorphism than Eastern, but it still shows plumage variation across its range. In the Northwest, birds can be brownish or even rufous (left), whereas the palest birds occur on the northeastern edge of the range (right).

Western Screech-Owl, southwestern CA, Mar (CM) (left); Western Screech-Owl, southeastern CA, Apr (BS) (right). In the southern half of Western Screech-Owl's range, birds are grayish, with variably dark upperparts and underparts. West of the Sierras, subspecies *M. k. bendirei* averages a bit browner overall, with finer markings below, yet shares the longer song of northern birds. In southeast California and across the interior West, the subspecies *M. k. aikeni* averages paler gray overall and sings the shorter song of southern birds (right).

Western Screech-Owl, AZ, Aug (BH) (left); Western Screech-Owl, Davis Mountains, TX, Jun (DH). Across the US-Mexican border region from southeast Arizona to Texas, birds average darker above and more coarsely marked below, and they sing the short song typical of southern birds.

from natal areas). Flammulated Owl, on the other hand, is highly migratory but is seldom encountered by birders during migration. Each of these owls is heard far more often than seen, so voice is the best tool for detection and identification. Silent birds pose problems, and day-roosting birds are not always positioned well for studied identification. All four are generally similar, but differences in plumage pattern, eye color, and bare parts exist, and most species segregate by range, and somewhat by habitat. These species are confusable mostly just with one another, but conceivably the diurnal Northern Pygmy-Owl or the tiny Elf Owl might be mistaken for one of the species covered here. But look closely at these little owls and consider that in the tropics new cryptic species are still being named, and that questions also remain about these birds here in North America. Are there new species right under our noses?

Hints and Considerations

- Voice is the best tool for detection and often for identification. Despite their name, screech-owls seldom screech but commonly give a distinctive series of gentle, hollow "toots"; Eastern Screech-Owl differs in giving a descending whinny also. Screech-owls have two song types: (1) a song to establish or advertise territory and (2) a courtship or pair-bonding song performed by both sexes in duet.[3] Males' voices are slightly lower pitched. Flammulated has a different vocal array, and pairs don't duet. Any owl species may give irregular barks, hisses, hiccups, and screeches, but these are seldom heard and little studied, and the sounds of juveniles remain inadequately studied.
- Like pygmy-owls in the West, Eastern Screech-Owls sometimes call in daylight, attracting mobbing passerines, and some birders imitate these calls to attract birds.
- From the Great Plains eastward, only Eastern Screech-Owl is typically encountered, but there are a handful of records of Flammulated Owl along the Gulf Coast (even from Florida), mainly during fall migration.
- West of the Great Plains, Western Screech-Owl overlaps with Flammulated Owl in range. Mostly they segregate by habitat, but at mid-elevations and in migration they may share habitat.
- In North America, Whiskered Screech-Owl's range is limited to southeast Arizona and southwest New Mexico, where its range overlaps at times with that of both Western Screech-Owl and Flammulated Owl.

Taxonomic Note:

Screech-owls were formerly placed in the genus *Otus*, with the smaller Old World scops-owls.[4] The taxonomic position of Flammulated Owl is unclear, and it may deserve its own genus, as it appears not to be especially closely related to the congeneric scops-owls, and perhaps only slightly more closely related to screech-owls.[5, 6]

Among the screech-owls (*Megascops*), little agreement exists as to the total number of species in the Americas, let alone subspecies. Screech-owls are largely nonmigratory and so show little gene flow, but they do show considerable geographic variation and polymorphism. Eastern and Western screech-owls were only just recognized as separate species in 1983;[7] hybrids occur rarely where ranges meet and may result from a lack of conspecific mates.[8] Whiskered Screech-Owl seems more closely related to the *Megascops* of South America than to either Eastern or Western screech-owls.[6] One form of Eastern Screech-Owl, *M. a. mccallii*, may merit species status, as it lacks the "whinny" call, does not occur in a red morph, averages smaller, and differs genetically from the others.[6] It occurs in south Texas from Big Bend National Park through the lower Rio Grande Valley and south into Mexico. Birds on the northern periphery of their range in the hill country of Texas are possibly intergrades or hybrids with Eastern, but more study is needed.

- Flammulated Owl has dark eyes; the screech-owls have yellow eyes.
- Screech-owls (*Megascops*) differ in their underparts pattern, and close examination of the breast and belly feathers, though differences are subtle, can be instructive. Bill color and foot size are also informative.

Identification

Sexes are similar, but in screech-owls females average larger. There is little seasonal variation, but worn birds (late spring/summer) may be paler and more washed out than fresh birds (fall/winter). All have ear tufts that are raised when birds are excited, or flattened, giving the head a rounder appearance. Occasionally, nestlings are discovered on branches near nests, and their downy plumage somewhat resembles that of the adults, but the feathers on the body and head are grayish, more loosely textured, and finely barred. Even at this early age Eastern Screech shows a pale bill, and Flammulated is best distinguished by its dark eyes.

EASTERN SCREECH-OWL: Ranging from the Great Plains eastward, Eastern Screech-Owl is fairly common and is generally the only small "eared" owl to occur. It overlaps with Western Screech-Owl in a few places, such as southeast Colorado, southwest Kansas, west Oklahoma, and Texas, and in these places gray morphs predominate, complicating identification. Eastern Screech-Owls occur in red, gray, and brown morphs, but the red and gray morphs are most common. The red morph is less successful in dry and dusty areas and is more common in warmer and/or humid areas, suburbia, and especially across the Southeast.[9, 10] It is rich reddish across the upperparts and fox red below. Gray morphs are more common in the northern and western portions of the range, and birds on the extreme northwest edge of the range (subspecies *M. a. maxelliae* of the northern Great Plains) are pale grayish overall. Gray morphs are rather like Western Screech-Owl, but note the generally narrower, dark vertical streaks below and the widely spaced yet distinct horizontal barring ("cross-hatching"). The brown morph is most common in the Southeast and Florida. In all morphs the bill is greenish or green gray with a horn-colored tip. Eastern Screech-Owl is generally browner than the others, but much variation exists. Its habits are very similar to those of Western, but Eastern prefers more humid woodlands. *Voice:* The monotone "trill" is a soft, even tremolo, lasting roughly five to seven seconds (sometimes falling in pitch and volume at the end) (ML Cat# 20434). The spooky descending "whinny" is often repeated in succession (ML Cat# 20427), especially later in the breeding season when used in territorial defense, often to expel alien juveniles searching for territory of their own.[10] Sometimes they also bark, hiss, chatter, and screech (especially when disturbed at the nest). In south Texas, "McCall's" Screech-Owl (*M. a. mccallii*), currently considered a subspecies of Eastern, lacks the whinny call and gives a different song that is faster and shorter than that of northern birds, sometimes with a somewhat more exasperated ending (ML Cat# 87462). At the northern periphery of its range in the hill country of Texas, this subspecies may breed with Easterns of the lower Great Plains (*M. a. hasbrouckii*), as birds there give a somewhat muted and restricted version of the whinny. More study is needed to clarify Eastern Screech-Owl subspecies.

WESTERN SCREECH-OWL: Very similar to its eastern counterpart, the Eastern Screech-Owl, Western is found mainly west of the Great Plains ranging from southeast Alaska south into Mexico. Western Screech prefers low-elevation woodlands, riparian areas, or desert washes and oases, and it is quite tolerant of humans, often nesting near houses or buildings. There is no red morph that rivals the fox-red morph of Eastern Screech-Owl, but about 7 percent of birds in the Pacific Northwest (*M. k. kennicottii*) are red-brown morphs (varying from dark fuscous to rich rufous).[11] Westerns have relatively large feet, which assist in the capture of small birds and rodents, and note its dark bill, which varies from being gray based with a pale tip to essentially black. Compared to that of Eastern, the vertical streaking below is bolder and wider, but the horizontal barring is finer and more closely spaced, creating a more complex pattern below. Western overlaps broadly in range with Flammulated Owl but is found generally at lower elevations, amid stands of deciduous trees or in more arid country. *Voice:* The most frequent call is a soft, staccato "bouncing ball song" that may run into a trill (ML Cat# 45181). They also give a soft, bubbling, two-part trill with a fast short trill, then a split-second pause, followed by a longer descending trill, perhaps transcribed as "brrrp-bu-bu-bu-bu-bu-bu" (ML Cat# 140262). They also give a series of burbling hoots, first rising and then descending, accelerating in the middle and slowing at the end: "bu-bup-bup-bu-bu-boo." This is generally longer in northern populations (eight to twelve notes) and shorter in the south (four to five notes); and these vocal differences remain in need of more study. They also give short "kek" notes (ML Cat# 47543).

WHISKERED SCREECH-OWL: A largely Central American species, this small screech-owl reaches the northern limit of its range in southeast Arizona and adjacent New Mexico. Only gray morphs are found in the United States. Whiskered Screech is less tolerant of human disturbance than Western, and its habitat requirements and the harshness of winter probably prevent it from ranging farther north. Compared to Western Screech, Whiskered is about 30 percent smaller and has smaller feet, as it feeds mostly on large arthropods. It prefers pine-oak woodlands at middle to upper elevations (3,000–9,000 feet) in canyons and riparian areas.[12, 13] It has stubbier ear tufts than Western, and the underparts are rather coarsely marked, more recalling an Eastern Screech-Owl but with darker and wider vertical shaft streaks. Both eye and bill color vary more than in other *Megascops*. The eyes are usually

Whiskered Screech-Owl, AZ, Apr (GV) (left) and (BS) (right). Whiskered Screech-Owl differs from Western in being more coarsely marked below and above, and in usually having a notably paler bill. Whiskered occurs at higher elevations, but there is broad overlap where both can be found together. In North America it occurs only in a gray morph, but some birds are tinged brown or buffy below, unlike the colder-colored, grayer Western Screech-Owls occurring nearby.

Whiskered Screech-Owls, AZ, May (left) and Apr (right) (BS). Unlike in Western Screech-Owl, eye color is somewhat variable in Whiskered Screech, ranging from typical yellow to tinged orange to strongly orange. Bill color is likewise variable but is generally pale.

Whiskered Screech-Owl, AZ, Apr (BS). Note variable head shape. Whiskered usually appears rounder headed than Western, with shorter ear tufts, but when raised the ear tufts can still be conspicuous. Field guides emphasize Whiskered's smaller feet (they eat more insects than Western), but this difference is very difficult to determine in the field, and even in photos.

Flammulated Owl, UT, Jun (BS) (left); Flammulated Owl, ID, Sep (AJe). Flammulated Owl is usually easily distinguished from the screech-owls by its dark brown eyes, and stubbier ear tufts that are usually held flat against the head, giving a typical smaller, round-headed appearance. Geographic variation is weak in Flammulated, but grayer birds (right) are more common across the interior West, while rustier birds predominate in the southern part of the range.

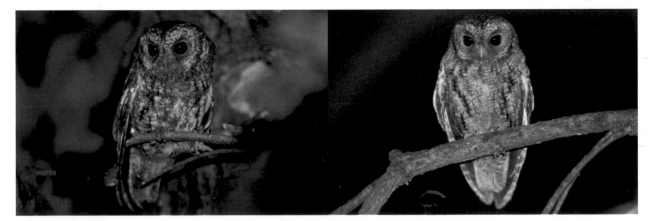

Flammulated Owls, AZ, May (BS). Flammulated Owl is fairly common throughout its middle-elevation habitats in the West, but it is seldom encountered by birders. It is a medium-distance migrant, wintering mainly in Mexico.

Flammulated Owl, AZ, May (BS) (left); Flammulated Owl, CO, May (CLW) (right). Like the screech-owls, Flammulated nests in tree cavities, and it readily takes to nest boxes. Unlike the screech-owls, Flammulated Owl is migratory, so vagrants do occur. The bird at right was at a migrant trap, and Flammulated has reached the Gulf Coast, Florida, and Texas on occasion. Is it overlooked as a vagrant to the East?

yellow but are sometimes orangish. Typically the bill is greenish, sometimes with a grayer tip, and paler than in Western. It averages more buffy and rufous tones overall than Western. The so-called whiskers (bristlelike extensions of facial disk feathers)[12] are not a useful field mark. *Voice:* The common song is a series of mellow monotone notes (six to eight), even-paced, rising slightly in the middle and trailing off a little at the end: "bu-bu-bu-bu-bu-bu-bu-bu" (ML Cat# 112622). When pairs duet they give a Morse code–like staccato "bu-dup-bu-bu, bu-dup-bu-bu" (ML Cat# 140238); the latter is frequently given in pair communication and pair bonding. Song pace varies and is perhaps faster when agitated.

FLAMMULATED OWL: This tiny migrant owl is not a screech-owl at all and is smaller even than the pygmy-owls; in North America it outsizes only the Elf Owl. Breeding in mature, mid- to high-elevation (1,500–3,000 feet, probably higher in places) forests of ponderosa pine, Douglas-fir, and to a lesser degree aspen and oak in western North America,[13, 14] it preys exclusively on insects, especially moths. Though seldom seen, it is fairly common, nesting from southern British Columbia south through the Rockies, but is absent on the immediate Pacific Coast. Flammulated Owl shows high fidelity at breeding sites, often returning to the same location for nesting,[14] and it too uses nest boxes.

Little is known of the wintering range in Mexico and northern Central America, and migration is poorly understood, but based on banding records routes seem to go mainly through the montane West. The most distinctive of these small owls, suffused with the eponymous rufous coloration, especially in the face and on the scapulars, unlike the screech-owls, Flammulated has dark eyes. Two morphs occur, a largely grayish one and a more rufous one, but the rufous markings and dark eyes distinguish it in all cases. Being a migrant, Flammulated has relatively longer wings compared to screech-owls, and its toes lack feathering, but this is rarely visible in the field. *Voice:* A unique structure to the syrinx allows deeper vocalizations than in the screech-owls.[15] The voice differs from that of *Megascops* in that Flammulated Owls do not duet or string notes together but instead give one or a series of deep, well-spaced (two to three seconds apart), single hoots (ML Cat# 47541). The sounds are reminiscent of, and at times confused with, those of Long-eared Owl. The loudest hoot is sometimes preceded by a short, doubled "ho-ho---hooo!" or just "ho-hooo!" Males call frequently early in the breeding season, but unmated males will continue broadcasting all summer. Both sexes give single ventriloquial hoots (contact calls), exceptionally hard to pinpoint, but females also give higher-pitched, whining, quavering calls.[16]

References

[1]Holt, D. W., and J. L. Petersen. 2000. Northern Pygmy-Owl (*Glaucidium gnoma*). The Birds of North America Online. A. Poole, ed. Ithaca, NY: Cornell Lab of Ornithology. http://bna.birds.cornell.edu/bna/species/494

[2]Howell, S.N.G., and M. B. Robbins. 1995. Species limits of the Least Pygmy-Owl (*Glaucidium minutissimum*) complex. Wilson Bulletin 107:7–25.

[3]Konig, C., F. Weick, and J. Becking. 1999. Owls: A Guide to Owls of the World. New Haven, CT: Yale University Press.

[4]Banks, R. C., C. Cicero, J. L. Dunn, A. W. Kratter, P. C. Rasmussen, J. V. Remsen, J. D. Rising, and D. F. Stotz. 2003. Forty-fourth supplement to the American Ornithologists' Union Check-list of North American Birds. Auk 120(3): 923–31.

[5] South American Classification Committee. 2003. Proposal #58: Elevate subgenus *Megascops* (New World *Otus*) to full generic status. http://www.museum.lsu.edu/~Remsen/SACCProp58.html

[6]Proudfoot, G. A., F. R. Gehlbach, and R. L. Honeycutt. 2007. Mitochondrial DNA variation and phylogeography of the Eastern and Western Screech-Owls. Condor 109(3): 617–27.

[7]American Ornithologists' Union. 1983. Check-list of North American Birds. 6th ed. Washington, DC: American Ornithologists' Union.

[8]Gehlbach, F. R. 2001. Western Screech-Owl (*Otus kennicottii*).

In Atlas of Texas Breeding Birds, edited by K. Arnold and K. Benson. College Station: Texas A&M University Press.

[9]Owen, D. F. 1963. Variation in North American screech owls and the subspecies concept. Systematic Zoology 2:8–14.

[10]Gehlbach, F. R. 1995. Eastern Screech-Owl (*Megascops asio*). The Birds of North America Online. A. Poole, ed. Ithaca, NY: Cornell Lab of Ornithology. http://bna.birds.cornell.edu/bna/species/165

[11]Marshall, J. T. 1967. Parallel variation in North and Middle American screech owls. Western Foundation of Vertebrate Zoology Monograph 1:1–72.

[12]Gehlbach, F. R., and N. Y. Gehlbach. 2000. Whiskered Screech-Owl (*Megascops trichopsis*). The Birds of North America Online. A. Poole, ed. Ithaca, NY: Cornell Lab of Ornithology. http://bna.birds.cornell.edu/bna/species/507

[13]Howell, S.N.G., and S. Webb. 1995. A Guide to the Birds of Mexico and Northern Central America. New York: Oxford University Press.

[14]Reynolds, R. T., and B. D. Linkhart. 1987. Fidelity to territory and mate in Flammulated Owls. In Biology and Conservation of Northern Forest Owls, edited by R. W. Nero, R. J. Clark, R. J. Knapton, and R. H. Hamre, 234–38. US Forest Service General Technical Report RM-142.

[15]Miller, A. H. 1947. A structural basis of the voice of the Flammulated Owl. Auk 64:133–35.

[16]Sibley, D. A. 2000. The Sibley Guide to Birds. New York: Alfred A. Knopf.

Nighthawks

Lesser Nighthawk (*Chordeiles acutipennis*)

Common Nighthawk (*Chordeiles minor*)

Antillean Nighthawk (*Chordeiles gundlachii*)

First Breeding:	1–2 years old
Breeding Strategy:	Seasonally monogamous (?); solitary nesters
Lifespan:	Up to 10 years

Natural History Note:

In very cold conditions that keep insect activity low, some nightjars (such as Common Poorwill and Whip-poor-will) have developed the ability to enter a state of reduced metabolic activity akin to hibernation, known as torpor. This ability to shut down all but the most basic life functions allows them to withstand periods when food is scarce, but nighthawks apparently enter torpor uncommonly,[13] and they appear poorly adapted to areas that are not warm enough to maintain a steady supply of insects.[4]

"Nighthawk" is an evocative word, but among birders it does not recall the slick, haunted "night owl" figures depicted in the famous Edward Hopper painting *Nighthawks*. For birders the word summons memories of warm orange sunsets, with agile nightjars erratically tracing silhouettes across a dusk sky, hawking insects and uttering alien sounds. But by any definition, nighthawks are cool.

Cryptically clad in brown, buff, and gray, they are fantastically camouflaged at roosts during the day, when they sit on tree branches or in gravel or sandy soil. And despite their name, these are not birds of prey but are instead members of the cosmopolitan nightjar family Caprimulgidae. Species in this enigmatic family are also referred to by the colorful yet misleading name "goatsuckers," and indeed, the word "Caprimulgidae" derives from the ancient and incorrect belief that these birds suckle milk from goats. In fact, nightjars are insectivores that use their small bills and very large mouths for capturing flying insects.

The nighthawks form a subfamily (Chordeilinae) of ten species, all confined to the New World, and compared to other nightjars, the nighthawks are more aerodynamic in shape, which facilitates their more aerial feeding habits. They also have smaller eyes and shorter rictal bristles (whiskers), and they are countershaded darker above and paler below. Not as strictly nocturnal as many other nightjars, nighthawks are sometimes active during the day, and they are most active at dusk and dawn. North American nighthawks are in the genus *Chordeiles*, which translates to "musical note at evening,"[1] a reference to the vociferous and crepuscular nature of these birds. In North America three species breed and each is migratory. From their nesting grounds they move south in the fall to spend winter in Central or South America, though some Lesser Nighthawks overwinter in California, Texas, and Florida. Their distribution away from breeding areas remains poorly understood, and winter sightings in the ABA Area are rare. Careful scrutiny should be applied to any vagrant nighthawk at this season.

Nighthawks are nearly always detected by voice, and in winter and fall they vocalize rarely or infrequently. Voice is also the chief means of identification, so when they aren't calling, determining species is difficult or even impossible in some cases. Fortunately, in North America nighthawks are found mainly in spring and summer, when they are vocal. Nesting and often roosting on open ground, because of their cryptic plumages they are surprisingly hard to spot in such areas. At dusk they take to the air, and in flight they move erratically but are buoyant and agile. Often seen hunting over open areas (even urban rooftops), nighthawks also frequent areas near railroad tracks or golf courses and forage over low scrub or brush.

Common Nighthawk is by far the most widespread and frequently encountered species, but Lesser Nighthawk is a common species in the arid Southwest from central California to south Texas. Antillean Nighthawk is a Caribbean species that barely reaches south Florida as a breeder and is foreign to most ABA Area birders. All three species stray on occasion, usually in autumn, and these migrants and vagrants pose real identification challenges.

Male Lesser Nighthawk, CA, Apr (BLS). Nighthawks are fascinating and enigmatic birds, unfamiliar to many birders because of their crepuscular nature, camouflaged plumage, and day-roosting behavior. Best identified by voice, they can be silent during migration, when several species' ranges overlap, making identification difficult. Subtle structural and plumage characters often help sort out silent birds, but distinguishing between Common and Antillean nighthawks is all but impossible, unless their vocalizations are heard.

Focus on: *Voice, Range, Migration timing, Primary extension, Plumage*

Nighthawks all have very small bills and very big mouths. In contrast to other nightjars, nighthawks lack long rictal bristles (whiskers) around the bill, and this helps quickly distinguish a perched nighthawk from other nightjars (LH).

Determining the age of nighthawks is relatively easy in summer when young first fledge, but it becomes increasingly difficult through fall as juveniles undergo a preformative molt and appear more adultlike before migration. Fresh juveniles have broad, pale fringes on the primary tips, and the primary tips are a bit more rounded than in adults. Overall, juvenile nighthawks exhibit a softer, more complicated plumage pattern than adults. In Common Nighthawk, geographic variation in juvenile plumage is pronounced, generally corresponding to broad patterns of variation in adults, but individual variation makes identification of any single nighthawk to subspecies problematic (BC, Aug, GB).

Hints and Considerations

- Compared to other nightjars, nighthawks are more crepuscular and social, and they have paler bellies, smaller heads, longer wings, shorter tails, and shorter rictal bristles. Nighthawks are more dynamic in flight, while nightjars feed only in darkness, sallying up from the ground or a tree to catch their prey.
- *Listen up!* Nighthawks are vocal and voice is the best tool for identification. The old common names are useful: Common Nighthawk was once known as "Booming" Nighthawk, and Lesser was formerly "Trilling" Nighthawk.
- The three nighthawks are similar in appearance, and silent perched birds are difficult to identify, but subtle patterns in the wings, and structural cues may permit identification.
- Antillean is rare in North America, regular only in the Florida Keys between April and September, and accidental elsewhere in North America. Common and Antillean appear nearly identical yet sound very different.
- Lesser Nighthawk differs in structure and plumage from the other two, possessing shorter, rounder wings, and spotted inner primaries.
- Lesser and Common differ in their migration timing, as in spring Lesser returns in late March/April, while Common appears later, in April/May. Both are early fall migrants, moving south in August/September. Any nighthawk found in North America from late December to mid-March is most likely a Lesser, but Common Nighthawks are being found with increasing regularity into December, so don't assume a later migrant is a Lesser.
- Different migration strategies mean different molt schedules, so Common Nighthawk (and probably Antillean too)[2, 3] replaces its flight feathers on the wintering grounds (November–January).[4] Lesser Nighthawk molts its flight feathers in late summer (July–September),[5] so a nighthawk seen in late summer that is molting its wing and tail feathers is almost certainly a Lesser.

Identification

All three nighthawks are cryptically plumaged in gray, black, brown, and buff with variable spotting and barring, and there is essentially no seasonal change in plumage, aside from wear and bleaching. All show notched tails, and when perched most show a small amount of white along the shoulder. Roosting on the ground, on posts, or on horizontal tree limbs, when in trees they orient themselves so as to be parallel to the branch. On roosting birds, the spacing of the primary tips may be a useful character, particularly the spacing between the first couple of primaries (but beware of molting birds).

An individual nighthawk can usually be categorized as belonging to one of three plumage types: male, female, or juvenile, but determining the age of nighthawks becomes difficult after early fall. After leaving the nest, juveniles wear a soft juvenile plumage, but this is soon replaced (in August–September) via a partial preformative molt of the head and body, after which they appear quite similar to adults. The juvenile flight feathers, however, are retained until the following late summer/fall[5] (until the second prebasic molt), and juveniles show nice crisp buffy-cinnamon edges to their primary tips.

The sexes differ subtly in plumage. Males have white throat patches, obvious white wing stripes, and a narrow white band on the underside of the tail. Females have less prominent wing stripes that are often more buffy in color, and their throat patches vary, being either reduced whitish or buff, or even appearing concolorous with the chest and chin. Females lack the thin white tail band, though this male character is difficult to discern in most field conditions. Though the differences may be difficult to judge in the field, some juveniles can be sexed when the wings, throat, and tail are seen to good advantage.

Studying sound recordings of the extremely distinctive vocalizations will allow you to quickly detect and identify nighthawks.

LESSER NIGHTHAWK: A widespread and largely Neotropical species, here in the ABA Area Lesser Nighthawk is confined to the arid Southwest, showing a strong association with creosote bush and dry desert washes. More a bird of the desert, Lesser winters primarily in Central America, though a very small number winter in southern California, and along the Gulf Coast of southern Texas and southern Florida. Exceptionally they are found elsewhere along the Gulf, and increasingly they are detected as vagrants away from these areas. Any nighthawk observed in North America from November through February is most likely a Lesser and should be carefully scrutinized, even if well out of range.

Male Lesser Nighthawk, CA, July (AM) (left); female Lesser Nighthawk, TX, Apr (TZ) (right). Differs from Common Nighthawk in having slightly shorter wings that fall usually even with or just short of the tail tip, a broader white wing band (males) that is situated closer to the wing tip and is usually visible past the tertials, and buffy spotting on the inner half of the primaries, which is variable but more prominent than on Common. Note also that the late July male is in heavy wing molt; most Common Nighthawks molt flight feathers on the wintering grounds.

Male Lesser Nighthawk, CA, Oct (JM) (left); female Lesser Nighthawk, AZ, Jul (BS) (right). Overall plumage pattern is less variable than in Common Nighthawk, usually spangled with buff or sometimes rust above. Males have white throats and broad white wing bands, as well as white tail bands. Females can have mixed white and buffy throats, or no white there at all, and they usually show buffy wing bands. All females lack white in the tail.

Male Lesser Nighthawk, CA, Apr (BLS) (left); juvenile Lesser Nighthawk, AZ, Jun (JR) (right). Lesser Nighthawk spends the day roosting on the ground or on horizontal tree limbs. Note the broad white wing band that is situated in the middle of the primaries, just past the tertials, and buffy spots on the primary bases. Juveniles have a soft, very cryptic plumage that is replaced by an adultlike plumage by late summer/early fall.

Lesser is the most distinctive of these three nighthawks, with a unique wing shape and wing pattern, and a relatively long tail. Even so, separating it from Common Nighthawk can be a problem, but where its breeding range overlaps with that of Common, Lesser is generally replaced by Common at higher elevations (~1,200+ feet). Preferring lower, warmer areas,[10] Lesser is less territorial than Common, ranging farther from breeding sites when foraging,[10] tending to fly lower when foraging, and having a more buoyant, fluttery, and less direct flight, with shallower wingbeats. Like Common, in migration Lesser often flies in loose, high flocks. Since it molts before migrating, a bird showing wing or tail molt in late summer is virtually always a Lesser rather than a Common (which molts its tail and wings in South America).

Compared to Common, Lesser is smaller and more compact and has more blunt-tipped wings that are less pointed (the outer primary, P10, is usually shorter than or equal to P9). The wing stripe is positioned farther toward the tip of the wing (about three-fourths of the way from the wrist to the wing tip) and spans the four outermost primary feathers (rather than five in Common). Importantly, Lesser shows buffy spotted inner primaries whereas those of Common and Antillean are usually plain. The underparts are warmer and buffier overall than in most Commons, and Lesser shows rows of buffy spots on the underwings (the other two are barred on the underwings). In resting birds the wing tips do not extend beyond the tail. In flying birds the wings appear broader than in Common and are especially broader beyond the wrist and in the hand area.

Male: These are similar to male Common except as noted above. Also, in resting birds the wing stripe is often visible below the tertials, whereas on Common the tertials usually conceal the wing stripe. *Female:* These are similar to female Common except as noted above. The wing stripe is narrow and buffy (not white) and is often visible below the tertials. *Juvenile:* Unlike juvenile Common Nighthawks, juvenile male Lessers show a white subterminal tail band,[3] though it may be less bold compared to that of an adult male.

Voice: The distinctive call given from the ground or a tree is a toad-like, soft, purring trill, droning on at length (often thirty or more seconds), occasionally sputtering out briefly before starting up again. This sound somewhat recalls the trill of an Eastern Screech-Owl but is much longer. In flight, it gives a gremlin-like giggle, or liquid sputtery chatter. Unlike Common, it does not perform a "boom" display.

COMMON NIGHTHAWK: The most widespread nighthawk and, not coincidentally, the most variable in plumage, this species breeds across nearly the whole continent, nesting on urban gravel rooftops and in open areas of woodlands, prairies, and rocky outcroppings. Its geographic variation is noticeable, and individuals breeding farther north tend to be larger than those at lower latitudes (i.e., Bergmann's Rule).[4] The upperparts average palest in the middle of the continent, darkest in the East, and intermediate in the West;[4] the density of barring on the chest and belly varies too, as does belly color, with eastern birds averaging buffier than individuals elsewhere. When examined closely, the variation between subspecies might seem dizzying, but when it comes to identification at the species level, the identifying characters hold up largely throughout the species' range.

Structural differences between the nighthawk species are subtle and difficult to appreciate in the field, but prolonged study of a Common Nighthawk may expose its relatively large size and longer wings. It is nearly identical in appearance to Antillean Nighthawk, and silent birds may prove unidentifiable to species (see Antillean below for more information). Lesser Nighthawk differs more palpably in shape and plumage. On Common, the outer primary is the longest, so the wings appear quite pointed, especially in flight. The pale primary bar is about midway between wrist and wing tip, and at rest, the longer wings project just beyond the tail tip.

The most oft-used colloquial name for Common Nighthawk is "bullbat," and given its erratic flight and crepuscular habits, confusion with bats is possible. In late summer and fall, sizable flocks of Common Nighthawks are occasionally seen in migration, the best places to see these flights being along the Great Lakes and the Atlantic Coast, when hundreds may be seen migrating at dusk.

Male: Marbled gray and black on the crown and back, adult males show a face that is streaked buff and blackish. Some males show rufous highlights on the back, shoulder, or crown. The breast and belly are barred with alternating bands of black and whitish, and the vent is whitish. The white throat patch is usually obvious but can be harder to see on roosting birds. Males show a broad band of white through the

Male Common Nighthawk, ON, Jul (GS) (left); female Common Nighthawk, BC, Aug (GB) (right). Note the bold white throat shown by males. Common Nighthawk's plumage varies across its broad range, with nine subspecies generally recognized, but identification of individual birds to subspecies is not advised. All are structurally similar, with long wings extending just past the tail. The white wing patch is often not visible on perched birds, as it is usually covered by the tertials. If visible, note its position, closer to the wrist than on Lesser, and usually appearing uneven, with narrower white on the outer primaries and broader white on the inners. These two birds are presumably of the generally dark, broad-ranging, nominate subspecies (*C. m. minor*).

Male "Pacific" Common Nighthawk, Sublette Co., WY, Jul (GV) (left); male "Sennett's" Common Nighthawk, CO, Jun (SB) (right). The "Pacific" Nighthawk (*C. m. hesperis*) averages paler dorsally and breeds across the Great Basin into California and east to western Wyoming and Colorado. "Sennett's" Nighthawk (*C. m. sennetti*) of the northern Great Plains averages the palest overall.

Unknown sex Common Nighthawk, NM, Jul, (BG) (left); male "Chapman's" Common Nighthawk, FL, Jun (DI) (right). Across the arid Southwest and the southern Great Plains, birds average paler, and some are as pale as typical Sennett's Nighthawks. "Chapman's" Nighthawk averages darker above and breeds across the Southeast and peninsular Florida.

Male Antillean Nighthawk, FL, Jul (LM) (left); female Antillean Nighthawk, FL, Jul (LM) (right). Antillean Nighthawk is sometimes very difficult if not impossible to distinguish from perched Common Nighthawk. In general, Antillean has a buffy belly and a contrastingly whiter breast, usually whitish scapulars, and pale gray tertials. Identification should be confirmed with voice.

Female Antillean Nighthawk, FL, Apr (KK) (left); female Antillean Nighthawk, FL, May (BM) (right). Even the best birders are tentative about the identification of perched Antillean Nighthawks. These two birds are more richly spangled rusty above than the resident Common Nighthawks in south Florida, and they show paler tertials, note also the whitish breast contrasting with buffier belly on the bird at left, though the pattern is subtle.

Antillean Nighthawk, Cayman Islands, Aug (RR) (left); female Antillean Nighthawk, Abaco, Bahamas, Aug (MT) (right). Geographic variation in Antillean Nighthawk is poorly understood. Birds nesting in the Bahamas and south Florida may be longer winged and longer tailed, and they average paler than those breeding throughout the rest of the Caribbean. But there is much overlap, and authorities have not agreed on this species' taxonomy.

Lesser Nighthawk (left column) and Common Nighthawk (right column). In the West these species occur together, especially during migration. Lesser is smaller, rounder and wider winged, and overall buffer in plumage when compared with most Common Nighthawks in the West. Lesser's white wing patch is farther out along the primaries, about halfway from the bend of the wing to the wing tip. The white patch is most prominent on adult males and tends to be buffer in females (bottom left). Females also have buffer throats. The shape of the white wing patch differs subtly as well, usually being broadest at the leading edge of the wing on Lesser, and tapering toward the rear; it is also less extensive than on Common, usually with white only on the outer four primaries. An important ID clue is the length of the outermost primary: in Lesser it is typically shorter than adjacent P9, but it's sometimes just as long; in Common it is usually longer than P9, giving the wing tip a more pointed look. Lesser usually shows boldly spotted inner primaries, whereas Common shows vague spotting or none at all. Females of both species lack the white tail band below and average less white in the wings and throat. Western Common Nighthawks range from being very dark in the Pacific Northwest to quite pale on the western Great Plains (all Lesser Nighthawk photos, BLS; Common Nighthawk: top two, SNGH; top middle and bottom right, SK; bottom left, MSt).

Common Nighthawk

Antillean Nighthawk

Common Nighthawk (left column) and Antillean Nighthawk (right column). These two species are virtually identical and are best distinguished by their vocalizations. Even so, where the two species occur together in south Florida, Common Nighthawk tends to be darker above and whiter below, whereas Antillean is frequently spangled with rufous above and has buffier underparts, often with a contrasting whiter breast barred with black. These differences can be good clues to identification, but they should be corroborated by vocal differences as well. In general, Antillean Nighthawk is slightly smaller and a bit stockier, with stiffer wingbeats than Common Nighthawk, though these differences are difficult to appreciate unless the two species are seen together (Common Nighthawk: top left, SNGH; top right and middle left small, TJ; middle right ventral, T; middle left and right dorsals, KK; bottom right, JC; Antillean Nighthawk: top left, MD; top right two small figures, MI; middle left ventral, T; middle right ventral, AHu; bottom, RR).

Common Nighthawk is a long-distance migrant that spends relatively little time in North America, so most do not molt their flight feathers here, instead undergoing a prebasic molt on the wintering grounds. There are some exceptions to this rule, however, most notably with breeders in peninsular Florida, which may begin their prebasic flight feather molt here in North America, perhaps suspending it for migration and completing it on the wintering grounds. This Florida breeder, photographed 23 July (DI), is just beginning to replace its inner primaries; a molting Lesser Nighthawk on this date would be more advanced in its wing molt (see plate).

base of the primaries, and a white subterminal tail band. *Female:* Similar to the male, the female usually has narrower and fainter wing stripes that also average buffier. The wing stripe is harder to see on a female at rest compared to a male. The throat shows a small amount of white or buff or is often concolorous with the chest and chin. Females at times show more buff or ruddy tones in the plumage compared to males, especially on the underparts. Rarely in the Southeast, females occur with body and head feathers marked mostly in rufous, where females normally appear gray.[7,8] *Juvenile:* Juveniles are quite variable. Compared to adults they show fresh flight feathers with relatively broad and crisp pale edges to the primary tips. Juveniles in the Great Plains are quite pale gray overall. In the Southwest, they can be very buffy or ruddy, appearing more similar to Lesser Nighthawk. Juvenile male Common Nighthawk differs from Lesser in replacing its tail feathers during the first winter; Lesser keeps its

juvenile tail feathers until its (prebasic) molt in late summer, at about one year old.[5] Interestingly, juvenile male Common Nighthawks lack a white tail band, while male Lessers are born with one. Commons attain theirs by the first spring, when ready to breed.

Voice: The common call is a nasal, abrupt "peent!" or "beert!" that somewhat recalls an American Woodcock, but nighthawks typically repeat their calls incessantly. On the breeding grounds, displaying males "boom" in flight, diving down and flexing their primaries to produce a dramatic, loud, accelerating "whooOOOMMMm!" before again turning skyward. Occasionally they make other sounds as well, particularly around the nest, including territorial wing claps.[9]

ANTILLEAN NIGHTHAWK: Nearly endemic to the West Indies, this species barely reaches the United States as a breeder, occurring in small numbers in the Florida Keys from April to August. It has also occurred as a vagrant to Louisiana and North Carolina, but Antillean is extremely similar to Common, so much so that many authorities consider them inseparable when they are not vocalizing. Until 1982 they were considered the same species[11] but then were split into two species, as they differ in egg color and clutch size, vocalizations (of both adults and nestlings), and also in the plumages of the nestlings and juveniles.[12] The wintering grounds for Antillean remain unknown,[3] and understanding its migration strategy and molt timing (both presumed similar to those of Common) could be useful in separating the two.

As noted, the physical differences between Antillean and Common are few and perhaps imperceptible, but Antillean averages smaller (by ~12 percent)[8] and has shorter wings. At rest the wings reach the tail tip but do not extend beyond it, as is typical of Common. Many times Antillean seems to show paler and largely grayish tertials that contrast with the rest of the upperparts, whereas Common usually has more extensive black marbling in the tertials, but this character is not always reliable, as some Antilleans show fairly marbled tertials. Antillean seems to average buffier below and more rufous above than Common, but Common is highly variable. Antillean often flies with more tense wingbeats, and with the wings held more often below horizontal (bowed), compared to Common.[8]

Voice: The call is a distinctive, rapidly delivered "pitti-pit-pit," often repeated at length. It also gives a Common Nighthawk–like "pit" that is usually doubled: "pit-pit." Like Common, Antillean performs a booming display, but Antillean's is weaker and higher pitched and does not carry to the same extent that Common's boom does.[12]

References

[1] Holloway, J. E. 2003. Dictionary of Bird of the United States. Portland, OR: Timber Press.

[2] Pyle, P. 1997. Identification Guide to North America Birds. Part 1: Columbidae to Ploceidae. Bolinas, CA: Slate Creek Press.

[3] Guzy, M. J. 2002. Antillean Nighthawk (*Chordeiles gundlachii*). The Birds of North America Online. A. Poole, ed. Ithaca, NY: Cornell Lab of Ornithology. http://bna.birds.cornell.edu/bna/species/619

[4] Brigham, R. M., J. Ng, R. G. Poulin, and S. D. Grindal. 2011. Common Nighthawk (*Chordeiles minor*). The Birds of North America Online. A. Poole, ed. Ithaca, NY: Cornell Lab of Ornithology. http://bna.birds.cornell.edu/bna/species/213

[5] Howell, S.N.G. 2010. Molt in North American Birds. New York: Houghton Mifflin.

[6] Zink, R. M., and J. V. Remsen. 1986. Evolutionary processes and patterns of geographic variation in birds. Current Ornithology 4:1–69.

[7] Howell, S.N.G., and S. Webb. 1995. Birds of Mexico and Northern Central America. New York: Oxford University Press.

[8] Sibley, D. A. 2000. The Sibley Guide to Birds. New York: Alfred A. Knopf.

[9] Weller, M. W. 1958. Observations of the incubation behavior of a Common Nighthawk. Auk 75:48–59.

[10] Latta, S. C., and M. E. Baltz. 1997. Lesser Nighthawk (*Chordeiles acutipennis*). The Birds of North America Online. A. Poole, ed. Ithaca, NY: Cornell Lab of Ornithology. http://bna.birds.cornell.edu/bna/species/314

[11] American Ornithologists' Union. 1982. Thirty-fourth supplement to the American Ornithologists' Union Check-list of North American Birds. Auk 99(3): Supplement 1CC–16CC.

[12] Stevenson, H. M., E. Eisenmann, C. Winegarner, and W. Karlin. 1983. Notes on Common and Antillean nighthawks of the Florida Keys. Auk 100:983–88.

[13] Fletcher, Q. E., R. J. Fisher, C.K.R. Willis, and R. M. Brigham. 2004. Free-ranging Common Nighthawks use torpor. Journal of Thermal Biology 29(1): 9–14.

Open-Country Birds

Yellow-bellied Kingbirds

Black Corvids: Crows and Ravens

Pipits

Longspurs

Cowbirds

This section comprises a diverse array of bird groups, most of which inhabit open country, particularly agricultural areas or grasslands, but several of which occur in arid semidesert or dry scrubby areas, and even somewhat suburban environments. The best methods for identification vary from group to group, but as is often the case with birds of open country, voice is useful in identification and detection.

Yellow-bellied Kingbirds

Western Kingbird (*Tyrannus verticalis*)

Cassin's Kingbird (*Tyrannus vociferans*)

Tropical Kingbird (*Tyrannus melancholicus*)

Couch's Kingbird (*Tyrannus couchii*)

Also: Thick-billed Kingbird (*Tyrannus crassirostris*)

First Breeding:	1 year old
Breeding Strategy:	Monogamous; highly territorial
Lifespan:	6+ years

Conspicuous birds of open country, kingbirds are admirably tyrannical, pugnacious, and famously territorial. They are tough birds, as their common and genus names suggest, characterized by large heads, flat bills, and strong and agile flight. On warm summer days they nimbly pursue insects through aerial sallies, often ending with an audible bill snap before swiftly returning to their perch. During the breeding season it is not uncommon to find kingbirds chasing birds that outsize them by ten times or more. Indeed, watching a kingbird hound and pester an otherwise brutish bird, such as a crow, vulture, or raptor, you may find yourself pitying

Natural History Note:

The world's birds are separated into two orders: the nonpasserines and the passerines. The passerines, or "perching birds," are further subdivided into two suborders, the oscines ("songbirds") and the suboscines. In North America, tyrannids are the lone representative of the suboscines, but the family reaches its greatest diversity in the New World tropics. The world's smallest passerine is a tyrannid; the Short-tailed Pygmy-Tyrant of South America is only about 2.5 inches long!

Suboscines differ from oscines in having a less complex syrinx (and often simpler songs), and they do not learn their songs but instead inherit them genetically. Because song is innate in flycatchers, vocal differences are useful in determining species limits. Partly because song is inherited, hybridization is rare among flycatchers, but it has been documented in the genus *Tyrannus* on several occasions, including a probable Couch's Kingbird × Scissor-tailed Flycatcher in New York;[4] several Western Kingbird × Scissor-tailed Flycatchers;[5] and Tropical × Couch's kingbirds in Mexico.[2, 6]

the larger bird, whose only crime was to cross paths with these ruthless tyrants. Kingbirds are the namesake group of the tyrant-flycatcher family Tyrannidae. Though the family is confined to the New World, representatives are found from Alaska to Tierra del Fuego, and it is in fact the most species-rich bird family in the world, comprising more than 430 species. The genus *Tyrannus* is home to thirteen species, and over half of these are "yellow-bellied types," showing grayish heads, green or gray backs, and darker wings and tails. Eight species of *Tyrannus* breed in North America (four of which are "yellow-bellied"), and a few others occur as vagrants.

These four "yellow-bellied kingbirds" of the American West are nearly always seen in edge or open habitats, especially along roadsides. Alert and agile, they perch on wires, fences, or treetops, from which they ceaselessly sally for insects, pausing only to call or to chase potential threats and drive them away from the nest area. Largely southwestern in overall distribution, most are migratory and so prone to vagrancy. Mostly present just during the warmer months when a steady diet of insects is assured, by winter these kingbirds have vacated the Lower 48 for warmer climes in Mexico or farther south, but small numbers winter in the southern portions of California,

Adult Cassin's Kingbird, CA, Mar (BLS). Cassin's Kingbird can be quite distinctive in fresh plumage, with its dark gray head, contrasting white throat, and whitish bordered tail, but these ID features are more difficult to assess on worn birds. In North America we see all four species in various states of wear, and identification of a bird out of range can be a real challenge. Subtle plumage and structural features help distinguish these species, as do their distinctive vocalizations.

Focus on: *Voice, Range, Tail shape/pattern, Breast pattern/color, Bill structure, Back color, Primary Spacing*

Kingbirds of all ages and both sexes share similar plumage, but they differ in the shape of the outer primary tips. Adult males have the most strongly "notched" outer primaries (left, KS), adult females are moderately notched (center, JTu), and juveniles (right, TJ) have little to no notch in the outer primaries. Western Kingbirds show the most strongly modified outer primaries among this group of species, with Cassin's, Couch's, and Tropical showing a degree less in each species and age/sex combination, respectively. The male Western Kingbird in this composite (left) is actually a first-summer that has replaced some but not all of its primaries in the preformative molt (note the retained juvenile P9 on the right wing, which is not strongly notched compared with the outermost feather on that wing).

Texas, and Florida. During colder times, like many flycatchers, kingbirds add fruit to their diet, and when away from breeding areas, they occasionally gather in communal roosts, sometimes involving multiple species.[1] Migrants are observed in spring and fall, but vagrants are detected most often in late fall or winter.

All four are quite similar to one another in plumage, and, Tropical and Couch's kingbirds are essentially identical in appearance and were considered the same species until 1983.[2, 3] Western Kingbird is the most widespread in the ABA Area and the most familiar species, breeding widely across the West, and is the only species found routinely in the East (where it is a scarce fall migrant). It is the species best used as a basis for comparison.

Given reasonable views, you can usually place a yellow-bellied kingbird into one of two groups, identifying it as either a "Western/Cassin's type" or a "Tropical/Couch's type." Specific identification beyond that can be a real challenge. Add to the already similar plumages the more subtle problems that arise from wear or molt, and it is a difficult situation for birders. All four behave similarly, but although habitat is useful and range is a good first clue, identification is best (and rather easily) reached using voice. When nesting, they are vocal, particularly at dawn and dusk; tyrant-flycatchers are unusual in performing more complex vocalizations at first light, called "dawn songs." Silent

birds require good views, but kingbirds remain active throughout the day and use exposed perches, allowing prolonged study. Bill structure and tail shape and pattern are good clues, with tail pattern usually best assessed from above (i.e., the dorsal side).

Take photos, pay attention to the breast and belly area, and note the quality of the color there and the degree of contrast. Distinguishing silent Couch's and Tropical is by far the most challenging problem, and some fall vagrants must simply be left unidentified. The spacing of the primary tips on the folded wing can be helpful for distinguishing these species; it is nearly impossible to see in the field yet may be visible in good digital photos. Certainly, voice is the best and most useful tool for separating these very similar species.

Hints and Considerations

- *Myiarchus* flycatchers, especially Ash-throated or Brown-crested, are at times confused with kingbirds. *Myiarchus* nest in cavities (e.g., woodpecker holes); are vocal, smaller, and browner; and perch more upright, generally preferring wooded riparian areas. But Ash-throated is also found in open arid areas, where it can be confused with kingbirds.
- *Listen up!* When possible, identify kingbirds by voice. In fall and winter they are quieter but still call, especially when agitated.

- None of the yellow-bellied kingbirds are generally expected in the East, but Western is a rare if regular fall migrant there, and a scarce winter visitor in Florida.
- Away from southeast Arizona and south Texas, Tropical Kingbird is very rare, but it is a regular vagrant to the Pacific Coast (north into Canada); after October, any Pacific Coast kingbird north of southern California is likely a Tropical. Tropical also strays rarely elsewhere.[7]
- Voice is the most reliable way to distinguish Tropical and Couch's kingbirds, but also look at the primary spacing on perched birds.
- Couch's Kingbird is accidental away from south Texas.
- Western and Cassin's kingbirds overlap broadly in breeding range but generally separate by habitat.[8, 9] Migrants and vagrants often occur in similar habitats.

Identification

The sexes are similar, but males have more emarginated (notched) outer primaries, and more extensive crown patches.[10, 11, 12, 13] In Tropical/Couch's, males show more deeply forked tails.[11, 12] Only males sing, but both sexes call. Like adults of other *Tyrannus*, adults in these species have concealed red crown feathers, revealed usually only in aggression.

Kingbirds generally appear similar regardless of age, but juveniles appear fresher in late summer, when adults often appear more worn and ragged in the process of completing their prebasic molt. Fresh juveniles have scalier upperparts, as the wing coverts are fringed with pale or rust, and they are paler yellow below. Juveniles undergo a variable molt of body and wing feathers in the first fall/winter, so by late winter/spring they appear similar to adults and can be aged safely only by molt limits in the wings (hard to see!).

Voice is key in identification, and the sounds are best learned in the field where you can gain a context for the vocalizations. You can learn a great deal by listening to recordings on the Internet, too, as you can develop your own mnemonics. Creating your own recordings of birds calling in the field really etches these sounds into your brain. Basic information on vocalizations is provided below, but text does these sounds little justice.

WESTERN KINGBIRD: One of the most familiar summer birds of the American West, this kingbird has among its most noticeable features a black tail with white outer tail feathers (outer webs of the outer rectrices) and a rather small bill. A bird of open country (even more so than the other yellow-bellies), it requires only a few odd trees, shrubs, or human-made structures (it loves utility poles) in suburban areas, for nesting or for hunting perches. Much more so than other kingbirds, Western is found in desert habitats and along dry creek washes, often nesting in yucca.[9]

In addition to its narrow-based, rather short bill and distinctive tail pattern, Western is the most migratory of these kingbirds and has the longest wings and primary projection. It also has a relatively short tail, and worn adults may have their white outer tail fringes worn away. In the other species the tail feather shaft (rachis) is pale, so if the outer webs are worn away, the rachis could appear as a whitish outer web. Still, on Western the tail should appear nearly black, or at least blackish brown. Also, compared to the others, Western is paler overall, paler gray about the head and chest, and paler yellow below. It shows more contrast between the dark wings/tail and the mantle. The degree of color can be difficult to assess on lone vagrants, which may be worn adults or molting juveniles, and in these cases it is helpful to focus on bill size, primary projection, and voice. On a perched Western, the browner primaries contrast somewhat with the blackish tail (more concolorous in other species), and the tail should appear more square tipped, lacking the notch shown by other species (but beware, molting birds can appear more fork tailed). Note also that Western tends to have darker wing coverts than the others, with less pale edging. In flight Western appears quite similar to American Robin and can be passed off as such by the unwary. Though Western is the most expected yellow-bellied kingbird in the East, the others occur as very rare vagrants. A Tropical/Couch's appears rangier and has a long, heavy bill; richer yellow underparts that extend into the upper breast; a longer, grayish, notched tail; and paler coverts that contrast less with a greener back. *Voice:* Western's song is "wik, wik-wik-wik, wikbreemehere." The introductory notes are staccato and squeaky. The call is a staccato "dik" or "wik," vaguely reminiscent of a Downy Woodpecker's call.

CASSIN'S KINGBIRD: A dapper kingbird, Cassin's is confined mostly to the Southwest but breeds sparsely into the shortgrass prairie of the western Great Plains. Its ecological separation from Western Kingbird remains a point of interest,[13] and at times the two share the same nest tree! In Texas and Arizona, they seem to separate

Couch's and Tropical Kingbirds show less strongly modified outer primaries by age/sex than Western and Cassin's Kingbirds. Couch's (left) shows slightly more emargination (notching) in the outer primaries than Tropical (right). In these composites adult males are at the top, adult females are center, and juveniles are at the bottom. Note the lack of notching in juveniles of both species. While difficult to see in the field, these differences can be helpful in identifying kingbirds and can often be seen well in digital photos (all photos, BLS).

by elevation and habitat. Compared to Western, Cassin's generally prefers more densely treed and hillier areas.[14] Cassin's also prefers higher elevations (more often above 4,000 feet), grasslands, and pine-oak-juniper woodlands.[8, 9] In Texas, Western usually nests below 4,000 feet, and the two seem to differ in nest placement as well, with Cassin's usually locating its nest in the upper canopy and Western placing its nest more often in the midcanopy of the nest tree,[8] but in Arizona they appear to differ little in this regard.[9]

In structure and appearance Cassin's is most similar to Western, but Cassin's is darker gunmetal gray on the head and chest and shows a noticeably contrasting pale whitish throat. The tail is dark but not quite as black as Western's, and Cassin's shows a thin pale terminal band. Fresh Cassin's can show narrow whitish outer webs, similar to those of Western, but this is seldom as noticeable or contrasting, and the color is often buffier. If tail pattern leaves you in doubt, examine the wing coverts, which are noticeably paler and grayer in Cassin's and show more pale fringing. The combination of this with the darker gray back and head and the small white throat patch should make most Cassin's identifiable. Cassin's seldom strays compared to Western and Tropical. Compared to Couch's/Tropical, the wings and tail are darker brownish, and the tail is darker and not so notched. *Voice*: The song is a harsh, low, burry, "chut, chut, chut, breemehrrr." The common call is "chee-BEER." They also give a sharp, quick "ka-deer" that is usually repeated four or five times or more. They also give a drawn-out "weeeeeerrrr."

TROPICAL KINGBIRD: A widespread and abundant Neotropical species found from central Argentina north to southeast Arizona, and sparingly into south Texas, Tropical Kingbird is rare in North America outside a few areas in these two states. Small numbers winter in coastal California (almost all are juveniles), and it strays more often and more widely than the others (except for Western Kingbird), especially in October and November. It is nearly identical to Couch's, but Tropical's distinctive twittering call helps separate it. It specializes in taking larger flying insects,[15, 16] evidenced by its large, wide-based, and very long bill; this perhaps allows it to coexist better with other *Tyrannus*, which take a wider variety of prey.[11] Similar to Couch's, it prefers more humid habitats than Western or Cassin's. Tropical is often found in areas near water with scattered trees, and it overlaps with Couch's somewhat

in breeding habitat, but Tropical prefers more open and human-altered landscapes, such as small towns, gardens, and golf courses. Vagrants and migrants are often found near the coast and are fond of beach scrub, savannah, tree-lined freshwater ponds, fallow fields and edges, and even semiurban environments.

Compared to the others, Tropical/Couch's show heavier bills and larger heads; long, brownish, notched tails; richer yellow underparts; and greener backs. From below, the gray of the head is less extensive than on Cassin's/Western, terminating on the throat (rather than on the chest), giving way more abruptly to the greenish or yellow chest. The dark auricular patch often appears more extensive as well.

Tropical Kingbird differs subtly in shape and habits from Couch's, but these differences may not be apparent in the field. Tropical usually shows a longer, narrower bill (more triangular when seen from below in Couch's), possibly darker wings with more distinct pale edgings to the coverts, a grayer back, and less evenly spaced primary tips on the folded wing.[14] More study is needed, but preliminary review of specimens suggests that the differences in primary spacing hold true across age and sex classes in these two species. Some Tropicals show some pale at the base of the mandible, and this appears to be rare in Couch's. Tropical averages slightly smaller and less vocal,[7] and it tends to look rangier and shows a more distinctly notched tail than is typical of Couch's, but these latter features are subject to change with behavior and posture. *Voice*: The song is high and twittering, "tic-tic tic-tic-tic, brreer, breeeeech, tic, tic." The song begins with sharp, shrill introductory notes, followed by an accelerating descending trill. The cadence (not tone!) might recall an attempt to start a failing lawn mower, which then sputters to a halt. Migrants may give calls that include a rapid three- or four-noted "tsi-tsi-tsi-tsi" that is very high pitched and thin, or an accelerating "pip-p-preeeeEEE" that is similar in quality; they also sometimes give individual "wik" notes.

COUCH'S KINGBIRD: This species is named for its discoverer, Lt. Darius Couch; he apparently pronounced his name "coach,"[17] but most birders pronounce it "couch," like the furniture piece. Though quite common in south Texas, this kingbird is probably the least studied of the four. Mostly a Mexican species that reaches its northern limit in the United States in Texas, it is strongly linked to thornscrub brushland habitat. Feeding mostly

Western Kingbird, AB, May (GV) (left); Western Kingbird, CA, Apr (BLS) (right). The quintessential "yellow-bellied kingbird," Western Kingbird is also the most widespread and familiar of the four species treated here, and it is the most prone to vagrancy. Western has a small, narrow-based, well-proportioned bill, relatively long wings, and a shortish black tail with white outer feathers. Western averages the palest overall of these kingbirds, with pale gray head and breast, and paler yellow underparts.

Western Kingbirds, CA, Jun (left) and Jul (right) (BLS). Western Kingbirds occupy arid environments in the West, so they become very worn by midsummer; note the broken tail feathers and generally washed-out plumage. The July bird has a mix of fresh greenish and worn grayish back feathers. At certain angles these worn Western Kingbirds can appear to have a whitish throat; beware of confusion with Cassin's Kingbird.

Juvenile Western Kingbird, AZ, Aug (BLS) (left); adult male Western Kingbird, CA, Apr (BLS) (right). Juveniles are similar to adults overall but are in uniformly fresh plumage in mid to late summer. By fall they undergo a preformative molt through which they replace much of the body plumage and a subset of wing and tail feathers. Fall/winter birds with two ages of flight feathers are typically aged as first-years. In flight Western Kingbird can be passed off as an American Robin, a species with which it often occurs as a fly-by vagrant in the East. This bird is an adult male, as indicated by its strongly notched outer primaries.

Cassin's Kingbird, CA, Mar (BLS) (left); Cassin's Kingbird, CA, Apr (TB) (right). Cassin's Kingbird is most similar in overall proportions to Western, but it is slightly shorter winged. It is darker overall, with a gunmetal gray head contrasting with a whitish throat, and a breast that is usually darker gray than in Western. The wings are browner than in Western, and they average broader paler fringing on the coverts. Cassin's tail is blackish with a buffy border, most notable as a buffy tip when folded.

Cassin's Kingbird, CA, Apr (BLS) (left); Cassin's Kingbird, CA, Jan (BLS) (right). Cassin's back is dark grayish green, more green in fresh plumage (right), and usually contrasts with paler brownish wings and a dark tail. The tail can appear pale tipped or bordered on all sides by buff.

Cassin's Kingbird, CA, Mar (BLS) (left); adult Cassin's (top) and juvenile Western Kingbirds, AZ, Aug (BLS) (right). In this flight shot note the dark gray head, greenish back, brownish wings, and pale-bordered blackish tail; beware of confusion with Western Kingbird, as many Cassin's show pale bordered tail feathers in fresh plumage. When seen together, Cassin's is obviously darker on the head and is more colorful overall than Western, and usually shows a more strongly contrasting whitish throat.

Tropical Kingbird, TX, Nov (BLS) (left); Tropical Kingbird, CA, Oct (BLS) (right). Tropical Kingbird is notably larger billed than both Western and Cassin's and is generally more colorful overall, with lemon-yellow underparts that extend up onto the breast. The head is pale gray, usually with a well-defined darker ear patch, and the back is gray green, often more distinctly green than in Western and Cassin's. The wings and tail are brown, and the tail is long and deeply notched at the tip. The wings are short and often appear rounded when folded.

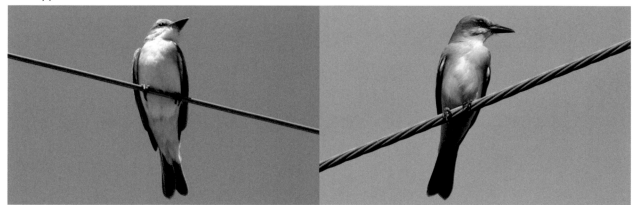

Tropical Kingbird, Baja California, Mexico, Sep (BLS) (left); Tropical Kingbird, Nayarit, Mexico, Jan (SNGH) (right). Tropical Kingbird is often seen around suburban areas, including small towns, pond edges, golf courses, etc. Note the extensive yellow underparts; the very large bill, which is notably wide based and which usually, but not always, has a distinctly hooked tip; and the long, notched tail. In contrast to Couch's, Tropical almost always seems to show a distinctly notched tail; Couch's is more variable in this regard.

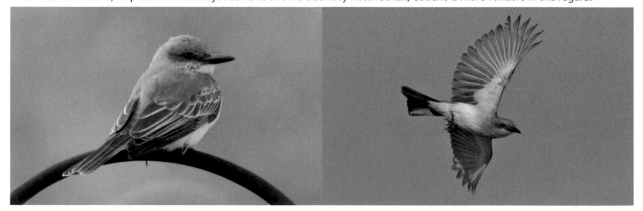

Tropical Kingbird, MD, Dec (BH) (left); Tropical Kingbird, PA, Jun (GLA) (right). Tropical Kingbirds are fairly common vagrants along the West Coast from midfall through winter, but on the Atlantic Coast they are much rarer, with only a few records, some from fall and a few from spring/summer. Note the large bill, short rounded wings, and long brown tail of the bird at left. The June bird can be safely aged as an adult male based on its notched outer primaries.

Couch's Kingbirds, TX, Feb (BLS). Couch's is most similar to Tropical Kingbird, and many silent birds are best left unidentified. However, on average Couch's appears somewhat intermediate between Tropical, with its extremely large bill and long, notched tail, and the more compactly built Western and Cassin's. Couch's bill frequently appears more proportional to the body, and the head appears bushy crested. The tail sometimes shows a distinct notch, but it is often held more tightly closed, hiding the notch and appearing more squared. The underparts are bright yellow up through the breast, as in Tropical.

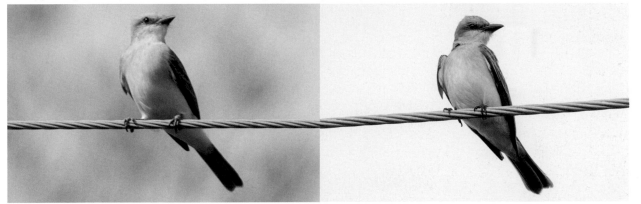

Couch's Kingbird, TX, Nov (BLS) (left); Couch's Kingbird, TX, Feb (BLS) (right). Compare these Couch's Kingbirds perched on a wire with the general shape and structure of the Tropical Kingbirds on the previous plate. Couch's tends to have a smaller and narrower bill, and it often holds its tail more tightly closed than Tropical, making for the appearance of a shallower notch at the tip. Plumage is identical to that of Tropical from this angle.

Juvenile Couch's Kingbird, TX, Aug (BH) (left); adult female Couch's Kingbird, TX, Feb (BLS) (right). Juveniles are very similar to adults but are in exceptionally fresh plumage in summer. Note the rusty tips to the greater coverts and the neatly pale edged wing coverts. In flight Couch's is probably indistinguishable from Tropical, but this bird is an adult female because of its narrow outer primaries with no notable notch.

Thick-billed Kingbirds, AZ, Jul (BS). In addition to being highly range restricted and not much prone to vagrancy, Thick-billed Kingbird is easily distinguished from the other yellow-bellied kingbirds treated in this chapter by virtue of its namesake thick bill! Other characters to note are dark grayish head and upperparts, and very pale yellow belly with white breast.

from and around the canopy of taller trees, it is rarely found away from extensive patches of trees, generally preferring denser, more native habitats than Tropical, and it is less tied to areas with water. Being mainly resident, Couch's strays less often but vocalizes more frequently than Tropical, though vagrants have occurred in the states bordering Mexico, and also in Arkansas, Louisiana, Alabama, and Florida,[7] and there are just a few records along the East Coast north of Florida. Most vagrants occur from midfall to early winter (as with other *Tyrannus*), but there are exceptions (e.g., Michigan in May). Many silent vagrants are left as Tropical/Couch's (and rightly so), so the true status of Couch's as a vagrant is still unclear.

Compared to Tropical, Couch's has a slightly shorter and thicker bill, and a rounder head with a slightly more bushy-crested look. It also appears more richly colored overall, with a greener back, more brownish (less grayish) wings, and a shallower tail notch, and it often holds its tail more horizontally and less vertically than Tropical. Couch's, rather than Tropical, is more likely to be confused with a Western Kingbird because of its posture and proportions. On the folded wing, the primary tips are evenly spaced, but this is usually visible only in photographs or in the hand. Voice is the best indicator as to species, but range and habitat are useful as well. *Voice*: Compared to those of Tropical, the calls are lower, squeaky (less twittering), and slightly throatier, with prominent burry "reel" or "gweer!" notes. The song might be interpreted as "ki-wip ki-wip Ki-WIP kit-choo." This is often repeated, with the low, harsh, burry "reel" calls interspersed. Sometimes the song is

a simpler "kip-kip-kip-kip-gweeerr" or "whik, breeerr." Their sounds are generally sharp and well separated and lack a twittering quality.

Other Yellow-bellied Kingbirds

Over half of the *Tyrannus* in the New World are "yellow-bellied" types. All are similar, and one wonders whether any of the South American kingbirds have graced North American soil but simply went unnoticed. These include the austral migrant form of Tropical Kingbird (*T. m. melancholicus*); one specimen from the Farallon Islands in California has been identified as this subspecies.[11] Tropical Kingbird may actually represent more than one species. Keep your ears (and mind) open, and pay attention to molt, habitat, and behavior.

THICK-BILLED KINGBIRD: For the most part the four kingbirds in this chapter are confused only with each other, but in southeast Arizona and southwest New Mexico the Thick-billed Kingbird should be considered. It is a mostly resident Mexican species whose breeding range only barely reaches the United States (including rarely in Big Bend, Texas). Juvenile Thick-billed especially is quite yellow below, but all Thick-billeds are very stocky and heavy, with a thick neck, a heavy head, and a very heavy bill. It is dark brown above with essentially no gray or green color there. All said, it is really rather different from the other four, but it strays rarely to areas where it could be confused with them, and vagrants have occurred along the Pacific Coast north into British Columbia during fall and winter.

References

[1] Anderson, B. H. 2006. Florida. North American Birds 60(2): 220–23.

[2] Traylor, M. A., Jr. 1979. Two sibling species of *Tyrannus* (Tyrannidae). Auk 96:221–33.

[3] American Ornithologists' Union. 1983. The American Ornithologists' Union Check-list of North American Birds. 6th ed. Lawrence, KS: American Ornithologists' Union.

[4] McGowan, K. J., and R. G. Spahn. 2004. A probable Couch's Kingbird × Scissor-tailed Flycatcher in Livingston Co., New York. Kingbird 54(1): 1–13.

[5] Regosin, J. V. 1998. Scissor-tailed Flycatcher (*Tyrannus forficatus*). The Birds of North America Online. A. Poole, ed. Ithaca, NY: Cornell Lab of Ornithology. http://bna.birds.cornell.edu/bna/species/342

[6] Binford, L. C. 1989. A distributional survey of the birds of the Mexican state of Oaxaca. Ornithological Monograph 43.

[7] Mlodinow, S. G. 1998. The Tropical Kingbird north of Mexico. Field Notes 52(1): 6–11.

[8] Ohlendorf, H. M. 1974. Competitive relationships among kingbirds (Tyrannus) in Trans-Pecos Texas. Wilson Bulletin 86:357–73.

[9] Blancher, P. J., and R. J. Robertson. 1984. Resource use by sympatric kingbirds. Condor 86:305–13.

[10] Gamble, L. R., and T. M. Bergin. 1996. Western Kingbird (*Tyrannus verticalis*). The Birds of North America Online. A. Poole, ed. Ithaca, NY: Cornell Lab of Ornithology. http://bna.birds.cornell.edu/review/species/227

[11] Stouffer, P. C., and R. T. Chesser. 1998. Tropical Kingbird (*Tyrannus melancholicus*). The Birds of North America Online. A. Poole, ed. Ithaca, NY: Cornell Lab of Ornithology. http://bna.birds.cornell.edu/review/species/358

[12] Brush, T. 1999. Couch's Kingbird (*Tyrannus couchii*). The Birds of North America Online. A. Poole, ed. Ithaca, NY: Cornell Lab of Ornithology. http://bna.birds.cornell.edu/review/species/437

[13] Tweit, R. C., and J. C. Tweit. 2000. Cassin's Kingbird (*Tyrannus vociferans*). The Birds of North America Online. A. Poole, ed. Ithaca, NY: Cornell Lab of Ornithology. http://bna.birds.cornell.edu/review/species/534

[14] Dunn, J., and J. Alderfer. 2006. National Geographic Guide to the Birds of North America. Washington, DC: National Geographic.

[15] Fitzpatrick, J. W. 1980. Foraging behavior of Neotropical tyrant flycatchers. Condor 82:43–57.

[16] Fitzpatrick, J. W. 1981. Search strategies of tyrant flycatchers. Animal Behavior 29:810–21.

[17] Gambone, A. M. 2000. Enigmatic Valor: Major General Darius Nash Couch (Army of the Potomac). Baltimore: Butternut and Blue Publishing.

Taxonomic Note:

Globally, the terms "raven" and "crow" have no taxonomic significance, but ravens are generally larger than crows.

Ravens: Common Raven is found across the Northern Hemisphere and is thus termed "Holarctic" in distribution. Within North America two lineages ("clades") of ravens occur, and the genetic distance between the two is comparable to that between many species.[4] One is widespread and quite similar (i.e., relatively close genetically) to those found in the Old World and is grouped with them in a "Holarctic" clade, while another, residing in the southwestern United States (centered in central California and the Sierras), is termed the "California" clade. The two behave similarly, but they differ genetically. The presence of these two raven lineages in North America seems most likely the result of isolation during an ice age, with each clade representing a separate colonizing event from Asia (across the Bering land bridge); the first event was about two million years ago, and another was perhaps around fifteen thousand years ago (the latter possibly coincided with migrations of humans and gray wolves).[5] Chihuahuan Raven seems an offshoot (diverging about one million years ago) of the earlier colonization that fostered the California clade.[4, 6] While Old World and New World (Holarctic) Common Raven populations appear to be evolving independently of one another,[6] the genetic gap between Holarctic ravens in North America and "California" ravens may be narrowing, if interbreeding regularly erodes these populations' genetic integrity.[6] But this is unclear, and more research on vocalizations and genetics might reveal biologically separate entities with only infrequent or occasional interbreeding. Determining the range limits of the "California" raven is an important next step in resolving our understanding of ravens in general. They may appear more similar to Chihuahuan Raven in structure (A. Jaramillo, pers. comm.) and could overlap with it in places.

Crows: Northwestern Crow is vexing. Some authors have argued for lumping it with American Crow,[7, 8, 9] but more often it is treated as a separate species.[10, 11, 12] Few if any consistent differences exist between the two, and they appear nearly (or actually) identical. (At the least, they seem to be each other's closest relative). The limits of their ranges remain unclear and their genetics are in need of more study, so whether "interbreeding" occurs or not is impossible to say. In essence, nobody really knows whether it qualifies as a species. Some postulate that all crows along the Pacific Coast between the Gulf of Alaska and southern California are the same taxon (i.e., species). This includes all "Northwestern" crows and "American" crows west of the Cascades and the Sierras (including the small western subspecies of American Crow, *C. b. hesperis*). These crows are isolated by mountain ranges, appear smaller, and sound throatier (particularly from the Seattle area north) (A. Jaramillo, pers. comm.). Others suggest that all crows west of the Great Plains should be treated as the same taxon (i.e., American Crow). The American Crow subspecies in peninsular Florida (*C. b. pascuus*) is quite distinct and seems to be in decline (A. J. Knue, pers. comm.). "Florida" Crows have larger bills, noticeably larger feet, and longer legs; seem less social; inhabit more rural areas (less suburban); and possess a greater vocal repertoire.[13] Fish Crow is not known to hybridize,[14] and it may be more closely related to crows from Mexico or the Caribbean than it is to American/Northwestern.

Black Corvids: Crows and Ravens

American Crow (*Corvus brachyrhynchos*)

Fish Crow (*Corvus ossifragus*)

Northwestern Crow (*Corvus caurinus*)

Common Raven (*Corvus corax*)

Chihuahuan Raven (*Corvus cryptoleucus*)

Also: Tamaulipas Crow (*Corvus imparatus*)
Eurasian Jackdaw (*Corvus monedula*)

First Breeding:	2–5 years old
Breeding Strategy:	Monogamous, form long-term pair bonds; "cooperative" breeding groups occur too
Lifespan:	< 29 years in the wild

Both feared and revered, crows and ravens have a storied history with humans. Often referenced in mythology and literature, in some places these large, vocal birds represent harbingers of war or death, while in other regions they are hailed as trickster gods. Many are the associations with crows, ravens, and jackdaws, and all too often they

American Crow, CA, Oct (BLS). Birders tend to give the "black corvids" short shrift, but there is a lot more to this group of birds than meets the eye. Each is clad in iridescent black plumage, so their structure and voices offer the best clues to identification. The taxonomy of some species remains unsettled, with unrecognized cryptic species possibly involved. The American Crow pictured here is the small western subspecies *C. b. hesperis*, which sounds and behaves differently than the bigger, more widespread nominate subspecies. But are these differences significant enough to warrant species status? More study is needed.

Focus on: *Voice, Range, Structure, Habitat/behavior*

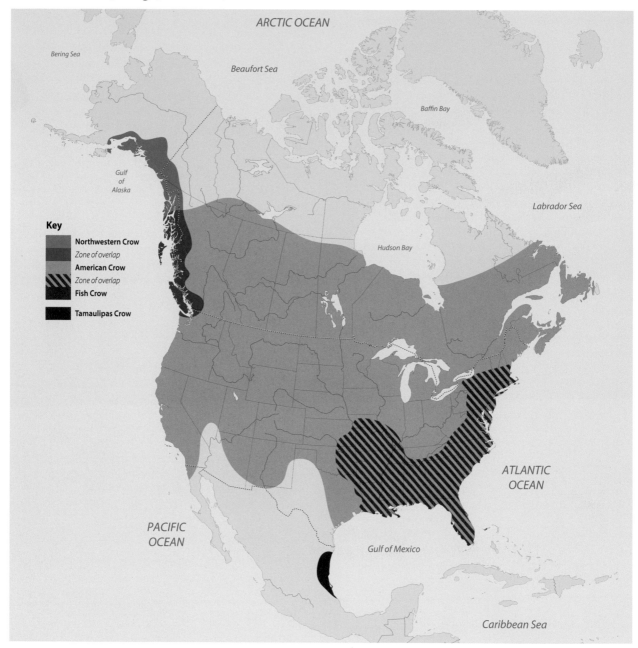

Luckily for birders, there aren't too many places where several species of crows overlap in range. Where the ranges do overlap, you need to pay special attention to crow identification, using a combination of voice and behavior to identify individuals.

are misperceived. One ancient Roman axiom said that "the swans will sing when the jackdaws are silent," which is to say that the wise will speak once the foolish have quieted down.[1] In fact, swans do not sing, and more to the point, corvids such as the jackdaw rank among the most intelligent animals on the planet! The intelligence of crows and ravens is comparable to that of parrots and even some primates.[2] Demonstrating a remarkable ability to learn and solve problems, most corvids are highly adaptable and omnivorous, subsisting on a remarkable variety of foods. In the end, for all their symbolism, crows and ravens are merely birds—but what birds they are!

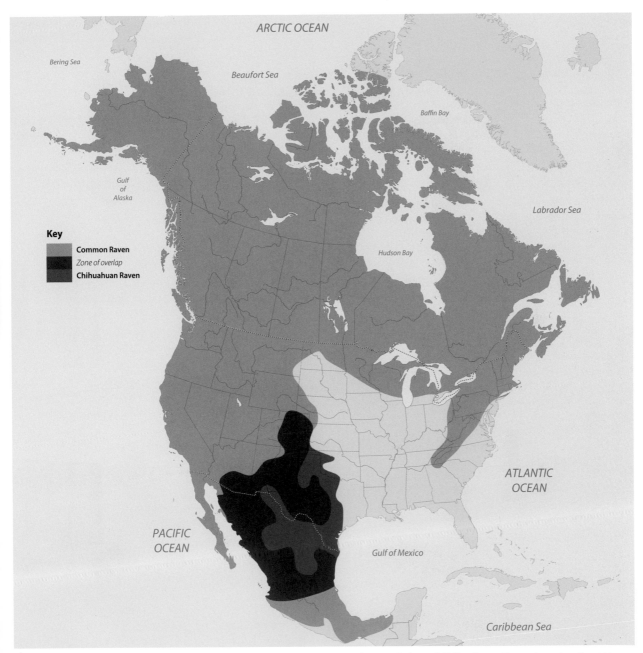

Common Raven is widespread across North America, and its range overlaps with that of Chihuahuan Raven in only a few places. In these places, you should identify ravens with caution, using a combination of voice, structure and plumage, and habitat and behavior.

All show long, stout, utilitarian bills and strong legs and feet to support their mostly terrestrial foraging habits. They are the largest of all the world's passerines (perching birds) and reside in the family Corvidae. This large, worldwide family also includes the jays, nutcrackers, and magpies, and collectively the members arc referred to as "corvids." A shared feature among the 120 or more species that occur worldwide is the elongated nasal bristles that extend forward to cover the nostrils.[3] The genus *Corvus* accounts for more than a third of the family's members, and in North America seven *Corvus* species are currently recognized.

Natural History Note:

In some crow populations, young from the previous year stay on to help their parents the next nesting season.[13, 14, 27] Helpers are usually one-year-olds but are sometimes two- to five-year-olds that delay breeding to help in their natal territories. These birds assist, but they also learn by experience. While parents forage, these helpers guard the nest (chase away rivals, deter predators) but also feed the incubating female and the nestlings.

Because they occur in large aggregations and are vocal, black corvids at least appear quite social, but it's unclear whether they are drawn together for social reasons, or merely because resources concentrate them in certain areas. The raucous roosts of these species are at times deemed a nuisance in some communities. But as scavengers, corvids remove a lot of decaying matter, and it's even been suggested that wild crows could be trained to dispose of trash in suburban areas.[28]

A complex social structure often indicates intelligence, and corvids are believed to be on par with some primates in intelligence.[2] Some ravens make their own toys,[25] and New Caledonian Crows commonly make tools (e.g., hooks) that they then use to obtain food.[29] Resourceful omnivores, corvids are hardy—ravens are even recorded on Christmas bird counts north of the Arctic Circle, when there is no daylight and no other birds are present. Black corvids are long-lived, and captive ravens have reportedly lived up to eighty years![30] Yet a number of crow species rank among the most endangered birds in the world, and several that are endemic to islands in the Pacific are in dire straits (e.g. Hawaiian, Mariana, and Banggai crows).

As generalists, the black corvids are encountered in a variety of habitats but usually prefer open country such as farm fields, ball fields, landfills, or shorelines. Many individuals go to large communal roosts in the evening and require not only open areas for feeding, but also areas with high points for roosting, such as woodlots, cliffs, or power lines; some species are at home in suburban areas. Sometimes found singly, just as often or more so they occur in groups, and though they are generally less social when breeding, flocks form at all seasons.

The corvid species in this chapter are similarly black overall, so attempts to distinguish them by plumage color or pattern are typically useless. Fortunately for birders, these corvids are highly vocal, and their calls are usually distinctive. Moreover, the most similar species segregate mostly by range. At times habitat offers a clue as well, but by and large, the black corvids are best identified using a combination of structure, voice, and range.

Hints and Considerations

- Black corvids are mistaken at times for hawks, and soaring ravens especially are confused with eagles, vultures, or other birds of prey.
- Range is a good first clue, and of the five main species covered here, three have relatively limited ranges. American Crow and Common Raven are widespread, but the others are rarely if ever encountered out of range.
- Two species of rare corvids occur in the ABA Area. Eurasian Jackdaw is extremely rare, with just a handful of records from the northeastern United States and eastern Canada, and Tamaulipas Crow was once regular in extreme south Texas but is now rare.
- Ravens and crows are often confused, but crows are smaller and more compact and have shorter, rounded wings; rounded, fan-shaped tails; and smaller bills. Ravens often occur in more remote areas and have wedge-shaped tails and longer, pointed "hands." Crows sometimes flare their tails when they call, but ravens do not.
- No more than two crow species occur in the same area.
- *Listen up!* American and Northwestern crows overlap in their sounds, but both differ notably from ravens. Fish Crow has a very distinctive voice. The voice of Chihuahuan Raven needs study, but it overlaps somewhat with that of Common Raven.
- Separating the two ravens is a real challenge. They overlap in range in western Texas, southern Colorado, New Mexico, and Arizona. Note the extent of the bill feathering and use a combination of range, habitat, and structure to distinguish them. Structural differences exist but are often difficult to assess, and the distinctive white bases of the neck feathers of Chihuahuan Raven are often well concealed.

Identification

Though males average slightly larger, the sexes appear mostly the same. The degree to which males and females differ vocally needs study.[15] Juveniles have more "loose" body feathering and lack glossy iridescence. Juveniles at the nest and recently fledged

The age of crows and ravens can typically be determined throughout the first year of life as either adult or first-year. Adults (left) have glossy, iridescent, black body plumage and flight feathers; juveniles (center) have duller brownish-black body feathers that lack the iridescence of adult feathers; and first-years (right) molt into an adultlike glossy body plumage yet retain the brownish, worn, and faded flight feathers of juvenile plumage (early fall through first summer). American Crows: Everglades, FL, Jan (BLS) (left); Bolinas, CA, Jul (SNGH) (center); Central Valley, CA, Feb (BLS) (right).

individuals of each species sound higher pitched than adults, causing confusion.

AMERICAN CROW: The quintessential corvid of North America, this adaptable, widespread species is found breeding throughout much of south and central Canada and is resident in most of the Lower 48, absent only in parts of the arid Southwest including southern Texas, southern New Mexico, Arizona (irruptions south occur in some years in these states), and southern/central California. Its status in northwestern Washington where its range meets that of Northwestern Crow is uncertain (see Taxonomic Note above). It often attends large roosts in winter but is less social when breeding.

American Crow prefers open, semiopen, agricultural, or urban habitats, and it averages larger than other crows and has broad wings, a shortish and rounded tail, and heavy legs and feet. A close inspection of the back feathers may reveal a more scaly appearance to the back compared to the more confiding Fish Crow.[16] Juvenile and immature Americans are sootier than adults, lacking the iridescence shown by adults. Though seldom useful in the field, digital photos of juvenile and immature Americans may reveal a pinkish mouth, rather than rather than the orange one of Northwestern Crow[17] (needs study).

Voice: American Crow has a varied and fascinating repertoire that includes mimicry of subjects such as Barred Owl, cats, dogs, and even humans.[13] The common call is the familiar and distinctive deep, raspy "caw" or "haw!" often repeated in quick succession several times. This is the sound used most often in long-distance communication[13] and there are at least eight variations;[18] the functions of each appear to change with the context (season, location, etc.). They also give a variety of clucks, rattles, grunts, and burbles. Of these perhaps the most commonly heard is the "dive-attack" rattle given when diving at other crows and raptors,[13] and a "ga-rok" rattle call in which the "r" is rolled. Be aware that juveniles sound more nasal and so can be confused with Fish Crow. Juveniles' nasal call is usually associated with begging, so once they leave the natal territory, a more regular voice is used. By early fall most juveniles have stopped making these nasal calls.

FISH CROW: This smallish, glossy-plumaged southeastern crow flourishes near humans and is often found in semiurban areas, around landfills (outnumbering American Crows there) and fast food joints, and along the coast. Usually near water, it is increasing inland along waterways, and common over much of the Southeast, throughout the Gulf States (east from east Texas), through Florida, Georgia, and the Carolinas, and north along the coast into Maine. Inland it occurs along the Mississippi Valley, including along the Arkansas River into western Oklahoma and Kansas (east of the Great Plains), and north to southern Iowa (mostly absent along the Ohio River). In the Northeast it is found inland especially along the

Adult American Crow, CA, Jan (BLS) (left); first-winter American Crow, CT, Mar (MS) (right). This plate shows all three common crow species together and highlights the subtlety of the differences between them; they are often impossible to identify visually, and are best identified by voice. American Crow may comprise several species, and the coastal Pacific population deserves special scrutiny: they are smaller, sound different, and behave more like Fish Crows than like typical American Crows.

Adult Fish Crow, FL, Mar (BLS) (left); adult Fish Crow, VA, Oct (GLA) (right). Fish Crows are best identified by voice and behavior. They are more social than American Crows where the two species occur together, and Fish Crows are more likely to be found picking garbage in a dumpster in a suburban setting. American Crows favor more pastoral settings in the East. Fish Crows have a distinctive voice, but beware of the nasal calls of begging juvenile American Crows, which can be heard from late spring through at least August.

Adult Northwestern Crow, AK, May (BLS) (left); first-spring Northwestern Crow, AK, May (BLS) (right). Northwestern Crow is not visibly different from the American Crows occurring farther south on the Pacific Coast. This taxon is still a matter of debate and may actually be a subspecies of American Crow. Northwestern Crow's voice averages a bit lower pitched and hoarser than that of American, but there is much overlap.

Susquehanna and Hudson rivers, all the way to Lake Erie, Lake Ontario, and even Lake Champlain.

The extent of its movements and migration remains poorly understood, but it is at most a short-distance migrant. Though its range is expanding, vagrants have occurred only as far as the Bahamas[19, 20] and north to Nova Scotia,[21] with no records west of the Great Plains. Certainly its similarity to American Crow clouds our understanding of the extent to which it may wander, but like many other southeastern bird species, Fish Crow appears not to stray often or dramatically.

Distinguishing Fish Crow from American Crow is difficult. Even for the most expert, the degree of confidence in identifying silent crows probably rests at 80 percent at best (personal observation).[16] Being intelligent birds, all crow species are wary and alert around humans, but Fish Crow seems more tolerant of humans compared to American, allowing photographers more leeway than does American Crow, for example. Though Fish Crow is slightly smaller than American Crow, assessing size is hard in the field. Similarly, the glossier purple plumage of Fish Crow can be tough to discern in certain light and is less obvious on worn birds. Fish Crows have shorter legs and smaller feet, too (this is especially noticeable compared to American Crows in Florida; see Taxonomic Note above). The upperpart feathers are fluffier and blend together more compared to those of American Crows, so Fish Crows appear less scaly above, and they often show a more pronounced hook at the end of the bill.[16] In flight Fish Crows often flap slightly faster, with somewhat floppier wingbeats, and show more pointed wings, with perhaps a narrower wing base and a longer tail. When perched and vocalizing, Fish Crows have a different posture than Americans; Fish Crows appear more hunched up and more bearded (with throat feathers erected), while American Crows usually extend their neck more and have a smoother-looking throat.[16]

Voice: Fish Crow is easily distinguished by voice. It has a far less varied repertoire than American, and its most common sound is a distinctive, nasal, and rather pessimistic "unh-uh" or "ah . . . ah-uh." The sound recalls a casual negative response to a question; an alternative to "nope." Fish Crows give a caw call like other crows, but it sounds more like "awk" or "ownk," and it's often repeated quickly. They frequently call in flight, and their sounds are noticeably higher pitched than those of Americans. Beware of juvenile American Crows (usually near the nest, accompanied by parents), which sound similarly high pitched and nasal but differ in cadence, trailing off more and lacking the pattern associated with Fish Crow.

NORTHWESTERN CROW: A confounding taxon (see Taxonomic Note above), Northwestern Crow is supposedly largely restricted to the coast from Alaska (Kodiak Island/Kenai Peninsula and south) through British Columbia and into northwest Washington. It is supposedly found up to about 5,000 feet in elevation, and along rivers sixty miles inland.[22] In the Puget Sound area, it comes into contact with American Crow, and there crow identification is problematic, to say the least! The two apparently interbeed,[8, 13] and they appear essentially identical.

Northwestern averages ~10 percent smaller[8, 13] and, perhaps owing to its smaller size, is said to flap slightly faster when it flies. The habits may differ slightly, with Northwestern being perhaps slightly more social and also preferring intertidal flats for foraging.[13]

Voice: As with physical characters, there seems to be no consistent difference in voice from that of American Crow.[15] Northwestern also produces an array of sounds, but these are generally described as lower pitched and hoarser than those of American, and perhaps it calls more rapidly, too.[23] Vocalizations need more study, but overlap with American seems extensive (complete?).

COMMON RAVEN: The world's largest passerine (songbird) occurs across much of the Northern Hemisphere and is one of the earth's most widespread, adaptable, resourceful, and intelligent birds. It can persist in remote wilderness and in places where few other animals survive, and it is one of the few species capable of wintering above the Arctic Circle. Yet it is also at home in mountainous areas, in the desert, and even in some urban settings.

Common Raven ranges throughout most of Canada and through most of the western United States, west of the Great Plains. East of there it occurs around the northern Great Lakes, through much of New England, and south along the Appalachians into northern Georgia, but it is largely absent from the Great Plains, the Midwest, and the Southeast. Away from Arctic and subarctic regions, Common Raven avoids flat, low country, except in parts of the Southwest and southern California. There it is found near human settlements with tall structures (which provide perches or nesting sites), and it also scavenges at landfills and along roads.

Adult Common Raven, CA, Jan (BLS) (left); adult American Crow, CA, Jan (BLS) (right). Distinguishing between Common Raven and American Crow is a challenge. These images are not to scale (raven is always larger), but note differences in head and bill structure, especially Common Raven's longer, heavier bill, glossier plumage, and shaggy neck feathers.

Common Raven, CA, Jan (BLS) (left); American Crow, CA, Jan (BLS) (right). When Common Raven is on the ground, note its larger, more imposing build, glossier plumage, and larger head and bill. Raven's wings are longer and reach the tail tip, whereas Crow's wings are shorter, falling well short of the tail tip.

Adult Common Raven, CA, Feb (BLS) (left); adult American Crow, CA, Oct (SNGH) (right). When Common Raven is in flight, note its more elongated appearance, larger head and bill, longer, wedge-shaped tail, and especially its longer wings, with notably longer and more pointed "hands" than in Crow. These shape differences can be applied to distinguishing either of the raven species from any of the crow species. Ravens also have deeper, more even-paced, rowing wingbeats, and they are much more aerial than crows, soaring and gliding in raptor-like fashion more frequently and extensively than crows.

Adult Common Raven (left) and Chihuahuan Raven (right) bill detail (BLS). In general, Common Ravens have deeper and longer bills than Chihuahuan; also, the nasal bristles extend out only halfway on the culmen on Common, and usually farther on Chihuahuan. There is overlap in this character and it is subject to the vagaries of wear and molt, as well as age-related differences, but if you see extensive nasal bristles it's a good indication of a Chihuahuan Raven. In general, Chihuahuan looks shorter and stouter billed, with less exposed culmen.

Adult Common Raven, CA, Apr (AJa) (left); immature Chihuahuan Raven, NM, Sep (BS) (right). The outward plumage appearance of these two is identical, so again, look at bill characteristics and note the voice.

Adult Common Raven, AK, May (BLS) (left); adult Chihuahuan Raven, TX, Apr (MM). Common Ravens in the northern and eastern parts of the species' range average larger and may represent a different species. Chihuahuan Raven used to be called "White-necked Raven" in reference to the white-based feathers of the neck (visible here). In reality, all the body feathers have white bases, not just neck feathers. Determining whether you're seeing white or pale gray can be difficult in bright sun, so be cautious.

Common Raven

Chihuahuan Raven

Black corvids are frequently seen in flight, and birders are often confronted with challenging identification situations involving these species. The four widespread species are depicted here, with the two ravens on this page, and American and Fish crows on the opposite page. Note both ravens' larger size and more elongated structure, including bigger head and bill, longer, wedge-shaped tail, and especially longer "hands." Common Raven (left column) is the largest of the four, often appearing raptor-like in flight. It is nearly identical to Chihuahuan Raven (right column) in flight, but note Chihuahuan's smaller size and somewhat slimmer build, with very slightly slimmer wings and narrower "hands." These shape differences are difficult to see here, and all but impossible to be sure of on a lone flying bird. To distinguish the ravens, note range, habitat, and especially voice. Through a combination of these, most birds should be identifiable (Common Raven images, BLS; Chihuahuan Raven images, NH).

American Crow

Fish Crow

American Crow (left column) and Fish Crow (right column) are very difficult to distinguish in flight if vocalizations are not heard. Luckily for birders, these birds frequently vocalize in flight, so keep your ears open. American Crow is slightly larger and flaps a bit more slowly. One structural difference that can be worth noting in photos is that on American Crow, P5 (P10 is the outermost primary on the wing) is quite a bit longer than P4, creating a more rounded wing tip. On Fish Crow, P5 is similar in length to P4, creating a more pointed wing. These differences are very subtle, and there is likely some overlap in this character—more study is needed. Fish Crow may average more round tailed, with its tail appearing more fanlike and having a narrower base, whereas American Crow is a bit more squarish tailed. Northwestern Crow (not pictured here) is identical to American Crow in flight (all photos, BLS).

Those in the eastern United States historically avoid areas inhabited by humans and seldom scavenge along roads, but their numbers are increasing in the East. In accordance with Bergmann's Rule, ravens at higher latitudes (e.g., Alaska) are noticeably larger than those farther south (California).

The movements of Common Raven remain poorly understood. Many seem resident or may make only relatively short migrations, but this highly aerial species tends to wander more than other black corvids do. Along the Atlantic Coast, from New Jersey to North Carolina, it occurs rarely and unpredictably as a vagrant. Vagrant Common Ravens also appear rarely in the Midwest or on the Great Plains. There are virtually no records from the Mississippi Valley, Alabama, the southern half of Georgia, or Florida. Though widespread in most of the West, it is inexplicably absent in a number of areas.

Distinguishing this raven from crows, particularly American Crow, is the most common problem, but where it overlaps with Chihuahuan Raven, distinguishing the two ravens is also tricky (see Chihuahuan Raven below). Compared to crows, Common Ravens are distinctly larger, with a longer tail, lankier wings, and a longer, heavier bill. When perched or walking, they have thicker legs than crows, and longer necks with more obvious "beards" (throat hackles; most apparent when calling), and ravens are more imposing birds overall. In flight they show a more graduated wedge-shaped tail, and longer, more tapered wings, soaring routinely, whereas crows soar only briefly and inefficiently. Ravens engage in aerial displays (including "rolling") more often than crows, and they rarely mob hawks, as crows do. Especially when soaring, and when seen from a distance or at an oblique angle, ravens can recall raptors, but their blackness and movements as they come out of a soar should separate them from raptors even at great distances. From a distance, ravens can look white above when sunlight reflects off their iridescent back feathers, but no raptor shows this effect.

Voice: Common Raven is another corvid possessing a large, varied vocal repertoire; its most common call is a "waah!" or "hah." This call varies in quality and urgency, at times sounding like an alarmed scream of horror, at other times more matter-of-fact and chatty. It also gives a sharp, deep "rok, rok, rok"; deep, croaking, and penetrating "krup" calls; and almost honking "howk" or "how-ik" calls, as well as an array of guttural rattles and clicks. Its voice averages deeper than that of Chihuahuan, but there may be some overlap.

CHIHUAHUAN RAVEN: The status of this poorly known corvid of the arid southwestern United States (and Mexico) is obscured in parts of its range by its similarity to Common Raven. Intermediate in structure between American Crow and Common Raven, it is best distinguished from the similar Common Raven by a combination of bill structure (including the extent of feathering on the culmen), range, habitat, and voice. The old name for this species is "White-necked" Raven, and indeed it possesses white bases on the neck feathers, but typically these are well hidden (hence the species name *cryptoleucus*) and are usually not useful in identification. In fact, not just the neck feathers but the entire body plumage has white bases in Chihuahuan, so any gust of wind can reveal these if you look carefully. Common Raven has gray-based feathers, and strong sunlight can make gray versus white surprisingly difficult to distinguish.

This species can be quite social (perhaps more so than Common), especially in winter, but flocks may form in both breeding and nonbreeding season. Roosts may number several hundred birds,[24] but it is just as often seen singly or in loose association with other individuals. Chihuahuan Raven ranges from northern Mexico north along the Rio Grande Valley, from the central coast of Texas west to southeastern Arizona. The heart of the species' range in the United States is from eastern New Mexico (except the northwest quadrant) and the western half of Texas north through the panhandle of Texas and Oklahoma to extreme southwestern Kansas and into the eastern half of Colorado, where it occurs north sparsely to Colorado Springs (and in winter to the Denver area). Vagrants out of range are seldom detected because Chihuahuan seems to seldom stray, or perhaps this is more because of its similarity to Common Raven. Chihuahuan Raven's range appears to be contracting.[24] Breeding in flat arid grasslands and desert scrub (with creosote, shinnery oak, and mesquite),[24] it frequents agricultural areas, landfills, or the outskirts of towns in winter. Sometimes it is also found in hilly areas of sparse piñon-juniper, and in riparian areas.

Though Chihuahuan Raven averages closer in size to American Crow, the differences in structure (larger size, longer wings and tail, more wedge-shaped tail, and heavier bill) make distinguishing it from Common Raven more of a challenge. Especially in flight, the two ravens are difficult or even impossible to tell apart. When Chihuahuan Raven is at rest, note that it is smaller, has a smaller and less angular head, a shorter, thicker bill,

Tamaulipas Crow, Mexico, May (LS). Tamaulipas Crow has bred sporadically in the very lower stretches of the Lower Rio Grande Valley, most recently around the Brownsville Airport. But it has not been seen there for about a decade, and birders frequently report Chihuahuan Ravens and Great-tailed Grackles as this species. Be on the lookout for any crows in this region, and note this species' glossy purple plumage, relatively small size, and uncharacteristically frog-like deep voice.

and a less obvious wedge shape to tail. The feathering on the nares is more extensive than in Common, extending to a point about two thirds of the way forward on the culmen (as opposed to halfway on Common), so that the exposed area of the culmen is less in Chihuahuan. Chihuahuan averages about 15 percent shorter in bill length and wing chord, and roughly 30 percent less in mass, compared to Common.[24, 25] Wind or preening may reveal the distinctive white bases to the neck feathers, but remember that Common has paler gray bases to these feathers (paler, but not white). The habits are little studied, but Chihuahuan seems to segregate from Common mostly by habitat. Common prefers foothills at higher elevation, whereas Chihuahuan prefers lower elevations in open desert, flat dry grasslands, or agricultural areas.

Voice: Vocalizations are in of need study, but they appear to overlap considerably with those of Common. The typical corvid "caw" call is a "raahk" or "waah," perhaps more nasal and higher in pitch than that of Common Raven. The vocal repertoire could be more limited than that of Common, but this needs confirmation.[24] Compared to that of American Crow, this species' caw call is lower, more guttural, and throatier.

Vagrants

Tamaulipas Crow is a Mexican species that ranges from Veracruz north along the Gulf Coast, rarely reaching extreme south Texas along the Rio Grande Valley. It was common at the Brownsville landfill through the 1980s and '90s[26] but has scarcely been recorded in the last decade. In 2000 it was readded to the Texas state review list. Formerly known as "Mexican Crow," this is a distinctive corvid that is small and noticeably glossy in plumage, and easily identified by voice. The typical call is a nasal, low-pitched, frog-like "arrrh." In Mexico it is a bird of open desert scrub.

Eurasian Jackdaw (a.k.a. Western Jackdaw) is a distinctive, dapper Eurasian corvid, known from just a few records in the ABA Area (nearly all from the 1980s), from the northeastern United States and Atlantic Canada. It once bred famously at a Lewisburg, Pennsylvania, penitentiary, but there have been very few records in the ABA Area since. Because this corvid is so small (much smaller than a crow) and has a white eye, a pale gray nape, and a rear crown that contrasts starkly with a dark crown, this species is unlikely to be confused with any other bird.

Eurasian Jackdaw, United Kingdom, Mar (AC). Eurasian Jackdaw is known from the ABA Area mainly from the 1980s, when several birds were scattered around the Northeast and the species actually bred in Pennsylvania. Since then there have been no records, and given how distinctive this species is, it seems unlikely to have gone overlooked.

References

[1] Mynors, R. A., trans. 1989. Collected Works of Erasmus: Adages: Ivi1 to Ix100. Toronto: University of Toronto Press.

[2] Emery, N. J., and N. S. Clayton. 2004. The mentality of crows: Convergent evolution of intelligence in corvids and apes. Science 306(5703): 1903–7.

[3] Madge, S., and H. Burn. 1994. Crows and Jays. Princeton, NJ: Princeton University Press.

[4] Feldman, C. R., and K. E. Omland. 2005. Phylogenetics of the common raven complex (Corvus: Corvidae) and the utility of ND4, COI and intron 7 of the β-fibrinogen gene in avian molecular systematics. Zoologica Scripta 34(2) (March): 145.

[5] del Hoyo, J., A. Elliott, and D. A. Christie. 2009. Handbook of Birds of the World. Vol. 14. Barcelona: Lynx Edicions.

[6] Omland, K. E., C. L. Tarr, W. I. Boarman, J. M. Marzluff, and R. C. Fleischer. 2000. Cryptic genetic variation and paraphyly in ravens. Proceedings of the Royal Society, Biological Sciences, Series B 267:2475–82.

[7] American Ornithologists' Union. 1931. Check-list of North American Birds. 3rd ed. Baltimore: American Ornithologists' Union.

[8] Johnston, D. W. 1961. The Biosystematics of American Crows. Seattle: University of Washington Press.

[9] Wahl, T. R., B. Tweit, and S. G. Mlodinow. 2005. Birds of Washington: Status and Distribution. Corvallis: Oregon State University Press.

[10] American Ornithologists' Union. 1957. Check-list of North American Birds. 5th ed. Baltimore: American Ornithologists' Union.

[11] American Ornithologists' Union. 1983. Check-list of North American Birds. 6th ed. Washington, DC: American Ornithologists' Union.

[12] American Ornithologists' Union. 1998. Check-list of North American Birds. 7th ed. Washington, DC: American Ornithologists' Union.

[13] Verbeek, N. A., and C. Caffrey. 2002. American Crow (Corvus brachyrhynchos). The Birds of North America Online. A. Poole, ed. Ithaca, NY: Cornell Lab of Ornithology. http://bna.birds.cornell.edu/bna/species/647

[14] McGowan, K. J. 2001. Fish Crow (Corvus ossifragus). The Birds of North America Online. A. Poole, ed. Ithaca, NY: Cornell Lab of Ornithology. http://bna.birds.cornell.edu/bna/species/589

[15] Spencer, A. 2012. North by northwest. Earbirding.com. http://earbirding.com/blog/archives/4139

[16] McGowan, K. J. 2005. How do you tell a Fish Crow from an American Crow? http://www.birds.cornell.edu/crows/FishCrow.htm

[17] Pyle, P. 1997. Identification Guide to North American Birds: Part 1. Bolinas, CA: Slate Creek Press.

[18] Parr, C. S. 1997. Social behavior and long-distance vocal communication in Eastern American Crows. PhD Thesis, University of Michigan.

[19] Norton, R. L. 1998. West Indies region. Field Notes 52:132–33.

[20] Norton, R. L. 1998. West Indies region. Field Notes 52:507–8.

[21] Godfrey, W. E. 1986. The Birds of Canada. Rev. ed. Ottawa: National Museum of Natural Sciences.

[22] Campbell, R. W., N. K. Dawe, I. McTaggart-Cowan, J. M. Cooper, and G. W. Kaiser. 1997. The Birds of British Columbia. Vol. 3, Passerines: Flycatchers through Vireos. Vancouver: University of British Columbia Press.

[23] Sibley, D. A. 2000. The Sibley Guide to Birds. New York: Alfred A. Knopf.

[24] Dwyer, J. F., J. C. Bednarz, and R. J. Raitt. 2013. Chihuahuan Raven (Corvus cryptoleucus). The Birds of North America Online. A. Poole, ed. Ithaca, NY: Cornell Lab of Ornithology. http://bna.birds.cornell.edu/bna/species/606

[25] Boarman, W. I., and B. Heinrich. 1999. Common Raven (Corvus corax). The Birds of North America Online. A. Poole, ed. Ithaca, NY: Cornell Lab of Ornithology. http://bna.birds.cornell.edu/bna/species/476

[26] Lockwood, M. W., and B. Freeman. 2004. The Texas Ornithological Society Handbook of Texas Birds. College Station: Texas A&M University Press.

[27] Verbeek, N. A., and R. W. Butler. 1999. Northwestern Crow (Corvus caurinus). The Birds of North America Online. A. Poole, ed. Ithaca, NY: Cornell Lab of Ornithology. http://bna.birds.cornell.edu/bna/species/407

[28] Klein, J. 2008. Technology Entertainment Design conference, March, New York University. Joshua Klein presented the potential use of a vending machine for crows. He suggested that the crows could be trained to pick up waste and the vending machine could be designed to give a reward in exchange for the trash.

[29] Pickrell, J. 2003. Crows better at tool building than chimps, study says. National Geographic News (April). http://news.nationalgeographic.com/news/2003/04/0423_030423_crowtools.html

[30] Ratcliffe, D. 1997. The Raven: A Natural History in Britain and Ireland. London: T. and A. D. Poyser.

Pipits

American Pipit (*Anthus rubescens*)

Sprague's Pipit (*Anthus spragueii*)

Red-throated Pipit (*Anthus cervinus*)

First Breeding:	First year
Breeding Strategy:	Monogamous; solitary, territorial
Lifespan:	5+ years

Small, slender, terrestrial birds of open country, pipits are inconspicuous and modestly attired. Their brown and buff plumage tones mix with bits of black and white, leaving them well camouflaged on the bare ground or amid the sparse grassy areas that they prefer. With relatively long legs they forage for insects, using their fine bills to pick prey from ground cover.

Over forty species of pipits exist worldwide; they make up a rather homogeneous and cosmopolitan group, and there are surely cryptic species still undescribed. All are in the genus *Anthus*, in the family Motacillidae,[1,2] a family shared with the dapper wagtails and the African longclaws. All members are noted for their strong flying ability, especially pipits, which have colonized many remote islands. North American pipits evolved from at least two waves of colonists (also called radiations) from the Old World. One wave likely came through Africa to South America, furnishing the *Anthus* of that continent, and Sprague's Pipit as well. Another wave reached North America through eastern Russia and spawned the tundra-breeding American Pipit and the related Red-throated Pipit, among others.[2,3,4]

Breeding areas for the North American pipits tend to be remote, so many birders see these species more frequently during migration or winter. Most familiar is American Pipit, which is widespread and locally common but also highly variable in appearance. Red-throated is primarily an Asian species, but it breeds sparsely in western Alaska. It is an irregular migrant to a small subsection of the continent and is famously irruptive, occurring in small numbers along the Pacific Coast, with records reaching even South America.[5] Though it could conceivably be overlooked elsewhere in North America, a record for eastern North America

seems possible. Sprague's Pipit breeds in the imperiled grasslands of the northern Great Plains, wintering in the southern Great Plains, the Southwest, and into Mexico. Seldom encountered, Sprague's is unfamiliar to most birders, so when you happen upon one, its rather drab appearance and skulking habits can cause confusion. Other species of pipit occur in North America as very rare vagrants from Eurasia, most often recorded in western Alaska.

Voice is key in the detection and identification of pipits. Often, these retiring birds flush from close by, exploding into the air, typically with a burst of strident, distinctive vocalizations, so pay attention to these sounds. When extended study is possible, you will see that these species resemble one another in shape but differ in plumage features and the coloration of bare parts. On a mystery pipit, remember range (in many places only one species is likely) but also focus on habitat, behavior, voice, and (if possible) plumage. Plumage details are of course helpful, but a combination of voice, behavior, and habitat clues may allow you to identify problematic pipits that you see only fleetingly.

Hints and Considerations

- Identification at breeding areas is usually straightforward but becomes tougher during migration or in winter when species overlap and vagrants occur. American Pipit is the default species, being widespread and less specific in habitat preferences.
- Finding Sprague's and Red-throated pipits requires real effort; seldom are they found serendipitously.
- Red-throated Pipit is rare outside western Alaska, and scarce even there. Periodic autumn "invasions" occur along the Pacific Coast from British Columbia to Baja, Mexico, particularly in coastal California. Nearly all are first-year birds, close to the coast. At times they associate with flocks of Americans.
- Sprague's is different, a bird of dry, open, barren areas and grasslands (usually away from water). It has more extensive white in the outer tail, and, unlike the others, does not bob its tail while foraging.
- Pipits are wary, and their flushing behavior can be informative. Spotting scopes help obtain prolonged study.

Nonbreeding American Pipit, western subspecies *A. r. pacificus*, CA, Oct (BLS). The American Pipit is widespread in winter across the Lower 48, though few birders are truly familiar with it. Extensive individual variation makes for some interesting identification challenges, particularly when it comes to understanding the subspecific differences in this species. Add to that the potential for a vagrant Sprague's Pipit or a pipit from the Old World, and you have a group of birds that typically receives little attention from birders and merits more scrutiny.

Focus on: *Voice, Range, Habitat, Plumage pattern, Behavior, Leg color*

American Pipit, CA, Oct (BLS) (left); Sprague's Pipit, CA, Feb (BLS) (right). Distinguishing American Pipit from Sprague's Pipit is fairly simple if the birds are seen well. They differ in plumage, structure, behavior, and habitat preferences. For typical winter habitat, American prefers wet, muddy fields, pond edges, beaches, and other open areas, whereas Sprague's occurs mainly in dry, grassy fields, typically with short or closely cropped grass, even cut lawns.

Breeding adult American Pipit, CA, Apr (BLS) (left); breeding adult Sprague's Pipit, ND, Jun (BS) (right). American Pipit has distinctive breeding and nonbreeding plumage, becoming buffy pink below in late spring, and grayish on the head and back. The amount of streaking and extent of pink below vary by subspecies. Sprague's looks similar year-round; note plain face with big dark eye, boldly streaked or scaled upperparts, and bright pink legs. American breeds on the tundra or at high elevation; Sprague's breeds in grasslands of the northern Great Plains.

Nonbreeding American Pipit, CA, Oct (BLS) (left); first fall Sprague's Pipit, KS, Oct (BLS) (right). Nonbreeding American Pipits vary substantially in plumage both within and among subspecies, but all show plain brownish-green upperparts, and streaked breast and flanks. Unlike American Pipits, juvenile Sprague's Pipits molt during fall migration, so first-fall birds can look quite disheveled, with messy upperparts and underparts as the preformative molt completes. Note the structural differences between these two, with Sprague's having an oddly skinny-necked appearance and a rounded head with a big eye.

Natural History Note:

When breeding, pipits perform aerial flight displays in which they sing persistently. In treeless expanses, these displays give males the prominence needed to establish territories and attract a mate. Sprague's Pipit in particular is known for its lengthy and vocal flight displays, which may run for nearly three hours and reach towering heights![17]

Why the long tertials? It is unusual for such strong-flying birds to have so little primary projection. Look at the nomadic finches in Fringillidae, or compare long-distance migrant wood-warblers or tyrant-flycatchers with those that migrate shorter distances, and you will nearly always see a correlation between strong, long-distance flying ability and longer wings. Longer wings usually translate to notably longer primary projection, but this isn't the case with birds in the family Motacillidae. In pipits, the primary tips are usually entirely covered by the unusually long tertials, so at rest they show zero primary projection or very little. Yet pipits are not short-winged birds; they just have long tertials. One wonders whether the aerial flight displays they perform on the breeding grounds are aided by their long tertials helping to keep them aloft longer. The exceptions in the group seem to support this idea, as those species showing some primary projection (Pechora, Tree, and Olive-backed pipits) differ slightly from the others in song delivery.[1]

Taxonomic Note:

American Pipit was split from Water Pipit (*A. spinoletta*) in 1989.[6, 7] The species now known as Water Pipit is confined to Eurasia and is unrecorded in North America. Confusing matters, however, is that Europeans refer to American Pipit by the common name Buff-bellied Pipit.

There are four subspecies of American Pipit,[8] three of which are confined to North America, and a fourth that breeds in east Asia. Some suggest that the species could be split into two or even three species.[1, 3, 9] In addition to the widespread nominate form, *A. r. pacificus* breeds along the Pacific Coast from the Aleutian Islands south to Oregon. The other two are:

A. r. japonicus, often referred to as "Siberian Pipit," breeds in northeast Russia and winters mainly in China and Japan. It differs from the others in plumage and leg color, is isolated from them by range, and also differs genetically;[9] it could be a separate species. It rarely strays to the Pacific Coast of North America but is regular in western Alaska (see Vagrants).

A. r. alticola breeds above tree line in the montane West from Montana south through Colorado, Utah, California, Arizona, and New Mexico.[10, 11, 12] It differs from the other taxa in breeding plumage (averaging less streaky and more rosy below), is isolated from them in breeding range, and differs genetically.[3] Studies of voice may reveal yet more differences.

- Confusion species: (1) Beware of juvenile Horned Larks. These are genuinely confusing birds, regularly mistaken for Sprague's Pipit. (2) Sky Larks can also cause confusion and are rare vagrants to Alaska, accidental in California, and introduced local residents on Vancouver Island.
- Pipits have long tertials. To distinguish a pipit from a confusion species (including sparrows such as Savannah, or longspurs), try to see the primary projection; most pipits show no primary projection.

Identification

Sexes are similar. Note that Sprague's Pipit shows little seasonal variation, and that juveniles differ only slightly from adults. American and Red-throated adults show distinct breeding and nonbreeding plumages.

Pipits undergo a complete prebasic molt on the breeding grounds prior to fall migration, and then a partial prealternate molt in March–April produces their breeding plumage. Pipits have a distinct juvenile plumage that is quickly molted in the late summer, so fall migrants more closely resemble adults. Determining the age of pipits during fall migration and in winter can be very difficult, as first-years and adults may appear similar. Some first-years are safely identified by a molt limit in the wing coverts; adults should have uniformly fresh wing coverts in fall.

The text below is focused on nonbreeding birds. Breeding birds are distinctive in plumage and are also usually easily separated by range and voice. Pipits migrate during the day, and flight calls are emphasized in voice descriptions.

AMERICAN PIPIT: Though it is widespread and common across North America, few birders take the time to study the American Pipit. Preferring barren fields, muddy margins of lakes and bogs, and coastal beaches, it often favors moist, bare ground near water, open sod, and tilled agricultural areas. It frequently bobs its tail when foraging and typically has darkish legs. When flushed, American Pipit usually rises rather

American Pipits, presumably of the nominate subspecies *A. r. rubescens*, TX, Nov (BLS). These two birds, photographed on the same day, show some of the individual variation in the nonbreeding plumage of American Pipit, even within a single subspecies. The bird at left shows some signs of breeding plumage, with a mix of pale gray and brown feathers on the head and back. The bird at right is more typical, with uniformly greenish upperparts. Note the variable dusky feather centers on the back, which don't give the back a streaked appearance as in some other pipits. Also note variation in leg color, which ranges from blackish to vinaceous in the North American breeding subspecies (but see *japonicus* plate).

Breeding adult American Pipit of the montane West, subspecies *A. r. alticola*, CO, Jun (LH) (left); nonbreeding American Pipit, TX, Nov (BLS) (right). In breeding plumage, the American Pipit subspecies differ in the general darkness and tone of the upperparts, the amount of streaking and extent of coloration below, and average size. Subspecies *alticola* of western alpine tundra averages larger and more richly colored below, usually with little to no streaking on the underparts. This pale Texas bird is likely a variant of the nominate subspecies, and birders are cautioned against trying to go too far with subspecies identification in nonbreeding American Pipits.

Nonbreeding American Pipit, western subspecies *A. r. pacificus*, CA, Oct (BLS) (left); American Pipit, CA, Oct (BLS) (right). American Pipits of the West Coast average buffer overall than nominate birds, and the streaking below is usually blurrier and often appears veiled in fresh plumage. In flight note the long blackish tail with white outer tail feathers, and dark necklace. Pipits call frequently in flight, and these sounds are great clues for both detection and identification.

Breeding adult Sprague's Pipit, SK, May (GB) (left); nonbreeding Sprague's Pipit, TX, Nov (KK) (right). During the breeding season there is no range overlap between Sprague's and American pipits. Note Sprague's pale face and underparts, streaked back, and bright pink legs. Sprague's has a very distinctive song that is given both on the ground and in skylarking flight displays. Nonbreeding Sprague's average more washed buffy overall. Note the patterned upperparts, which can appear either scaled or streaked depending on the angle.

Sprague's Pipit, TX, Mar (TJ) (left); Sprague's Pipit, CA, Oct (LS) (right). Sprague's Pipit lives in open country, usually in very short grass, so it is exposed to strong sun much of the time. By spring (left) birds become worn, faded, and paler than when fresh in fall (right). Note typical posture with the bird looking over its shoulder, crouching or walking away from the observer!

Sprague's Pipit, CA, Feb (BLS) (left); Sprague's Pipit, KS, Oct (BLS) (right). Sprague's Pipit relies on its cryptic plumage and mouse-like habits to camouflage itself from potential predators. Sprague's is more apt to crouch down in the grass or run mouse-like away from you than it is to flush. When it does flush, it is usually from close underfoot; birds typically rise in a spectacular stair-stepping skyward flight, giving their distinctive "squit-squit" flight calls before descending back into the grass, often not far away. On birds in flight note the finely streaked necklace as well as the more obvious white in the outer tail than on American Pipit.

Breeding Red-throated Pipit, AK, Jun (BS) (left); first-winter Red-throated Pipit, Mexico, Oct (SNGH) (right). Unlike American Pipits, adult Red-throated Pipits look similar year-round. But most North American records, especially during fall migration, involve first-fall birds (right). Note heavily streaked underparts, blackish malar, streaked upperparts, pink legs, and black median wing coverts with bold white fringe. The fun thing about Red-throated Pipit is that it occurs with enough frequency that well-informed birders can actually hope to find one, if they are in the right place at the right time (coastal California or Baja in October).

First-fall Red-throated Pipit, CA, Oct (BLS). Among American Pipits, Red-throated Pipit really stands out. Most show strongly marked underparts that look as if someone took a black Sharpie pen and drew on the bird. The upperparts are more variable but always appear streaked. Leg color is less variable than on American Pipit, typically a bubble-gum pink, including the feet.

First-fall Red-throated Pipit, Mexico, Oct (SNGH) (left); Red-throated Pipit, CA, Oct (BLS) (right). Note the bold blackish streaks on the back of this bird, created by the extensive blackish feather centers. American Pipit can have narrow dusky feather centers but doesn't approach this pattern. Note that Red-throated Pipit's back can appear even more boldly streaked than this, often appearing black and white instead of black and brown, as in this bird. On birds in flight note Red-throated's slightly more compact appearance, and especially listen for its distinctive flight call, an explosive "speeee".

deliberately, descending again at some distance. It often occurs in flocks, at times with other open-country species such as Horned Lark, Savannah Sparrow, Lapland Longspur, and even occasionally with the rare Red-throated Pipit.

Juveniles and adults appear essentially similar by fall, and nonbreeding-plumaged birds are less variable in appearance than breeding birds, but they still vary in color (especially on the underparts) and in the degree of streaking on the chest. Nonbreeders are olive brown above and the back is usually plain, but heavily marked birds may show a hint of fine, dark streaking there (but never bold as on Red-throated and Sprague's). The greater upperwing coverts are dusky gray at the center but fringed with buff (not bold white), creating variable wing bars. The latter are hidden at times or may wear away. The underparts are pale, ranging in color from buff white to brownish buff, often with browner flanks, and with variable dark streaking on the chest and flanks. The streaking may appear fine or rather heavy, but it often forms a necklace contrasting with a paler whitish throat. The throat is bordered by darker mustache-like stripes that connect with the chest streaking below and become weaker near the bill. Head pattern is useful also. Most show a fairly obvious whitish eye ring, a pale supercilium, and darkish auriculars offset by a pale malar. *Voice:* The flight call is a whispered "spi-pit," wheezing and breathy (ML Cat# 131478). The calls of birds in flocks run together.

SPRAGUE'S PIPIT: A strictly North American species, Sprague's is easily identified with reasonable views and a little caution. It is seen singly or in small groups, and nearly always in dry grasslands. Unlike the others, it doesn't bob its tail, and it doesn't typically forage on open ground, preferring to stay amid grassy cover. Notably "mousy" in its behavior, Sprague's runs through the grass furtively, often with only its head periscoping above the vegetation. It prefers to run and hide from a threat and doesn't usually flush until nearly underfoot. When it does flush, it does so quite explosively, often rocketing skyward in escalating flight before folding up and plummeting down, sometimes landing near its initial taking off point.

Compared to the others, Sprague's is short tailed and shorter legged, a little more plump, and less elongate. The pale face (whitish lores and buffy auriculars) makes the dark eye look big and prominent. The shorter tail also has more extensive white compared to that of the others. Juveniles resemble adults but have scaly backs, and possibly yellower gapes, but regardless of age, Sprague's shows a more patterned back (darkish mixed with white buff) than American. Sprague's has a streakier crown, too. On the underparts, fine streaks are concentrated on the breast and sides of the upper breast, with little or no streaking on the lower flanks. On singing breeders in display flight high overhead, note the pale translucent flight feathers. The legs are pinkish. *Voice:* Sprague's performs long, high, aerial song flights; it gives a mechanical, draining, spiraling "spweeee-spweeee-spweeee" while gliding, between periods of flapping in circles. It is difficult to see when singing, but easy to hear. When flushed, it emits a distinctive explosive "squit" or doubled "squit-squit" (ML Cat# 45225).

RED-THROATED PIPIT: Quite rare in North America and seldom seen, this species nests occasionally or sparsely in western Alaska and is also a regular migrant there (late August to late September). It is a rare fall migrant along the Pacific Coast from southern British Columbia to Baja California (especially California), where periodic autumn irruptions occur. Away from the coast the species is accidental (as far inland as Arizona). Even during noninvasion years there are a few reports in coastal California and Baja. Pacific migrants or vagrants occur between late September and early November; winter and spring records from along the Pacific are very rare.

The red throat itself is rarely ever seen in North America (outside Alaska), as a majority of migrants are first-fall birds that lack red altogether. It is fairly distinctive when present, but note that some breeding American Pipits (especially *A. r. alticola*) have pinkish or rosy coloration on the underparts. The red throat on Red-throated Pipit is featured on adults, though some adult females lack red, and a very few first-winters (presumably males) show a small amount of red.[1] In hue it is less a true red, and more a pinkish or rufous.

Red-throated is slightly more "sawed off" compared to American Pipit, with a slightly shorter tail and bill. These subtle structural differences are perhaps most noticeable in flight, especially when the two are together. Otherwise they are quite similar in structure and habits. Red-throated is a bit more shy, often opting for a little more cover, favoring pastures, and grassy areas at the fringe of wet or muddy areas. But it will also frequent open sod and tilled agricultural fields, where it may mingle with American Pipits. It occurs singly or in small flocks, again, at times with Americans. When flushed, Red-throated behaves similarly to American, lurching upward in a jarring manner before landing again, sometimes only a moderate distance away.

First-fall/winter Red-throated Pipits are distinctively marked with heavy dark streaking below, and also with moderate vertical streaking on the back. The back streaking (alternating light and dark) usually includes a couple of fairly striking buffy "braces." Head pattern is also useful, and note the relatively short, pale supercilium that ends abruptly behind the eye, and how the dark olive-brown auriculars contrast noticeably with the pale malar. The pale throat is bordered by (and contrasts sharply with) the distinctly black mustache-like stripes that blur into dark heavy streaking at the side of the neck and continue down the flanks. These clusters of dark streaks at the sides of the neck are often readily noticeable but sometimes are more subdued. The crown has thin black streaks, and the nape is unstreaked brownish. The greater upperwing coverts are blackish, bordered by contrasting white. The legs are typically pink. *Voice*: The distinctive flight call is a loud yet thin, single, descending "speeee," explosive when close (ML Cat# 140688).

Vagrants

The following Old World species have occurred as vagrants in North America, mostly from Asia to western Alaska, but a few are also accidental vagrants farther south. All are extremely rare, and claims undocumented by photographs must be met with skepticism.

"Siberian" Pipit (*A. r. japonicus*) is currently regarded as a subspecies of American Pipit (taxonomy is vexed). Like Red-throated Pipit, Siberian Pipit is irruptive; it is a rare but regular stray to western Alaska, and very rare in California and Mexico. Its occurrence may coincide with irruptions of Red-throated Pipits along the Pacific Coast.[13, 14] It is particularly similar to *A. r. pacificus*, the subspecies of American Pipit from Alaska and western North America (and birds appearing intermediate occur). Compared to nonbreeding *A. r. pacificus*, Siberian has slightly darker and browner upperparts (some show mantle streaking), a whiter ground color below, relatively heavier streaking below, and, most noticeably, pale and pinker legs (some Americans show dusky pink legs). On Siberian the malar stripe is dark and broad, and the greater upperwing coverts are darker centered yet whiter fringed (so more like a Red-throated). The flight call needs study, but it may differ slightly from that of other American Pipits.[1]

Olive-backed Pipit (*A. hodgsoni*) has occurred in spring and fall in the Bering Sea. It is accidental in Nevada, California, and Baja. It shows a plain olive back that is faintly streaked with black, a buffy breast streaked with black, a white belly, and pale legs. The

Olive-backed Pipit, China, Dec (DI) (left); Pechora Pipit, AK, Sep (BLS) (center); Tree Pipit, Belgium, Aug (BLS) (right). All three of these are very rare vagrants. On Olive-backed note the bicolored eyebrow, which is yellow in front of the eye and white behind; pale and dark auricular spots; white belly with buffy breast and flanks; faintly streaked olive back; and neatly streaked underparts. On Pechora note the wing tips extending past the tertials (the only pipit in which this occurs); tawny upperparts, including crown; streaked back; and underparts similar to those of Olive-backed, with buffier breast and flanks (cf. Red-throated). Pechora has a boldly streaked back, like Red-throated, and is more patterned above than both Olive-backed and Tree Pipit. Tree Pipit is similar to Olive-backed, but note plainer head pattern (typically) and more boldly streaked back.

Nonbreeding "Siberian" American Pipit (*A. r. japonicus*), Japan, Dec (ID) (left); nonbreeding "Siberian" American Pipit, Japan, Jan (DS) (right). The "Siberian" Pipit is an enigmatic taxon that occurs in North America only as a vagrant, though it can be a regular migrant on the western Alaskan islands. Its pattern of occurrence farther south is similar to Red-throated Pipit, though it is detected less often and may be overlooked by birders. It should be looked for mainly during fall migration, especially in years when numbers of Red-throated Pipits are being reported in California and Baja. Note heavily streaked underparts, pale legs with darker feet, plain greenish back, and importantly, blackish wing coverts with bold white edges.

23.14. Nonbreeding "Siberian" American Pipit, CA, Nov (BLS). "Siberian" American Pipits usually occur in the company of American Pipits. They stand out from the crowd by being more heavily streaked below with a bolder blackish malar, and they usually have paler pinkish legs and feet. On most birds, at least the median coverts are black with white edges, and on some the greater coverts are blackish with white edges. Vocal differences between the two are not obvious.

"Siberian" American Pipit, CA, Oct (CR) (left); "Siberian" American Pipit, CA, Oct (CM) (right). On these two California vagrants note the general characters that set "Siberian" Pipit apart from American Pipit, including the more heavily streaked underparts, paler legs, and blackish wing coverts with bold white fringes. There are plenty of "tweener" pipits out there that can't be identified to subspecies, and it is likely that we are identifying only the more extreme examples of *A. r. japonicus* among the variably plumaged *A. r. pacificus*.

head pattern is unique, with a bold white supercilium, yellowish lores, and a black and a white spot at the rear of the auriculars. Like Pechora Pipit (see below), it is less likely than other pipits to call when flushed, and unlike the others it sometimes flushes into the tree canopy. Olive-backed bobs its tail when foraging. The flight call is a slightly buzzy, single "spizzz." It may sometimes give a mechanical, electric "zeepp."

Pechora Pipit (*A. gustavi*) is very rare in western Alaska. It is a very shy and quiet species. Pechora is quite similar to first-winter Red-throated, but it shows a slightly heavier bill, a buff wash on the breast, a distinctive head pattern with a tawny-brown ground color, and a crown with black streaks that extend onto the nape. The wing bars and back braces tend to be more prominent than on Red-throated, and the dark loral line is often bolder, too. Pechora is the only pipit that shows noticeable primary projection (on birds at rest, the primaries extend beyond the tertials). This mark is hard to see in the field, but photos often confirm it. Pechora usually flushes quietly but sometimes gives a distinctive buzzy, static-sounding "tziip" or "tchitt." When flushed, it usually flies a short distance and often hovers briefly before landing.[1]

Tree Pipit (*A. trivialis*) is a nondescript species, closely related to Olive-backed and similar in habits. It has occurred just a few times in western Alaska.[15, 16] It shows a white belly and a buffy breast with bold, thick streaking on the chest that becomes finer toward the flanks. The legs are pale. The brown back is moderately streaked brownish black. The flight call is similar to that of Olive-backed.[1]

References

[1] Alstrom, P., and K. Mild. 2003. Pipits and Wagtails. Princeton, NJ: Princeton University Press.

[2] del Hoyo, J., A. Elliott, and D. Christie. 2004. Handbook of the Birds of the World. Vol. 9, Cotingas to Pipits and Wagtails. Barcelona: Lynx Edicions.

[3] Voelker, G. 1999. Molecular evolutionary relationships in the avian genus *Anthus* (Pipits: Motacillidae). Molecular Phylogenetics and Evolution 11:84–94.

[4] Howell, S.N.G. 2010. Molt in North American Birds. New York: Houghton Mifflin.

[5] Brinkhuizen, D. M., L. Brinkhuizen, A. Keaveney, and S. Jane. 2010. Red-throated Pipit *Anthus cervinus*: A new species for South America. Cotinga 32: OL 15–17. http://www.neotropicalbirdclub.org/html/toc_32.html

[6] Knox, A. 1988. Taxonomy of the Rock/Water Pipit superspecies *Anthus petrosus*, *spinoletta* and *rubescens*. Breeding Birds 81:206–11.

[7] American Ornithologists' Union. 1989. Thirty-seventh supplement to the American Ornithologists' Union Check-list of North American Birds. Auk 106:532–38.

[8] Verbeek, N. A., and P. Hendricks. 1994. American Pipit (*Anthus rubescens*). The Birds of North America Online. A. Poole, ed. Ithaca, NY: Cornell Lab of Ornithology. http://bna.birds.cornell.edu/bna/species/095

[9] Zink, R. M., S. Rohwer, A. V. Andreev, and D. Dittman. 1995. Trans-Beringia comparisons of mitochondrial DNA differentiation in birds. Condor 97:639–49.

[10] American Ornithologists' Union. 1957. Check-list of North American Birds. 5th ed. Baltimore: American Ornithologists' Union.

[11] Parkes, K. C. 1982. Further comments on the field identification of North American pipits. American Birds 36:20–22.

[12] Miller, J. H., and M. T. Green. 1987. Distribution, status and origin of Water Pipits breeding in California. Condor 89:788–97.

[13] Sullivan, B. L. 2004. The changing seasons: The big picture. North American Birds 58:14–29.

[14] Hamilton, R. A., M. A. Patten, and R. A. Erickson. 2007. Rare Birds of California. Camarillo, CA: Western Field Ornithologists.

[15] Lehman, P. E. 2005. Fall bird migration at Gambell, St. Lawrence Island, Alaska. Western Birds 36:2–55.

[16] Kessel, B. 1989. Birds of the Seward Peninsula, Alaska: Their Biogeography, Seasonality, and Natural History. Fairbanks: University of Alaska Press.

[17] Robbins, M. B. 1998. Display behavior of male Sprague's Pipits. Wilson Bulletin 110:435–38.

Longspurs

Lapland Longspur (*Calcarius lapponicus*)

Smith's Longspur (*Calcarius pictus*)

Chestnut-collared Longspur (*Calcarius ornatus*)

McCown's Longspur (*Rhyncophanes mccownii*)

First Breeding:	First year
Breeding Strategy:	Monogamous and territorial, but Smith's is polygynandrous
Lifespan:	Up to 6 years

Unfamiliar to many birders, longspurs are small, sparrow-like songbirds of open country that feed on the ground and use their stout, conical bills to crack seeds. Along with Snow and McKay's buntings (genus *Plectrophenax*), they compose the family Calcariidae.[1] All four of the world's longspurs occur in North America, and three are endemic to the continent. Lapland is Holarctic (occurring worldwide in the Arctic), and named for a region in northern Scandinavia. McCown's Longspur differs from the others in being the sole member of the genus *Rhynchophanes*, and although it is genetically more closely related to the *Plectrophenax* buntings, it is more similar in appearance to the longspurs (*Calcarius*). In all but Smith's, breeding male longspurs perform dramatic and conspicuous aerial flight displays to project their songs while simultaneously advertising for mates and defining their territories. For Lapland Longspurs, this behavior has led the Unangan (Aleut) people of Alaska to affectionately refer to them as "gliders."

Smith's and Lapland are tundra breeders of the high Arctic, whereas Chestnut-collared and McCown's longspurs are prairie grassland breeders. McCown's breeds sparsely in the northern Great Plains and prairie provinces, where it overlaps broadly with Chestnut-collared Longspur. Smith's and Chestnut-collared longspurs are most closely related to one another.[1, 2] All four are migratory to varying extents: tundra breeders are long-distance migrants, and prairie breeders are short- or medium-distance migrants. In winter, longspurs inhabit vast open areas, especially between the Rockies and the Appalachians, with the highest diversity and concentrations occurring on the

Natural History Note:

Nesting in treeless expanses, longspurs often perform flight displays to project their song. The only species that doesn't do this is Smith's Longspur because it differs from the others in its breeding strategy. Smith's is not territorial; instead, it occupies home ranges where both males and females have multiple mates, making them one of the few polygynandrous bird species in North America. Broods of mixed parentage often result, and family groups with multiple males provisioning the same female and young are the norm.[3] Male Smith's may have testes twice the size of those of male Lapland; this is apparently a result of "sperm competition," in which males produce large volumes of sperm to secure paternity.[4] One Smith's Longspur was observed copulating over six hundred times in six and a half days![5]

southern Great Plains. There they occur in large roving flocks, typically flushing many meters before you can take a position to study them. When they are close, however, the eponymous long hind claw may be visible. This character is shared with other strong-flying birds of open country, including *Plectrophenax* buntings, Horned Lark, pipits, and wagtails, and provides greater purchase on the ground in high winds.

Because of their skittish habits and generally remote nesting areas, longspurs are both unfamiliar and sought after among birders. In winter, especially on the southern Great Plains, all four species can occur together, but mixed flocks of two or three species are more typical. Somewhat ironically, vagrant longspurs often provide better opportunities for study, sometimes allowing closer approach than is typical for the group. Being strong fliers, longspurs stray regularly, frequently turning up at various "migrant traps" around the country. Breeding males, with their dapper plumage patterns and skylarking song displays, are rather easily identified, but females are duller and more cryptic, with subdued patterns that create camouflage during nesting. In winter, however, both sexes become more subdued overall, as the buffy tips of freshly molted feathers veil the gaudy breeding colors and patterns, and at this time longspurs present a significant ID challenge for birders, so in this chapter we'll focus on distinguishing the longspurs in winter plumage. Good views are a must, and careful study

Adult male Lapland Longspur, AK, June (GV). Male longspurs are striking, with flashy plumage and amazing breeding displays. They are easy to identify so this chapter focuses more on nonbreeding males, females, and immatures, which are drabber overall, clad in buff, brown, black, and white, and make for a real identification challenge. In addition to plumage details, shape and voice provide helpful identification clues.

Focus on: *Head pattern, Wing pattern, Overall color/streaking, Voice, Primary projection, Tail pattern*

Longspur topography, showing key areas of focus for accurate identification (GB).

Plumage progression of adult male Lapland Longspur. In fall (upper left), they are at their freshest, having just completed molt. The breeding pattern is almost completely obscured by buffy or white feather tips (CA, Nov, BLS). By spring (upper right) the breeding pattern becomes obvious, mostly through a combination of wear and limited prealternate molt (CA, Apr, BLS). By midsummer (lower right) they are in peak breeding plumage (AK, Jun, GLA). By late summer (lower left) they are in heavy molt, with breeding plumage being replaced again by buffy-tipped, fresh feathers (AK, Aug, BLS).

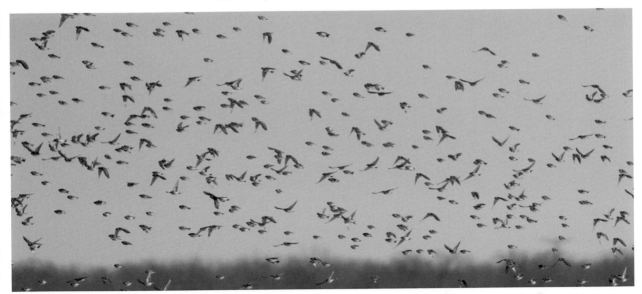

Longspurs are foreign to many birders because they breed on the tundra or the northern Great Plains and winter mainly in the middle part of the continent, in areas less populated by people. In such places longspurs form massive mixed- or single-species flocks, such as this flock of Lapland Longspurs in MO, Feb (TJ). Longspurs associate with other open-country birds in winter, most notably with Horned Larks, and often these large flocks comprise larks and several species of longspurs.

of both structure and plumage is required to arrive at an accurate identification. Structure is helpful, and primary spacing can be useful too, but with longspurs a "feather-by-feather" analysis of key parts of the bird is required for identification.

Hints and Considerations

- Range is an important first consideration. Lapland Longspur is the default longspur across much of the country in winter, whereas the others have more restricted breeding and winter ranges. Become familiar with Lapland and use it as a basis for comparison with the others.
- In winter, longspurs are more social, flocking at times with Horned Larks, Snow Buntings, Savannah Sparrows, or other nomadic open-country birds. Note that Smith's Longspurs are more homogeneous, seldom flocking with other species.
- Longspurs can be confused with other open-country birds such as Savannah and Vesper sparrows, or Lark Bunting. Larger sparrows, such as Lark or Harris's, might cause confusion, but they virtually never overlap in habits or habitat with longspurs.
- In western Alaska and along the Pacific Coast, furtive Asian *Emberiza* buntings occur extremely rarely and can be confused with longspurs.

- Even in winter many adult longspurs show hints of breeding plumage.
- Many encounters with longspurs involve birds inadvertently flushed from the ground, or flying birds. They call often in flight, and voice and tail pattern are useful tools.
- When close study is permitted, note the head pattern, the general overall color, the extent and quality of streaking below, and primary projection. Arctic breeders (Smith's and Lapland) are long-distance migrants, while prairie breeders (Chestnut-collared and McCown's) are medium-distance migrants, so the more migratory Arctic breeders generally have longer wings and longer primary projection.

Identification

In late summer (July–August), adults undergo a complete molt, resulting in a fresh, veiled fall/winter plumage. Breeding plumage is acquired through a combination of wear over the course of winter and early spring, as the brown-gray tips abrade to reveal richer breeding colors by late spring,[6] and a limited prealternate molt (most notably in Smith's). During winter, males appear more subdued and similar to adult females, but they are usually richer in color and often show hints of breeding plumage. First-winter females are overall drabbest, but

Breeding female Lapland Longspur, AK, Jun (GV); nonbreeding Lapland Longspur, NJ, Dec (BLS). Breeding females look similar to nonbreeding birds of both sexes. Note the rusty nape and bold dark auricular border, as well as the long wings extending past the tertials. Nonbreeding birds can be hard to age and sex, but all typically show bold dark streaked flanks, broad rusty notches on the tertials, and a bold dark auricular border. Lapland Longspurs are the longest winged of the longspurs, with 5–7 primary tips typically visible past the tertials.

Nonbreeding Lapland Longspur, BC, Oct (GB) (left); nonbreeding Lapland Longspur, CA, Oct (EM) (right). These two birds show typical variation in the auricular border pattern of nonbreeding Lapland Longspur, with some birds showing broken auriculars (cf. Smith's Longspur) and some with a border pattern that is muted altogether (cf. Chestnut-collared and McCown's).

Nonbreeding Lapland Longspur (right) with Horned Lark, CA, Nov (BLS) (left); juvenile Lapland Longspur, AK, Jul (ID) (right). Lapland Longspurs frequently associate with Horned Larks, and birders should carefully check flocks of Horned Larks for this species. Beware of juvenile Horned Larks, which are frequently confused for longspurs. Juvenile plumage in longspurs is kept for only a few brief months in late summer/early fall. Note the generally streaky plumage and lack of head pattern—longspurs become more adultlike through a preformative molt, usually prior to fall migration.

Adult male Smith's Longspur, IN, Apr (RSa) (left); adult female Smith's Longspur, MB, Jul (AJ). Breeding male Smith's Longspur is a striking bird, and in April, spring migrants move northward, molting into breeding plumage as they go. These birds show a mix of drabber nonbreeding and bold breeding plumage. Breeding females are much drabber than males. Note the typical features of Smith's, such as the buffy underparts with fine streaks, bold auricular border that is broken at the rear, and long wings (not as long as in Lapland!).

Nonbreeding Smith's Longspur, ME, Sep (LB) (left); nonbreeding Smith's Longspur, NJ, Jan (SG) (right). Birders should be on the lookout for vagrant longspurs. On these two vagrants, most likely first-year females, note the dark-bordered auriculars broken at the rear, long primary extension with uneven spacing between primary tips, buffy underparts that are finely streaked and lack a strongly contrasting white belly, and rufous-fringed tertials that lack the strongly notched effect of Lapland. Smith's can migrate in juvenile plumage, so vagrants found earlier in the fall (left) might retain more of the streaky juvenile plumage than those found later.

Nonbreeding Smith's Longspur, KS, Mar (SG) (left); nonbreeding Smith's Longspur, NJ, Jan (SG) (right). Smith's is a bit unusual in that during winter it forms single-species flocks, tending to not mix with other open-country birds or even with other longspurs. Birds hide furtively in dense grass, allowing close approach before explosively flushing. In flight, Smith's shows bold white wing bars on the upper wings (cf. Chestnut-collared) and has more white in the outer tail than Lapland.

Breeding female Chestnut-collared Longspur, ND, Jun (BLS) (left); nonbreeding Chestnut-collared Longspur, CA, Oct (BLS) (right). Breeding females are typically drab overall but can show quite a bit of chestnut on the nape, and black below. Nonbreeding birds are harder to age and sex, and even adult males can be very drab in fresh basic plumage. Often, however, adult males show some hint of the breeding plumage pattern, especially in the nape, face, or underparts. In general, nonbreeding Chestnut-collared is buffy overall like Smith's, with a small bill and variable, though generally short, primary projection. The tertials are similar to those of Smith's, though they average a bit more muted in pattern.

Nonbreeding male Chestnut-collared Longspur, TX, Nov (MK) (left); nonbreeding Chestnut-collared Longspur, AZ, Nov (DV). Some nonbreeding males show obvious signs of adulthood (left), with extensive blackish underparts. But more often, nonbreeding birds are overall buffy, with little head pattern and little color to work with. Note the small bill, very muted tertial pattern, and relatively short primary projection (right), with just three primary tips visible past the tertials.

Juvenile Chestnut-collared Longspur, WY, Jul (SB) (left); adult male Chestnut-collared Longspur, ND, Jun (BLS) (right). The prairie-breeding longspurs are more likely to be encountered as juveniles in the short late summer–early fall window; note streaked body and upperparts, and muted head pattern. In flight, Chestnut-collared shows lots of white in the tail (cf. McCown's), and bold white upper wing bars (cf. Smith's Longspur). The flight call of Chestnut-collared is unlike the others, a squeaky "queedle".

Breeding female McCown's Longspur, MT, Jun (BS) (left); nonbreeding McCown's Longspur, CA, Oct (LS) (right). McCown's differs from the rest of the longspurs in being more heavily built, with a bigger, flatter head, and especially a bigger, deeper bill. Breeding females are variable, and some appear similar to nonbreeding males. Nonbreeding birds are the plainest of all longspurs, at times recalling a giant female House Sparrow. Note the thick, pale bill with dark tip, plain head pattern and tertial pattern, and medium-length primary projection (highly variable).

Nonbreeding McCown's Longspur, BC, Oct (PK) (left); nonbreeding McCown's Longspur, TX, Nov (SF) (right). Note the big pink bill with dark tip, and variable but generally weak tertial pattern shown by both of these birds. Primary projection is variable and can be difficult to assess depending on the bird's position, but both of these birds show medium-length primary projection past the tertials. Adult male and some female McCown's can show wholly rusty median upperwing coverts; immatures, such as these, show broad buffy fringes to the median upperwing coverts.

Juvenile McCown's Longspur, WY, Jul (SB) (left); adult male McCown's Longspur, WY, Apr (SB) (right). Juveniles can be confusingly patterned with scaly upperparts and streaked underparts, but most are adultlike by early fall. In flight, McCown's shows the most white in the tail, which has a dark tip and dark central tail feathers creating an inverted T pattern, which can be difficult to ascertain in the field. As always, pay attention to flight calls. Note the row of rufous median upperwing coverts on this adult male; winter males (and some females) also show this.

determining the age of longspurs in fall/winter can be difficult, as there is much overlap in the general appearance of older females and first-winter males.[7] First-spring/summer birds appear similar to adults but generally retain a few signs of immaturity (e.g., white mottling on otherwise solid black plumage areas). Juveniles of all four species have a streaky, dusky overall plumage that is held only briefly in late summer, and molted prior to fall migration. The descriptions below exclude the distinctive breeding males and instead focus on females, nonbreeding males, or juveniles and first-winter birds.

LAPLAND LONGSPUR: One of the most abundant passerines in the Northern Hemisphere, and the most widespread longspur in North America, it is the least specific in its choice of winter habitat, occurring in a variety of areas with open ground. In winter on the Great Plains, Lapland frequently flocks with the prairie longspurs or Horned Larks, but it also makes use of coastal beaches, where it is often found with Snow Buntings. Lapland always shows considerable chestnut in the wings, especially in the greater coverts, but also in the tertials, which are rather broadly edged with chestnut. Laplands have *tertials that are strongly notched with chestnut*, not merely fringed with chestnut as in Smith's. Head pattern is useful, and almost all individuals show ear coverts boldly bordered with black, such that the cheeks (auriculars) are completely rimmed in black, most noticeably so on the rear auriculars. Most Laplands have heavy streaking along the flanks, which is usually dark and blurry, but some individuals are more faintly streaked. When visible, the primary projection is distinctive, being exceptionally long. This character can be tough to discern in the field (though now it is easier with digital photos), but Lapland shows five to seven primaries extending past the tertials—the longest of any longspur. In flight the outermost tail feathers are white, but the tail is otherwise dark, so the bird appears largely dark tailed with just a small amount of white in the outer tail. *Voice:* The flight call is a sharp, rattling "tic, tic, tic" interspersed with Snow Bunting–like, descending "teuw" notes.

SMITH'S LONGSPUR: This longspur is the buffiest below, differing from the others by preferring short grazed grass in flat areas, and also by occurring in flocks that are usually homogeneous.[8] It is most similar to Lapland Longspur but generally doesn't overlap with that species in habitat. Chestnut-collared can be similarly buffy below with fine streaks, but note its very short primary projection, extensive white in the tail, usually more obvious broken auricular bar, and weaker malar stripe. Compared to all other longspurs, Smith's has a warm buffy ground color, a narrow whitish eye ring, and white wing bars (white lesser coverts, best seen in flight). Some are strikingly rich buff below, whereas others are only pale buff, and most show light thin streaking across the upper chest and along the flanks. Compared to Lapland, Smith's has a less distinct dark border to the auriculars that is usually broken at the rear (rarely broken in Lapland). Importantly, Smith's has *dull chestnut fringes on the tertials*, not appearing as extensive or as strongly "notched" as on Lapland. The wings are also slightly shorter than those of Lapland, with uneven spacing among the exposed primary tips. In flight, the outer two tail feathers are white, and the rest of the tail is dark. *Voice:* This is similar to that of Lapland but lacks the interspersed "teuw" notes between rattles.

CHESTNUT-COLLARED LONGSPUR: The smallest longspur, inhabiting denser grasslands than the others, Chestnut-collareds at times cluster at remote water sources in winter, and they also inhabit desert grassland.[9] They often flock with Horned Larks and other longspurs in winter. Confusion with McCown's is most likely, as both appear rather drab gray brown overall and have weak head patterns with rather plain faces, but Chestnut-collared is smaller and darker billed and has shorter wings. Its primary projection is the shortest of all longspurs, with the wing tips projecting just beyond the tertials. The tertials are only lightly edged with brown, contrasting little with the darker inner webs. More so than other longspurs, winter/fall male Chestnut-collared often shows some breeding plumage aspects, with obvious black below, some buff in the face, and/or some chestnut on the nape. In flying birds, the tail is largely white and similar to that of McCown's, but with a narrow black wedge at the center. Similar to Smith's, Chestnut-collared has bold white wing patches visible on the upperwing. *Voice:* When flushed or flying, it gives a distinctive explosive "queedle."

McCOWN'S LONGSPUR: This palest and drabbest longspur exhibits a stout, pale bill, short tail, and moderately long primary projection. It prefers short grass, high prairie, dry lakebeds, and overgrazed areas with sparse vegetation and only a close crop of ground cover.[10] In winter, it often flocks with other longspurs, Horned Larks, and occasionally Sprague's Pipits. Fall and winter vagrants might recall a female House Sparrow, with a drab sandy-gray ground color, a broad pale supercilium on the plain face, and a nearly unstreaked grayish chest with a whitish belly. The large, pale bill often shows a dark tip, and the bill is a good feature to use for separating this species from others. The chestnut shoulder patch that is so evident on breeding males is often present to a degree on many nonbreeding males. The distinctive tail pattern is most easily studied when the tail is fanned, or in flight. The outer tail is extensively white but contrasts with the darker central tail area. This mark becomes an inverted black *T* pattern in adults. *Voice*: This is similar to that of Smith's, an overall dry rattle, lacking the "teuw" notes of Lapland.

References

[1] Chesser, R. T., R. C. Banks, F. K. Barker, C. Cicero, J. L. Dunn, A. W. Kratter, I. J. Lovette, P. C. Rasmussen, J. V. Remsen Jr., J. D. Rising, D. F. Stotz, and K. Winker. 2010. Fifty-first supplement to the American Ornithologists' Union Checklist of North American Birds. Auk 127:726–44.

[2] Klicka J., R. M. Zink, and K. Winker. 2003. Longspurs and snow buntings: Phylogeny and biogeography of a high-latitude clade (*Calcarius*). Molecular Phylogenetics and Evolution 26(2): 165–75.

[3] Briskie, J. V. 2009. Smith's Longspur (*Calcarius pictus*). The Birds of North America Online. A. Poole, ed. Ithaca, NY: Cornell Lab of Ornithology. http://bna.birds.cornell.edu/review/species/034

[4] Briskie, J. V. 1993. Anatomical adaptations to sperm competition in Smith's Longspurs and other polygynandrous passerines. Auk 110(4): 875–88.

[5] Tudge, C. 2008. The Bird: A Natural History of Who Birds Are, Where They Came From, and How They Live. New York: Crown Publishers.

[6] Howell, S.N.G. 2010. Molt in North American Birds. New York: Houghton Mifflin.

[7] Pyle, P. 1997. Identification Guide to North American Birds: Part 1. Bolinas, CA: Slate Creek Press.

[8] Dunn, E. H., and R. B. Dunn Jr. 1999. Notes on behavior of Smith's longspurs wintering in Oklahoma. Bulletin of the Oklahoma Ornithological Society 32(3): 13–20.

[9] Hill, D. P., and L. K. Gould. 1997. Chestnut-collared Longspur (*Calcarius ornatus*). The Birds of North America Online. A. Poole, ed. Ithaca, NY: Cornell Lab of Ornithology. http://bna.birds.cornell.edu/review/species/288

[10] With, K. A. 2010. McCown's Longspur (*Rhynchophanes mccownii*). The Birds of North America Online. A. Poole, ed. Ithaca, NY: Cornell Lab of Ornithology. http://bna.birds.cornell.edu/bna/species/096

Cowbirds

Brown-headed Cowbird (*Molothrus ater*)

Bronzed Cowbird (*Molothrus aeneus*)

Shiny Cowbird (*Molothrus bonariensis*)

First Breeding:	1–2 years old
Breeding Strategy:	Monogamous or promiscuous; brood parasites
Lifespan:	Up to 16 years

"It's a cowbird . . ."

Usually such a declaration is met with displeasure, disappointment, and sometimes even contempt or outright disgust. When we think of cowbirds we think of sneaky brood parasites, scourges of the avian community taking advantage of our favorite birds. Always on the make, cowbirds are ready to boot another bird's eggs out of a nest to replace them with their own. That they also leave their young for another, often smaller, species to care for is flat out repugnant. Simply put, cowbirds, are unpopular. A more objective view, however, reveals some incredibly interesting characteristics.

Reproductive strategy among cowbirds is fascinating and depends on their population densities. Brown-headeds may be monogamous, or both sexes may be highly promiscuous;[1] pair bonds appear difficult to maintain in densely populated areas.[2] Bronzed Cowbirds, like some hummingbirds and shorebirds, employ an "exploded lek" breeding strategy. Compared to "classic leks," in which many males gather within sight of one another and perform visual displays and engage in physical contests (e.g., grouse), exploded leks are driven by vocalizations from males spaced farther apart.[3] The Bronzed Cowbird displays in open areas with scattered trees, and both sexes are promiscuous, but males outnumber females (by five to one in Texas).[4] The courtship display of the Bronzed Cowbird is one of the most magnificent of any North American bird and includes exaggerated bowing, wing fluttering, "helicoptering," sky pointing (an aggressive posture given near rival males), and other dramatic poses. Each of these affected positions is made more

Natural History Note:

As North America's most widespread brood parasite, the much-maligned Brown-headed Cowbird has had a population boom that is largely the result of human disturbance. The species has merely taken advantage of the increased habitat (i.e., fragmented woodlands) available as a result of human activities.

Female Brown-headed Cowbirds find nests by locating a host perching or singing near a nest, or in the process of nest building.[1,7] The female ejects one or two eggs, replacing the ejected egg(s) with one of her own, at times spoiling the remaining host egg(s).[1] Females are uniquely adapted to produce eggs nearly continuously for two months, and they lay about forty eggs on average per season! Some ornithologists have thus characterized them as "passerine chickens." Many hosts have developed defenses against cowbirds, and 97 percent of eggs/nestlings never reach adulthood, even though, compared to their host's nestlings, nestling cowbirds hatch earlier, grow faster and larger, and call more loudly and persistently, thus monopolizing the food supply at the nest.[8]

Bronzed Cowbird is known to have parasitized > 101 species (though fewer successfully), but it favors oriole nests.[8] Brown-headed Cowbird has parasitized > 220 species, with favorite hosts including Yellow Warbler, Song Sparrow, and Red-eyed Vireo, among others.[1] Cowbirds have become a threat to several endangered songbirds, such as Kirtland's and Golden-cheeked warblers and Black-capped Vireo. Reducing cowbird parasitism in the range of the Kirtland's Warbler does not appear to have resulted in an increase in the warbler's population, suggesting that habitat availability may be a stronger limiting factor.[4]

striking by the erectile feathers of the neck ruff, breast, and back. Add to this that the song of the male Brown-headed Cowbird is the highest-frequency sound made by any North American bird, and contains the broadest frequency range,[5] and we have a truly interesting group of birds.

Cowbirds are part of the New World family Icteridae, which comprises about one hundred species and includes the blackbirds, orioles, meadowlarks, Bobolink, and grackles. The genus *Molothrus* includes all three North American cowbirds, the endangered Bronze-

Adult male Brown-headed (left) and Bronzed cowbirds, Mexico, Feb (SNGH). Typically objects of disdain in the birding community, cowbirds are unfairly derided for taking advantage of human-altered landscapes to better practice their fascinating nesting habits and behaviors. Adult males are easily identified, but females and immatures can pose interesting identification challenges. Brown-headed is widespread, but the other two species are range restricted in North America, and both occur as vagrants.

Focus on: *Range, Voice, Bill, Structure, Overall color/pattern, Eye color*

This plate shows the plumage progression of male Brown-headed Cowbird from juvenile to adult male. All three cowbirds molt from a streaky/scaly juvenile plumage into an adultlike plumage by way of a preformative molt in the late summer and early fall. By late fall and early winter, most birds cannot be safely aged, though sometimes a few juvenile flight feathers are retained through the first spring/summer (most obvious on males). First-winter males can either be identical to older males or appear a bit drabber and less glossy, but more study is needed. Juvenile Brown-headed Cowbird, CA, Aug (SNGH) (left); first-fall male Brown-headed Cowbird, CA, Oct (SNGH) (right).

Molting first-fall male Brown-headed Cowbirds, CA, Oct (BLS). These birds, photographed the same day at the same location, show males in various stages of molt. Note the retained brown juvenile flight feathers on the mostly black bird at right.

Adult male Brown-headed Cowbird, CA, Mar (BLS). Once this plumage aspect is reached, males appear similar year-round, with the only plumage changes a result of wear and molt. Prealternate molts are not well understood in cowbirds, but this bird appears to be actively molting its head feathers.

brown Cowbird (*M. armenti*) of northern Colombia, and the Screaming Cowbird (*M. rufoaxillaris*) of temperate South America. These birds are most closely related to the grackles and their allies,[6] which include the blackbirds in the genera *Agelaius* and *Euphagus*. In North America, two species of cowbird are common, and one is rare. The Brown-headed is widespread and familiar, occurring throughout the Lower 48 and much of Canada. Bronzed Cowbird is a largely Central American species that reaches its northern limit in the southwestern United States. The Shiny Cowbird is a bird of South America and the Caribbean that is rare if regular in south Florida and has strayed widely in the eastern half of the United States (especially the Southeast).

Cowbirds are conspicuous, preferring edge habitat and open country with scattered trees, but birders don't very often study them, so when you encounter a lone female or an immature cowbird, it may suddenly cause confusion. All three species have shown the ability to wander, especially in fall. Males are usually straightforward, but females and juveniles can be very hard (even impossible) to identify. Females and juveniles are drab, nondescript, and brown, with few prominent field marks. They are confused not only with each other but also with other birds. Range and voice are often the two first and best clues, but overall structure and bill shape are useful, too. Most show subtle plumage patterns that can be helpful, as well.

Hints and Considerations

- Other icterids are often confused with cowbirds. Brewer's Blackbird has a finer bill, longer tail, longer legs, and (in adult males) yellow eyes. Rusty Blackbirds have yellow eyes and are similar to Brewer's Blackbird in structure. Grackles have longer, heaver bills and long, keel-shaped tails, and usually pale yellow eyes. A juvenile cowbird might be confused with a female House Finch.
- Brown-headed is the most widespread cowbird and so provides a good basis for comparison with the others. The range of Bronzed overlaps with that of Brown-headed from southern Louisiana west along the US-Mexico border to the Colorado River. Shiny Cowbird is annual only in south Florida. It is rare or accidental elsewhere.
- *Listen up!* Cowbirds are vocal with distinctive sounds. Males give songs with usually two components: low gurgling introductory notes, and a variable liquid whistle as the primary component. Males also give shorter high-pitched whistles (especially in flight) but do not "chuck" like other blackbirds in flight. Females emit hard rattles, but these are very similar across species and take practice to distinguish.
- On female and juvenile birds, focus on structure and general color, head and eye color, and bill structure. Note the distribution of paler and darker plumage, and any streaking. In some instances distinguishing these species in these plumages may prove impossible.
- Brown-headed Cowbird flocks in flight are rounder and less linear than blackbird or grackle flocks.

Identification

The structural characters associated with each species are useful in all plumages. Flight calls are not described here but are useful in identification.

Adult males are usually easy to identify. They show distinctive, glossy, iridescent plumage. First-year males show patches of this but also retain some browner juvenile feathers until the following summer/fall (first prebasic molt).

Females appear similar to juveniles in general plumage, but females are plainer overall, and less streaky below. They also are less scaly above, lacking the pale edges to the upperparts found on juveniles. Like adult males, adult females undergo a complete prebasic molt in the fall, so the effects of wear are usually at their worst in the late summer.

Some cowbirds disperse after fledging while still in juvenile plumage, and identifying these birds to species is difficult or impossible, though Bronzed stands out by structure. Juvenile males and females resemble one another prior to the preformative molt and often show some yellow or orangish at the gape. Juveniles undergo the preformative molt in the fall[10] (usually August–October), after which first-year birds become easier to identify as they begin to show their first signs of adulthood (making it easier to distinguish between the sexes). Some first-year birds retain juvenile flight feathers until the following summer/fall (first prebasic molt). Juvenile Bronzed Cowbirds have duskier eyes than adults, and the eye color remains darkish through at least the first winter; first-winter males also tend to be less glossy than adults.

Head and bill detail of male Brown-headed Cowbird, MD, Feb (BH) (left); adult male Bronzed Cowbird, AZ, Jul (BS) (right). This plate focuses on distinguishing adult males. Note that Brown-headed has a stout bill, yet it is both shallower and shorter than in Bronzed Cowbird. Brown-headed usually shows a more obvious forehead and is usually rounder headed. While these structural clues aren't necessary to identify adult males, they carry over to females and immatures.

Adult male Brown-headed Cowbird, TX, Apr (GLA) (left); adult male Bronzed Cowbird, TX, Apr (BLS) (right). Note the general shape differences between the two: Brown-headed is more slimly built and well proportioned, with a "normal" neck and head, whereas Bronzed (this bird is half displaying) is bulkier, with a thick neck, big head, hefty bill, and red eyes.

Adult male Shiny Cowbird, Puerto Rico, Apr (GLA) (left); first-spring male Shiny Cowbird, FL, May (RH) (right). Adult male Shiny Cowbirds are overall glossy iridescent purple, with dark eyes and a finer bill than in the other two species. Note the retained brown juvenile primaries on the bird at right, an indication that this bird is a first-spring. Retained feathers like this are rare, and most birds cannot be safely aged by late fall/early winter of the first year.

Female Brown-headed Cowbird, CA, Oct (BLS) (left); adult female Bronzed Cowbird, AZ, July (BS) (right). Females are trickier to identify, and there is geographic variation to consider in both Brown-headed and Bronzed cowbirds. Western Brown-headed Cowbirds (left) tend to be paler overall and smaller billed than birds of the Great Basin and farther east. Bronzed Cowbird females of western and eastern populations differ; western birds are grayer overall, and eastern birds (see below) are blackish brown and more like immature males (but note adult female's bright red eye).

Female Brown-headed Cowbird, TX, Apr (GLA) (left); adult female Bronzed Cowbird, TX, Apr (BS) (right). Brown-headed Cowbird females average darker on the Great Plains, and female Bronzed Cowbirds are dusky blackish in Texas and in the western Gulf Coast region.

Female Brown-headed Cowbird, MD, Feb (BH) (left); female Shiny Cowbird, FL, Apr (GLA) (right). On this eastern female Brown-headed Cowbird, note the deeper, heavier bill than on the western Brown-headed female above. Shiny Cowbirds are notably slimmer billed than eastern Brown-headed Cowbirds and in general have a more uniformly brown plumage lacking the subtle contrasts of female Brown-headed.

Juvenile Brown-headed Cowbirds, CA (left) and Baja California, Mexico (right), Sep (SNGH). Brown-headed Cowbirds disperse long distances after fledging and can appear in odd places in full juvenile plumage. It might surprise you to learn that it is one of the most commonly encountered passerines offshore on West Coast pelagic trips, especially in August and September (left). There is considerable variation in juvenile plumage; some birds are very pale (typical), while others can approach a blackish-brown general coloration. Juvenile Brown-headed Cowbird is perhaps one of the most frequently misidentified birds in North America.

Adult female (left) and immature female Bronzed Cowbird, Mexico, Feb (SNGH) (left); adult male Brown-headed (right bird) and Bronzed cowbirds, TX, Mar (TJ) (right). Determining the age and sex of Bronzed Cowbirds can be difficult, and more study is needed. In general, first-winter birds have duller eyes, and males lack the bright glossy iridescence of older birds; eye color may be the only way to age females. Brown-headed and Bronzed cowbirds are obviously different when seen together, but lone vagrants can be more difficult to judge. Focus on head and bill shape, and general structural differences.

Mixed blackbird flock, NJ, Oct (GLA). Cowbirds, blackbirds, and grackles often form huge mixed-species flocks in fall and winter, sometimes numbering in the millions. Vagrants of all three species have been discovered in large mixed-species flocks.

BROWN-HEADED COWBIRD: As a widespread species, often mixing with blackbirds when feeding and roosting, Brown-headed Cowbird shows variation across its range in both size and (in females) general darkness of plumage (see photos). It is intermediate in structure between the more slender Shiny and the heftier Bronzed (but note that Brown-headed in the Great Basin area averages larger than elsewhere and is closer to Bronzed in proportions). It is most similar to Shiny Cowbird, but Brown-headed is shorter tailed and has a larger, rounder head with a steeper forehead. The stout bill usually shows a slightly swollen arch to the culmen, but some appear straighter. As the most migratory cowbird, it also shows longer, more pointed wings (perhaps noticeable in flight, or in photos).

Adult males are glossy greenish black or bluish black, with a distinctive chocolate-brown head. Females are nondescript brown or gray, drab and dull in color and pattern. Usually the throat is pale, whitish, or buff (averaging paler than on Shiny) and contrasts somewhat with the darker auriculars and chest. Some show a hint of a whisker, or lateral throat stripe. The dark eye is usually more prominent against the generally paler face, compared to that of Shiny. Most show a gray or horn-colored base to the mandible. Most females show extremely thin but crisp pale fringing on their primaries. These may be hard to see or may wear away by summer, but they are absent on Shiny, or contrast much less noticeably. Juveniles are paler brown than females and usually show noticeable streaking below, and when fresh they are scalier above than in the other species. Even the flight feathers are narrowly edged with pale, and some individuals may show a more patterned head, too, with more noticeable lateral throat stripes. *Voice:* They have a complex song beginning with several low, liquid, gurgling notes, trailing off into a very high quavering whistle.

BRONZED COWBIRD: This bull-necked, hulking cowbird is usually distinguished from the others on structure alone, but also by the adults' red eyes. Juveniles have brown eyes, but the characteristic hunchbacked appearance, combined with the heavy, swollen bill and the rather blocky head, sets this species apart from the others. Note how the bill appears swollen and has an arched, decurved culmen. This is not only the largest and stockiest cowbird, it also appears plump and big legged and shows a relatively short tail. It is seldom encountered outside its normal range, but it strays east along the Gulf Coast to south Florida, and rarely to the West Coast. It is accidental north of its normal range. There are two subspecies of Bronzed Cowbird in the region: the Southwestern *M. a. loyei* found in southern Arizona and New Mexico south into Mexico, and the nominate *M. a. aeneus* found along the Gulf Coast of Texas and Louisiana, south to Panama.[9] These two overlap in west Texas and differ primarily in the plumage of the female (see below).

Adult males are distinctive, being especially large and having a thick neck ruff and (especially in the breeding season) a bronzy sheen on the nape, neck, and upper back, while the wings are a contrasting iridescent blue. When males are puffed up, their legs may appear relatively small because the birds appear "inflated." Females are brownish black in the East and grayer brown in the West, but note that wear and bleaching may affect this. Note the structural features above, as well as the eye color. First-spring males are larger than females and have a bit of a neck ruff, but they show less iridescence than adult males and may show some red in the eye, or even entirely red eyes. Juveniles are pale gray brown, with noticeable streaking on the chest and underparts, and they lack a ruff but still look heavy billed and strong legged. On some juveniles the large bill may appear to almost engulf the head; in other juvenile cowbirds the bill looks more like it was just stuck onto the face. In flight, Bronzed shows relatively rounded wings. *Voice:* This somewhat recalls that of Great-tailed Grackle, or an electrified and complex vireo song. The repeated phrases at different pitches are more electric and run together more than in Brown-headed.

SHINY COWBIRD: Rarely seen away from south Florida (and very scarce even there), Shiny Cowbird is most similar to Brown-headed in appearance. It averages smaller than Brown-headed and often appears slimmer, with a smaller head and a more sharp-tipped bill. Shiny Cowbird first appeared in North America in Florida in 1987,[11] arousing great concern over what seemed an inevitable invasion and range expansion (similar to what has transpired with Eurasian Collared-Dove), but it failed to gain a foothold, and the feared invasion never materialized. Shiny has occurred west along the Gulf Coast to Texas and was rare if regular north along the Atlantic Coast to North Carolina, but today is occurs erratically in south Florida. Vagrants have occurred to Oklahoma and Maine, but records of strays since the mid-1990s have diminished remarkably.

In addition to being the smallest (on average) of these cowbirds, it is also the most elegant in shape. A somewhat longer tail may add to this impression, as does the less steep and more sloping forehead, and also the relatively long, pointed bill. The bill is usually entirely dark (lacking the gray base visible on most Brown-headeds), and the culmen usually appears straight and not swollen.

Adult males are entirely glossy blue black, with the wings and tail being darkest. Adult females are typically a dark gray brown but occasionally show a buffy tinge to the neck and chest. They usually seem slightly less buff or sand colored (at least when relatively fresh) and are generally a shade darker, and a slightly richer brown than Brown-headed. The head and crown especially seem darker, and the face too, such that the eye is less prominent than it often appears in Brown-headed, and the throat contrasts less noticeably and averages darker than in Brown-headed. First-spring males are patchy, a mixture of dark grayish/brownish feathers and adultlike glossy purplish or bluish-black feathers. Juveniles are similar to adult females but are paler below, usually with some streaking (at times only faint). Fresh juveniles show pale fringes to the upperparts but are darker than the warmer-colored juvenile Brown-headed (which also shows more obvious pale fringes on the flight feathers).

Noticeably dark female cowbirds should be studied closely, and scrutinized for other marks consistent with Shiny. Beware of female Brewer's Blackbirds, which could overlap in parts of the Southeast, but Brewer's prefers muddy fields, while Shiny is usually in open grassy areas or at feeders. Brewer's always appears even more slender, with a longer, finer bill. *Voice:* This species has probably the most distinctive song of the three, beginning with a mechanical, low-pitched bubbling of roughly three phrases, followed by a sharp, high-pitched whistle—so high and different, it's hard to believe it's part of the sam/e song! The hard rattle of the female is similar to that of Brown-headed, but perhaps slightly higher and faster.

References

1 Lowther, P. E. 1993. Brown-headed Cowbird (*Molothrus ater*). The Birds of North America Online. A. Poole, ed. Ithaca, NY: Cornell Lab of Ornithology. http://bna.birds.cornell.edu/bna/species/047

2 Yokel, D. A. 1989. Intrasexual aggression and the mating behavior of Brown-headed Cowbird: Their relation to population densities and sex ratios. Condor 91:43–51.

3 Morales, M. B., F. Jiguet, and B. Arroyo. 2001. Exploded leks: What bustards can teach us. Ardeola 48(1): 85–98.

4 Jaramillo, A., and P. Burke. 1999. New World Blackbirds: The Icterids. Princeton, NJ: Princeton University Press.

5 Byerley, B. 2013. Brown-headed cowbird. Animal Diversity Web. http://www.biokids.umich.edu/critters/Molothrus_ater/

6 Lanyon, S. M., and K. E. Omland. 1999. A molecular phylogeny of the blackbirds (Icteridae): Five lineages revealed by cytochrome-b sequence data. Auk 116(3): 629–39.

7 Banks, A. J., and T. E. Martin. Host activity and the risk of nest parasitism by Brown-headed Cowbirds. Behavioral Ecology 12(1): 31–40.

8 Cornell Lab of Ornithology. Birds in forested landscapes. http://www.birds.cornell.edu/bfl/speciesaccts/bnhcow.html

9 Ellison, K., and P. E. Lowther. 2009. Bronzed Cowbird (*Molothrus aeneus*). The Birds of North America Online. A. Poole, ed. Ithaca, NY: Cornell Lab of Ornithology. http://bna.birds.cornell.edu/bna/species/144

10 Howell, S.N.G. 2010. Molt in North American Birds. New York: Houghton Mifflin.

11 Smith P. W., and A. I. Sprunt. 1987. The Shiny Cowbird reaches the USA: Will the scourge of the Caribbean impact Florida's avifauna too? American Birds 41(3): 370–71.

Index

Note: boldface refers to images

316

Vaux's Swift (*C. vauxi*), **223**, 225–226

Western Kingbird (*T. verticalis*), 255, **258**, **259**

Western Screech-Owl (*M. kennicottii*), **233**, 235

Whimbrels
    subspecies, 151, **152**, 154
    "Eurasian" (*Numenius p. phaeopus, N. p. variegatus*), **152**, 154
    "Hudsonian" (*N. p. hudsonicus*), **148**, **150**, 151, **152**, 154, **154**
    "Siberian" (*N. p. variegatus*), **152**

Whiskered Screech-Owl (*M. trichopsis*), 235, **236**, 238

Whistling Swan. *See* Tundra Swan

White-collared Swift (*S. zonaris*), **227**, 228

White Herons, 69–73
    hybrids, 69, 71, **78**, **79**
    subspecies, 71
    Cattle Egret (*B. ibis*), **70**, **72**, 73, 75, **77**
    Great Egret (*A. alba*), **70**, **72**, 73, **76**, **77**
    "Great White" Heron (*A. herodias occidentalis*), **74**, 79
    Little Blue Heron (*E. caerulea*), **70**, **74**, 75, **75**, **76**, **77**
    Little Egret (*E. garzetta*), 79, **79**
    Reddish Egret (*E. rufescens*), **70**, **74**, 75, 76, **76**
    Snowy Egret (*E. thula*), **70**, **72**, 73, **76**, **77**
    Wurdemann's Heron, 71, **78**, 79

White-throated Needletail (*H. caudacutus caudacutus*), **227**, 228

White-throated Swift (*A. saxatalis*), **222**, 226

Whooper Swan (*C. cygnus*), **46**, 52

Winter Wren (*T. hiemalis*), **190**, 194–195

Wrens, small, 175, 187–189
    subspecies, **188**, **191**, **193**
    House Wren (*T. aedon*), **188**, 189, **193**, 194, **194**
    Marsh Wren (*C. palustris*), **186**, **193**, 196
    Pacific Wren (*T. pacificus*), **191**, 195
    Sedge Wren (*C. platensis*), **192**, 195–196
    Winter Wren (*T. hiemalis*), **190**, 194–195

Wurdemann's Heron, 71, **78**, 79

Yellow-bellied Kingbirds, 253–255
    subspecies, 262
    Cassin's Kingbird (*T. vociferans*), **252**, 255–257, **259**
    Couch's Kingbird (*T. couchii*), **256**, 257–262, **261**
    Thick-billed Kingbird (*T. crassirostris*), 262, **262**
    Tropical Kingbird (*T. melancholicus*), **256**, 257, **260**
    Western Kingbird (*T. verticalis*), 255, **258**, **259**

Yellow-billed Loon (*G. adamsii*), 40–42, **41–42**

Zino's Petrel (*P. madeira*), 146